Forensic Medicine Investigation in M

England has traditionally been understood as a latecomer to the use of forensic medicine in death investigation, lagging nearly two hundred years behind other European authorities. Using the coroner's inquest as a lens, this book hopes to offer a fresh perspective on the process of death investigation in medieval England. The central premise of this book is that medical practitioners did participate in death investigation—although not in every inquest, or even most, and not necessarily in those investigations where we today would deem their advice most pertinent. The medieval relationship with death and disease, in particular, shaped coroners' and their jurors' understanding of the inquest's medical needs and led them to conclusions that can only be understood in context of the medieval world's holistic approach to health and medicine. Moreover, while the English resisted Southern Europe's penchant for autopsies, at times their findings reveal a solid understanding of internal medicine. By studying cause of death in the coroners' reports, this study sheds new light on subjects such as abortion by assault, bubonic plague, cruentation, epilepsy, insanity, senescence, and unnatural death.

Sara M. Butler is Professor of History at Loyola University New Orleans. She has written on the subjects of marital violence, suicide, abortion, and divorce in medieval England. In 2007, she was awarded the Sutherland Prize by the American Society for Legal History.

Routledge Research in Medieval Studies

1 **Agrarian Change and Crisis in Europe, 1200–1500**
Edited by Harry Kitsikopoulos

2 **Pluralism in the Middle Ages**
Ragnhild Johnsrud Zorgati

3 **Theorizing Medieval Geopolitics**
War and World Order in the Age of the Crusades
Andrew A. Latham

4 **Divorce in Medieval England**
From One to Two Persons in Law
Sara M. Butler

5 **Medieval Islamic Historiography**
Remembering Rebellion
Heather N. Keaney

6 **The Jewish-Christian Encounter in Medieval Preaching**
Edited by Jonathan Adams and Jussi Hanska

7 **Forensic Medicine and Death Investigation in Medieval England**
Sara M. Butler

Previous titles to appear in Routledge Research in Medieval Studies include:

The Generation of Identity in Late Medieval Hagiography
Speaking the Saint
Gail Ashton

Performing Virginity and Testing Chastity in the Middle Ages
Kathleen Coyne Kelly

Women Pilgrims in Late Medieval England
Susan S. Morrison

Forensic Medicine and Death Investigation in Medieval England

Sara M. Butler

LONDON AND NEW YORK

First published 2015
by Routledge

2 Park Square, Milton Park, Abingdon, Oxon OX14 4RN

711 Third Avenue, New York, NY 10017, USA

Routledge is an imprint of the Taylor & Francis Group, an informa business

First issued in paperback 2016

Library of Congress Cataloging-in-Publication Data

Butler, Sara M. (Sara Margaret), author.
Forensic medicine and death investigation in medieval England / by
Sara M. Butler.
p. ; cm. — (Routledge research in medieval studies ; 7)
Includes bibliographical references and index.
I. Title. II. Series: Routledge research in medieval studies ; 7.
[DNLM: 1. Forensic Medicine—history—England. 2. Coroners
and Medical Examiners—history—England. 3. History, Medieval—
England. W 611 FE5]
RA1022.G3
614′.10942—dc23
2014016350

ISBN: 978-1-138-80981-9 (hbk)
ISBN: 978-1-138-22307-3 (pbk)

Typeset in Sabon
by Apex CoVantage, LLC

Contents

Figure

Tables

Royal Statutes

Abbreviations

AHR	*American Historical Review*
AJLH	*American Journal of Legal History*
AS	*Acta Sanctorum*
BIHR	*Borthwick Institute of Historical Research*
C	Chancery
C&C	*Continuity & Change*
CCR	*Calendar of Close Rolls*
CIM	*Calendar of Inquisitions Miscellaneous*
CPR	*Calendar of Patent Rolls*
EHR	*Economic History Review*
JBS	*Journal of British Studies*
JHMAS	*Journal of the History of Medicine & Allied Sciences*
JLH	*Journal of Legal History*
JMEMS	*Journal of Medieval and Early Modern Studies*
JUST 1	Eyre and Assize Rolls
JUST 2	Coroners' Rolls
KB	King's Bench
L&HR	*Law & History Review*
MH	*Medical History*
P&P	*Past & Present*
PIMS	Pontifical Institute of Mediaeval Studies
PRME	Parliament Rolls of Medieval England
SC	Special Collections, Ancient Correspondence of the Chancery and Exchequer
SHoM	*Social History of Medicine*
SR	Statutes of the Realm
SS	Selden Society
TNA PRO	The National Archives, Public Record Office
UP	University Press
Y.B.	Year Book

Acknowledgments

In many respects, this book is a product of my fascination with the coroners' rolls; thus I would be remiss if I did not thank Roy F. Hunnisett, whom I have never met, but whose work I devoured with great interest as an eager doctoral students some years ago. Cynthia J. Neville, my doctoral advisor, was the first to nurture my passion for the coroner's inquest. Krista J. Kesselring, one of the few people I've met who reads a coroner's report with an equal amount of enthusiasm, has not only eagerly shared odd archival finds over the years, but she also happily read the first draft of this manuscript and offered many fruitful suggestions and reinterpretations. I am greatly indebted to her for her keen mind and her friendship. Katherine D. Watson, who self-identified as one of the anonymous reviewers of my book manuscript, deserves much credit for her meticulous editing and rigorous review. Both manuscript reviewers for Routledge offered cogent suggestions for improvement, and I have done my best to respond to their proposals.

For financial support, I would like to thank Loyola University New Orleans's Grants and Leave Committee for the travel funds necessary to complete this project. Thanks to Ina Gravitz and her hard work in producing the index to this book. For intellectual stimulation, many thanks must go to Alice Clark, Mark Fernandez, Helen Good, David Moore, John Sebastian, the participants of the 21st British Legal History Conference at Glasgow University, and my colleagues at the History Department at Loyola University New Orleans who kindly listened to me obsess on the subject of death investigation. For emotional support, many thanks to my beloved family who patiently tolerate my work habits: my children (Cade, Genevieve, and Miranda), my parents Brian and Carol Butler, as well as my husband, Mark. Especial thanks must go to my husband, who manages to convince our children that life is a party when Mommy is at the archives.

Some of this material has appeared in print in other formats. Chapter Four includes three pages from a previous publication entitled: Sara M. Butler, "Abortion by Assault: Violence against Pregnant Women in Thirteenth- and Fourteenth-Century England," *Journal of Women's History* 17.4 (2005): 9–31. Copyright ©2005 *Journal of Women's History*. Reprinted with permission by Johns Hopkins University Press.

Chapter Four also includes five pages from a previous publication entitled: Sara M. Butler, "Representing the Middle Ages: The Insanity Defense in Medieval England," in *The Treatment of Disabled Persons in Medieval Europe: Examining Disability in the Historical, Legal, Literary, Medical, and Religious Discourses*, ed. Wendy Turner and Tory Vandeventer (Wales: The Edwin Mellen Press, 2011), pp. 117–34. Reprinted with permission of The Edwin Mellen Press.

Introduction

Few books on the study of the law have garnered as much attention as Thomas A. Green's 1985 publication of *Verdict According to Conscience: Perspectives on the English Criminal Trial Jury, 1200–1800*.[1] Green's provocative work on jury discretion explores the curious transition from medieval England's highly active jurors, men purportedly drawn from the scene of the crime who entered court wholly informed and prepared to pass judgment, to today's passive jurors whose ignorance is prized above all other virtues, left to the mercy of lawyers to hand-feed them the relevant evidence.[2] Green's monograph prompted the collective writing of one of the most cited tomes in the field, J.S. Cockburn's and Thomas A. Green's *Twelve Good Men and True: The Criminal Trial Jury in England, 1200–1800*,[3] at least one conference dedicated entirely to the subject as well as the publication of that conference's proceedings, and numerous articles relating to the trial jury.[4] More recent landmark publications by Anthony Musson, John Bellamy, Daniel Klerman, Mike McNair, and James Masschaele attest to the continuing vitality of the subject, despite the passage of time since Green's book first appeared.[5] The ensuing intellectual discourse has sharpened our understanding not only of the shift in the trial jury's function, but also of its origins, its rapport with other juries (including overlap in membership), and its behavior. Significantly, Green's influence has extended far beyond the trial jury, inspiring scholars to set their sights on various other forms of juries. Bernard McLane's analysis of presentment juries has vividly transformed our understanding of the place of indictment in the legal process.[6] Sherri Olson, Maureen Mulholland, and Peter Larson offer an evolving and much-needed reassessment of manorial jurors.[7] James Masschaele highlights the political side of jurors' work by refocusing the lens on sworn inquests.[8] Even jurors who sat on inquisitions post-mortem have received their share of attention with Matthew Holford's most recent work.[9] Among this flurry of publications, the one jury that historians have continually overlooked or undervalued is the medieval coroner's jury.

The medieval English understood the coroner primarily as a figure of criminal law enforcement. His chief responsibility was to investigate sudden or unnatural deaths; in the medieval context, this meant primarily homicides, although the records include also deaths by misadventure, the occasional suicide or death by disease, and deaths in prison. In addition, the coroner played a key role in views of wounding and rape, and he recorded the confessions of felons prepared to abjure the realm. In terms of authority, the coroner was second only to the sheriff within the county. Indeed, much of their work overlapped, and the crown expected the two to act as each other's moral compass. The one major distinction between the two was that the coroner's office pertained primarily to criminal law, while the sheriff's office was much more diverse in its aims. The authority of the coroner in criminal matters is measured also by the weight of the inquest's verdict: in cases of homicide, the law treated the finding of a coroner's inquest as an indictment.[10] The coroner did not reach any conclusion unassisted: he worked in cooperation with a jury of twelve to twenty-four men drawn from *vicini*, that is, men living in the areas neighboring those where the death occurred. Coroners' jurors functioned as witnesses rather than lay judges: while not necessarily eyewitnesses, they were "hearsay witnesses" or "neighbor-witnesses."[11] Stationing themselves at the scene of death, in the presence of the body of the deceased and surrounded by neighbors who presumably knew precisely what had happened, their inquiries led them to draw a preliminary verdict. In cases of homicide, their on-the-ground investigative work laid a solid foundation for the resultant trial procedure. Particularly in the later medieval period, when trial juries were less exclusively self-informing, the written indictments of coroners' juries, supplying usually far more detail concerning the circumstances surrounding the crime than anything one might find in an assize roll, were crucial in assisting trial juries to decide how to cast their vote. The findings of the coroner and his jury had an extended life not only because of the written record, but also because of the critical role played by some coroners outside the normal parameters of their duties. Coroners often did double-duty as keepers of the peace, involving them even more deeply in the trial process.[12] In addition, "[c]oroners provided some of the most regular jurors" for trial juries.[13] Since coroners were required to attend sessions of jail delivery, in the event royal justices needed to reference the coroners' rolls, coroners were "natural candidates" for the jury when some of those summoned for jury duty failed to appear.[14] Given the centrality of the coroner and his jury to the outcome of the criminal process, it is somewhat surprising that this renewed attention to juries and juror discretion has not expanded to the initial stage of the process in the criminal investigation in cases of homicide.

In large part, the reluctance of historians to revisit the coroners and their juries stems from a sense that the work is already done. The spirit of Roy F. Hunnisett casts a heavy shadow over the field. As the Assistant Keeper of the Public Records for a good part of the twentieth century, he published extensively and meticulously on the subject of the coroner,[15] leading some to conclude that he "has left few aspects of the coroner's work unexplored."[16]

Unquestionably, Hunnisett's scrupulous and painstaking research into the coroners' rolls and the office of the coroner itself are fundamental to any understanding of the medieval criminal justice system. This monograph does not presume to replace his work. However, if Hunnisett was writing his work today, rather than in the 1950s and 1960s, it is likely that he might be asking different questions of his sources. Hunnisett's chief interest was the office of the coroner and its changing role over the course of the Middle Ages. His work was critical to understanding the precise nature of the coroner's position. The focus, though, was always on the coroner. Hunnisett very much understood the jury as an entity wholly subservient to the needs and will of the coroner: the coroner asked the questions, jurors answered. Yet, the work of Green and others has demonstrated to us that medieval jurors were not that submissive. What meager light historians have shone on the coroners' juries since that time reinforces the perception of juror activism. Those who have looked to the coroners' juries have done so in a very piecemeal fashion, analyzing them through a particular and often narrow lens: looking specifically at rates of crime in the English village,[17] children and the family,[18] suicide verdicts,[19] and the reliability of the records.[20] But there is no equivalent to Green and Cockburn's fine collection for the coroner's jury.

Notwithstanding, the coroner and his jury have received much criticism for their work. This is especially true in terms of legal medicine. On the Continent, medieval courts of law regularly exploited the expertise of medical professionals to determine causes of death, to assess the damages incurred by an assault, and to address various other legal issues of a medical nature. In contrast, conclusions drawn about the state of forensic medicine in medieval England construct an exceedingly bleak picture. "[F]orensic practice was at best ad hoc and at worst non-existent," and "Britain lagged nearly two centuries behind Continental Europe in developing a science of forensic medicine."[21] The expansive role played by the coroner in the initial investigatory process into a death has garnered the lion's share of the blame for England's failure to keep abreast of Continental advances in legal medicine.

Granted, it is critical to acknowledge that the impetus for the creation of the coronership in 1194 was chiefly financial. From the crown's perspective, medieval death was highly profitable. Death investigation produced the following revenues:

1. The English crown confiscated felons' and outlaws' landed property for a year, a day, and waste, and all chattels permanently.[22] It was the coroner's responsibility to inventory those properties and assess their value for the escheator.
2. In deaths by misadventure, if an object (called *deodand*) was in any way responsible for the death, it was forfeit to the king. For example, if a child was mauled to death by a pig, the crown removed the pig from the community. The coroner assessed the value of the pig, the escheator sold it, and the profits went either to the crown or to one of his loyal

subjects as a token of royal patronage. Weapons used in a homicide or suicide were considered a special form of deodand called *bane* (in Middle English, "destroyer"); they were subject to the same process.

3. Procedural faults created a multiplicity of opportunities for profit. Communities as a whole were subject to amercements for:

    a) failure to attend an inquest.
    b) failure to raise the hue and cry.
    c) removal of the body or burial before the arrival of the coroner.
    d) failure to arrest (that is, attach by surety). It was the coroner's responsibility to attach first finders, nearest neighbors, and eyewitnesses by two pledges to ensure that they would appear at the eyre for the presentation of the indictment.
    e) false appraisal of property.
    f) false appraisal of the deodand.
    g) nonattendance at eyre by those attached at inquest.

4. Finally, if the community was incapable of proving the "Englishry" of the dead, the crown also imposed a *murdrum* fine.

Indeed, when legal historians speak wryly of the "profits of the law," they are referring primarily to crown pleas (that is, criminal trials). Anne and Edwin DeWindt's study of the Huntingdonshire eyre of 1286 substantiates this fact. At that eyre, civil pleas brought in "little more than £40"; crown pleas increased the king's holdings by a total of £190 10*s*. 5*d*. Fines for procedural faults, which more often than not relate to criminal trials, brought in an additional £229.[23]

Because of the explicitly financial overtones of the office, medieval coroners had no formal or informal training in medicine. The medieval English considered the position to be an honor: the coronership was an appointment for life and bestowed on the elite in society, involving mostly travel and record keeping. The simple fact that the position was unsalaried underscores its privileged nature. The crown expected coroners to be sufficiently affluent to afford the expenses of the office; it also prohibited coroners from charging for their services. While the county coroner was literate and was assisted by a scrivener (that is, an expert in court hand), he had no training in the field of medicine, nor did he have state-funded resources to hire someone trained in medicine. Yet, the crown instructed the coroner and his jury to diagnose medical conditions on a daily basis. Of course, this was true of laymen throughout the English legal system:

> [j]urors and expert lay witnesses in royal courts were accustomed to determining whether or not plaintiffs had been raped or mutilated, if they were pregnant, impotent, insane, senile or simply absent-minded, virginal, paralytic, blind, capable of trial by combat (despite fervent protestations to the contrary), or if their claims for damages because of physical injury had been grossly exaggerated.[24]

The difference lies in the proportion of medically relevant work: while most jurors were faced with knotty medical decisions, the vast majority of the work executed by the coroner and his jury centered on medical diagnoses. The fundamental concern was to determine whether a death occurred through natural or unnatural means. For those without training in healthcare, this was not necessarily an easy task. For example, in the event that an assault occurred prior to a man's death, the crown relied on jurors to deduce whether injuries incurred during an assault precipitated death, even if the incident happened weeks or months prior to the decedent's demise. This undertaking was not so onerous when the wound involved a knife to the chest; but what happened when the injuries were primarily internal? Were a headache and fever appearing soon after a blow to the head and eventually culminating in the victim's death necessarily a result of the blow, or just a coincidence? Because voicing a suspicion of guilt led to the accused felon's incarceration until trial, a coroner's jury had to be confident in its decision. The determination of unnatural death was just one facet of the job; coroners and their juries tackled many other matters requiring judgments of a medical nature.

When death was the product of homicide, coroners' juries often had little evidence upon which to base their judgment. Medieval felons typically fled after committing a crime. Moreover, because the medieval English functioned entirely on the goodwill and energies of communities to police crimes, "a felon could consider himself distinctly unlucky if he were captured by the authorities."[25] This cynical assessment seemingly paints an image of an inefficient and failing legal system: yet, in many respects, flight and subsequent outlawry fell distinctly in line with communal expectations of justice. "Publicity and exclusion" were a community's twin aims in criminal law: flight and outlawry then not only led to a public identification of the felon, but also to his expulsion from community life.[26] For a homicide investigation, however, this convention meant relying on a small pool of evidence: a corpse and its wounds, perhaps a weapon or a trail of blood, and, if they were fortunate, an eyewitness or two.

The performance of a post-mortem autopsy could have resolved countless questions provoked by the inquest process. However, even though some Continental authorities sanctioned autopsies and their medical practitioners regularly performed them, the English did not. The reluctance of the English to do so has nothing to do with traditional scholarly assumptions about the sacred nature of the body. In reality, the English had been dissecting royal and aristocratic corpses, even boiling the bones, for multiple burials since at least the high Middle Ages. King John, for instance, had his entrails buried at Crokestone and his body at Worcester.[27] Katharine Park credits the cult of relics with the northern domestication of dismemberment.[28] As an alternative explanation for English discomfort with autopsies, she argues it derives from

> a whole complex of contrasting attitudes toward the recently dead body . . . while Italians envisaged physical death as a quick and radical separation of body and soul, northern Europeans saw it as an extended and

> gradual process, corresponding to the slow decomposition of the corpse and its reduction to the skeleton and hard tissues, which was thought to last about a year. Thus, while Italians tended to see the recently dead body as inert or inactive, northerners treated it during this liminal period as active, sensitive, or semianimate, possessed of a gradually fading life.[29]

Park employs this hypothesis to clarify some of the more bizarre northern folkloric beliefs, such as revenants, the resurrection of stillborn infants for baptism, cruentation (that is, the idea that a corpse will bleed in the presence of its murderer), as well as the north-south divide relating to funerary practices. While the legal sources offer no evidence to support Park's theory, her explanation provides key insight into the northern mentality, and helps us to understand why neither coroners nor any other crown officeholders were carrying out autopsies.

The crown relied on coroners and their juries to craft medical assessments in at least two other critical situations. First, where the perpetrator was not of sound mind at the time of the crime, jurors might declare that he was *non compos mentis*, and thus the court might not hold him accountable for his actions. Because the law distinguished accountability by the nature of the mental incompetence (from birth, or temporary versus permanent insanity), the law required jurors to prepare a reasonably accurate medical history of the assailant before concluding whether the perpetrator was, indeed, mentally incompetent, and if so, insane enough to justify excusing his or her actions. Second, abortion by assault,[30] while not common, occurred with some regularity. An abortion by assault transpired when an individual physically attacked a pregnant woman, inducing a miscarriage. The law categorized such an assault as a homicide providing it had taken place after the quickening (the first fetal movements). In order to make their determination, jurors had to establish a correlation between assault and miscarriage. Investigations of this nature depended on a sound knowledge of medical theory; and while the English eschewed autopsies, abortions by assault typically involved a physical examination of the fetus itself for clues pertaining to the nature of the assault and fetal development.

How coroners and their juries negotiated the evidence in these challenging scenarios and came to a conclusion without the benefit of a trained medical practitioner has been a puzzle for legal historians. In this respect, the nature of the English records complicates the problem. Once again, the coroners' rolls are financial records, intended to ensure that the king received the profits of the law. The term "coroner" itself is a reminder of that fact: coroner derives from the Latin term for crown (*corona*), emphasizing that he was a crown employee looking out for the crown's best interests by handling crown pleas (criminal investigations). As a result, almost the entire legal process is omitted from the record. While we can assume the law expected jurors to seek out eyewitnesses and learn from their testimonies, there are no witness depositions in the coroners' rolls. The assize rolls (which document indictments by presentment, or grand, jurors) and jail delivery rolls (records of the trials themselves) are even less helpful: they offer no courtroom transcripts, no witness lists, no weighty jury deliberations. Once again, these were not trivial decisions: in cases of homicide, for example, the judgments of coroners' juries acted as indictments in the legal process, and had a significant influence on the outcome of the trial. Given the centrality of their decisions, and the coroner's lack of formal medical training, how could they possibly have come to any conclusion with assurance?

Here, it is pertinent to note that while medieval England's historians have generally glossed over this enigma, early modernists have shown great interest in the medical dimensions of death investigation. Nonetheless, their findings sometimes provoke more questions than answers. Thomas R. Forbes is the early modern era's counterpart to R.F. Hunnisett. An anatomist and endocrinologist working out of Yale's Medical School, Forbes's many publications are indispensable to any understanding of the development of forensic medicine in England.[31] Yet, Forbes's estimation of early modern death investigation is highly critical and tinged by modern expectations. He states, "[t]he records, in most cases kept by laymen, are confused not only by medical misconceptions of the period but by the layman's inevitable ignorance of medicine itself."[32] His opinion of coroners is even more damning: he believes that coroners regularly failed to investigate deaths, especially those falling into the category of suicides and deaths by misadventure.

More recently, both Krista Kesselring and Carol Loar have delved more deeply into the process of death investigation by looking beyond the coroner's inquest to news reports intended for popular consumption. With the development of broadsides in the mid-sixteenth century, the English population discovered an affordable means to satiate its desire for news of a bloody nature. Stories of murder trials and gallows speeches dominated broadsides. Popular accounts of homicide provide us with an opportunity to gain a clearer understanding of the investigative process than what appears in the more formulaic and terse legal record. Kesselring draws our attention to the 1598 pamphlet entitled *The Examination, Confession and Condemnation of Henry Robson, Fisherman of Rye, who poisoned his wife in the strangest manner that ever hitherto hath been heard of*. Robson's wife had been murdered four years earlier while Robson was serving time in prison for debt. On the advice of a fellow prisoner, Robson resolved to slay his wife during an overnight visit to him in jail by inserting a combination of ground glass and arsenic into her "privy parts" while she slept. The slow and painful nature of her death clued local physicians into the likelihood that something was amiss. They requested permission to perform an autopsy on her body, at which point they discovered the cause of her death and confronted Robson who subsequently confessed. What is perhaps most critical about this case is the simple fact that the legal record itself mentions nothing about the autopsy. More to the point, Kesselring observes that "the author of the pamphlet did not portray the participation of physicians in revealing the crime as especially noteworthy."[33] Indeed, Loar argues that this discrepancy between the process of death investigation and the legal record was normal. In the period after the 1580s, when autopsies were becoming more common in the English setting, she observes that the inquest records "generally make no reference to that fact in the formal reports"; yet, diaries and popular newspapers both confirm that coroners ordered autopsies in those same deaths.[34] It is not hard to imagine the same disjuncture in medieval coroners' reports.

Helen Brock and Catherine Crawford's study of coroners' juries in seventeenth-century Maryland is especially relevant here. Maryland's inquest juries commonly included surgeons. Moreover, as jurors, they utilized their positions to proffer evidence of a medical nature. Although the study's sample size is small, involving only a handful of individuals, the participation of surgeons on inquest juries is significant enough to persuade the two authors that "awareness of the potential value of medical opinion presumably came from knowledge of its use in contemporary courts in England."[35] When empanelling a jury for an inquest involving complex medical evidence, why wouldn't a coroner ask a medical practitioner to serve on the jury?

This monograph strives to answer the question of how coroners and their jurors deciphered the body's signs of physical distress in order to determine cause of death without 1) appointing physicians as coroners, and/or 2) disbursing funds to pay a cadre of medical practitioners for their expertise. The central premise of this book is that medical practitioners did participate in death investigation—although, not in every inquest, or even most, and not necessarily in those investigations where we today would deem their advice most pertinent. The medieval relationship with death and disease, in particular, shaped coroners' and jurors' understanding of the inquest's medical needs and led them to conclusions that can only be understood in context of the medieval world's holistic approach to health and medicine. Admittedly, coroners' rolls do not typically document the involvement of medical practitioners in an obvious or straightforward manner. Nonetheless, a faint presence can be detected through a careful analysis of jury lists, nearest neighbors, and first finders; through a rigorous examination of the framework of death investigation and its needs; and above all, close scrutiny of the jury's verdicts as they relate to the field of medicine. In the process, this monograph offers a solid reassessment of the medical side of English common law and the development of legal medicine in late medieval England, as well as fresh insight into the process of crime detection.

THE MEDICO-LEGAL CONTEXT

To understand the importance of a study of death investigation in medieval England, it is critical to place it in the larger context of legal and medico-legal advances in Christendom. Prompted by the rediscovery of Justinian's *Corpus Juris Civilis*, the Legal Revolution of the twelfth century marks the turning point in the history of European law, in which England branched off from the Continent as a whole by rejecting the Roman law that eventually laid the base for canon law and the *ius commune* across Europe. Of course, the process of adoption was spread over a period of time and highly regionalized: at no point did the law function uniformly across the Continent. The Holy Roman Empire, for example, did not formally adopt Roman law until 1495.[36] Moreover, throughout Europe, Roman law coexisted alongside a body of customary law that sometimes overrode Rome's learned mandates. Nor is the story of England's adherence to custom that simple. Despite officially rejecting Justinian's code, much of England's legal content and jurisprudence have been influenced by contact with the law through ecclesiastical and Continental sources.

Nonetheless, the Legal Revolution, which culminated in the pontificate of Innocent III, an experienced canon lawyer, marks a number of critical procedural changes that distinguished Continental trials from their English counterparts. By prohibiting the clergy from participating in judicial ordeals, previously the normal method of trying accused felons when the evidence was insufficient to convict, Pope Innocent III propelled Christian nations into a process of experimentation. Without access to God's testimony, courts of law were required to look elsewhere for evidence. The English embraced trial by jury. Traditionally, legal historians have emphasized that torture was the Continent's response to the abolition of the ordeal. However, Richard Fraher explains that this was just one solution among many.[37] Indeed, to meet Rome's high standards of evidence, judges turned to whatever sources of authority were available in order to provide a sound judgment. Medical expertise was one of those newfound sources.

Innocent's pontificate witnessed changes also in the method of prosecution. Before the thirteenth century, much of the onus for prosecution rested with the victim or his/her family. It was the victim's responsibility to plead a suit at law. Prosecution was accusatorial: meaning that whichever party offered the best argument won the suit. Innovations of the thirteenth century included both denunciation and the birth of inquisitorial justice. Denunciation was a byproduct of the growth of royal power. Under denunciation, the victim reported the crime, but the state assumed responsibility for prosecution. This approach permitted church and crown alike to launch campaigns against crime in a way that they were not able to do so previously. England also participated in this transition, moving emphasis away from the individual appeal to the jury of presentment. The truly momentous change in Continental procedure, however, was in the development of inquisitorial justice that transferred the locus of fact finding from the litigants to the judge. The Continent fostered "judge-led trials"[38] in which the responsibility to assemble a case by questioning witnesses and gathering evidence fell to the judge. Judgment also belonged to the judge: assessing the evidence, he formed an opinion and rendered a sentence. England, instead, relegated fact finding to the jury, and without any boldly articulated law of evidence, it was up to

the jury to decide whether the evidence was sufficient to determine innocence or guilt. This distinction in process is critical. Medieval incursions into forensic medicine derive principally from the structure of Romano-canon law adopted by Continental authorities: the law entrusted judges with the responsibility to establish the facts of a case. Confronted with a plethora of assaults and homicides, judges turned to medical practitioners for the necessary advice to close their cases.

Throughout this evolution there was much interchange between canon law and the *ius commune*. Indeed, canonical procedure often acted as the spur to civil law's experimentation with forensic medicine. The English church's decision to implement tests for impotence in suits for annulment has been cited as the inspiration for civil law's move toward legal medicine.[39] The same can be said for autopsies. Many of the first autopsies were, in fact, "holy autopsies," that is, inspections of the internal organs of alleged saints in order to seek out "corporeal signs of sanctity." For example, the 1308 autopsy of Chiara of Montefalco, carried out by her fellow Umbrian nuns, unearthed a small crucifix and miniature instruments of the Passion embedded in her heart, as well as three stones in her gallbladder representative of the Trinity.[40] The popularity and prestige of medical expertise stems in part from the role it played in canonization trials. From the thirteenth century on, the church regularly summoned medical practitioners as witnesses to healing miracles in order to evaluate the otherworldly nature of the cure.[41] The physician's ability to recognize and pronounce a miracle not only enhanced the discipline's reputation, but it also created an ironclad case for sanctity. After all, if a medical practitioner declared a condition beyond the capacity of human healthcare, then how could any critic naysay a miracle? Physicians became more deeply embedded in the practices of the law after Pope Gregory IX's 1234 *Nova Compilatio Decretalium* in which he made medical practitioners responsible for overseeing the application of judicial torture by ecclesiastical tribunals.[42]

In Continental Europe, courts of law began to exploit the wisdom of expert witnesses as early as the 1250s.[43] Bologna seems to have been the first to foray into the realm of legal medicine, but other kingdoms and states soon followed suit: Manosque (in Provence) by at least 1262, the Crown of Aragon in 1275, Venice in 1281, Paris in 1311.[44] Medical experts were central to criminal investigations, testifying chiefly to cause of death and the impact of an assault, although occasionally courts even employed medical experts to rule on allegations of poisoning.[45] In this respect, the Continent's openness to human dissection greatly assisted them in their detective work.

The extent to which the law became medicalized varied tremendously across the Continent. Venice was by far the most formalized in its relationship between law and medicine. Beginning in the thirteenth century, a medical practitioner wishing to work in Venice had to register his services with the government. The city government then monitored his practice. If his treatment with a patient was unsuccessful, and that patient died, he was expected to certify the cause of death. In addition, the city employed select physicians as municipal public health officers, whose contracts included free healthcare to the city's poor.[46] Beginning in at least 1281, a medical practitioner attending a patient whom he suspected to be the victim of violence was required to inform local police.[47] Moreover, all victims of homicide and those fatalities where the nature of death was unclear were subject to autopsies. Diversity existed across Europe also in basic practices relating to post-mortem examinations. For example, in the kingdom of Aragon, the court targeted the assault victim's attending physician to assess the severity of a wound and offer a prognosis.[48] In Manosque, the court strove instead for impartiality. It ordered the names of all possible physicians to be written on pieces of parchment and then placed in a sack: a neutral person then plucked out the names of two physicians whom the court assigned to assess the victim's wounds.[49]

The medical practitioner was paid handsomely to prepare a statement concerning the assault victim's state of health, or the nature of the homicide victim's demise. Yet, Joseph Shatzmiller cautions that a medical man's evaluation should not be conceived as definitive, incontestable testimony in the way it often is viewed today. Rather, the medieval courts considered the medical practitioner's statement "as an opinion, a crucial and very appreciated one," but also one with which the judge might disagree or find lacking.[50] Over time, many of these prepared statements were published as collections, referred to as *consilia*, to act as a template for future medical practitioners in their work. These statements are far from scientific in their nature: indeed, Nancy Siraisi warns that *consilia* read "very like that of a miracle story."[51] In essence, they are stories of self-aggrandizement. "Characteristically, the stories emphasize the skill and success of the author's cures, concluding triumphantly with the complete recovery of the recipients of apparently fatal wounds, previously given up for dead by bystanders, family members, or rival practitioners."[52]

The close cooperation between the state and the medical profession in criminal investigations laid the groundwork for the growing field of Western forensic medicine.[53] It was also mutually beneficial: "the law helped validate (and maybe even drive) the development of medical professionalism with new legal expectations of medical expertise."[54] Physicians and surgeons achieved the professionalization of medicine by asserting the elite and specialist nature of their knowledge. Over time, the rhetoric of elitism sparked a growing and widespread belief that "certain matters could only properly be advised on by these specialists."[55] Without the backing of the state, the medium of state legislation, and the process of state licensing, professionalization of medicine would have foundered. Elite medical practitioners relied heavily on cooperation with the state to assert their superiority in the medical marketplace, making them the official assessors of acceptable medical practice.

Professionalization of elite medicine inevitably led to marginalization: of women, of Jews, of nonacademic medical practitioners (sometimes surgeons, but especially barbers, stone-cutters, tooth-pullers)—all those whose medical training did not fit with the expectations of learned medicine. Yet, professional medicine failed to convince everyone that physicians were the only possible experts. As Sylvia De Renzi writes, "judges would routinely seek specific expertise where general consensus placed it: for example, competence on female bodies remained with midwives well after learned physicians had launched their attack on women's knowledge, and surgeons were the main port of call in cases of violent death."[56] Women, in particular, stand out in this respect. Medieval society traditionally associated women with the body, men with the soul. As such, courts of law awarded laywomen with no formal training places of prestige in legal medicine. "Old women" were typically responsible for physical examinations of rape victims, particularly when the victim was a virgin.[57] In Scotland, and later also in England, laywomen became "searchers of plague," tasked by the state to identify residents who fell sick with plague and have them quarantined.[58] In doing so, the law empowered ordinary women: "the searchers' responsibility to read living bodies for signs of plague, a responsibility which effectively put them in charge of quarantine" (which lasted anywhere from twenty-eight to forty days), made the searcher, marked out by her red wand, a fearsome character in the medieval landscape.[59]

Laywomen were not the only nonmedical professionals called upon to act as medical experts in the legal setting. In Catalonia, for example, it was the city fathers who determined whether an assault was connected with a man's subsequent demise.[60] In *iudicium leprosorum*, the judgment of lepers—a legal procedure by which a person was judged to be leprous—priests were often assigned as judges.[61] In Aragon, the bailiff filled this role.[62] When it came to evaluations of the insane, across Europe courts assigned laymen as judges. Perhaps the most intriguing example comes from holy autopsies: Katharine Park observes that nuns, not medical practitioners, performed fourteenth-century autopsies of purported saints.[63] All of this is a potent reminder that the education and experience of the professional medical cadre complemented but did not replace lay participation in the medieval courts.

ENGLAND IN THE LARGER CONTEXT

How aware were the English of what was going on in Continental Europe? The English may have been isolated geographically, but the English Channel did little to thwart the spread of knowledge. English medical practitioners were aware of the central role medicine played in the Continental courts. England did not begin educating its own physicians until the fourteenth century, and even then, it produced so few practitioners that French and Italian physicians played a key role in England's elite medicine.[64] Because of the mobility and intellectual curiosity of its practitioners, learned medicine was "European in scope." "National boundaries" in medicine were "permeable, in a state of flux, or intellectually non-existent."[65] This broader consciousness extends also to autopsies: in the English gentleman Henry of Lancaster's fourteenth-century *Le Livre de Seyntz Medicines*, he articulated an unmistakable familiarity with continental practices, praying that "he might be cut and opened before the Lord just as the bodies of executed criminals are dissected by physicians in the schools at Montpellier."[66] In no way did England's geographical isolation parlay into intellectual isolation or ignorance. Surely, England's medical practitioners were aware also of the prominence and affluence many of their Continental counterparts had achieved in their alliance with municipal governments.

The English were also alert to the fact that Continental courts worked differently, especially that royal officials elsewhere were paid salaries. Yet, quite astutely, the English feared that payments for service tainted an official's objectivity. Instead, the English strived to achieve something better. They hoped to guarantee impartiality by appointing or electing those whose finances were already secure. Members of Parliament reasoned that electing coroners from among the knightly class assured that they would have no need of bribes. While the English rationalization may have failed to account for human nature, Continental sources substantiate that English fears were well founded. There is plentiful evidence to demonstrate that Continental officeholders and expert witnesses engaged in extortion. Surgeons hired by the Crown of Aragon to assess the state of a wound in cases of assault proved to be highly vulnerable to bribery.[67]

Scholars have attributed England's failure to keep up with the Continental advance in legal medicine to a number of factors. England's standards of proof have received much attention in this respect. England depended primarily on jurors as witnesses; the enterprise of fact finding belonged to the jury, not the judge. In addition, the English never adopted Romano-canon law's rigorous evidentiary requirements: where Continental legal systems adhered to the rule of needing a confession or two eyewitnesses to convict, the English needed only a unanimous verdict from the jury, and the crown left it largely to the jurors to set their own standards of proof.[68] As a result, witnesses played a more fundamental role in the Continental courts than they did in English courts. It was only in the sixteenth century that witness testimony became an established part of common law proceedings.[69] England's late recognition of the centrality of witness testimony to a criminal trial coincides with the decline of the self-informing jury: as the courts were less able to rely on jurors as witnesses, they needed to search elsewhere for information. This transfer of knowledge gradually led to a sharpening of distinction between jurors and witnesses, opening a path for expert witnesses in the courtroom setting.[70] In terms of legal medicine, scholarly tradition has credited the "adversarial revolution" with its genesis. Prior to this, criminal trials purportedly took place without the presence or even advice of counsel: when lawyers penetrated the criminal courtroom, this paved the way also for the cross-examination of witnesses. Nonetheless, it is critical to acknowledge a major social change as a prerequisite to this eighteenth-century procedural innovation. The early modern English experienced a growth of specialist occupations in order to produce a crew of individuals uniquely qualified to comment on medical evidence.[71]

Common law itself has been targeted as being "inhospitable to the development of forensic medicine as a learned science."[72] Because "facts were determined by juries," the English did not have the same need to "ground their factual judgements in doctrines about proof and procedure" as the Continental judges did.[73] Where Continental judges enlisted the services of medical practitioners to construct a solid evidentiary base, the English jury eliminated any need for medical expertise. Rather, "[i]n England, juries became finders of fact and based their decisions on oral eyewitness testimony; there was no formal mechanism for obtaining evidence from anyone who had not been a direct observer of the events in question."[74] This perception of English history is essentially correct. Yet, the conclusions are far more definitive than our records permit. Because no one has scrutinized the process of how coroners' jurors collected their evidence, we really do not know whether they sought the advice of medical practitioners. While "there was no formal mechanism for obtaining evidence from anyone who had not been a direct observer of the events in question," in reality, English common law included few formal mechanisms relating to evidence at all! This investigation requires us to embrace the versatility of a law that is unwritten, and realize that without such rigid boundaries, royal officials and their juries had much more discretion at their disposal. As Chapter One will discuss in some depth, statute law did not explicitly require coroners to enlist the support of medical practitioners; nor did it prohibit them from doing so.

The function of jurors as witnesses further undermines this conception of medieval English law. No term existed for "expert witness" in common law until after 1790.[75] Granted, the medieval English had no need for one. Why summon expert witnesses to testify before a court of law when the jurors themselves were witnesses? Even if medieval England had no term for expert witness, it was no stranger to the idea. English law founded the special jury precisely on this premise. In many respects, medieval London was the testing ground for this practice. The mayor appointed special juries to address a whole host of issues. In January of 1389, when the aldermen caught wind of the sale of "unwholesome fish," the city assigned a jury of six fishmongers the task of reporting on the condition of the fish and determining who sold it. With their inside knowledge, they had little difficulty in discovering who was at fault. They announced that the fish belonged to Salamon Salamon, a mercer, who had already been in trouble with the law once before for the sale of "stinking fish" found at the bottom of a well near "Wallokesbernes."[76] The special jury was valuable also in cases involving medical expertise. In February of 1354, Thomas of Sheen complained to the mayor that he had hired John the Spicer of Cornhill to care for his wounded jaw but that "through want of skill on the part of the said John the Spicer, the said injury under his care has become apparently incurable." In response, the mayor appointed three surgeons (Master Paschal, Master Adam of the Poulter, and Master David of Westmorland) to investigate the allegations. They sided with the plaintiff.[77] London's mayoralty addressed a similar grievance in 1424. William Forset complained of the negligence of John Harwe (a surgeon), John Dalton (a barber), and Simon Rolf (a barber), whom he had hired to heal his mutilated hand. The city assembled a jury stocked with medical practitioners from a wide variety of backgrounds: Master Gilbert Kymer, physician and rector of the medical men of London; John Sombreshete, inceptor of medicines; Thomas Southwell, physician and surveyor of the Faculty of Physic in London; John Corby, physician; Thomas Morstede, surgeon; William Bradwardyne, surgeon; Henry Asshborne, surgeon; John Forde, surgeon. The jury also sought the testimony of John Parker, a barber-surgeon. After a thorough investigation, they exonerated the three defendants, declaring that they had behaved in a "surgically correct manner and had made no error." Not only did they acquit the three of all charges, but they also imposed upon William Forset "perpetual silence on this matter" in order to restore the defendants' good reputations.[78] Medical practitioners sometimes served on special juries in matters of a broader scope relating to public health. For example, in November of 1471, the mayor ordered barrels and pots of treacle suspected of being unwholesome brought to the Guildhall for investigation. The special jury he appointed included two Doctors in Medicine and several apothecaries.[79] The jury declared on oath that the treacle was unwholesome.[80] Once again, it seems ludicrous to suggest that the courts recognized the value of expert testimony in these instances, but saw no need for it in coroners' inquests.

The unpaid nature of the coroner's position acts as a sizeable stumbling block for a number of historians trying to understand how medical expertise might have come to play a part in the English legal process. Working on the supposition that medical practitioners, like their Continental counterparts, would only lend their services to the crown in exchange for good wages, historians have asked what motivation coroners had to pay medical experts from their own purses. Presumably, the answer is "none." The medieval crown's failure to establish a policy to compensate medical witnesses is regarded as a serious flaw. Indeed, if payment was the necessary foundation, then coroners had an "absence of incentive" to conduct any investigation until the Act of 1487 required payment of a fee to each coroner for conducting homicide inquests.[81] Of course, this act created additional problems: what enticement, then, did coroners have to investigate accidental deaths, or deaths of a sudden nature? It should come as no surprise that forensic medicine in England emerged as a discipline only after the English crown in the nineteenth century legislated an "incentive," by requiring that medical experts be paid to participate in trials.[82] Nonetheless, these conclusions are most relevant in a capitalist society, governed by the ideology that we all have capital in our own labor. Medieval England did not perceive labor in these terms. Rather, the genius of the medieval crown is that it created a system of administration, of not only law, but also government and the military, which functioned chiefly on unpaid labor by convincing the English population that service to the king was prestigious.[83]

In terms of the criminal justice system, this strategy ensured that the crown was able to reap the profits of justice and maintain peace within the realm, all without depleting the king's coffers. The main exception to the rule were royal justices, who did receive reasonable salaries; of course, because there was never more than a handful of royal justices at a time, the expense was not burdensome for the state. The king also expected most crown officials to foot the bill for their own expenses with respect to travel in performance of the king's justice—and they did. While such a system may seem derisory and unfeasible today, unpaid labor was the foundation of medieval English law and governance. Not only the aristocracy competed for judicial positions; even at the lower levels of society the peasantry (both free and unfree) were eager to represent their villages as (unpaid) jurors. Indeed, as Sherri Olson has suggested, "[t]he possibility that officeholding might have seemed unprofitable, too time-consuming or too little rewarding to tempt men to serve, is one that counters most views of village government, particularly for the later medieval period."[84]

One might well ask why anyone would be willing to take on such onerous work without remuneration. Clearly, the answer is that officeholding had its own rewards, if not always financial, then instead in communal standing and influence. The leet juror, one of the most burdensome and seemingly thankless offices of the medieval era, illustrates this point best. Yet, men were eager to serve, believing the office "wielded genuine power."[85] A village juror had the opportunity to assume the position of "village spokesman, an instrument of the court in its communal / collective dimension, the most important mouthpiece for that '*vox communitatis*' that overrode individual dissent or desire."[86] The opportunity to shape one's community and uphold the peace was more than sufficient reward for most men who chose to hold office. Consequently, we cannot assume that any medieval officeholder, such as the coroner, performed his tasks in a shoddy manner because he was not paid. Nor can we assume that medical practitioners were unwilling to participate in a coroner's inquest because there was no wage waiting for them at the end of the day. The medieval English were well accustomed to the "idea of the responsible private citizen whose participation is necessary to the maintenance of the common peace."[87]

THE RECORDS

Because of the chiefly financial nature of the coroners' reports, they present many challenges in discerning the process of death investigation. However, taken as a whole, they let us identify the main features of the process as well as the coroner's and jurors' priorities. Thus, the nucleus of this study is formed by surviving coroners' reports and communications, wherever they might be found: JUST 2, KB 9, Calendars of Inquisitions Miscellaneous, Ancient Petitions, patent rolls, and close rolls.[88] England's written legal tradition acts as a useful supplement to augment our knowledge of English process. Legal treatises (*Bracton*, *Britton*, *Fleta*, and *The Mirror of Justices*) as well as statute law offer an abundance of evidence concerning the role of the coroner and his jury in death investigation. The Year Books, in particular, furnish a wealth of information regarding the unique obstacles presented by death investigation. While Maitland perpetuated the myth that Year Books address only civil process, more recently David Seipp has rescued them from the dustbins of criminal historians by stressing the large percentage of debates relating to criminal issues found in these medieval textbooks. This plethora of legal insight derives from what Seipp sees as a misunderstanding concerning the process of criminal trial. Despite received wisdom that the crown denied legal counsel to individuals who stood accused of felony, Seipp confirms that lawyers regularly counseled and defended criminal defendants. As a result, the Year Books needed to address issues of a criminal nature in order to teach future lawyers and pleaders the criminal process.[89] Finally, this monograph will exploit also England's surviving records of canonization trials. For those saints who specialized in bringing back the dead (such as Becket and de Cantilupe), witness depositions have much to say about the regular process of death investigation. More important still, because they were compiled for adjudication by Roman clergy, the records are careful to explain English process for an audience unfamiliar with it.

Because coroners' rolls form the base of this study, it is vital to acknowledge the context in which they were written, and how that context shaped their form and survival. Frederick Pollock, one of the great minds of legal history, once wrote:

> The habit of preserving some written record of all affairs of importance is a modern one in the north and west of Europe. But it is so prevalent and so much bound up with our daily habits that we have almost forgotten how much of the world's business, even in communities by no means barbarous, has been carried on without it. And the student of early laws and institutions, although the fact is constantly thrust upon him, can hardly accept it without a sort of continuing surprise.[90]

While Pollock directed his remarks toward the Anglo-Saxon world, the sentiment holds equally true for England in the later medieval period. Unlike what we see going on in Continental Europe at this time, the "formation of literate habits was relatively slow [to develop] in England."[91] English government officials in the fourteenth century were far more comfortable creating lists than writing letters, and oral testimony garnered a confidence that written documents could not evoke.[92] Proofs of age illustrate the medieval

English reluctance to embrace the written record, even if it might save money and time. When an heir reached the age of majority, he needed to provide proof of age. Rather than rely on written certification of birth, the medieval English adopted an elaborate and expensive process of bringing witnesses before royal justices to testify collectively to an heir's age by stirring up memories of contemporary events that might situate the heir's birth in a clear chronology.[93] Royal justices had even greater concerns about the written record. England's preference for collective oral testimony over written record was grounded distinctly in fears of micromanagement, believing that each case should properly "be judged on its merits, unrestricted by precedents in writing."[94] Perhaps most importantly, the English aversion to relying too heavily on the written word extended well beyond the medieval era.

This distinctly English predilection for oral evidence is the key to understanding medieval coroners' rolls. The responsibilities of the coronership were twofold. First, the crown expected the coroner to be his financial representative in the county, guaranteeing that the king would receive his due. Second, in the interests of upholding the peace, an indispensable royal obligation, the state assigned coroners the task of carrying out competent death investigations in order to restore harmony to the locality of the visne. Generally, the coroners' rolls are a much better reflection of the former than the latter. Yet, because England was in the midst of transitioning from a primarily oral culture to a more document-driven one, this should come as no surprise. The precision evident in the coroners' rolls as it relates to monies owed to the king emanates from the English comfort with listing. A full, step-by-step narrative of the investigation surely seemed extraneous to most Englishmen. It is significant also that where the coroners' rolls went, so too did the coroner. The crown obligated the coroner to attend the general eyre (later the assize) to read out the coroners' rolls. Coroners may well have regarded their documentation merely as a mnemonic device to remind them of the essential details of a case when called upon to discuss it more fully in a courtroom setting.

If we separate the coroner from his documentation, it is clear that the rolls themselves held a distinct purpose to act as a check on the presentments of the hundred jurors: that is, if the hundred jurors failed to present on deaths that appeared in the coroners' rolls, the crown fined the entire community for concealment. The poor survival rate of coroners' rolls is integrally related to this function. So few coroners' rolls have survived the medieval period because once they were used to check the hundred jurors' presentments they were cancelled. There was little reason to preserve the coroners' rolls once they had fulfilled their purpose.[95] Here, M.T. Clanchy offers a powerful reminder about the nature of societies on the cusp of literacy. He writes, "[d]ocuments do not automatically become records. Writing may be done for ephemeral purposes without any intention of keeping the documents permanently."[96] Carrie Smith provides a useful measure of the proportion of coroners' rolls that have gone missing. For the county of

Hampshire, she notes that a mere twelve coroners' rolls are extant from the reigns of Edward III and Richard II (a period of roughly seventy-two years). Yet, the close rolls record the appointments of forty-seven other coroners during that period: what happened to their rolls?[97] In addition, some coroners' reports were never enrolled. Coroners or their clerks drew up their initial reports on scraps of parchment or wax tablets. Prior to the meeting of the general eyre, coroners charged their clerks with collating these materials into a proper roll, England's peculiar approach to record management.[98] If a coroner died in office, there was a good possibility that his records might never be enrolled, even though common law charged his heirs to do so.

Given the transitional nature of the records, it is no wonder that such variety exists in the structure and level of completion apparent in the coroners' enrollments. In general, medieval coroners were no more keen on paperwork than are bureaucrats today. Indeed, some enrollments expose a coroner with a distinct hostility to paperwork, intent to spend as little time as possible recording the details of his investigations for the unfortunate scrivener who would later transform the heap of hastily drafted files into a formal roll. The following enrollment, drawn from a Lincolnshire coroner's roll, provides an illustration of a coroner who documented only the barest of detail:

> Gainsborough, Scawby, Donington.[99] Jurors present on their oath that Gilbert Bertranus of Tankersley, tenant at See [Sea End?], on the Sunday closest before the feast of Saint Swithin [July 2] in the xvi year of the reign of King Edward the iii since the conquest [1342] feloniously slew Idonea, wife of the said Gilbert of Tankersley, at See. And after the fact he fled.[100]

With the inclusion of so few specifics, this enrollment supplies no glimpse of the investigative process, leaving the reader without answers to a number of key questions: were there witnesses? What did they discover at the scene of the crime? What did they learn from the post-mortem examination? How did they manage to reach a verdict in order to compose an enrollment with (seemingly) such little evidence? The record discloses even less information about the fundamentals of the crime: how did he kill her? Was there a weapon? Where did he kill her (in someone's home, in the street?)? What was his motivation? The deficiency of the documentation has often led historians to believe that medieval coroners adopted an equally sloppy approach to the investigation itself. However, such a conclusion is not demonstrable or even reasonable. Coroners recognized the investigation as the first priority. The record, which was primarily for financial purposes, was somewhat of an afterthought. Once again, because the crown required coroners to attend sessions of the eyre (and later assizes), coroners were present in court to correct any misinformation perpetuated by such a pithy record. In addition, while coroners had useful guidelines concerning the investigative process, how to compose the record was not part of that instruction. Nor did formularies address the issue. Parliament failed to set any guidelines until the 1413 Statute of Additions, and even those requirements were minimal and applied only in instances when the enrollment acted also as an indictment.[101] The statute stipulated that indictments must include the following: the name of the defendant, his or her estate/degree/mystery, and place of residence. Given the low expectations of the state in terms of documentation, historians should greet any extraneous detail relating to the investigative process as a windfall.

Thankfully, some coroners relished the investigative process and ostensibly viewed the documentation as an opportunity to record their achievements for posterity. Here is an example of a much more comprehensive enrollment:

> At the county of Suffolk, taken at Gipping on the Monday after the feast of Pentecost in the xxxth year of King Edward the iii since the Conquest [1356]. G. Seintcler then sheriff. The villes of Hasketon, Melton with Ufford, Great Bealings, and Little Martlesham present that on the Tuesday after the feast of Saint John before the Latin Gate in the abovesaid year a certain contention arose between William the Piper of Woodbridge, aged xxiiii years and more, and John Scalon of the same, and they punched each other with their hands and after this came John Bray, chaplain, and others and the said John Bray took the said John Scalon by the neck by which he resisted from his said malice and to this came the same William and struck the said John Scalon while he was being held and forthwith the said John Scalon took a knife called "broche" out of the sheath of the said John Bray without the said John Bray knowing it and struck the said William feloniously with a wound in the chest ix inches deep, i inch in latitude from which wound the said William died, languishing for ix days following [the dispute]. The inquisition was taken at Woodbridge over the body before Richard of Martlesham, coroner of the king for the said county, on Saturday after the feast of Saint Dunstan in the abovesaid year by xii [jurors] and [representatives from the] iiii [neighboring vills]. Who say on their oath that nothing other can be inquired except that the said John Scalon feloniously killed the said William le Piper as above. And after the felony had been committed, he immediately fled and evaded [the law] in defect of the vill of Woodbridge the value of the weapon which was used in the killing is xviii *d.* for which the vill of Woodbridge responds. Asked of the goods and chattels of the felon, lands and tenements, they say on their oath that he had chattels worth xl *d.* for which the vill of Woodbridge responds and he had no lands or tenements. Alice wife of the said William was with him in his home when he died. Her pledges are John Vynce and William of Brustleham. Nearest neighbors are John Shepherd, Reginald the Cook, Henry the Smith, John the Baxter. Whose pledges are Peter Ole, Thomas Crane, John of Bokenham, John Collesson, Hugh le Cravet, William Roc, John Holdelong, John the Shepherd.[102]

The only element missing from this record is a jury list, but jury lists were often missing. As this last example should illustrate, despite the frequent grumbling of medieval historians over the laconic nature of English royal records, enrollments of a more complete nature have much to offer.

The uneven nature of the coroners' reports creates some sizeable problems for the historian. Among others, while this monograph examines the coroner and his jury from the origin of the office in 1194 to the end of the fifteenth century, the nature of the records coupled with poor survival rates have had a profound impact on our ability to measure changes over time. First, the great disparity in coroners' enrollments witnessed above makes it difficult to discern whether a coroner's actions are the product of changes in practice, or simply an individual coroner's reporting style. For example, the first enrollment above mentions nothing about pledges for the nearest neighbors. A newcomer to the coroners' rolls might conclude that the practice of taking pledges must have developed in the fourteen-year period between the two above enrollments, when in reality these enrollments are merely products of two very different approaches to recording the results of an inquest.

Second, the survival rate of coroners' rolls produces a skewed vision of the evolution of the coronership. The vast majority of coroners' rolls date to the thirteenth and fourteenth centuries. After the general eyre ceased to exist in the fourteenth century,[103] the crown processed coroners' rolls centrally, first before a visitation of the itinerant King's Bench, then after King's Bench ceased to perambulate in the early fifteenth century, coroners submitted them directly to Westminster.[104] Without the regular threat of a looming eyre, coroners had less incentive to assemble their reports on a regular basis. Moreover, because of the "intrinsically sporadic" collection of coroners' rolls, "large numbers of records were never sent to Westminster even if they had been formally engrossed in the first place."[105] The irregular preservation of documentation means that for the thirteenth and fourteenth centuries, there is a good corpus of extant coroners' rolls; but after that, they are few in number and often preserved in unexpected places. These two factors together make it near impossible to track in any definitive way changes over time in the practices of the coroner or his reporting.

A WORD OF CAUTION

The temptation to draw comparisons between modern law enforcement (i.e., what we know best) and its medieval counterpart is sometimes overwhelming. Yet, comparisons between the two in general encourage an uncomplimentary view of the medieval criminal justice system, that is, if we fail to take into account differences in context and process. To offer a pertinent illustration: the turn toward the social sciences in the 1960s produced widespread criticism for medieval England's tolerance for felony, evidenced by high acquittal rates (roughly 70–80% for medieval felony trials)[106] and a distinct reluctance to send murderers to the gallows. Furthermore, medieval England's readiness to release known murderers back into the general population only to wreak further havoc has created unimaginably violent perceptions of the medieval landscape. English scholars have argued in favor of high levels of interpersonal violence: "every person in England in the thirteenth century, if he did not personally witness a murder, knew or knew of someone who had been killed."[107] "[I]n medieval London or Oxford, the man in the street ran more of a risk of dying at the hands of a fellow citizen than he did from an accident."[108] Yet, these conclusions rest on untenable comparisons. Acquittal rates over such vast distances of time cannot be compared on equal terms. While the English crown embraced execution as the only acceptable penalty for felony, today's courts offer a broad menu of punishments. As a result, in modern America, 94% of indicted felons plead guilty, while few medieval felons chose to do so.[109] This discrepancy immediately invalidates any meaningful statistical comparison.

Manpower and procedural differences in terms of law enforcement also create immeasurable distinctions in the nature of those who appeared before the courts in medieval England. Working without the benefit of a modern police force, those medieval felony suspects who knew the evidence stacked against them was sufficient to result in a conviction (that is, roughly 72%) fled the scene of the crime and were never heard from again.[110] Thus, many of those individuals who did not flee after a crime did so because they were confident in their innocence, or, at least assured that they would not be convicted.[111] Medieval courts of law also pursued different aims. While courts today strive for conviction, often medieval juries were content to interpret time served in prison awaiting trial as sufficient punishment for a felon's actions.[112] This is a critical point. We cannot judge the medieval system of law as being any better or worse than the modern system, when in reality it was just profoundly different. Instead of evaluating the common law by modern standards, we need to gain a clearer understanding of how the legal system worked in its own time and place. Of course, none of this prevents us from indulging in drawing comparisons with modern systems of law enforcement, providing we understand that, in effect, we are comparing two very different models.[113]

With such a project, we need also to address what has been referred to alternately as the "tech effect" or the "*CSI* effect."[114] The 21st century is a period of technological revolution in which technology (at least in the popular mindset) presents itself as the ultimate solution to almost every fathomable problem. The ubiquity of technology as the decisive factor in crime scene investigations is most evident in American television programming. *CSI*, *Law and Order*, and *Bones*, for example, have not only heightened our expectations of "the quantity, quality and availability of scientific evidence," but they may also have had a very real impact on courtroom trials. Lawyers today labor under the anxiety of disappointing the jury when prosecuting or defending a case in which forensics play little role.[115] Moreover, because of the focus on forensics in television programs, the lay public holds to unrealistic perceptions of case completion. While television depicts a 94% solution rate, in reality only 40% of crimes are ever solved.[116] For the purposes of this study, these perceptions act as a useful reminder not to set an unrealistic bar for medieval criminal justice.

THIS STUDY IN BRIEF

How better to deconstruct the process of death investigation than to begin with the personalities involved? Chapter One will focus on the coroners, beginning with the legal evidence. What did the crown expect of its coroners? How did the English define the position and scope of the office? More important still: what kind of men became coroners? And, did their backgrounds prepare them for posts in law enforcement? This chapter tackles also a number of fallacies about the coroner. Foremost, aspersions of corruption and negligence have dominated studies of the coroner, although, as this chapter will make clear, the evidence is slim and unrepresentative. Scholarly tradition has perpetuated an ideal hierarchy of officeholding that relegates the coronership to a position of minor authority, even though it was manned by a corpus of former (and sometimes current) mayors, sheriffs, and bailiffs. Even with men of high social standing and authority executing the office, the inevitable conclusion to be drawn from the crown's recommendations for the coronership is that the position was too large for one man. Coroners had no choice but to rely heavily on their jurors in order to meet the expectations of the law.

Chapter Two asks the critical question: who served on coroners' juries? Medieval England's customary approach to jury service was to reserve important issues to important people. Thus, knowing more about the kinds of people who served on inquests will help us to understand more precisely the place and priority of the inquest in the legal process. In this respect, scholarly tradition has faltered. There is no consensus in the field about the status of coroners' jurors. Historians have proposed equally convincing arguments for juries of elite status and for the unfree. Others have ignored status altogether and placed precedence instead on proximity, claiming death investigation was all about neighbors. This chapter hopes to draw some tentative conclusions by juxtaposing crown expectations for juror qualifications in terms of income, locality, and moral rectitude with a study of coroners' jurors drawn from the city of York in the years 1363 to 1378. A rigorous analysis of jury lists side by side with poll tax evidence and the register of freemen suggests that jury duty on a coroner's inquest was a position of prestige with great appeal to the upper middling ranks of York. Nonetheless, there is little reason to believe that coroners sacrificed knowledge to status. Coroners were determined to meet the needs of the office by appointing also jurors whose unique knowledge, through familiarity with the deceased, awareness of the law, or medical expertise, would contribute to an efficient and effective inquiry.

Death investigation is always a contentious process. Assigning meaning to death has enormous implications for the family, the community, the participants in the investigative process, and the crown. Thus, coroners had to tread lightly, negotiating a whole host of conflicting, yet equally compelling, concerns. Chapter Three walks the reader through the process of death investigation. Medieval inquests shared much with their modern counterparts. Today, integrity of body and scene are top priorities; so, too, were they for medieval coroners and communities. Although the English did not sanction the use of autopsies, the inquest's post-mortem examination was much more hands-on and informative than scholars have previously imagined. Testimonial evidence assumed a variety of forms: eyewitnesses, character witnesses, confessions, and dying declarations. What is perhaps most intriguing, however, is the coroners' desire to protect the identity of those witnesses, in the hopes of curbing future violence. An overall assessment of the investigative process highlights coroners and jurors willing to exploit all the tools at their disposal in order to conduct an effective investigation.

For jurors, some inquests presented greater challenges than others did, and most of those centered on questions of a medical nature. Chapter Four explores the medical dimension of the coroner's inquest. Some degree of medical competence was required from the moment a community became aware of a death in its midst. The crown tasked coroners with investigating all sudden and unnatural deaths, but the coroner only initiated an investigation after local authorities sent for him. How did localities define a death as unnatural and thus deserving of investigation? Obviously, the larger question behind this is: why these deaths? Why do the coroners' rolls include some deaths to the exclusion of others? Second, the primary task of the investigators was to determine cause of death, but not all deaths transpired in the presence of witnesses or produced physical evidence of an unambiguous nature. In cases of assault, this was particularly crucial as their verdict might cost the perpetrator his life. It was the responsibility of the jury to establish a causal connection between assault and homicide. This matter was even more complicated when the victim was pregnant. Jurors had the unenviable task of calculating exactly how much force was required to cause a woman to miscarry. Finally, the crown did not hold all felons responsible for their actions. Common law classified the mentally incapacitated alongside children and beasts: lacking moral discretion, they could not be held criminally accountable. But how did medieval jurors negotiate that line between sanity and mental incapacity?

Chapter Five articulates the value of exploiting legal documents for medical historical purposes. The coroners' rolls have much to tell us about contemporary perceptions of disease and medical practices. For example, despite the reticence of historians to interpret *pestilencia* as bubonic plague, seeing instead that it referred to any mortal disease, the coroners' rolls suggest just the opposite. In common parlance, *pestilencia* did indeed mean bubonic plague. Similarly, the rolls shed light on the average person's understanding of epilepsy and senescence. Most of our historical knowledge of medical practices is drawn from medical treatises, written by elite practitioners. The coroners' rolls open a window into daily medical practices, revealing general perceptions of curettage, bloodletting, the accountability of medieval practitioners under the law, and the treatment of the elderly. Altogether, the coroners' rolls construct a powerful argument for medical historians' taking a fresh look at the legal materials.

NOTES

1. Thomas A. Green, *Verdict According to Conscience: Perspectives on the English Criminal Trial Jury, 1200–1800* (Chicago: University of Chicago Press, 1985).
2. Thomas R. Forbes reminds us that it was only two centuries ago that the basis for a verdict was limited to evidence presented in court. See his *Surgeons at the Bailey: English Forensic Medicine to 1878* (New Haven: Yale UP, 1985), p. 23.
3. J.S. Cockburn and Thomas A. Green, eds., *Twelve Good Men and True: The Criminal Trial Jury in England, 1200–1800* (Princeton: Princeton UP, 1988).
4. The Fourteenth British Legal History Conference held in Edinburgh in July of 1999 boasted the theme of "Parliaments, Juries, and the Law," and was a direct response to the stimulating work of Green and others. This conference resulted in the monograph edited by John W. Cairns and Grant McLeod, "*The Dearest Birth Right of the People of England": The Jury in the History of the Common Law* (Oxford: Hart Pub., 2002).
5. Anthony J. Musson, "Twelve Good Men and True? The Character of Early Fourteenth-Century Juries," *L&HR* 15.1 (1997): 115–44; J.G. Bellamy, *The Criminal Trial in Later Medieval England: Felony before the Courts from Edward I to the Sixteenth Century* (Toronto and Buffalo: University of Toronto Press, 1998); Daniel Klerman, "Was the Jury Ever Self-Informing?" *Southern California Law Review* 77:123 (2004): 123–49; Mike McNair, "Vicinage and the Antecedents of the Jury," *L&HR* 17 (1999): 537–90; and James Masschaele, *Jury, State, and Society in Medieval England* (New York: Palgrave Macmillan, 2008). McNair's article elicited a forum within the same volume of *L&HR*. Respondents included Charles Donahue, Jr., "Biology and the Origins of the English Jury," 591–96, Patrick Wormald, "Neighbors, Courts and Kings: Reflections on Michael McNair's *Vicini*," 597–601, and concluding remarks by Mike McNair, "Law, Politics and the Jury," 603–7.
6. Bernard W. McLane, "Juror Attitudes toward Local Disorder: The Evidence of the 1328 Trailbaston Proceedings," in Cockburn and Green, *Twelve Good Men and True*, pp. 36–64.
7. Sherri Olson, *A Chronicle of All That Happens: Voices from the Village Court in Medieval England* (Toronto: PIMS, 1996); Maureen Mulholland, "The Jury in English Manorial Courts," in Cairns and McLeod, *The Dearest Birth Right*, pp. 63–74; Maureen Mulholland, "Trials in Manorial Courts in Late Medieval England," in *Judicial Tribunals in England and Europe, 1200–1700*, ed. Mulholland and Brian Pullan, 2 vols. (Manchester: Manchester UP, 2003), v. 1, pp. 81–101; Peter L. Larson, "Village Voice or Village Oligarchy? The Jurors of the Durham Halmote Court, 1349–1424," *L&HR* 28.3 (2010): 675–709.
8. Masschaele, *Jury, State, and Society*.

9. Matthew Holford, "Thrifty Men of the Country? The Jurors and their Role," in *The Fifteenth-Century Inquisitions Post-Mortem: A Companion*, ed. Michael Hicks (Woodbridge: Boydell, 2012), pp. 201–22.
10. C.J. Neville, "Common Knowledge of the Common Law in Later Medieval England," *Canadian Journal of History* 29.3 (1994): 475. Eventually indictment became a more formalized process performed before a grand jury; however, at this time indictments were laid in three tribunals: sheriff's tourns, sessions of the peace, and coroners' inquests. In many respects, the transition process began in the late fourteenth and fifteenth centuries. See Bellamy, *The Criminal Trial*, p. 23.
11. Klerman, "Was the Jury ever Self-informing?," 138; John Marshall Mitnik, "Neighbor-Witness to Judge of Proofs: The Transformation of the English Civil Juror," *AJLH* 32.3 (1988): 201–35.
12. Anthony J. Musson, *Public Order and Law Enforcement: The Local Administration of Criminal Justice, 1294–1350* (Woodbridge: Boydell, 1996), p. 153.
13. Edward Powell, "Jury Trial at Gaol Delivery in the Late Middle Ages: The Midland Circuit, 1400–1429," in Cockburn and Green, *Twelve Good Men and True*, p. 90. Musson and J.B. Post have drawn comparable conclusions; see Post, "Jury Lists and Juries in the Late Fourteenth Century," in Cockburn and Green, *Twelve Good Men and True*, p. 68; Musson, *Public Order and Law Enforcement*, pp. 130–31, 190–91.
14. Musson, *Public Order and Law Enforcement*, p. 191.
15. R.F. Hunnisett, "An Early Coroner's Roll," *Bulletin of the Institute of Historical Research* 30 (1957): 225–31; "Sussex Coroners in the Middle Ages. In 3 parts," *Sussex Archaeological Collections* 95 (1957): 42–58, 96 (1958): 17–34, and 98 (1960): 44–70; "The Origin of the Office of the Coroner," *Transactions of the Royal Historical Society* 5th series, v. 8 (1958): 84–104; "The Medieval Coroners' Rolls," *AJLH* 3 (1959): 95–124, 205–21, 324–59; "Pleas of the Crown and the Coroner," *Bulletin of the Institute of Historical Research* 32 (1959): 117–37; *The Medieval Coroner* (Cambridge: Cambridge UP, 1961); "The Reliability of Inquisitions as Historical Evidence," in *The Study of Medieval Records: Essays in Honour of Kathleen Major*, ed. D.A. Bullough and R.L. Storey (Oxford: Oxford UP, 1971), pp. 206–35. This list does not include also his myriad transcriptions and translations of coroners' rolls for the counties of Bedford, Sussex, and Nottinghamshire.
16. C.J. Neville, "'The Bishop's Ministers': The Office of Coroner in Late Medieval Durham," *Florilegium* 18.2 (2001): 47.
17. Barbara A. Hanawalt, *Crime and Conflict in English Communities, 1300–1348* (Cambridge, MA: Harvard UP, 1979).
18. Among others, Barbara A. Hanawalt, *The Ties That Bound: Peasant Families in Medieval England* (New York: Oxford UP, 1986); Hanawalt, *Growing up in Medieval London: The Experience of Childhood in History* (New York: Oxford UP, 1993). Dr. Hanawalt has written many pieces on the subject of the medieval family, juxtaposing the evidence of the coroners' rolls against gaol delivery rolls and literary works. See also Sara M. Butler, *The Language of Abuse: Marital Violence in Later Medieval England* (Leiden: Brill, 2007).
19. Gwen Seabourne and Alice Seabourne, "The Law on Suicide in Medieval England," *JLH* 21.1 (2000): 21–48; Sara M. Butler, "Degrees of Culpability: Suicide Verdicts, Mercy, and the Jury in Medieval England," *JMEMS* 36.2 (2006): 263–90; Butler, "Local Concerns: Suicide and Jury Behavior in Medieval England," *History Compass* 4.5 (2006): 820–35; Butler, "Women, Suicide, and the Jury in Later Medieval England," *Signs: Journal of Women in Culture and Society* 32.1 (2006): 141–66; and Butler, "Cultures of Suicide? Regionalism and Suicide Verdicts in Medieval England," *The Historian* 69.3 (2007): 427–49.

20. Carrie Smith, "Medieval Coroners' Rolls: Legal Fiction or Historical Fact?" in *Courts, Counties and the Capital in the Later Middle Ages*, ed. Diana E.S. Dunn (New York: St Martin's Press, 1996), pp. 93–115.
21. Katherine D. Watson, *Forensic Medicine in Western Society* (London and New York: Routledge, 2011), p. 43; Catherine Crawford, "Legalizing Medicine: Early Modern Legal Systems and the Growth of Medico-legal Knowledge," in *Legal Medicine in History*, ed. Crawford and Michael Clark (Cambridge: Cambridge UP, 1994), p. 89.
22. Technically, outlaws had not been declared guilty; however, flight from the scene of the crime was considered evidence of guilt.
23. Anne Reiber DeWindt and Edwin Brezette DeWindt, *Royal Justice and the Medieval English Countryside: The Huntingdonshire Eyre of 1286, the Ramsey Abbey Banlieu Court of 1287, and the Assizes of 1287–88*, pt. 1 (Toronto: PIMS, 1981), pp. 101–3. From this total, it is worthy of note that a little over £14 came from deodands, roughly £18 from *murdrum* fines, and £80 came from the confiscation of felons' property.
24. Carole Rawcliffe, *Leprosy in Medieval England* (Woodbridge: Boydell, 2006), p. 167.
25. J.G. Bellamy, *Crime and Public Order in England in the Later Middle Ages* (London: Routledge & Kegan Paul, 1972), p. 201.
26. Simon Walker, "Order and Law," in *A Social History of England 1200–1500*, ed. Rosemary Horrox and W. Mark Ormrod (Cambridge: Cambridge UP, 2006), p. 111.
27. Katharine Park, "The Life of the Corpse: Division and Dissection in Late Medieval Europe," *JHMAS* 50.1 (1995): 111.
28. Park, "The Life of the Corpse," 115.
29. Park, "The Life of the Corpse," 115.
30. "Abortion by assault" is not the term that was employed in this period; rather, the medieval English would have referred to this as an abortion. However, since abortion today has a far different meaning, I have chosen to refer to this form of abortion specifically as abortion by assault. For a more detailed discussion, see my "Abortion by Assault: Violence against Pregnant Women in Thirteenth- and Fourteenth-Century England," *Journal of Women's History* 17.4 (2005): 9–31.
31. Thomas R. Forbes, "By What Disease or Casualty? The Changing Face of Death in London," *JHMAS* 31.4 (1976): 395–420; *The Crowners Quest* (Philadelphia: The American Philosophical Society, 1978); *Surgeons at the Bailey*.
32. Forbes, "By What Disease or Casualty?," 396.
33. K.J. Kesselring, "Detecting 'Death Disguised,'" *History Today* 56.4 (2006): 24–5.
34. Carol Loar, "Medical Knowledge and the Early Modern English Coroner's Inquest," *SHoM* 23.3 (2010): 479–81.
35. Helen Brock and Catherine Crawford, "Forensic Medicine in Early Colonial Maryland, 1633–83," in Crawford and Clark, *Legal Medicine in History*, pp. 40–41.
36. Watson, *Forensic Medicine in Western Society*, p. 18.
37. See Richard Fraher, "Conviction According to Conscience: The Medieval Jurists Debate Concerning Judicial Discretion and the Law of Proof," *L&HR* 7.1 (1989): 23–88.
38. Trevor Dean, *Crime in Medieval Europe* (Edinburgh: Longman, 2001), p. 4.
39. Michael R. McVaugh, *Medicine before the Plague: Practitioners and Their Patients in the Crown of Aragon 1285–1345* (Cambridge: Cambridge UP, 1993), pp. 200–205.
40. Katharine Park, "Holy Autopsies: Saintly Bodies and Medical Expertise, 1300–1600," in *The Body in Early Modern Italy*, ed. Julia L. Hairston and Walter Stephens (Baltimore: Johns Hopkins, 2010), p. 62.

41. J. Ziegler, "Practitioners and Saints: Medical Men in Canonization Processes in the Thirteenth to Fifteenth Centuries," *SHoM* 12.2 (1999): 191–225.
42. Watson, *Forensic Medicine in Western Society*, p. 35.
43. McVaugh, *Medicine before the Plague*, p. 208.
44. Joseph Shatzmiller, ed., *Médecine et Justice en Provence Médiévale: Documents de Manosque, 1262–1348* (Aix-en-Provence: Publications de l'Université de Provence, 1989); McVaugh, *Medicine before the Plague*, p. 200; Guido Ruggiero, "The Cooperation of Physicians and the State in the Control of Violence in Renaissance Venice," *JHMAS* 33 (1978): 159; Crawford, "Legalizing Medicine," p. 93.
45. Shatzmiller, *Médecine et Justice*, pp. 132, 63; Andrée Courtemanche, "The Judge, the Doctor and the Poisoner: Medical Expertise in Manosquin Judicial Rituals at the End of the Fourteenth Century," in *Medieval and Early Modern Ritual: Formalized Behavior in Europe, China, and Japan*, ed. Joëlle Rollo-Koster (Leiden: Brill, 2002), pp. 105–23.
46. Ruggiero, "Cooperation of Physicians," 158.
47. Ruggiero, "Cooperation of Physicians," 159.
48. McVaugh, *Medicine before the Plague*, p. 211.
49. Joseph Shatzmiller, "The Jurisprudence of the Dead Body: Medical Practition at the Service of Civic and Legal Authorities," *Micrologus* 7 (1999): 225.
50. Shatzmiller, "Jurisprudence of the Dead Body," 224, 230.
51. Nancy G. Siraisi, "Girolamo Cardano and the Art of Medical Narrative," *Journal of the History of Ideas* 52.4 (1991): 594.
52. Siraisi, "Girolamo Cardano," 589.
53. Watson, *Forensic Medicine in Western Society*, p. 1.
54. Monica H. Green, "Integrative Medicine: Incorporating Medicine and Health into the Canon of Medieval European History," *History Compass* 7.4 (2009): 1227.
55. Déirdre M. Dwyer, "Expert Evidence in the English Civil Courts, 1550–1800," *JLH* 28.1 (2007): 114.
56. Silvia De Renzi, "Medical Expertise, Bodies, and the Law in Early Modern Courts," *Isis* 98.2 (2007): 318.
57. Hiram Kümper, "Learned Men and Skillful Matrons: Medical Expertise and the Forensics of Rape in the Middle Ages," in *Medicine and the Law in the Middle Ages*, ed. Wendy J. Turner and Sara M. Butler (Leiden: Brill, 2014), pp. 88–108.
58. Karen Jillings, "Plague, Pox, and the Physician in Aberdeen, 1495–1516," *Journal of the Royal College of Physicians of Edinburgh* 40.1 (2010): 70–76.
59. Richelle Munkhoff, "Searchers of the Dead: Authority, Marginality, and the Interpretation of Plague in England, 1574–1665," *Gender & History* 11.1 (1999): 10.
60. McVaugh, *Medicine before the Plague*, p. 217.
61. Elma Brenner, "Recent Perspectives on Leprosy in Medieval Western Europe," *History Compass* 8.5 (2010): 395.
62. McVaugh, *Medicine before the Plague*, pp. 219–22.
63. Park, "Holy Autopsies," p. 65.
64. Faye Getz, *Medicine in the English Middle Ages* (Princeton: Princeton UP, 1998), p. 24.
65. Margaret Pelling, *Medical Conflicts in Early Modern London: Patronage, Physicians, and Irregular Practitioners 1550–1640* (Oxford: Clarendon Press, 2003), p. 9.
66. Naoë Yoshikawa, "Holy Medicine and Diseases of the Soul: Henry of Lancaster and *Le Livre de Deyntz Medicines*," *MH* 53 (2009): 403.
67. McVaugh, *Medicine before the Plague*, pp. 211–14.

68. Crawford, "Legalizing Medicine," p. 96.
69. Barbara J. Shapiro, *A Culture of Fact: England, 1550–1720* (Ithaca: Cornell UP, 2000), pp. 11–12.
70. Shapiro, *Culture of Fact*, p. 12.
71. Dwyer, "Expert Evidence," 114. See also Carol A.G. Jones, *Expert Witnesses: Science, Medicine and the Practice of Law* (Oxford: Clarendon Press, 1994), p. 19.
72. Crawford, "Legalizing Medicine," p. 105.
73. Crawford, "Legalizing Medicine," pp. 100, 98.
74. Watson, *Forensic Medicine in Western Society*, p. 9.
75. Dwyer, "Expert Evidence," 96.
76. Reginald R. Sharpe, ed., *Calendar of Letter-Books of the City of London*, 11 vols., (London: John Edward Francis, 1899–1912), v. H, pp. 344–54.
77. H.T. Riley, ed., *Memorials of London and London Life: In the 13th, 14th and 15th Centuries* (London: Longmans, 1868), pp. 273–75.
78. A.H. Thomas, ed., *Calendar of Plea and Memoranda Rolls of the City of London, 1413–1437* (Cambridge: Cambridge UP, 1943), pp. 174–75. The requirement for perpetual silence on a matter of reputation was common in defamation suits. See Ian Forrest, "Defamation, Heresy and Late Medieval Social Life," in *Image, Text and Church, 1380–1600: Essays for Margaret Aston,* ed. Linda Clark, Maureen Jurkowski, and Colin Richmond (Toronto: PIMS, 2009), p. 145.
79. It is not clear how many apothecaries were on the jury. The word "apothecaries" appears after a list of seventeen names, so it is entirely possible that all seventeen were apothecaries, or that only the last few were apothecaries.
80. Sharpe, *Calendar of Letter-Books*, v. L, pp. 100–110.
81. J.D.J. Havard, *The Detection of Secret Homicide: A Study of the Medico-Legal System of Investigation of Sudden and Unexplained Deaths* (London: Macmillan, 1960), p. 35.
82. Crawford, "Legalizing Medicine," p. 109. Mary Beth Emmerichs has also made this point. See her "Getting Away with Murder? Homicide and the Coroners in Nineteenth-Century London," *Social Science History* 25.1 (2001): 96. See also Watson, *Forensic Medicine in Western Society*, p. 40.
83. Scott Waugh, "Reluctant Knights and Jurors: Respites, Exemptions, and Public Obligations in the Reign of Henry III," *Speculum* 58.4 (1983): 937–86.
84. Olson, *A Chronicle of All That Happens*, p. 104.
85. Anne Reiber DeWindt, "Local Government in a Small Town: A Medieval Leet Jury and Its Constituents," *Albion* 23.4 (1991): 628.
86. Olson, *A Chronicle of All That Happens*, p. 128.
87. Heather Kerr, "'Romancing the Handbook': Scenes of Detection in *Arden of Faversham*," in *'This Earthly Stage': World and Stage in Late Medieval and Early Modern England*, ed. Brett Hirsch and Christopher Wortham (Turnhout: Brepols, 2010), p. 178.
88. A complete inventory of extant coroners' rolls appears in Jeremy Gibson and Colin Rogers, *Coroners' Records in England and Wales*, 3rd ed. (Bury, Lancs.: The Family History Partnership, 2009).
89. David J. Seipp, "Crime in the Year Books," in *Law Reporting in Britain*, ed. Chantal Stebbings (London and Rio Grande, OH: Hambledon, 1995), pp. 15–34.
90. F. Pollock, "Anglo-Saxon Law," *English Historical Review* 8.30 (1893): 239.
91. M.T. Clanchy, *From Memory to Written Record: England 1066–1307*, 3rd ed. (Malden, MA: John Wiley & Sons, 2013), p. 187.
92. Given the number and ease of forgeries in the medieval period, this attitude is a pragmatic one. See Clanchy, *From Memory to Written Record*, p. 298.

93. See Margaret McGlynn, "Memory, Orality and Life Records: Proofs of Age in Tudor England," *Sixteenth Century Journal* 40 (2009): 679–97.
94. Clanchy, *From Memory to Written Record*, p. 99.
95. David Crook, *Records of the General Eyre*, Public Record Office Handbooks, no. 20 (London: PRO, 1982), p. 36. Coroners' rolls were used to check oral testimony in the county courts as early as 1202. See Clanchy, *From Memory to Written Record*, p. 72.
96. Clanchy, *From Memory to Written Record*, p. 147.
97. Smith, "Medieval Coroners' Rolls," pp. 97–98.
98. Clanchy, *From Memory to Written Record*, p. 137. Continental governments preferred to keep records in book form.
99. This is a reference to the neighboring vills represented at the inquest.
100. TNA PRO JUST 2/64, m.15.
101. "Statute of Additions," 1 Hen. V, c. 5 (1413); *SR*, v. 2, p. 171.
102. TNA PRO JUST 2/173, m. 3.
103. English justice worked on the model of bringing the courts to the people. Under the general eyre, itinerant justices traveled the counties of England holding eyres at intervals of six or seven years. The eyres were multi-competent: royal justices addressed complaints of both a civil and criminal nature. On the criminal side, the eyre heard presentments and tried accused felons. By the fourteenth century, the sheer volume of business for the general eyre was overwhelming. In order to create a more efficient judicial system to better serve the needs of the people, the fourteenth century witnessed the crown's implementation of a period of innovation, experimenting with new models of justice. Eventually, the crown settled on assize commissions. Assize justices continued to work on an itinerant basis; however, they visited the counties much more frequently, and with a specific commission. The crown tasked assize justices with four responsibilities: 1) *oyer* and *terminer* (also popularly referred to as "trailbaston"), 2) jail delivery, 3) *nisi prius*, and 4) peace. This short summary of England's judicial system does not account also for vast changes in local justice as well as England's central judicial courts (that is, King's Bench, Common Bench, and the development of equity courts). For an excellent summary in changes to the medieval judicial system, see Chapter Two of Masschaele, *Jury, State, and Society*, and for the experimentation of the fourteenth century in particular, see Musson, *Public Order and Law Enforcement*.
104. Keith Challis, "Drowned in 'A Whyrlepytte': The River Trent in the Nottinghamshire Coroners' Inquests of 1485–1558," *Transactions of the Thoroton Society of Nottinghamshire* 108 (2004): 115–6.
105. J.B. Post, "Crime in Later Medieval England: Some Historiographical Limitations," *C&C* 2.2 (1987): 216.
106. Richard W. Ireland, "Theory and Practice within the Medieval English Prison," *AJLH* 31.1 (1987): 64.
107. J.B. Given, *Society and Homicide in Thirteenth-Century England* (Stanford: Stanford UP, 1977), p. 40.
108. Barbara A. Hanawalt, "Violent Death in Fourteenth- and Early Fifteenth-Century England," *Comparative Studies in Society and History* 18 (1976): 302. Andrew Finch sees that perceptions of violence in the medieval context are skewed primarily because we focus on homicide as the ultimate measure. See his "The Nature of Violence in the Middle Ages: An Alternative Perspective," *Historical Research* 70.173 (1997): 249–68.
109. Sean Rosenmerkel, Matthew Durose, and Donald Farole, "Felony Sentences in State Courts, 2006-Statistical Tables," *Bureau of Justice Statistics* (December 2009), 1. http://bjs.gov/index.cfm?ty=pbdetail&iid=2152. Accessed Apr. 3, 2013.

110. McLane, "Juror Attitudes," p. 56.
111. McLane, "Juror Attitudes," p. 56.
112. For a good discussion of this belief, see Ireland, "Theory and Practice," 56–67.
113. In terms of statistical analysis, this study adopts a cautious approach not only because of differences in process between medieval and modern, as well as the low survival rate, but also because of the challenges in reading medieval coroners' rolls. Many are grotty, full of holes and smudges, and at times the writing is cramped, miniscule, even illegible. It is entirely possible that the occasional case has missed being counted as a result. In the grand scheme of things, a few missed cases will not have any impact on the arguments of this monograph.
114. Steven M. Smith, Veronica Stinson, and Marc W. Patry, "Fact or Fiction? The Myth and Reality of the *CSI* Effect," *Court Review* 47 (2011): 4–7.
115. Smith, *et al.*, "Fact or Fiction?," 4.
116. Smith, *et al.*, "Fact or Fiction?," 6.

1 The Coroners

Any study of medieval death investigation inescapably begins with the coroner. The coroner existed at the center of the process. When death was sudden or unnatural, the law barred family and neighbors from removing or burying the body of the dead until the coroner arrived to view it, and the few surviving amercements of communities who failed to adhere to this regulation confirm that the crown vehemently defended the needs of the coroner. This proscription held firm even when the district's county coroner had to journey across vast distances to reach the scene of the crime, and also in the heat of the summer when having a decomposing corpse around for any great length of time was unenviable.[1] Given the intermediacy of the coroner, it is noteworthy that historians have had little constructive to say about this royal official. Many view him merely as a "tax gatherer," failing to acknowledge that the job involved more than just delivering the king's profits.[2] Carelessness and indolence are the traits that dominate scholarly depictions of the medieval coroner. Much of the fault for this negative perception must be laid at the feet of R.F. Hunnisett himself. Not only did he see coroners as crooked and extortionate, he also distrusted their documentation, cautioning historians to be wary of submitting their findings to statistical analysis. His suspicion of coroners' rolls rested on the following premises:

1) Precedent books so dictated the nature of the enrollments that coroners had no leeway to incorporate extraneous details.
2) Coroners regularly altered the dates of inquests to make themselves appear more conscientious in the execution of their office.
3) Coroners commonly mislaid their files before they properly enrolled the relevant information, and thus much of the detail is missing from the records.[3]

Carrie Smith has since established that Hunnisett's concerns regarding the coroners' rolls are misplaced. Medieval formularies had little to say about the structure and composition of the coroners' rolls. If coroners falsified the documentation to make themselves appear more diligent, then they did not do a particularly good job at it. Finally, the sparse detail evident in various coroners' rolls is not a result of missing files, but rather of coroners' intent to meet only the minimum standards of statutory requirements.[4] While Smith's revision has renewed confidence in medieval coroners' rolls as a meaningful historical source, admittedly, her view of the coroner is no more optimistic than is Hunnisett's. The coroner was not only corrupt, he was also lazy: even when a community bothered to notify the coroner, "he might be both less willing to turn out and more prepared to turn a blind eye if the weather was particularly bad."[5] Hunnisett and Smith are not alone (by far) in their pessimism. J.B. Post writes "the further from a main road that a death occurred, the less likely it was to reach the ears of the coroner and the less likely he was to travel for the purpose of an inquest."[6] Like Smith, he also supposes that the winter's lower rate of homicide has less to do with patterns of criminality than that "the coroner was less diligent, as the weather got worse."[7] J.D.J. Havard sees the problem less in terms of lethargy than in moral rectitude: he expresses his fears most eloquently by saying that "the coroners had contracted from the sheriffs the disease which it had been intended they should cure—corruption."[8]

These conclusions are galvanized by the grumblings of Parliamentary discourse. Sessions of Parliament entertained a profusion of complaints about royal officials. Contrary to perceptions fostered by England's corpus of outlaw literature, the English crown was highly responsive to fears about the quality of its officeholders, even if it was not always capable of enforcing compliance. In fact, the introduction of the coronership owed much to contemporary apprehensions about the early sheriffs' autonomy. The crown intended coroners to act as "watchdogs on the sheriff," hoping to check any oppressive behavior by imposing accountability through the coroner and his documentation.[9] Even so, medieval Parliament oversaw a whole host of complaints about coroners relating to unlawful distraint,[10] false records,[11] absenteeism,[12] selling or suppressing indictments,[13] creating false indictments,[14] losing coroners' rolls,[15] maintenance,[16] and extortion.[17] To achieve the appropriate perspective, we must acknowledge that the legal lens inexorably provides a view of the coroner at his worst. Assuredly, some coroners were corrupt. Some coroners took bribes, and some coroners did so regularly. Some coroners were apathetic. Yet, we do not know that *all* coroners took bribes, or even that *most* coroners did; nor do we know that most coroners stayed home, lazing by the hearth and sipping a hot beverage rather than do their jobs in the bitter cold of England's winters. The law exists to punish offenders, not to reward honesty and hard work. Thus, complaints and legislation, on their own, are an insufficient basis on which to assess the coroners as a whole.

Why is any of this relevant? Indeed, the quality of the coroners does matter. If we assume that most coroners were unscrupulous, looking out only for their own best interests, then by extension we must also infer that death investigation was conducted, at best, in a mediocre fashion—a supposition that, as this chapter will demonstrate, is not corroborated by the documentation. Moreover, as this chapter contends, coroners belonged to a cast of individuals with substantial experience in law enforcement. Coroners belonged to families who, over multiple generations, dedicated their careers to upholding the peace. Surely, some of these individuals were attracted to the position out of a desire to serve the kingdom, rather than glimpsing an opportunity for graft. The goal of this chapter is not to redeem the medieval English legal system, but to argue that the history of the coroner needs a fresh start. We need to approach the subject with an open mind and realize that medieval coroners were entirely human. Some of them were corrupt; but others were conscientious and hard working. By looking to the parameters of the office as the legal documentation articulates it, we can gain a much better sense of how the ideal coroner functioned in the process of death investigation, what guidelines the crown had to offer, and the nature of the obstacles he might encounter while executing his duties.

THE SOURCES

Because English common law is unwritten, the corpus of legal writing weighs much more heavily on our understanding of the practice of the law. This chapter draws mainly, but not exclusively, from three forms of legal writing: statutory law, legal treatises, and the Year Books. First, statutory law exists outside common law. Statutes are legislation promulgated by Parliament primarily in response to a perceived problem not already addressed by common law procedures. While statute law predates Edward I, historians credit his reign with "one of the greatest outbursts of reforming legislation in English history until the nineteenth century."[18] Edward I promoted a positive reception to new law, a foreign concept to a law thought to be grounded in ancient tradition. England's royal justices were typically well versed in statute law out of necessity. Because collections of statutes for reference purposes did not circulate until the mid-fourteenth century, royal justices memorized the body of statute law by rote.[19] As the coronership was created by statute, not by the Anglo-Saxons, members of Parliament employed statutory law for the continuing regulation of the position. Consequently, statute law has much to offer concerning expectations for the office. In particular, its instructions relating to the process of investigation are astonishingly thorough. From the historian's perspective, what is most striking is that the legislation does not privilege the financial aspects of the office at the expense of a thorough investigation. Indeed, the coroner is both financial officer and death investigator. The two go hand in hand.

Second, the legal treatises, founded in part on the performance of English law, supply us with some of the best insight into the workings of the English judicial system. Four English treatises address the subject of the coronership specifically. *On the Laws and Customs of England*, traditionally associated with and maybe even penned by, Henri de Bracton (c. 1210–1268), a renowned royal justice and cleric, is the first to discuss the office.[20] The treatise is sometimes considered problematic in that its author drew a sizeable portion of its content from Roman law rather than English custom.[21] However, as the coronership was an English innovation, these passages are free of Continental borrowings. The other three treatises in order of appearance are *The Mirror of Justices*, *Fleta*, and *Britton*. There has been much contention about the dating and origin of each treatise. The most persuasive scholarship locates all three as "late thirteenth-century updates and abridgements" of *Bracton*, all of unknown authorship, and most likely written "within the space of ten or fifteen years."[22] *The Mirror of Justices*, in particular, has been the target of much ridicule and abuse by historians, largely because of its openly Christian viewpoint. Once dismissed by Maitland and Pollock as "speculation or satire,"[23] under David Seipp's guidance the treatise has returned to its proper place in history as a "reformist textbook on law."[24] *Britton* presents its own challenges in that it professes to have been composed at the command of King Edward I and is even written in the first person plural as if it were the king's authorized code of law. Yet it, too, is clearly an abbreviated version of *Bracton*. Together, all four treatises, which vary in interesting ways, enhance our vision of the medieval coroners, whom *Britton* describes as "the principal guardians of our peace" in every county.[25]

Finally, with the rise of sergeants and pleaders in the thirteenth century, a new genre of literature surfaced in order to prepare them for their careers in common law: the Year Books. Drawn from actual cases and courtroom dialogues from England's myriad courts of law, royal justices intended these annual publications to clarify the law's known ambiguities and to model good judicial decision making. Medieval English common law did not function according to precedent. Nonetheless, close study of the compilation of cases included in these texts achieved much the same effect. Pleaders acquired a sense of how best to defend their clients by looking to the successes and failures of past cases. The vast majority of Year Book cases involve civil suits. The meager assemblage of crown pleas included in the publications, however, offer fruitful insight into the coroner and his office.

Collectively, all three facets of the legal literature have much to tell us about the coroner and his role in death investigation.

WHO WERE THE CORONERS (IN THEORY)?

The crown imagined coroners as knights. The 1194 article that concocted the position expressed this stipulation quite clearly. It stated there should be four "keepers of the peace" (that is, coroners) in each county: three knights and one cleric (*clericus*).[26] The inclusion of a cleric in this grouping, ostensibly, was to guarantee that at least one among them was capable of enrolling the indictment. The expenses associated with the office were held up as justification for requiring knighthood. Much like justices of the peace or other crown officials, the king anticipated that coroners would bear the costs involved in the execution of their office. Coroners who were insufficiently affluent to finance their travels were more likely to resort to dishonesty. Nonetheless, in practice, only a minority of coroners belonged to England's coterie of knights. Throughout much of the period, England experienced a shortage of knights. Although many men met the property qualifications, they avoided applying for knighthood because of the burdens of service that went with it.[27] Even if Parliament had to compromise on status, independent wealth always remained a key qualification articulated in the statutes as a safeguard against corruption. This is confirmed by a statute from 1340 mandating that "no Coroner be chosen unless he have Land in Fee sufficient in the same County, whereof he may answer to all manner of People."[28] Describing the coroner as "sufficient" is a polite euphemism for knighthood (or, the equivalent in landholdings).

The more pressing concern evoked by this legislation is that coroners must reside in the county in which they assumed office. This provision had discernible benefits. The locality of shire officials "guarded against corruption through the mechanism of answerability: appointees with a stake in their bailiwicks would be less likely to offend their neighbours or 'betray the interests of their class' for fear of retribution."[29] A 1354 statute reiterates this condition by impressing that coroners were to be "chosen in the full Counties by the Commons of the same Counties, of the most meet and lawful People that shall be found in the said Counties to execute the said Office."[30] Residency requirements remind us of the contentious place coroners assumed in local administration. While the crown understood coroners as a bridge between the center and the locality, most hundreds doubtless viewed the county coroner as an outsider interfering in micro-politics—even if he did own property in that county, the majority of deaths occurred outside his immediate home village. Medieval England was highly regional in terms of outlook, custom, and even law.[31] The prevalence of England's multitude of franchises, liberties, and independent boroughs only served to intensify regionalized identities at the most basic level. While the jury might compensate for a coroner's ignorance of village politics, tensions revolved around the fact that the coroner was ultimately in control of the enrollment and he might well choose to disrespect the hundred's concerns and hierarchy. A skilled coroner was required to navigate the "politics of place" by forging a relationship of trust with the various localities belonging to his district. Residency in the county, at the very least, facilitated this aspect of the office.[32]

Statute law was concerned also to check unsuitable overlaps in personnel. Chapter Twenty-Four of the Magna Carta insisted that "[n]o sheriff, constable, coroner or bailiff shall hold pleas of our crown," meaning that no coroner might undertake the duties of a royal justice and stand as judge over those cases he indicted. This injunction was reiterated in various forms at intervals throughout the period. In 1317, the crown forbade coroners from becoming justices of assize, jail delivery, or oyer and terminer; this was confirmed again in 1355.[33] Predictably, the reasoning behind this legislation falls into the same category as the 1351–1352 act intended to limit overlap between indicting and trial jurors.[34] As the treatment of actual (as opposed to theoretical) coroners later on in this chapter will clarify, the Magna Carta's efforts achieved roughly the same degree of success: coroners commonly served as justices of the peace throughout the medieval period, and in practice, if not in theory, the crown seems to have sanctioned this overlap. Admittedly, it is not surprising that coroners sometimes did double-duty as justices of the peace. After all, a coroner often behaved as one in carrying out the duties of his office. Coroners not only indicted accused felons and ordered their arrests, but the legal treatises acknowledge that coroners also had the power to perform summary justice. As *Britton* explains:

> If any man be found killed, and another be found near him with the knife or other weapon in his hand all bloody, wherewith he killed him, the coroner shall be presently fetched, and in his presence the felon shall, upon the testimony of those who saw the felony done, be judged to death. The like when a person is found in a house, or other place where one shall be found killed, and the person found alive is neither hurt, nor wounded, and has not raised the hue and cry, and has not charged any with the felony, and shall not be able to do so.[35]

If coroners might be held responsible for ordering the execution of fellow countrymen, they could not be men of lowly or even middling rank. Indeed, status was a necessary shield to preclude them from becoming a target for local recrimination.

BECOMING A CORONER

Upon assuming office, the crown mandated the coroner to swear an oath on the Holy Gospel, pledging not only due diligence in the execution of his office, but also loyalty to the crown. This ritual was not merely *pro forma*. In predominantly oral societies such as medieval England, oath swearing was more than a simple promise to do one's best. The ceremony submitted one's reputation to public scrutiny. Failing to live up to an oath endangered one's communal standing, indeed one's sense of self. Oaths were the keystone of English law, such that the primary method of proof for much of the Middle Ages relied upon oaths, not just compurgation and pledging, but also jury trial, manned by twelve *sworn* men. That society deemed only some men and women to be "oathworthy," and thus eligible to testify in court, speaks to just how integrally oath taking, personal honor, and social credit were linked together in the medieval mindset. Oaths were in no way restricted to the courtroom setting. The English swore oaths to initiate an apprenticeship or service relationship, create political alliances, mark entrance into tithings and guilds, contract marriage, conduct business, and make simple purchases. One might even make a case for confession as a distinct form of oath, as well as sponsorship, confirmation, and last rites. An individual with a reputation for "falseness" not only stood to be ostracized by his resident community, but he also endangered his prospects for daily survival.[36] The medieval English understood oaths as quasi-sacral moments. Thus, it was not only the process of oath swearing that was meaningful, but also the phrasing of the words, the earnestness of expression, and the performance of ritual gestures (perhaps a kiss to seal a compact, the exchange of a token gift, or a handshake). Richard Firth Green puts it best: "[i]n an oral society the precise words of the oath, at the moment that they are spoken, bind speaker and listener by virtue of an inherent performative power which resists translation or paraphrase."[37] All of this is a useful reminder for our study of the coroner. When a man contracted to perform the duties of the coronership, he, too, was putting his reputation on the line. While the ceremony certainly did not eliminate the possibility of extortion or laziness, it encouraged the man who valued his honor sufficiently to think long and hard before breaking his oath.

Regrettably, the general oath sworn by county coroners has not survived the Middle Ages, but at least two of those sworn by borough coroners have. Coroners' oaths provide precious insight into not only the expectations of the office, but also what coroners believed their priorities should be.

Example A (London, *c.* 1309–1314):

You shall swear that you will well and truly serve the King and the City of London in the office of Coroner. And that you will well and honestly entreat the people that shall come before you. And that neither for gift nor for favor, for promise nor for hate, you shall fail but that you shall do equal justice as far as in you lies to all manner of people, as well poor as rich, denizens as well as strangers, that shall have anything to do with you by force of your office, and that all the things that shall be done or said before you by force of your office you shall truly record, and diligently cause them to be enrolled, and copies of the said Rolls you shall cause to be written each year by a clerk, at the cost of the City, and to be delivered to the Common Clerk in the Chamber of the Guildhall, there to remain of record. And that no inquest, abjuration, or other great matter shall you do or record without the presence of the Sheriffs or their substitute, according to the custom of the City. And ready shall you be at the command of the Mayor and governors of the City at all times when necessity shall arise for coming and doing your office. And that you suffer not to be put in inquests that shall be held before you any suspect persons nor partisans, but good, true, and indifferent persons. And that you take nothing whereby the King incurs a loss or his right to be prejudiced. And that the City, as far as in you lies, you will preserve harmless, and all the customs and liberties thereof according to your power maintain. And in all other things to your office appertaining you will well and truly have you. So God you help and the Saints.[38]

Example B (Coventry, 1452):

You shall duly and truly occupy and exercise the office of Coronership of the Shire of the City of Coventry, and duly be at the Counties [*that is*, county courts] of the said Shire held within the said city every month on the Tuesday, and truly record exigents and inquisitions taken before you, and all other things before you also as far as law requires. And also execute and return all manner [of] writs, precepts, and warrants that shall be to you directed, or by you to be executed. And all things shall do that belong to your office of Coronership of the said Shire when you be thereto required to do it. You shall duly occupy and exercise [the office of] clerk of recognizance of debts within the said City to be taken after the form of Statutes for Merchants made from the time that it happens the office of any such Clerk within the said City by any cause to be void. And duly deliver the people in that that in you this, that will sue for any such recognizance.[39] And that you compel no man to pay more for any recognizance than according to the statutes thereupon made, without that he will of his own free will and agreement any more pay. And you shall be demeaned in all things touching your said offices that the mayor for the time being by the advice of his Council will command you, which is lawful, honest, and [of] profit to this City. All these shall you do to your power and cunning [*that is*, knowledge], during the time that you stand in the said offices, so help you God and holy dame.[40]

Putting these oaths side by side best highlights the scope of the office. The two oaths have much in common. Both enunciate the centrality of formalities: because of the value of the coroner's roll as a counter-check on the sheriff's behavior, any lapse in the coroner's efficiency might redound negatively on the person and reputation of the sheriff. Yet, the burden of paperwork for coroners extended well beyond their rolls to include also the response and return of royal mandates, maintaining steady communication between the center and the locality. Both articulate the need for "honesty," defined principally by honor in this period as opposed to truthfulness. However, the London oath furnishes a much more extensive anticorruption guarantee, citing a litany of potential abuses that the coroner must eschew. Both oaths also delineate the coroner's place in the municipal hierarchy. While in office, he is duly subservient to the mayor and the city council.

Perhaps what is most striking are the differences between the two, reminding us that the duties of the office varied greatly from place to place. In Coventry, the coroner doubled as the clerk of recognizances, that is, the municipal clerk in charge of formally enrolling loans between private parties, including the amount of debt involved and the date of expected repayment. While this may seem like an odd coupling of responsibilities, the coroner was, in actual fact, the ideal person to fill the position because of his regular presence in court, his ability to write, and his availability. After all, medieval Coventry was not so large as to keep the coroner occupied daily with the business of death investigation. In all likelihood, combining the two offices permitted the city to endow the coroner with a full-time position and a salary. London's quasi-democratic promise of "equal justice," regardless of rank or provenance, stands out as the most curious element of the two pledges. However, it, too, originates in the city's distinctive needs. Medieval London was populated by a highly transient and diverse population, including many resident and nonresident foreigners. In this atmosphere, a coroner must subordinate the usual medieval distrust of strangers to the greater needs of effective law enforcement.[41] Such an oath must have imbued London's constituents with a sense of confidence that the city held its coroners to high standards.

Both oaths exist in the vernacular. The survival of London's oath in the French language is a potent reminder that coroners belonged to the upper ranks of society, that is, those who spoke French rather than English. The English of the Coventry oath does not undermine the status of the coroner; rather, it represents the oath's much later date, at a time when English was more widespread and had become the kingdom's "national" language.[42] The vernacularity of these oaths attests that coroners understood the parameters of the crown's expectations, an element that would not be guaranteed if they existed only in the more scholarly Latin.

THE DUTIES OF THE CORONER

The 1275–1276 statute referred to as *Officium Coronatoris*, although somewhat belated in its recognition of the office, provides a summary of the nature of the coroners' duties. The excerpt below focuses on his responsibilities as they relate to criminal acts:

> First, he shall go to the Places where any be slain, or suddenly dead, or wounded, or where Houses are broken, or where Treasure is said to be found and shall forthwith command four of the next Towns, or five or six, to appear before [him] in such a place: and when they are come thither the Coroner upon the Oath of them shall inquire in this manner, that is to wit; [If they know where the Person was slain, whether it were in any house, field, bed, tavern or company,] and who were there: Likewise it is to be inquired, who were culpable either of the Act, or of the Force, and who were present, either Men or Women, and of what age soever they be, if they can speak, or have any Discretion: and how many soever be found culpable by Inquisition in any of the manners aforesaid. . . . If it fortune any such Man be slain, which is found in the

> Fields, or in the Woods, first it is to be inquired, whether he were slain in the same Place or not; and if he were brought and laid there, they shall do so much as they can to follow their steps that brought the body thither, whether he were brought upon a horse, or in a cart: It shall be inquired also, if the dead Person were known, or else a Stranger, and where he lay the night before. . . . In like manner it is to be inquired of them that be drowned, or suddenly dead: and after, [such Bodies are to be seen] whether they were drowned, or slain, or strangled, by the sign of a cord tied straight about their necks, or [about any of their members, or upon] any other hurt found upon their Bodies: whereupon they shall proceed in the Form abovesaid: and if they were not slain, then ought the Coroner to attach the Finders, and all other in the company. A Coroner also ought to inquire of Treasure that is found, who were the Finders, and likewise who is suspected therof; and that may be well perceived where one liveth riotously, haunting Taverns, and hath done so of long time; hereupon [he] may be attached for this suspicion by four, or six, or more Pledges [if he may be found.] Further, if any be appealed of Rape, he must be attached, if the Appeal be fresh, and [they must see] apparent sign of truth by Effusion of Blood, or an open Cry made; and such shall be attached by four or six Pledges, if they may be found: if the Appeal were without Cry, or without any manifest Sign or Token, two pledges shall be sufficient. Upon Appeal of Wounds and such like, especially if the Wounds be mortal, the Parties appealed shall be taken immediately and kept until it be known perfectly, whether he that is hurt shall recover, or not; and if he die, [the Defendant] shall be kept; and if he recover health, they shall be attached by four or six Pledges, after as the Wound is great or small. If it be for a Maim, he shall find no less than four Pledges; if it be for a small Wound, two Pledges shall suffice; also all Wounds ought to be viewed, the Length, Breadth, and Deepness, and with what Weapons, and in what Part of the Body the Wound or Hurt is; and how many be culpable, and how many Wounds there be, and who gave the Wound, all which things must be inrolled in the Roll of the Coroners. Moreover if any be appealed [of any Act done, as Principal,] they that be appealed of the Force, shall be attached also [and] surely [kept in Ward,] until the Principals be attainted [or delivered.] Concerning, Horses, Boats, Carts, [&c.] whereby any are slain, that properly are called Deodands, they shall be valued and delivered unto the Towns, [as before is said.][43]

This synopsis of the coroner's duties best represents the ideals at the time of its writing. The duties of the office were not set in stone. Inquiring into treasure trove,[44] for example, is a charge that county coroners generally performed only on an *ad hoc* basis.[45] Likewise, a mere twenty years after this statute, county coroners ceased to have any jurisdiction in the related realm of wreck of the sea.[46] At a 1305 session, Parliament decreed that coroners relinquish their responsibility over this aspect, transferring it instead to sheriffs.[47] A contemporaneous petition concerning William le Poer, county coroner in Cornwall, appointed to receive and guard wreck for the island of Scilly, explains their decision. The petition describes how "the men of the island prevent, appropriate and lay waste this wreck, and do not permit the same coroner to perform his office with regard to it, threatening to drown and butcher him."[48] The reallocation of responsibility from coroner to sheriff reflects the sheriff's prominence in the county as well as the manpower at his disposal. This example also helps us to appreciate the changing nature of the coroner's duties. A reduction in the reach of the office does not automatically imply profiteering or ineptitude. Indeed, expediency is sometimes the best justification.

Treasure trove and wreck of the sea are not the only matters in which the statute departs from the coroner's reality. While coroners participated in the view (i.e., witnessing) of wounds in both assault and rape, they did not direct the investigation, nor did they have any oversight in matters of housebreaking. These duties fell squarely within the sheriff's jurisdiction. Most notably, the statute neglects any mention of the coroner's obligations toward felons in sanctuary and approver's appeals. If the rolls afford any measure, coroners spent an inordinate amount of time hearing felons' confessions in sanctuary and arranging for them to be escorted to the port of their choice in order to abjure the realm. Approvers' appeals also consumed a good portion of the coroner's time. An approver is one who turned king's evidence, that is, who chose to betray his criminal accomplices in exchange for the king's clemency. If royal justices convicted all of those he accused, the law permitted the approver to live. If any of his accomplices were acquitted, he was hanged, as was most often the case.[49]

Despite these trifling misconceptions, the statute lays out a comprehensive blueprint for the coroner's participation in the investigatory process. Typically, the discovery of a body and the raising of the hue and cry (what the statute refers to as "hue and steps") by the first finder initiated the investigation. "Hue and cry" was the technical term for alerting the authorities. Although the statutes fail to define the phrase, an instructive passage included in the miracles of Saint Thomas de Cantilupe, former Bishop of Hereford, with the intention of clarifying the process of English death investigation for the benefit of its Roman judges, illuminates the procedure:

> whoever first discovered a dead body (of one slain or drowned as it might be) had to publish the fact and raise the hue and cry. All those who heard it must follow the discoverer from vill to vill until they got to the place where those in charge of the area's jurisdiction lived. The discoverer had then to announce the said homicide or drowning, whereupon he would be held until he could produce a pledge that he would appear before the king's justices when they next came to those parts, and submit to judgment in their presence.[50]

The hue and cry itself involved a great deal of shouting and trumpeting. Pollock and Maitland explain that the proper cry was "Out! Out!," at which point the "neighbours should turn out with weapons such as bows and arrows, and amidst much shouting blow a horn so that the 'hue' will be 'horned' from vill to vill."[51] Chaucer's highly democratic vision of a hue and cry in "The Nun's Priest's Tale," incorporating not only men and women, but also dogs, cows, ducks and bees, paints a similar, if somewhat poetic, picture:

> And crying, 'Out! Harrow! And well-away!
> Ha! ha! the Fox!' and after him they ran
> And each with staves many another man.
> Ran Colle our dog, and Talbot and Gerland,
> And Malkyn, with a distaff in her hand;
> Ran cow and calf, and each the very hogs,
> So feared for the barking of the dogs
> And shouting of the men and women each,
> They run so them thought his heart break.
> They yelled as fiends down in hell;
> The ducks crying as men would him quell;
> The geese for fear flew over the trees;
> Out of the hive came the swarm of bees.
> So hideous was the noise, God bless us all!
> Certainly, he Jack Straw and his many
> Never made shouts half so shrill
> When that they would any Fleming kill,
> As this day was made upon the fox.
> They brought trumpets of brass, and of box,
> Of horn, of bone, in which they blew and pooped,
> And therewithal they shouted and they hooped.
> It seemed as that heaven should fall.[52]

As this passage from the *Canterbury Tales* underscores, the hue and cry was a communal activity. While one man or woman was responsible for raising the hue in the first place, once the cry was issued it could not be ignored. The hue and cry was a critical part of the process, transforming simple villagers into a body of witnesses whose testimony formed the base of the coroner's enrollment. Although they were not necessarily witnesses to the death itself, notified so soon after the death, they could speak to fresh wounds, torn and/or stained garments, discarded weapons, trailing blood, as well as the first finder's state of mind.[53]

Once local authorities were alerted to the situation, a summons was sent to one or two of the relevant coroners. Before his arrival, the local bailiff assembled a jury of those living closest to the scene of the death, as well as representatives from the four neighboring vills, those who participated in the hue and cry.[54] However, these were not the only individuals present at the inquest. The crown commanded all males over the age of twelve from the four neighboring vills to attend inquests. Thus, coroners arrived to discover a body of potential witnesses awaiting direction.[55] Indeed, the legal treatises regard all attendees as witnesses. *Britton* instructs the coroner to "swear the townships upon the Holy Evangelists." The *Mirror* makes a comparable remark.[56] The questioning of neighbors and witnesses was a vital part of death investigation. Faced with a sizeable crowd, coroners had to adopt a systematic approach in order to create a productive interviewing process. *The Mirror of Justices*[57] directs coroners to separate witnesses by rank into "panels of the better folk by themselves, the mean folk by themselves, and the small folk by themselves."[58] Sequestration of this nature was to prevent any group from intimidating or influencing another. Therefore, "no dozen may speak to another, but each jury must answer for itself."[59] In an era so rigidly defined by hierarchy and reputation, in all probability this method of questioning was the only means to uncover the truth: how else could an individual contradict the word of his social superior? Segregation was critical also given the nature of criminal activity in medieval villages. In her landmark study on the subject, Barbara Hanawalt professed that crime in the village setting sprang from "competition for power and survival." A necessary byproduct of this rivalry was the dominance and manipulation of the judicial system by what she refers to as "primary villagers."[60] In order to uncover the facts of the crime, the coroner had to find some way to separate those in direct competition, as well as destabilize the ascendancy of the village elite. In this respect, the *Mirror's* recommendation would certainly fit the bill.

The statute above speaks to the kinds of questions coroners should pose to witnesses about the existence of eyewitnesses, the crime location, interference with the corpse, and the method of death. *Fleta* enhances our vision of the interview process by including also an example of the "articles of enquiry," that is, a list of matters that the crown anticipated the coroner would discuss with his jurors. The coroner should address:

> whether so-and-so was slain abroad or at home, at a tavern or at a wake or at some other gathering; and who was present at the slaying, man or woman, adult or child; and which of them were guilty as principals and which as accomplices, in counselling, aiding or directing, or who were in any way the cause of the deed; and whence came the wrong-doers and whither they have departed.[61]

The treatises propose additional lines of questioning. In cases of homicide, *Fleta* underscores the imperative to discover where the accused felon lodged the night before the crime, instructing the coroner to hunt down his host to learn whether s/he harbors any relevant information about the perpetrator and his whereabouts.[62] In those cases where assault led to a death,

Bracton reminds the coroner to probe also into the character of the dead, inquiring whether he may have courted death out of a desire for revenge. Thus, coroners needed to find out whether "a wounded man could escape death by medical care" but "he refused to be cured."[63] It is hard to imagine that many victims deliberately disobeyed medical advice out of vengeance. Yet, it was the coroner's duty to make certain that the dead was not responsible, even in part, for his own demise. The treatises anticipate also that the coroner will summon the deceased's next of kin, in the event that a member of the family was not already present. The purpose was to establish proof of Englishry.[64] Imposing a *murdrum* fine for the homicide of anyone of Norman descent was a relic from the days of the Conquest. As with most antiquated legal practices, proof of Englishry persisted as a means to channel funds into the king's coffers.[65] If the coroner was incapable of contacting a member of the family, then he was to inquire into the deceased's lineage by some other means.[66] In terms of the quality of the investigation, at the very least, this provision meant that coroners, much like their modern equivalents, had to take an active interest in the background of the deceased. In doing so, he might well uncover more clues as to how he or she died.

The 1275–1276 *Officium Coronatoris* stresses the value of the post-mortem examination of the corpse. However, the manner in which it communicates the requirements is somewhat muddled. In explaining the view of wounds in assault cases, the statute declares coroners must record the "Length, Breadth, and Deepness" of the wound, "with what Weapons, and in what Part of the Body the Wound or Hurt is," "how many Wounds there be, and who gave the Wound." While this was the principle component of the view of wounds, coroners also regularly recorded these measurements in homicides (that is, mortal assaults). Why was the crown eager to see a record of the number of wounds and their dimensions? Faye Getz rationalizes these expectations as "relics of an earlier time when the victim was compensated by the size and location of the wound."[67] In the hopes of curtailing private feuds, the early medieval crown imposed injury tariffs as an alternative. In the spirit of "an eye for an eye," the law assigned each body a price, a *wergeld* ("man-gold") paid to the family in the event of a homicide. Compensation was not restricted to homicide. The law also assigned value to body parts in an effort to craft a just system of reparation for injury through assault. Most relevant here, the *Laws of Æthelberht*[68] include provisions for compensation per inch for a stab wound: "If a person stabs through a thigh, for each thrust 6 shillings. If [the width of the wound] is over an inch, a shilling. For two inches, two [shillings]. Over three [inches], 3 shillings."[69]

While a legal hangover is the most rational explanation for such stringent requirements, medical practitioners elsewhere in Europe were meeting similar benchmarks with their post-mortem examinations, and thus, England's expectations were no more backward than those of other European kingdoms.[70] For example, in the Manosquin medical reports for the thirteenth and fourteenth centuries, court-appointed physicians habitually recorded the length, width, and depth of wounds. The surviving documentation even discloses their methodology, remarking that physicians probed the wound with a candle in order to gauge accurately its depth.[71] The coroners' rolls themselves propose an alternate explanation for the continuation of such seemingly archaic practices. Coroners and jurors analyzed the size and appearance of the wound to learn more about the circumstances surrounding a death, particularly when no eyewitnesses came forward. To offer a case in point: in the inquest of Henry Colburn of Barford (*Beds.*) held in 1266, an exhaustive inspection of the various wounds on the dead's body led jurors to identify the nature of the weapons employed in the homicide. The seven wounds inflicted near Henry's heart and stomach were made with a knife, "as it appears" (*ut patebat*). They linked the four wounds on his head to a pickaxe. Unfortunately, they were unable to identify the object used to produce the mixture of wounds on his throat, chin, and also on the head penetrating to the brain.[72] While these discoveries did not aid jurors in narrowing the pool of candidates to one particular perpetrator in this instance, in many others, knowing the murder weapon assisted jurors in identifying the felon.

The legal treatises are unanimous that "[n]o matter how they died," the dead should be viewed by the coroner and his jury "naked and uncovered."[73] While this may seem commonsense to us today, the medieval world was much more wary of the sinfulness associated with the human body. Reticence to put the body on display even made its way into the practice of the law: the unwillingness to try women by the ordeal of cold water may have had much to do with the prescribed dress for probands.[74] Similarly, many Continental authorities stipulated decapitation as the method of execution for the affluent. The medieval world viewed hanging as a vulgar, undignified form of capital punishment, chiefly because one tended to lose control of bladder and bowels in the process.[75] Given the tendency to make modesty a priority, the provision for such a public unveiling of the body is somewhat unexpected. To their credit, the treatises put the needs of the investigation first. None of them makes exception to protect the modesty of women or the well heeled.

Exactly what were coroners looking for when they viewed the body? The legal treatises explain that the coroner was to document any visible "marks and tokens" that might offer clues into whether the death took place by felony, misadventure, or naturally.[76] Specifically, the coroner and his jurors were to look for "external signs, as where open wounds are found or bruises which have not broken the skin, as where they have been strangled, which may be inferred from the mark of the impress of the rope around the neck."[77] *Bracton*'s treatments of assault and rape are also helpful in this respect. The law's definition of wounding precluded appeals from those who suffered "nothing except a scratch or a bruise," or "contusions made by a club rather than an edged weapon"—quite simply, injuries of this nature did not meet the standards of assault.[78] This perception is relevant also to homicide investigations. As a fatal assault, jurors were plainly expecting wounds of a much more grievous appearance, betraying that they had little understanding of the dangers of internal bleeding. With victims of rape, the treatises direct the coroner to assess "the blood and her clothing stained with blood, and her torn garments" for signs of struggle. Presumably, these same elements came into play in determining whether a death was a homicide.[79]

An early sixteenth-century oath book from the borough of Doncaster (*Yorks.*) illuminates one facet of the coroner's physical inspection. In dealing with deaths by drowning, the book astutely advises coroners not to leap to conclusions. After all, drowning might be a convenient cover for murder. The oath book recommends that the coroner "sit upon a body drowned" in order to "search if he were slain afore by throttling with cord or other thing or wounded."[80] Sitting on the corpse had its benefits. If the lungs expelled water under the subdiaphragmatic pressure of the coroner's weight, he would know whether the perpetrator drowned his victim (a process that would fill the lungs with water), or merely threw the body into the water after the homicide (in which case, the lungs would be generally free of water).

With respect to the body as evidence, the one critical element omitted in the 1275–1276 statute was the obligation in cases of homicide to distinguish which was the mortal wound. Again, this expectation was routine across Europe. In doing so, coroners and their juries expressed the need to acknowledge that there was a causal connection between wounding and death, and thus establish that a felony had actually taken place. Procedurally, this was significant for two reasons. First, English courts only held those who struck mortal blows responsible for the homicide; all others were merely accomplices.[81] While the law punished accomplices with the same vigilance as principals, the principal had to be tried and convicted first. If the court acquitted the principal, his accomplices were acquitted by default. Second, the crown also confiscated as *bane* only the weapon used to inflict the mortal wound.

Communities sometimes proceeded to the burial of the dead without awaiting the arrival of the coroner. When a coroner encountered this obstacle, the treatises instructed him to carry on as usual. The body must be disinterred and "viewed openly by both the jurors and the townships," regardless of the impact on communal or familial sentiment.[82] In practice, the crown fined the entire community for the poor judgment of those who buried the body without view of the coroner. The *Mirror*, however, advocates a more individual punishment, declaring it was the coroner's responsibility to record "the names of the buriers" for reprimand when the justices next arrived in eyre. The treatise's diatribe on the subject expands far beyond illicit burial. It condemns also those who removed the body from the scene of the crime, or those who, through "careless keeping" failed to preserve the body so that "one cannot tell how death happened."[83] All of this reminds us that the body was the focal point of the investigation. The crown was resolute to guarantee the quality of the investigation by preserving the evidence.

But the body was not the only locus of investigation. If homicide was suspected, the treatises expected the coroner and his jury to carry out a methodical investigation of the death scene, looking for "presumptive clues, such as the dripping of blood" (if the perpetrator was wounded), as well as "cart tracks or the like."[84] If the coroner and his jury came across any "traces left by the malefactors," the treatises instruct them to follow them, "by pursuing the tracks of a cart, the hoof-marks of horses, the footprints of men" in the hopes of discovering where the felon might have fled.[85]

Anyone in the community who disappeared subsequent to the crime opened themselves up to investigation. *Fleta* recommended the coroner go directly to that person's house to interview his neighbors and ascertain whether his flight was linked to responsibility for the death.[86] When a homicide involved multiple perpetrators, the *Mirror*, *Fleta*, and *Britton* all underscore the need for the coroner to discriminate the principal from the accessories. *Fleta* furnishes some directive as to the kinds of questions a coroner should ask about the nature of the accessory's participation, whether it was "counselling, aiding or directing, or who were in any way the cause of the deed."[87] The *Mirror*, which elevates the distinctly medieval tendency to catalog to an art form, elaborates on the subject by supplying a list of the nine kinds of accessories. This list includes: "[t]hose who command, those who counsel, those who hire or are consenting thereto, those who send, those who aid, those who are partners in the gain, those who acquiesce and do not disturb the offenders by word or deed, and those who knowingly receive them, and those who go out armed."[88] Such a comprehensive inventory provides instructive insight into the practice of the law.

Most helpfully, *Britton* outlines every conceivable manner of death and explains what the coroner must do in each scenario. The instructions are highly specific. For example, *Britton* proffers the following directive in the case of a drowning death:

> Of such as are drowned within our realm by falling from a vessel not at sea, our will is, that the vessel and whatsoever shall be found therein be appraised as a deodand and enrolled by the coroner, that is to say, whatsoever was moving; for if a man happens to fall from a ship under sail, nothing can be deemed the cause of his death, except the ship itself and the things moving in it; but the merchandise lying at the bottom of the ship, is not presumed to be the occasion of his death, and so in like cases. And of those drowned in fountains and wells, we will, as in the other cases, that the coroners admit to mainprise the first finders, and enroll their names and the names of their pledges.[89]

This passage emphasizes the centrality of the *deodand* to the coroner. The deodand, which literally translates as "to be given to God," is an object implicated in one way or another in the negligent death of an individual.[90] It was the duty of the coroner and his jury to identify

relevant deodands and appraise their value. The crown then confiscated all runaway carts and murderous pigs with the objective of putting them to some pious use in atonement.[91] The law defined the offending object as "whatever moved in the thing which caused the accident."[92] The deodand serves as an "early form of liability for death."[93] Parents of children mauled to death by a neighbor's dog wanted justice. Removing the dog from the community not only provided some measure of revenge for the victim's family, but it also ensured the future safety of the village's children and acted as a potent reproof to its careless owner.[94] The punitive nature of the deodand is illuminated in drowning deaths that took place in private wells. In order to prevent future fatalities, the crown ordered the well filled at the owner's expense. Granted, as the passage above implies, a jury's judgment might be contentious. No mariner would react kindly to the confiscation of his ship, even if the merchandise he was transporting was exempt. Confiscation from the less prosperous might also jeopardize a family's livelihood. A miracle story from the canonization of Saint Thomas de Cantilupe makes this point explicit. When an oxcart belonging to Robert and Leticia Russell inadvertently crushed their son Geoffrey to death, the horrified and grief-stricken parents reacted by hiding their son's body in bed out of fear of the "danger and injury to come at the royal court." They knew what happened in accidental deaths. Once the death became public, not only would Robert and Leticia be held in prison until the sheriff was certain the death was by misadventure, but they would also suffer permanent loss of their wagon and oxen. Happily for the Russells, Saint Thomas was on hand to answer their prayers. At dusk the same day, the boy rejoined the world of the living, putting their fears to rest.[95] To avoid acrimony within the community yet still meet the spirit of the law, jurors shied away from confiscating costly items. For example, they preferred to claim as deodand the sails rather than the whole ship; the mill wheels rather than the mill itself.[96]

The treatises also expand on a coroner's duties, but in a somewhat unexpected fashion. The *Mirror* reports that "Coroners were wont also to hold their views in cases of sodomy, and on infant monsters who had nothing of humanity, or who had more of the beast than the man in them; and these the coroners caused to be buried. But the holy faith grows stronger every day, whereby folk do not burden their souls with such horrible sins so commonly as they used."[97] Conforming to Maitland's unfavorable assessment of the *Mirror*, ostensibly motivated by Maitland's distaste for the boldly religious tenor of the work, historians have traditionally dismissed this passage as mere fantasy. Certainly, Seipp's reminder that "[e]very legal treatise, to one degree or another, states law as the author thinks it should be" is relevant here.[98] However, the *Mirror* is not alone in its condemnation. *Fleta* offers some corroborating evidence. Although it does not enumerate this among the coroner's duties, it declares that those who are guilty of sodomy "should be buried alive in the ground, provided they be taken in the act and convicted by lawful and open testimony."[99] In point of fact, the surviving coroners' rolls boast no evidence of coroners working in either capacity. Yet, we must also recognize that our documentation represents only a "tiny proportion" of the inquests actually held in the Middle Ages.[100] Without the complete corpus of coroners' inquests, it is impossible to rule out unequivocally the likelihood that coroners performed these duties. It is also important to ask, if the crown assigned these responsibilities to anyone in the legal system, which official would be as qualified? Coroners were already intervening in rape cases, a sex act of a different kind, and the deaths of children. Granted, research into the prosecution of sodomy establishes that medieval men and women were notoriously hesitant to accuse anyone of sexual deviance.[101] Because of the church's expansive perspective of sexual deviance as a category, most individuals held back from accusations, fearing that it might redound on them. Thus, if coroners did inquire into sodomy, surely those cases were few and far between. The argument for infant monstrosity is much stronger. Medieval tradition interpreted monstrous births as a sign from God. The infant's deformity was a physical representation of the moral depravity of the parent(s). A woman who conceived outside of marriage or within the bounds of an adulterous relationship might expect to give birth to a monster, and thus have her immorality exposed publicly.[102] Given the association of monsters with dishonest conception, the *Mirror* was probably referring here to the stereotypical abortion: the mother-to-be independently pursuing a course of action intended to expel the fetus and thus avert the birth of an illegitimate child. If that is, indeed, the case, then the *Mirror* was correct. Coroners did have jurisdiction over abortions, providing there was a body (or a fetus) for him to view, and the records provide many examples of this kind to confirm that coroners did indeed carry out investigations of this nature.

The Year Books have little to add to this perspective of the coroner and his duties. However, as textbooks are wont to do, the Year Books tend to overlook the mundane in favor of the unusual, and thus present us with not one but two references to a remarkable jurisdictional quandary that, presumably, most coroners never had to address. In 1313, a corpse washed up on the shores of Essex. The county coroner presided over the inquest, and the jury concluded that an individual named here only as Stephen was guilty of homicide. Local authorities arrested him. When Stephen later appeared before justices of assize, he was acquitted. Soon after, a Middlesex grand jury indicted Stephen for the same homicide. At his trial, Stephen admonished the justices of jail delivery for trying a man twice for the same homicide. In response, they declared that the first inquest had been in error. Because Stephen purportedly slew the man in Middlesex, an Essex jury did not have jurisdiction over the death, even though they were the ones to discover the body.[103] Justices at the trial of a 1490 homicide clarified what needed to be done when coroners encountered this bizarre situation. A London grand jury indicted a man for homicide after he struck another with a shovel in the county of Middlesex, causing the man to die within the year. The court dismissed the case, noting that a London jury could not inquire about a blow struck in Middlesex. Rather, justices remarked that the "usage has been, after the death, to bring the deceased, that is the body, into the county where he was struck" and hold an inquest there.[104]

CORONERS AND CORRUPTION

The majority of statute law relating to the coronership centers on the misdeeds of coroners. Here, keep in mind that statute law acts as a corrective. It is a legislative response to an existing problem otherwise irresolvable by common law procedures. The late medieval age tended to dramatic expressions of anxiety concerning social order. Petitions to Parliament regularly depict the kingdom "on the verge of anarchy," although it is still unclear whether there was, in fact, an epic rise in rates of crime or simply in a sense of unease.[105] The implication for historians is that in addressing the grievances of the commons, statute law produces an image of the coroner at his worst. Historians' censorious perceptions of the coroner originate in concerns enunciated by Parliament. The first statute to address coroners' corruption materialized in response to the Hundred Roll inquiry of 1274–1275, targeted at investigating the dishonest behavior of local officials.[106] Adopting a firm stance, Chapter Nine declares boldly that sheriffs, coroners, or bailiffs who "conceal, consent or procure to conceal, the Felonies done in their Liberties, or otherwise . . . shall have one Year's Imprisonment, and after make a grievous Fine [at the King's pleasure, if they have wherewith;] and if they have not whereof, they shall have Imprisonment of [three] Years."[107] Somewhat unexpectedly, the statute puts the coroner in the spotlight. Following immediately on the heels of this warning, Chapter Ten reiterates the necessary qualifications of a coroner: counties must elect their coroners from "persons honest, lawful and wise." The statute insists that sheriffs keep "Counter-Rolls with the Coroners" as a precautionary measure (a condition that mirrors the coroner's actual role with respect to the sheriff). Finally, the statute addresses also payments for service, stipulating that "no Coroner [shall] demand nor take any thing of any Man to do his Office, upon pain of great Forfeiture to the King."[108]

Legislation and surviving petitions concerning crooked coroners convinced Hunnisett that corruption was universal. He argues that coroners' bribes for performing services "had become an established and invariable fee," and that coroners "practised extortion regularly, if moderately."[109] Carrie Smith draws a similar conclusion, noting that communities likely paid coroners an "unofficial fee" for their services.[110] A 1354 complaint put forward by the commons regarding the coronership spells out just how extortion worked with coroners determined to profit from their position. The House of Commons protested that

> whereas coroners are usually chosen from the great and most respected men of each county and area where they dwell, now some come to procure this office to their own profit, giving generously of themselves in order to have the office; telling the people that they give a great farm for the same, when our lord the king usually gave it to them for keeping the said office well; and they also go into the country, and by pretext of this office fabricate indictments to be brought before them, and attach or take various people in various parts of their bailiwicks and detain them in prison until the said people have made fine to the said coroners at their will, to the great damage and impoverishment of all the people.[111]

Despite the impassioned plea for just coroners, realistically, the surviving evidence does not support ubiquitous extortion.

That is not to suggest that medieval coroners were never paid. Indeed, there are a number of reasons to believe coroners did receive some honest remuneration for their work. First, the Parliamentary evidence implies it. A mandate by the king in January 1401 commanded "the coroner not take more than was duly taken in ancient times," creating the distinct impression that coroners did receive some sort of fee.[112] One way around statutory strictures was for the king himself to reward the coroner for his service, as the above petition hints, rather than payment by the locality or family of the dead. Second, in many regions of England, the coronership was a paid position.[113] Many localities exhibited great resourcefulness in finding the means to subsidize their coroners' activities. For example, Shrewsbury required its coroners also to be superintendents of town works, duties that garnered them a weekly salary of six pence.[114] In Leyland hundred in Lancashire, custom dictated that coroners have the upper garment from the deceased, supplying the coroner with a mortuary fee of sorts.[115] The bishop of Durham's coroners received a portion of the corn levied in each ward within the palatinate as a salary.[116] At the very least, coroners were sometimes compensated for the expenses pertaining to their office. The records of the city of Norfolk include a 1397 notation for payment to the coroner for his "expenses in going to Bukenham-Ferry, to sit upon 2 women drowned there 13*s.* it being within the city liberty."[117]

Many of these customs probably originated in extortion and over time came to be seen as honest graft. These subsidies nonetheless provided coroners with the necessary funds to cover their travel costs. How universal these practices were is impossible to gauge. Once again, the medieval coronership was highly regionalized. Even a coroner's duties varied sometimes quite radically depending on the locality. Given the circumstances, the statute of 1487 should be re-evaluated. Historians have greeted Parliament's decision to afford coroners a set fee of 8*s.* 4*d.* for each homicide inquest, drawn from the goods and chattels of the perpetrator, as belated recognition that efficiency is tied to income: a coroner who is paid for his labor may be inclined to work harder than one who labors only for prestige. Instead, the motivation behind the statute's creation may have been to standardize the irregular nature of these payments across England.[118]

The legal treatises also tackle the subject of corruption. *Fleta* dedicates an entire chapter to the various ways coroners might abscond with the king's rightful property. Much of this anxiety centers on the goods and lands of the killer. It is ironic that the 1487 statute mandates fees for homicide inquests be paid from the felon's goods and property. Homicides were a considerable source of profit for the crown. A felon's goods were forfeit permanently to the king; his lands, including any leases on land, escheated to their lord after the king had taken waste and profits for a year and a day.[119] It was the coroner's responsibility to inventory the accused felon's lands and goods; the escheator did the actual confiscation. Preparing an inventory gave the coroner an opportunity to steal from the dead before anyone had a chance to discover it. Given the impressive sums garnered by crown pleas on behalf of the king, the fears that the coroner might abscond with the crown's profits were legitimate enough.

Cheating the king was not *Fleta*'s only source of apprehension. Mercifully, the treatise evinced also some concern for how an extortionate coroner might lead to the miscarriage of justice, while recognizing that greed was not the only motivation. *Fleta* identified also intimidation, kinship, and local bias as potential pitfalls for which coroners and communities must beware.[120] *Britton* lays out the various ways in which coroners might err in their ways:

> We forbid every coroner, upon pain of imprisonment and heavy ransom, to make his inquests of felonies accidents or other things belonging to his office, by procurement of friends, or to remove a juror on the challenge of any party, or to take anything by himself or other, or suffer anything to be taken by his clerk or any person belonging to him, for executing his office; or to erase, or alter, or practice any kind of fraud in his rolls, or suffer it to be done.[121]

The legal treatises showed especial concern for a coroner's rolls, shedding some light on the haphazard condition of the rolls as they exist today. *Fleta* explains that a coroner may always add new information to his rolls, but he "may in no wise diminish them." Indeed, any hint of an erasure in his rolls might well lead to the coroner being imprisoned and fined on the assumption that he was paid to hide evidence.[122] As a safeguard, the coroner sealed his rolls after enrollment. They were not opened again until the eyre in order to prevent any tampering with the official record. This insight returns us momentarily to the oath of the London coroner, which places great emphasis on the coroners' records as ultimately belonging to the state and not the coroner. This is a significant point. The irregular survival of coroners' rolls has sometimes been blamed on the "ancient custom of inquest papers being regarded as the personal property of the coroner in question."[123] This was not the case in medieval England. English coroners understood the public nature of their documentation, and the crown was more than willing to sue coroners or their heirs who failed to return the rolls upon demand.[124]

While the statutes and the treatises speak about corruption in hypothetical terms, the Year Books provide concrete examples. At the 1313 eyre, justices convicted John of Oveney, county coroner for Kent, for taking half a mark (that is, 13*s.* 4*d.*) from a woman before he would permit the burial of her husband. The court ordered that he make restitution to the victim, and pay her damages, although it did not specify the amount. He was to go to prison until he made fine.[125] The crown punished the same coroner also for appropriating the dead's "upper garment" in three separate inquests, presumably a local customary fee that did not meet with crown approval.[126] Royal justices fined another two unnamed coroners in 1353 for extorting half a mark for performing the duties of their office.[127] These specific incidents aside, the Year Books otherwise evince little concern over the dishonesty of coroners, and certainly not enough to suggest widespread corruption. What is more significant is that the Year Books clarify the harsh punishment that awaited coroners who failed in their duties. In 1329, when a coroner misplaced the enrollment of a homicide, Chief Justice Scrope sentenced him to prison until he made fine.[128] Even more egregious, Justice Stanton commanded royal officials to seize John de Wangrave's wife and children as hostages when the London coroner failed to appear in court in response to a summons in 1321. Stanton justified his pronouncement by saying that a coroner "ought to be always ready and present."[129]

Scrope's reaction to the loss of one enrollment (presumably a high-profile homicide?) shines some light on the process of record keeping as well as the difficulties associated with it. The various coroners of a county worked as a team, safeguarding each other's documentation. A presenting jury at the Northamptonshire eyre of 1329 clarified the process. In response to a complaint that a coroner had not returned his roll to court, the jury replied that the loss of one set of coroners' rolls meant little because coroners worked together to create duplicates of each other's inquests. Thus, any "one, two, or three of its four coroners could act in the absence of the others, that those who were absent would upon their return enter in their rolls the acts of the others taken in their absence." The king's justices were not at all pleased to hear this. They "criticized the practice of having a coroner record business at which he was not present."[130] While the king's justices had good reason for disparaging this practice, undoubtedly the coroners were looking out for their own best interests. If the crown was willing to send a coroner to prison over a single lost enrollment, how much worse might the penalty be for a coroner who lost an entire roll? Coroners were also well aware that their obligation to safeguard the records of their investigations did not cease after their deaths. That responsibility fell to their heirs, who might also suffer punishment at the hands of the king.

Admittedly, the crown implemented numerous safety measures to ensure the moral probity of its coroners. Coroners not only acted as a check on the sheriff's behavior, but the sheriff did the same for the coroner. As *Britton* explains, the sheriff is to be the coroner's "controller in every part of his office."[131] The jury of presentment acted as an additional precaution. The articles of eyre upon which jurors were to present addressed directly the misdeeds of coroners. Jurors were to speak:

> Of coroners who take money or anything by way of bribe for discharging their office, and whether they have concealed, or have kept for their own use, the chattels of felons or fugitives, and how much and into whose hands these have come.
>
> Of sheriffs, coroners and other bailiffs, dwelling both within franchises and without, who, for prayer, price or favour or for any kinship, have concealed or procured the concealment of felonies committed in their bailiwicks or have avoided arresting any wrongdoers.[132]

Fleta also expected juries of presentment to comment on whether their coroner "freely and without delay" visited scenes of death.[133]

More important still, the treatises acknowledge that sometimes it was not the coroner who was deceitful, but his jurors. If a coroner imagined his jury was hiding evidence, the treatises recommend due diligence. According to *Britton*, "if the coroner on the first inquiry suspect concealment of the truth, or that there is need of further inquiry, and that by others, let inquiry be made again and again."[134] Similarly, the *Mirror* advocates that the coroner be flexible when addressing concealment. While empanelling a new jury might seem like the best option, he should also consider the possibility of holding the inquest in a new location, or holding multiple inquests with multiple juries, if he thinks he can "thereby discover more as to the concealed facts."[135]

All of this needs to be put in perspective. Statute law and the treatises reflect a real-life situation in which some coroners, although certainly not all, charged illicitly for their services, or falsely appraised felons' goods in order to keep some profit for themselves. Did dishonesty in these forms necessarily have an impact on a thorough investigation? Indeed, many of the instances of corruption documented in the Year Books suggest nominal fees were not demanded until after that service was rendered. Thus, while the crown did not in any way condone it, it was nevertheless still possible for a crooked coroner to carry out a legitimate investigation.

The evidence of legal tradition (that is, statute law, legal treatises, and the Year Books collectively) presents a comprehensive perspective of crown expectations for the coroner. It is significant that this literature does not describe the coroner only as a financial officer. Tradition acts as a useful corrective to scholarly perception. Because of the financial undertones of England's succinctly expressed coroners' rolls, often historians have reduced the medieval coroner to an accountant, rather than both a financial officer and an officer of law enforcement. Barbara Hanawalt's query springing from the narrative format of coroners' rolls reveals how ingrained this viewpoint has become. She asks, "Why do these people tell complete, detailed stories when all the bureaucrats want to know is who or what did what to whom and how much the Crown can collect?"[136] Drawing on what she sees as analogous examples from anthropological sources, she concludes that medieval communities were determined to tell their stories as an experience of communal therapy, even if the law had no desire to hear them. "Fortunately, medieval coroners and their clerks seem to have had a high tolerance not only for narrative but also for writing it down."[137] Indeed, "[t]he community was not content with the Crown's requirement simply to give essential facts; it had to have its story spoken out and recorded."[138] Hanawalt's hypothesis of the "persistence of narrative needs" largely in spite of the crown's financial concerns finds no support whatsoever in the legal tradition.[139] While the king's sights ultimately were set on the profits of the law, the literature evinces a genuine conviction to uphold the law that in no way can be interpreted as mere rhetoric for efficient and effective justice.

The legal literature constructs the impression that the crown set high standards. It expected coroners to be men of honesty, guaranteed by wealth, and diligent in their duties. The list of the coroners' obligations also makes it clear that this could be a busy job. Coroners not only headed up death investigations, but they had a wide array of related and unrelated duties concerning abjuration of the realm, approver's confessions, wounding and mayhem, attendance at court, rape, treasure trove, wreck of the sea, and perhaps even sodomy. On top of all this, the crown relied on the coroner to supervise the morality of the sheriff—an individual who technically outranked him in the administrative hierarchy. Certainly some of those complaints presented at Parliament about the inadequacy of the coroners are best explained by the expectations of the job. The mountain of tasks set before the coroner required a man of exceptional vigor and integrity.

WHO WERE THE CORONERS (IN PRACTICE)?

The coroner's duties placed him squarely at the nexus of law and medicine. Yet, neither the statutes nor the legal tradition prescribes appointing coroners with training in either discipline. Indeed, few coroners had experience in the realm of medicine.[140] The crown did not see experience in medicine as a prerequisite for the coronership. In terms of law, the absence of any mandatory training is not entirely surprising. Much like justices of the peace, medieval coroners needed no formal education in law to perform their duties because, in such a legally minded society, instruction in the field was not considered a necessity. As Morris Arnold has noted, law was a "habit" in medieval England. "In the fourteenth century a man became a man of law the same way he learned to be a smith or a skinner or a bowyer: he watched master craftsmen at work, sought their advice, and did his best to imitate them."[141] Even lawyers were not university trained. Medieval universities specialized in Roman and canon law. Common law was taught at the Inns of Court in a manner far more similar to an apprenticeship.[142] Even still, most coroners did not start their careers as lawyers, climbing a chain of command toward the coronership. Only two coroners have been discovered to have possessed a lawyerly background. John Everard of Stratford-sub-Castle in Wiltshire brought his skills as a lawyer to the post of county coroner, a position he held for at least the period 1341–1355, although he probably continued in this post until his death in 1361.[143] During this time, he also performed service on a wide range of shire commissions. He was appointed sheriff of Wiltshire in October of 1354, and he also served as county escheator in 1355.[144] John de Wangrave, described above as the London mayor who worked as deputy coroner for many years, also had a lawyer's background. In 1304, he worked as London's recorder.[145]

Even if few men had formal training in the law, most coroners had already gained considerable experience in the field prior to assuming office. Englishmen usually followed one of two paths on the road to becoming coroner. First, many coroners were born into families of officeholders. Thus, they were raised in an environment that offered a firsthand view of the law in action. In select regions, coronerships were actually hereditary. This was true of the county of Northumberland, the liberty of Durham, and the liberty of the Bishop of Ely.[146] Elsewhere, even if the position was not properly hereditary, coroners hailed from administrator families. Thomas Belhous, a coroner for fourteenth-century Essex, illustrates this pattern of familial officeholding.[147] His great-grandfather, Thomas Belhous, was seneschal of Pontieu in the thirteenth century; his grandfather, Thomas Belhous, was sheriff of Cambridge from 1281 to 1288 and also of Hungtingdonshire in 1286; while Richard de Belhous (presumably another relation) was sheriff of Norfolk and Suffolk in 1289.[148] Two fourteenth-century coroners emerged from Yorkshire's influential Darell family. Marmaduke Darell was county coroner for the North Riding in the 1340s; William Darell was coroner for the liberty of the abbot of Whitby for most of the second half of the century.[149] The Pope family produced two coroners for Gloucester: John Pope in the 1360s and Stephen Pope from 1384–1395 (presumably they were father and son).[150] The Pope family also dominated the office of bailiff, occupying the post for eleven years during the period 1377 to 1397; and it sent four family members (John Pope I, Robert Pope, Stephen Pope, and Thomas Pope) as representatives to a total of ten Parliaments during the period 1376 to 1397.[151] The Compton family was a virtual powerhouse of coroners. Robert of Compton raised two sons while he was Warwickshire's county coroner.[152] Both followed his example: Edmund in Warwickshire,

Thomas in nearby Gloucestershire.[153] These few men are representative of the scores of other families who dominated these offices.[154] Admittedly, at times, the interrelatedness of officeholders presented procedural problems. For example, the Year Books report that when an escheator was indicted for traverse of office (that is, making a defective inquisition into lands or goods) in 1489, a representative for the king challenged the jury. Purportedly, the sheriff who empanelled the jury was a "cousin" (that is, family member) of the escheator: thus, he could not be trusted to put together an impartial jury. Accordingly, the job fell to the coroner. There were seven available coroners: three of them were also cousins to the sheriff and the escheator. Consequently, the king's representative requested one of the four coroners not related to either individual be commanded to empanel a new jury.[155] As this example illustrates, coroners came by their passion for law enforcement honestly. In each of these situations, their home lives functioned as an apprenticeship in the administration of the law. How better to learn the law than to grow up surrounded by it?

Second, the office of coroner was usually one of the last positions a man held in the administration of the law.[156] Among others, men held positions as member of Parliament, escheator or sub-escheator, royal justice, tax collector for the crown, bailiff, and verderer (who often served as coroner for the royal forests), before moving on to the coronership. Consequently, by the time a man became coroner, he was well acquainted with the needs of the office. Philip of Lutley, a county coroner in mid-fourteenth-century Staffordshire, offers a good example of a career spent in the administration of the law. He was a commissioner of beer and wheat in 1324; in 1332 he served as member of Parliament for Staffordshire; by 1345 he was acting as bailiff to the Staffordshire sheriff, John of Aston (who also later became a county coroner); for a time he was verderer of Kinver forest; he served on a wool commission in 1347; he also worked as a justice of the peace and a commissioner of an array in 1352. Finally, he became coroner in 1352, the year in which he was slain while performing his duties levying a distraint for the sheriff.[157]

As the careers of many of these men imply, there was a close association between coronership, bailiwick, and shrievalty. Given the shared ground between them, as the three offices most closely concerned with criminal law enforcement, this connection is both reasonable and predictable. Sheriffs knew better than anyone else what they were getting themselves into when accepting election to the office of coroner, a weighty decision given the post was for life. Once again, because the crown envisioned coroners as a safeguard against shrieval corruption, coroners and sheriffs worked side by side in scores of their myriad duties.[158] Because so much of their work overlapped, coroners regularly stepped in to perform a sheriff's duties when he was suspected of being partial.[159] A man who took pleasure in the work of sheriff and had that experience to bolster his reputation was an ideal candidate for coroner. The bailiff, as the sheriff's right-hand man, shared many of the same perquisites and was in a similar position. This reality challenges traditional scholarly beliefs concerning local officeholding. As Richard Gorski explains it, "[m]edieval local government is conventionally perceived as a hierarchy, with sheriffs, knights of the shire and justices of the peace at the top. Coroners and verderers at the bottom and other officials somewhere in between."[160] This perception of the administrative hierarchy has led many to believe that coroners were usually of a "lower social stratum" than sheriffs, escheators, and justices of the peace.[161] Yet, channeling men of a lower social standing into the coronership would have undermined the purpose of the office. The coroner existed as a check on the behavior of the sheriff. How might a man of lesser standing confidently report on the performance of a social superior and expect the crown to believe him? At the very least, when the crown or the church charged a community with overseeing the behavior of their local authorities (either a sheriff or a parish priest, for example), the expectation is that it was too difficult for a group of individuals to form a united front around a lie. The coroner was on his own. The medieval English conceived of officeholding as a means to advance in society: but a lower-ranked coroner who betrayed a sheriff of superior rank was engaging in social suicide.

More important still, this vision of political administration does not reflect the coterie of men who parlayed a term in the shrievalty into a lifelong career as coroner. To offer a few examples: John Filliol was sheriff of Essex in 1373, roughly a decade before the men of Gloucestershire elected him county coroner. His extant roll reveals that he was resident in that post by 1382, and despite an order to the sheriff to have him replaced in 1384, he was still working in this capacity in 1390.[162] The career of William Harvey of London proves just how wrong-headed this perception of the local hierarchy actually is. Harvey was sheriff of London and Middlesex twice before he became king's chamberlain (the chamberlain assumed the role of coroner in London early on, although it eventually became the duty of the king's butler): first in 1254–1255, then again in 1265–1266.[163] He then moved on to the position of bailiff in 1267 and for a second time in 1268. In 1269, he became chamberlain once again and held that post for two years; finally, he was elected mayor of London in 1271.[164] Many other men followed this route, shifting seamlessly between shrievalty and coronership.[165] A position as bailiff also frequently acted as a stepping-stone to a coronership.[166] For some, the positions overlapped: William Reyne was bailiff of Colchester eight times, both before and after he became coroner of the liberty.[167]

A pluralistic approach to officeholding, as evidenced by the careers of men such as William Reyne who was bailiff and coroner simultaneously, was not unusual in this period.[168] What is perhaps most remarkable is that several coroners held the position of sheriff while they were also coroners. For example, William of Bleesby was coroner from at least 1354 to 1404 when the crown commanded the sheriff of Lincoln to replace him, yet he was also sheriff of the city of Lincoln in 1382.[169] William Norton, a draper from London, also seems to have held both positions concurrently. His surviving coroners' rolls demonstrate that he held that office by at least 1381; nonetheless, he also held the post of sheriff of London and Middlesex in 1408, and there is no evidence that he stepped down from being coroner.[170] Robert Whittington was sheriff of Gloucestershire multiple times while coroner: his coroner's roll covers 1392–1393, but he was sheriff for three terms: 1402, 1407, and 1412.[171] Once again, scores of other men seem to have followed this route.[172] Having one man in both positions would certainly undercut the coroner's ability to act as a check on the sheriff; the king's council also expressly forbade it. Again, a memorandum from 16 April, 1317, notes that "no sheriff or coroner shall be made a justice to take assizes, deliver gaols, of oyer and terminer, or to do any other office of justice, because they ought to be intendent to other justices appointed in their county, and if it happen that the king order the contrary, the chancellor shall inform him of this agreement of the council before he do anything."[173] The number of coroners who wore multiple hats affirms that countless exceptions existed to this rule.

Why did the English endorse such a pluralistic approach to the administration of the law? Hunnisett answers this question by arguing that "the pluralist tendency existed in all towns because the number of possible candidates for local office was limited."[174] If towns and hundreds had been resolved to hold fast to the statutory requirements for a coroner's credentials, Hunnisett's conclusion would be well founded. However, as he observed, after 1300, knights rarely filled the position of coroner because, quite simply, "there were not enough knights to go round."[175] Innumerable requests for the replacement of unqualified coroners extant in the close rolls indicate that adhering to the property qualifications stipulated in the statutes was not a high priority in elections. This was not simply a matter of rejecting the idea of knighthood: many men with sufficient lands to apply for knighthood chose not to do so. Rather, requests for replacement of coroners indicate that the English were willing to consider an even larger pool of candidates than that articulated within the law. Thus, Hunnisett's view that there were simply not enough qualified candidates around is untenable. It is much more likely that the same men filled these positions continually because they wanted to do so, and they had the experience to prove to their peers that they were uniquely qualified. This also explains why some men were coroner of more than one county: Edmund of Weedon was coroner of Buckinghamshire before he became coroner of Bedfordshire.[176]

Also in defiance of the 1317 memorandum, many other coroners worked as escheators or justices of the peace both before and during their terms as coroners. Richard of Gaddesby (*Leics.*) worked as a justice of the peace on numerous commissions before and after he began his career as coroner around 1361.[177] John Bredeford worked as escheator in Essex (1383) and Hereford (1383) during his time as coroner of Essex.[178] Thomas Cole acted as a justice of the peace in Gloucestershire on numerous occasion while also coroner; in the 1390s he worked as clerk to the justices of the peace; he was also undersheriff of the city of Gloucester, all while he was also one of the county's coroners.[179] The crossover between escheator and coroner may have seemed like a logical extension of a coroner's duties. While coroners and their juries assessed the value of deodands and a felon's goods and lands, the escheator executed the confiscation and was accountable to the king for their value. Employing one man for both tasks was surely the most efficient, although not necessarily reliable, approach. Similarly, coroners who worked also as royal justices probably believed they were pursuing the enforcement of the law in another venue. Here, it is worthy of note that common law set strenuous property requirements of £20 per year for sheriffs, escheators, and royal justices alike.[180] The more rigid property requirements for these offices would seem to substantiate an administrative hierarchy that organized along property lines. Yet, the number of coroners who also served in these capacities turns this assumption on its head.

That some mayors eventually became coroners demonstrates that the coronership was not relegated to the less substantial men in gentry society. William Catour was mayor of Reading (*Berks.*) several years before he became coroner.[181] Five London mayors in total went on to occupy the coronership: Geoffrey of Ruxley (mayor 1275–1282 and 1285–1286; chamberlain, 1275–1278), Stephen of Abingdon (mayor 1315–1316; chamberlain, 1316–1325); John de Wangrave of London (mayor 1316–1319; deputy coroner 1315–1319); Henry Picard (mayor, 1356–1357; king's butler, 1350–?); and John of Stody (mayor, 1357–1358; king's butler, 1359–?).[182] John of Owthorpe was mayor of Lincoln in 1348, a couple of decades before he became coroner.[183] The Wakelyn family of the city of Northampton produced two men who pursued both posts. William Wakelyn was mayor prior to becoming coroner: first in 1357 and again in 1367; he served as coroner in the 1370s. Thomas Wakelyn chose the opposite route. He was borough coroner in the later 1370s, and then became mayor in 1382 and again in 1394.[184] Like many of London's mayor-chamberlains, William Wakelyn was probably coroner and mayor at the same time; other men also filled both roles at once. Peter of Kent of the town of Leicester chose this path. He was mayor of Leicester twice, first in 1319–1320, next in 1321–1322, both while he was also coroner of the borough. Lawrence the Seller, another mayor of Leicester, also held the two positions concurrently.[185] Certainly, any man who had worked as mayor would have had a good appreciation for the services of a hard-working coroner and have come to realize how valuable the position was to the functioning of a peaceful and well-run borough. The need for a good coroner was clearly well appreciated in the borough of Doncaster (*Yorks.*) where a 1467 charter authorized the mayor to assume the role of coroner for the borough. This duality continued until the *Municipal Corporations Act* of 1835.[186] That English communities expected a man with some experience to assume office is emphasized also by a complaint registered in *Fleta*. The legal treatise bewails that "[w]hereas young and inexperienced men have commonly been elected to the office of coroner in times past," he calls on counties to choose more "suitable coroners."[187]

The careers of these men lead us to two distinct conclusions. First, for some, the office of coroner was a reward for a long and active career in service. Gilbert Wace's experience exemplifies this.[188] Gilbert Wace of Ewelme held many posts in government. He was the joint sheriff of Oxfordshire and Berkshire four times (1371, 1374, 1379, 1387).[189] He was also an escheator in Oxfordshire, Berkshire, and Westminster in 1378.[190] He was a commissioner of the peace in 1383; he served on a commission of oyer and terminer later that same year. In 1386, he became one of Oxford's two members of Parliament.[191] Somewhere toward the end of his career he was also elected coroner: his roll comprises 1391–1396, and a royal mandate from November of 1398 seeks his replacement because of age and illness.[192] Wace's long and ambitious career made him the ideal candidate for a coroner; but also, surely after so many annual posts, he had earned the job stability of the coronership? Second, many men like Wace moved into the coronership because they had an indispensable background, and although they might have preferred to continue on as sheriff or bailiff, this was not the nature of those offices. Positions like sheriff, bailiff, and even mayor were limited to a year at a time; while some mayors served multiple terms, although never consecutively, the opportunities to do so were constrained by popular fears of tyranny. The office of coroner, on the other hand, was a life appointment. And as the multiple requests for substitution extant in the close rolls imply, it was not very easy to uproot a coroner from his post. Hunnisett argues that most calls for replacement emanated from the coroner himself wanting to step down. Yet if a coroner was desperate to resign, would he not have been more proactive in pressuring the county sheriff to find a replacement? Rather, surviving royal mandates leave the distinct impression of men intent on dying in office. The crown issued four separate commands for the replacement of William Hales of Kirton (*Lincs.*), the first three (1383, 1388, and 1394) on the grounds of insufficient qualifications, the third in 1399 because he was too sick and aged to perform the office.[193] Similarly, there are four requests for the replacement of Robert Holme of Lincoln: once in 1360 because he "has no lands to qualify him"; twice in 1378 for being insufficiently qualified; one again in 1380 because he was too sick and infirm to do the job.[194] Ralph Beler of Kettleby held on to his position as coroner of Leicestershire despite repeated requests addressed to him in his other capacity as sheriff that he stand down. As these examples confirm, a man who knew that he enjoyed a life in law enforcement probably saw the coronership as the model office, an ideal means to finish out one's career as an officeholder with dignity.

Admittedly, coroners who fought to remain in office did so to their own detriment. The coronership exposed its holders to a wide variety of perils.

Investigating death, especially during outbreaks of disease, left the coroner vulnerable. The Black Death hit coroners harder than it hit any other crown employees. Three of the twelve clerks of Chancery died in the course of 1349, as well as nine recording clerks in Common Pleas, ten recording clerks in King's Bench, and four sheriffs, but "no less than twenty-nine serving coroners were reported dead" that year.[195] Exposure to disease is just one of the hazards of the job. Homicide investigation was certain to garner enemies for any coroner. A coroner for the borough of Northampton discovered this the hard way in 1329 when three locals conspired to have him removed from office.

> They entered the house of one who was coroner of the town and beat him and trampled upon him and dragged him out of the house by the hair and made him come to the Gildhall the next day and removed him from the office of coroner and forced him to swear that he would never again hold office in the town unless upon the king's command.[196]

The trio of conspirators initially defended their actions by asserting that they were merely carrying out the king's command. The coroner was unsuitable for his job, and thus the king had sent a writ to the sheriff requesting his replacement. These men were merely helping the coroner out of office. They eventually abandoned this pretense, but tried their best to deny the allegations of conspiracy and battery. Chief Justice Scrope made sure the three paid heavily for their crimes.[197]

This example is not an anomaly. The Parliament rolls include numerous complaints regarding coroners who were prevented from doing their jobs by the machinations of an individual or groups of individuals. For example, in December of 1321, the coroner of the king's household and many other ministers of the king, sent to take horses for carrying victuals from Caldwell to Burton Bridge, found themselves the target of the local vicar's anger. The coroner and his men were soon fleeing quarrels (crossbow bolts) and stones aimed in their direction.[198] In 1303, the crown responded to complaints that "the whole community" of Norwich "made an assault by force and arms upon Roger of Hales, the king's coroner of co. Norfolk," while he was trying to conduct an inquest. The townsmen "beat, wounded and maltreated" the coroner, the bailiff, and the inquest jurors. That their concern centered on the nature of the inquest's findings is revealed by their actions. The townsmen "withdrew the coroner's rolls from [the coroner's] hands and tore and stamped upon them, and did not permit the coroner to execute what pertained to his office." In order to discern the reasons for such widespread "contempt," the crown sent in two justices of the peace to investigate more fully into the matter.[199] The coroners for Staffordshire became repeated victims to the tyranny of a local knight, Roger of Swynnerton, and his personal army. In 1314, Swynnerton and his men marched into the county court, halted all business by force, and compelled the sheriff and coroners to pay fines for indicting him in the death of Henry of Salt. Because Roger of Aston, one of the coroners, had written up the indictment, he was penalized with a fine of £100, where the sheriff and other coroners only had to pay 50 marks each. Then, in 1321, Swynnerton and his men prevented Henry of Cresswell, another county coroner, from carrying out an inquest on the body of Henry Persoun, also purportedly slain by Richard of Swynnerton.[200]

As the account of Roger of Hales above illustrates, not only coroners, but also their records became the targets of violence. A complaint registered by Norwich's city coroners in 1264 illustrates just how troublesome an official record of a crime might become. Fatigued after a harrying day working two separate crime scenes, Norwich's coroners sat down at Roger the Coroner's home to enter the records into a formal report. The drafting of their rolls was curtly interrupted by the arrival of a group of armed men headed by two ringleaders, one a clerk, the other presumably a knight, who "threatened to cut the Coroners into little pieces" if they did not surrender their documentation. When the coroners refused, they seized Roger, dragged him back into his home and wrested the record he was hiding in his shirtfront. Abandoning the startled coroners, the men proceeded to the church of Saint Peter Mancroft where they cut the record into pieces.[201] At times, attacks on the coroner were motivated instead by the deodand. In 1285, Thomas Bek, a former chancellor, was pardoned for having impeded a coroner from seizing a house, from which a clerk's servant had fallen to his death, as deodand.[202]

While most coroners had little recognized training in law or medicine, they did not need it. Indeed, neither do many coroners today. While the modern English and Welsh require coroners to have five years of practice as a lawyer or a physician, throughout much of the English-speaking world, the coronership continues to be an elected or appointed position that requires no experience in either discipline. Rather, the coroner is a government official who manages the institution responsible for determining cause of death. A good coroner hires medical practitioners and legal consultants to do the relevant work for him. This situation is not necessarily very different from what happened in medieval England. As this chapter has attempted to show, the English crown had lofty expectations for the coroner in terms of the broad scope of the office and the needs of the investigative process. Today, the work of the medieval coroner is carried out by an assembly of homicide detectives and police technicians, a coroner and his office of medical practitioners and pathologists, and a lawyer or two.[203] If we follow Hunnisett's lead and place all the responsibility for the coroners' expansive jurisdiction squarely on the shoulders of the coroner, then clearly it was far too large a job for any man. But medieval coroners did not (and could not!) work alone. Without the hard work and expertise of their jurors, it is difficult to imagine that any medieval homicide investigation would have concluded in a conviction.

NOTES

1. Although each county ideally had four coroners, some counties were quite large (such as Yorkshire). Depending on where the coroner lived in the county, the distance from his residence to the scene of death might still be substantial. Hunnisett discusses the nature of coroners' districts and the number of coroners per county (in fact, as opposed to theory) in Chapter Eight of *The Medieval Coroner* (Cambridge: Cambridge UP, 1961).
2. Paul Matthews, "Involuntary Manslaughter: A View from the Coroner's Court," *Journal of Criminal Law* 60 (1996): 189.
3. R.F. Hunnisett, "The Reliability of Inquisitions as Historical Evidence," in *The Study of Medieval Records: Essays in Honour of Kathleen Major*, ed. D.A. Bullough and R.L. Storey (Oxford: Oxford UP, 1971), pp. 206–35.
4. As summarized in Carrie Smith, "Medieval Coroners' Rolls: Legal Fact or Historical Fiction?" in *Courts, Counties and the Capital in the Later Middle Ages*, ed. Diana E.S. Dunn (New York: St. Martin's Press, 1996), pp. 93–95.
5. Smith, "Medieval Coroners' Rolls," p. 100.
6. J.B. Post, "Crime in Later Medieval England: Some Historiographical Limitations," *C&C* 2.2 (1987): 219.
7. Post, "Crime in Later Medieval England," 219.
8. J.D.J. Havard, *The Detection of Secret Homicide: A Study of the Medico-Legal System of Investigation of Sudden and Unexplained Death* (London: Macmillan, 1960), p. 29.
9. Anthony J. Musson, *Public Order and Law Enforcement: The Local Administration of Criminal Justice, 1294–1350* (Woodbridge: Boydell, 1996), p. 153.
10. 1327, *PRME*.
11. 1327, *PRME*.
12. 1399, *PRME*.
13. 1411, *PRME*.
14. 1376, *PRME*.
15. TNA PRO SC 8/136/6799 (*c*. 1318–*c*.1324): Matthew de Redmane reports that his grandfather's coroner's rolls were lost during the invasion of Lancashire by the Scots.
16. TNA PRO SC 8/11/514 (1330): Robert of Haugham, coroner of Essex, is accused by Rose, daughter of John le Setersteyn of Fyfield, of maintaining a band of robbers.
17. 1401, *PRME*; TNA PRO SC 8/37/1831 (c. 1331): the Abbot of Bindon complains that a monk, John de Montagu, maintains the coroner and has made him his steward.
18. Theodore Plucknett, *A Concise History of the Common Law*, 5th ed. (London: Butterworths, 1956), p. 27.
19. Richard Firth Green, *A Crisis of Truth: Literature and Law in Ricardian England* (Philadelphia: University of Pennsylvania Press, 1999), p. 137.
20. Henri de Bracton, *De Legibus et Consuetudinibus Angliae*, ed. George Woodbine, ed. and trans. Samuel E. Thorne, 4 vols. (*SS*, 1976). There is still a heated debate over whether Bracton is the author, reviser, or contributor to the text. See J.L. Barton, "The Authorship of *Bracton*: Again," *JLH* 30.2 (2009): 117–74; Paul Brand, "The Date and Authorship of *Bracton*: A Response," *JLH* 31.3 (2010): 217–44.
21. See J. L. Barton, *Roman Law in England*. (Mediolani: Giuffrè, 1971).
22. David J. Seipp, "The Mirror of Justices," in *Learning the Law: Teaching and the Transmission of the Law in England, 1150–1900*, ed. Jonathan A. Bush and Alain A. Wijffels (London and Rio Grande, OH: Hambledon, 1999), p. 91.

23. F. Pollock and F.W. Maitland, *A History of English Law before the Time of Edward I,* 2nd ed., 2 vols. (Cambridge: Cambridge UP, 1898), v. 1, p. 28.
24. Seipp, "Mirror of Justices," p. 112. F.W. Maitland and W.J. Whittaker, eds., *The Mirror of Justices* (*SS*, v. 7, 1895).
25. F.M. Nichols, ed., *Britton: The French Text Revised with an English Translation*, 2 vols. (Oxford: Clarendon Press, 1865), v. 1, p. 8.
26. William Stubbs, ed., *Select Charters and Other Illustrations of English Constitutional History*, 8th ed. (Oxford: Clarendon Press, 1900), p. 260.
27. Scott L. Waugh, "Reluctant Knights and Jurors: Respites, Exemptions, and Public Obligations in the Reign of Henry III," *Speculum* 58.4 (1983): 937–86.
28. 14 Edw. III, c. 8 (1340); *SR*, v. 1, p. 283.
29. Richard Gorski, *The Fourteenth-Century Sheriff: English Local Administration in the Later Middle Ages* (Woodbridge: Boydell, 2003), p. 82.
30. 28 Edw. III, c. 6 (1354); *SR*, v. 1, p. 346.
31. For example, despite the prevalence of primogeniture throughout England, the county of Kent continued to practice gavelkind, a unique form of tenure that included partible inheritance, throughout the medieval period. Under the rules of gavelkind, the crown could not confiscate the lands of a convicted felon.
32. Elizabeth Hurren, "Remaking the Medico-Legal Scene: A Social History of the Late-Victorian Coroner in Oxford," *JHMAS* 65.2 (2010): 209.
33. *CCR*, 1313–1318, p. 463; "November 1355," *PRME*.
34. 25 Edw. III, c. 3 (1351–52); *SR*, v. 1, p. 320.
35. *Britton*, v. 1, pp. 36–37.
36. For a discussion of "falseness," see Chapter One of Derek G. Neal, *The Masculine Self in Late Medieval England* (Chicago and London: University of Chicago Press, 2008). The centrality of oaths in medieval society helps us to understand the plethora of "breach of contract" suits in both ecclesiastical and royal courts.
37. Green, *Crisis of Truth*, p. 60.
38. Reginald R. Sharpe, ed., *Calendar of Letter-Books of the City of London*, 11 vols. (London: John Edward Francis, 1902), v. D, pp. 1–2. The spelling has been modernized.
39. The first part of the sentence feels like a word is missing. In Middle English, it reads: "And duly delyuer the pepull in that that in you his, that will sue for ony suche reconysaunse."
40. Mary Dormer Harris, ed., *The Coventry Leet Book: Or Mayor's Register: Containing the Records of the City Court Leet or View of Frankpledge, A.D. 1420–1555, with Divers other Matters*, 2 parts (London: Kegan Paul, Trench, Trübner, Co., Ltd., 1908), pt. 2, pp. 274–75. The spelling has been modernized.
41. In many respects, suspicion of foreigners was institutionalized, even in London. A 1243 municipal legislation stipulated that foreigners attached for homicide in London were to put themselves on the verdict of "two-and-forty men sworn of the three Wards next adjoining," a task that would have been impossible for most foreigners. See H.T. Riley, ed., *Chronicles of the Mayors and Sheriffs of London: 1188–1274* (London: Trübner, 1863), p. 10.
42. For an interesting discussion, see Jill C. Havens, "'As Englishe is comoun langage to oure puple': The Lollards and Their Imagined 'English' Community," in *Imagining a Medieval English Nation*, ed. Kathy Lavezzo (Minneapolis and London: University of Minnesota Press, 2004), pp. 96–131.
43. "Office of the Coroner," 4 Edw. I (1275–1276); *SR*, v. 1, pp. 40–41.
44. *Black's Law Dictionary* defines "treasure-trove" as: "Literally, treasure found. Money or coin, gold, silver, plate or bullion *found* hidden in the earth or other private place, the owner thereof being unknown." *Black's Law Dictionary*, 6th ed. (St. Paul, MN: West Publishing, 1990), p. 1501. Given the propensity

of the Roman-British, the Anglo-Saxons, and the Vikings to bury hoards, such a finding was more common than one might think.

45. For some franchisal coroners, such as those for county Durham, it was part of their regular business.
46. *Black's Law Dictionary* defines wreck of the seas as: "Goods cast ashore from a wrecked vessel, where no person has escaped from the wreck alive; and which are forfeited to the crown, or to persons having the franchise of wreck. But if claimed by the true owner within a year and a day the goods, or their proceeds, must be restored to him, by virtue of statute." (*Black's*, p. 1608). Wreck of the sea is not mentioned in the above excerpt from the statute, but it appears in the following paragraph on p. 41.
47. "Original Documents: Edward I Parliaments: Roll 12, #151," *PRME*.
48. "Original Documents: Edward I Parliaments: Roll 12, #113," *PRME*.
49. For a further discussion of approvers, see Anthony J. Musson, "Turning King's Evidence: The Prosecution of Crime in Late Medieval England," *Oxford Journal of Legal Studies* 19.3 (1999): 467–79.
50. *AS*, p. 610. Translation drawn from Valerie I.J. Flint, "The Saint and the Operation of the Law: Reflections upon the Miracles of St Thomas Cantilupe," in *Belief and Culture in the Middle Ages: Studies Presented to Henry Mayr-Harting*, ed. Richard Gameson and Henrietta Leyser (Oxford: Oxford UP, 2001), p. 344.
51. Pollock and Maitland, *A History of English Law*, v. 2, pp. 578–79.
52. Chaucer, "The Nun's Priest's Tale," lines 4570–90, in *The Canterbury Tales*. The English spelling has been modernized here.
53. For an interesting discussion of valid and invalid hues and cries, see Miriam Müller, "Social Control and the Hue and Cry in Two Fourteenth-Century Villages," *Journal of Medieval History* 31 (2005): 29–53.
54. In practice, there was great variety in the number of jurors and their affiliation. See Chapter Two.
55. The 1267 Statute of Marlborough reiterates this requirement. See "Statute of Marlborough," c. 24 (1267); *SR*, v. 1, p. 25.
56. *Britton*, v. 1, p. 9; *Mirror of Justices*, p. 30.
57. The treatment of the subject in the *Mirror* is somewhat puzzling initially, as it refers to juries by the dozens. Yet, if we understand "juror" more generally as "witness," rather than exclusively those twelve men enrolled as the coroner's jury, the passage in the *Mirror* makes considerably more sense.
58. *Mirror of Justices*, p. 30.
59. *Mirror of Justices*, p. 33.
60. Barbara A. Hanawalt, *Crime and Conflict in English Communities, 1300–1348* (Cambridge, MA: Harvard UP, 1979), p. 261.
61. H.G. Richardson and G.O Sayles, eds., *Fleta*, 3 vols. (*SS*, 1953–1983), v. 2, p. 64.
62. *Fleta,* v. 1, p. 65.
63. *Bracton*, v. 2, p. 356.
64. *Britton*, v. 1, pp. 16–17.
65. *Murdrum* fines themselves originated with Canute and were originally intended for the homicide of Danes. When William usurped the throne, he revived the custom in order to punish those who rebelled against their Norman conquerors.
66. *Mirror of Justices*, p. 35. This custom was abolished by statute. See 14 Edw. III, c. 4 (1340); *SR*, v. 1, p. 282.
67. Faye Getz, *Medicine in the English Middle Ages* (Princeton: Princeton UP, 1998), p. 75. For an excellent discussion of this genre of law, see Lisi Oliver, *The Body Legal in Barbarian Law* (Toronto and Buffalo: University of Toronto Press, 2011).

68. On the dating of these laws, see Lisi Oliver, ed., *The Beginnings of English Law* (Toronto and Buffalo: University of Toronto Press, 2002), pp. 41–57.
69. Cited in Oliver, *Beginnings of English Law*, p. 77.
70. Injury tariffs were a universal feature of early medieval law, not an Anglo-Saxon peculiarity. See Oliver, *Body Legal.*
71. Joseph Shatzmiller, "The Jurisprudence of the Dead Body: Medical Practition at the Service of Civic and Legal Authorities," *Micrologus* 7 (1999): 225–27. The statutory provisions also mirror what medical examiners today do in homicide investigations.
72. TNA PRO JUST 2/46, m. 1.
73. *Bracton*, v. 2, p. 344.
74. Robert Bartlett, *Trial by Fire and Water: The Medieval Judicial Ordeal* (Oxford: Clarendon Press, 1986), p. 94.
75. This is addressed by Florike Egmond, "Execution, Dissection, Pain and Infamy—A Morphological Investigation," in *Bodily Extremities: Preoccupation with the Human Body in Early Modern European Culture*, ed. Egmond and Robert Zwignenberg (Aldershot: Ashgate, 2003), pp. 106–08.
76. *Fleta*, v. 1, p. 66.
77. *Bracton*, v. 2, p. 344.
78. *Bracton*, v. 2, p. 409.
79. *Bracton*, v. 2, p. 415.
80. Doncaster Archives AB 4/4 (oath book: early sixteenth century), as cited in Jenny Moran, "By the Instigation of the Devil: The Doncaster Borough Coroner's Records," in *Aspects of Doncaster: Discovering Local History*, 2 vols., ed. Brian Elliott (Barnsley: Wharncliffe, 1997), v. 1, p. 210. I have modernized the spelling for ease of access.
81. Naomi D. Hurnard, *The King's Pardon for Homicide Before AD 1307* (Oxford: Oxford UP, 1969), p. 108.
82. *Britton*, v. 1, p. 9.
83. *Mirror of Justices*, pp. 29–30.
84. *Fleta*, v. 1, p. 64.
85. *Bracton*, v. 2, p. 343.
86. *Fleta*, v. 1, p. 65.
87. *Fleta*, v. 1, p. 64.
88. *Mirror of Justices*, p. 31.
89. *Britton*, v. 1, p. 16.
90. *Bracton* includes an interesting passage to explain why it is not homicide if an animal causes a human's death. He writes: "If it is done by an ox, a dog or some thing it will not properly be termed homicide. For it is called 'homicide' from '*homo*' and '*caedo, caedis*,' 'man-killing,' so to speak." See *Bracton*, v. 2, p. 340.
91. *Fleta* claims that deodands, "as the price of blood," were distributed "for the souls of the king's ancestors and all faithful departed"; however, the reality is that kings viewed deodands as a franchise, a right of collection that might be distributed to their adherents to reward loyalty. See *Fleta*, v. 1, p. 65.
92. *Mirror of Justices*, p. 31. Some jurors adhered strictly to this requirement. When a miller died after getting too close to his millwheel, the jury reported that "every moving part of the mill was adjudged deodand." See Donald W. Sutherland, ed., *The Eyre of Northamptonshire, 3–4 Edward III 1329–30)*, v. 1 (*SS*, v. 97, 1983), p. 185.
93. Teresa Sutton, "Nature of the Early Law of Deodand," *Cambrian Law Review* 30 (1999): 9.
94. Elsewhere in Europe, the solution was usually to put the animal on trial. See Esther Cohen, "Law, Folklore and Animal Lore," *P&P* 110 (1986): 10–37; or

Peter Dinzelbacher, "Animal Trials: A Multidisciplinary Approach," *Journal of Interdisciplinary History* 32.3 (2002): 405–21.

95. *AS*, p. 621.
96. The death of the mariner Elias Ide in 1336 confirms that coroners and their juries took their charge seriously, but hoped to minimize the damage inflicted by their verdict. Drunk while climbing a rope to reach the mast of his ship, Elias slipped and fell to the deck below: the fall killed him instantly. According to the jury, the rope was solely to blame: "neither the ship nor anything belonging to it was moving or being moved except the rope." Reginald R. Sharpe, *Calendar of Coroners' Rolls of the City of London, A.D. 1300–1378* (London: R. Clay & Sons, Limited, 1913), p. 177.
97. *Mirror of Justices*, p. 32.
98. Seipp, "Mirror of Justices," p. 97.
99. *Fleta*, v. 1, p. 72.
100. Smith, "Medieval Coroners' Rolls," p. 97.
101. Of the 21,000 defendants who came before the London church courts between 1420 and 1518, only one of them stood accused of sodomy. See Jeffrey Richards, *Sex, Dissidence and Damnation: Minority Groups in the Middle Ages* (London and New York: Routledge, 1991), p. 148. Michael Rocke argues that severe penalties for sodomy in Renaissance Florence acted as a deterrent to denouncers who might have come forward with a complaint had the implications been less severe. See Chapter One of Michael Rocke, *Forbidden Friendships: Homosexuality and Male Culture in Renaissance Florence* (Oxford: Oxford UP, 1998).
102. An association between birth defect and moral stain goes back at least as far as Augustine's *City of God* and his discussion of Cain. See Stephen C. Bandy, "Cain, Grendel, and the Giants of *Beowulf*," *Papers on Language and Literature* 9 (1973): 238. See also Dudley Wilson, *Signs and Portents: Monstrous Births from the Middle Ages to the Enlightenment* (London and New York: Routledge, 1993).
103. Y.B., term uncertain, 6 Edw. II; as cited in William Craddock Bolland, ed., *Year Books of Edward II*, v. 5 (*SS*, v. 24, 1910), pp. 127–28.
104. Y.B., term Mich., 6 Hen. VII, fo. 10a. In recounting the history of the coronership, Matthew Hale reports that this was standard practice in "ancient times." See his *History of the Pleas of the Crown: Concerning the Coroner and his Court, and His Authority in the Pleas of the Crown* (London: T. Payne, 1800), p. 65.
105. Simon Walker, "Order and Law," in *A Social History of England 1200–1500*, ed. Rosemary Horrox and W. Mark Ormrod (Cambridge: Cambridge UP, 2006), p. 101.
106. Hunnisett, *Medieval Coroner*, p. 118. This had been an ongoing problem. The 1258–1259 special eyre of Surrey and Kent concluded that "each coroner of this county took rewards for view of the dead." See Andrew H. Hershey, ed., *The 1258–9 Special Eyre of Surrey and Kent* (Surrey Record Society, 2004), p. 179.
107. "Statute of Westminster I," c. 9 (1275); *SR*, v. 1, p. 29.
108. "Statute of Westminster I," c. 10 (1275); *SR*, v. 1, p. 29.
109. Hunnisett, *Medieval Coroner*, pp. 121, 118.
110. Smith, "Medieval Coroners' Rolls," p. 100.
111. "Edward III: April 1354," *PRME*.
112. "Henry IV: January 1401," *PRME*.
113. Fitzherbert's Abridgement is sometimes cited as proof that coroners were paid for their services. Fitzherbert references a statute, supposedly dating to 3 Edw. III, stating that a penny is to be paid to the coroner by each visne. However, if

this statute ever really existed, the medieval evidence for it has vanished. See Anthony Fitzherbert, *La Graunde Abridgement* (London: John Rastell and Wynkyn de Worde, 1516), "coroners," item 372.

114. Hunnisett, *Medieval Coroner*, p. 94.
115. Hunnisett, *Medieval Coroner*, p. 122.
116. C.J. Neville, "'The Bishop's Ministers': The Office of Coroner in Late Medieval Durham," *Florilegium* 18.2 (2001): 54. Surviving documentation from Nottingham does not clarify the borough's own peculiar custom, but it regularly mentions payments to coroners for "their fee" of 6*s*. 8*d*. *Records of the Borough of Nottingham*, 3 vols. (London: Quaritch, 1882–1885), v. 2, p. 380; v. 3, pp. 70, 279, 320, 416. This custom did not change even after the 1487 statute. Unfortunately, the record does not indicate the nature of the service supplied, but a remark from 1500 hints that this was the sum of the annual wages for both borough coroners. See *Borough of Nottingham*, v. 3, p. 71. A surviving petition to the king dating to 1318–1324 implies that the office of coroner for Holderness (*Yorks*.) was also a salaried position. Hoping to compensate for his losses fighting the crown's enemies, John of Fawdon begged the king to consider granting him the office, claiming that it brought an annual income of 26 marks, although he did not explain how local government generated the necessary income. TNA PRO SC 8/260/12952.
117. Francis Blomefield, *An Essay towards a Topographical History of the County of Norfolk* (London: William Miller, 1806), v. 3, pt. 1, p. 114.
118. "An Acte agaynst Murderers," 3 Hen. VII, c. 2 (1487); *SR*, v. 1, p. 511.
119. The process of felony forfeiture is often misunderstood. For an impressive discussion of this subject, see K.J. Kesselring, "Felony Forfeiture in England, c. 1170–1870," *JLH* 30.3 (2009): 201–26.
120. *Fleta*, v. 1, p. 44.
121. *Britton*, v. 1, p. 14.
122. *Fleta*, v. 1, p. 64.
123. Moran, "By the Instigation of the Devil," v. 1, p. 216.
124. Hunnisett, *Medieval Coroner*, pp. 101–11.
125. Y.B., term uncertain, 6 Edw. II, fo. 24; as it appears in Bolland, *Year Books of Edward II*, v. 5, pp. 94–95.
126. Bolland, *Year Books of Edward II*, v. 5, pp. 150, 155–56.
127. Y.B., term uncertain, 27 Edw. III, fo. 134b.
128. Y.B., term uncertain, 3 Edw. III; as cited in Sutherland, *Eyre of Northamptonshire*, p. 176.
129. Helen M. Cam, ed., *Year Books of Edward II*, v. 26, pt. 2, (*SS*, v. 86, 1969), p. 126.
130. Y.B., term uncertain, 3 Edw. III, fos. 45–56. As the coroners' rolls attest, medieval coroners regularly adopted this "team" approach to documentation. Being a team had implications also outside of the official record. For example, the coroners' rolls include examples of situations in which one coroner filled in for another. John Peverell, coroner for the city of Winchester, conducted the inquest into the death of Thomas Spyneye in November of 1383 in the absence of the county coroners, John Waryn and Thomas Canteshangre. See TNA PRO JUST 2/155, m. 10.
131. *Britton*, v. 1, p. 17.
132. *Fleta*, v. 1, pp. 48, 54.
133. *Fleta*, v. 1, p. 42.
134. *Britton*, v. 1, p. 10.
135. *Mirror of Justices*, p. 33.
136. Barbara A. Hanawalt, "The Voices and Audiences of Social History Records," *Social Science History* 15.2 (1991): 160.

137. Hanawalt, "Voices and Audiences," 161.
138. Hanawalt, "Voices and Audiences," 162.
139. Hanawalt, "Voices and Audiences," 160.
140. William of Hastings, a fourteenth-century coroner for the county of Sussex, was also a surgeon. Hunnisett, *Medieval Coroner*, p. 177. A mandate for the replacement of William of Hastings because of illness survives in *CCR* (October 1304), p. 185.
141. Morris S. Arnold, "Law and Fact in the Medieval Jury Trial: Out of Sight, Out of Mind," *AJLH* 18.4 (1974): 279.
142. Paul Brand, "Courtroom and Schoolroom: The Education of Lawyers in England prior to 1400," *Historical Research* 60.142 (1987): 147–65.
143. His surviving roll, TNA PRO JUST 2/195, comprises this period.
144. Gorski, *Fourteenth-Century Sheriff*, p. 8; *CCR* (1355), p. 155. John Everard may also have come from a coroner's family. A John Everard filled the post of coroner for neighboring Somerset in the early fourteenth century as well. A request for his removal from office appears in the close rolls for 1317, citing that "he does not reside continuously within the county." *CCR* (July 1317), p. 488.
145. Recorders acted as the mayor of London's right-hand men, recording and pronouncing judgments. Barristers invariably occupied this post, many going on to impressive careers as sergeants. H.T. Riley, ed., *Liber Albus: The White Book of the City of London* (London: Richard Griffith & Co., 1861), p. 38. See John Noorthouck, *A New History of London: Including Westminster and Southwark* (London: R. Baldwin, 1773), pp. 893–94.
146. Hunnisett, *Medieval Coroner*, p. 150.
147. Thomas Belhous is associated with TNA PRO JUST 2/33A (1376–80).
148. Thomas Wright, *The History and Topography of the County of Essex* (London: George Virtue, 1836), p. 400; Anne Reiber DeWindt and Edwin Brezette DeWindt, *Royal Justice and the Medieval Countryside: The Huntingdonshire Eyre of 1286, the Ramsay Abbey Banlieu Court of 1287, and the Assizes of 1287–88* (Toronto: PIMS, 1981), pt. 1, p. 10; *List of Sheriffs for England and Wales From the Earliest Times to A.D. 1831, Compiled from Documents in the Public Record Office* (London: HMSO, 1898; repr. New York, 1963), pp. 12, 86.
149. Marmaduke is associated with TNA PRO JUST 2/210 (1340–1344), William with JUST 2/216 (1356–1385).
150. John is associated with TNA PRO JUST 2/35 (1368–1371), Stephen with JUST 2/38 (1384–1388) and JUST 2/40 (1387–1395).
151. J.S. Roskell, L. Clark, and C. Rawcliffe, eds., *The History of Parliament: The House of Commons 1386–1421* (Woodbridge: Boydell, 1993), www.historyofparliamentonline.org/volume/1386-1421/constituencies/gloucester. Accessed March 12, 2013.
152. Arthur Collins, *Collins's Peerage of England: Genealogical, Biographical, and Historical* (London: F.C. & J. Rivington, Otridge & Son, 1812), v. 3, p. 225.
153. Edmund is associated with TNA PRO JUST 2/188 and JUST 2/190, Thomas with JUST 2/45 (1395–1398). This pattern of family officeholding holds true even for the earliest coroners. Robert de Crevequer, one of Bedfordshire's thirteenth-century coroners, came from a family of administrators stretching back to the Conquest (Robert de Crevequer is associated with TNA PRO JUST 2/4, 1275–1276.) His grandfather, Hamo de Crevequer, was sheriff in Kent during the time of King William I; his father, also named Hamo, held posts both as the constable of Dover Castle and warden of the Cinque Ports. See Edward Hasted, *The History and Topographical Survey of the Count of Kent*, v. 1 (Canterbury: W. Bristow, 1797), p. 177; Hasted, *History and Topographical Survey*, v. 9, pp. 475–548.

154. Family relationships are visible also in the repetition of names among offices. For example, Alan Botiler was coroner for the county of Gloucester in 1392–1398 (his extant roll is TNA PRO JUST 2/43), while another Alan Botiler was county sheriff in 1274. See *List of Sheriffs*, p. 49. John Trye was county coroner in Gloucestershire in 1395–1398 (TNA PRO JUST 2/45); another John Trye was sheriff in 1448 (*List of Sheriffs*, p. 50). Robert of Wyville was followed by his son, also Robert of Wyville, in office as coroner of Leicestershire, making it difficult to distinguish the two coroners from each other. See Philip Lloyd, "The Coroners of Leicestershire in the Early Fourteenth Century," *Transactions of the Leicestershire Archaeological and Historical Society* 56 (1980–1981), p. 27. An Adam Hobeldod filled the office of coroner for Cambridgeshire from 1375–1384 (TNA PRO JUST 2/24); John Hobeldod (possibly his son?) was county sheriff in 1403 and again in 1407 (*List of Sheriffs*, p. 13). There are far too many examples of these interrelationships to include in a footnote.
155. Y.B., Hil. term, 4 Hen. VII, fos. 3a–3b.
156. Hunnisett made a similar argument in 1961 concerning the Sussex coroners. Of the sixty-six known Sussex county coroners, he observed that thirty-seven served in other offices before they became coroners. See Hunnisett, *Medieval Coroner*, pp. 170–71.
157. *Collections for a History of Staffordshire*, ser. 3 (Stafford: Staffordshire History Society, 1917–18), p. 10.
158. Hunnisett, *Medieval Coroner*, pp. 84–86.
159. Hunnisett, *Medieval Coroner*, pp. 87–92.
160. Gorski, *Fourteenth-Century Sheriff*, p. 70.
161. Hunnisett, *Medieval Coroner*, p. 171.
162. Gorski, *Fourteenth-Century Sheriff*, p. 174; Filliol is associated with TNA PRO JUST 2/33A (1382–1390); *CCR* (December 1384), p. 492. Filliol was clearly from a family of some influence. Essex sent MPs with the last name Filliol in 1290, 1295, 1297, 1300, and 1301.
163. Martin Weinbaum, ed., *The London Eyre of 1276* (London: London Record Society, 1976), pp. 42–49.
164. Riley, *Chronicles of the Mayors and Sheriffs*, p. 236.
165. John Joce was sheriff of Gloucestershire in 1373 (*List of Sheriffs*, p. 50); his extant coroner's roll (TNA PRO JUST 2/45) shows that he was coroner during the period 1397–1398. William Worthin was sheriff of Shropshire in 1383 and 1395 (*List of Sheriffs*, p. 118); his period as coroner spanned at least the period 1392–1400 (TNA PRO JUST 2/146).
166. Men who followed this path include: Thomas Compton (*Glos.*), *CCR* (1402), p. 119. John Norman was bailiff of the borough of Leicester for 1279–1280; see Mary Bateson, ed., *Records of the Borough of Leicester* (London: Clay & Sons, 1899–1905), v. 1, p. 192. Robert of Holme was a bailiff of Lincoln in 1380; he is associated with TNA PRO JUST 2/70 (1361–1376). John le Wedour was bailiff of Northampton during 1310–1311; *A Descriptive Catalogue of Ancient Deeds*, v. 2 (London: HMSO, 1894), pp. 327–37. He is associated with TNA PRO JUST 2/108A (1312–1315). Ralph of Calverton was bailiff of Nottingham during 1361–1362. He is associated with TNA PRO JUST 2/118 (1376–1378).
167. William Reyne is associated with TNA PRO JUST 2/331 (1380–1389). He was bailiff in 1360, 1361, 1363, 1373, 1375, 1377, and 1391. See Janet Cooper, *A History of the County of Essex: Volume 9: The Borough of Colchester* (Oxford: Institute of Historical Research, 1994), pp. 374–78. The medieval town of Ipswich offers numerous examples of men who assumed the positions of coroner and bailiff. See John Wodderspoon, *Memorials of the Ancient Town of Ipswich* (London: Pawsey, 1850), pp. 106–10.

168. In fourteenth-century Dunwich, the same two men filled the positions of coroner and bailiff simultaneously. See Hunnisett, *Medieval Coroner*, p. 161. It is difficult to know how common this approach was. P.F. Mellen has made a similar observation of the pluralism of coroners in mid-eighteenth-century Massachusetts. See his "Coroners' Inquests in Colonial Massachusetts," *JHMAS* 40.4 (1985): 469.
169. TNA PRO JUST 2/67 (1354–1362); *CCR* (February 1404), p. 256.
170. William Norton is associated with five rolls: TNA PRO JUST 2/96 (1381–1386), JUST 2/97A (1386–1390), JUST 2/98 (1391–1394), JUST 2/99 (1395–1396), and JUST 2/100 (1397–1398); *List of Sheriffs*, p. 203.
171. TNA PRO JUST 2/42; *List of Sheriffs*, p. 50.
172. Ralph of Goldington was coroner of Bedfordshire by the 1260s (TNA PRO JUST 2/2, for 1268–1272), but he was also the county sheriff in 1282 (*List of Sheriffs*, p. 1). Thomas Torel was coroner of Cambridgeshire by 1363 (TNA PRO JUST 2/21, for 1363–1370), and he was county sheriff in 1374 (*List of Sheriffs*, p. 13). Robert Somervile was coroner of Gloucestershire by 1393 (TNA PRO JUST 2/44, for 1393–1398); he was also sheriff during 1402 (*List of Sheriffs*, p. 50). Andrew Landwhat was coroner of Northamptonshire during the period 1343–1363 (TNA PRO JUST 2/113); he was also county sheriff in 1358 (*List of Sheriffs*, p. 92). John del More was county coroner for Yorkshire during the period 1377–1393 (and presumably also afterwards, TNA PRO JUST 2/236); he was also sheriff of the city of York in 1396 (*List of Sheriffs*, p. 230).
173. *CCR* (April 1317), p. 463.
174. Hunnisett, *Medieval Coroner*, p. 162.
175. Hunnisett, *Medieval Coroner*, p. 173.
176. R.F. Hunnisett, ed., *Bedfordshire Coroners' Rolls* (Bedfordshire Historical Record Society, v. 61, 1960), p. xviii.
177. Richard of Gaddesby is associated with TNA PRO JUST 2/48 (1361–1363) and JUST 2/49 (1362–1366). References to his work as a JP survive in *CPR* (April 1356), p. 395; *CPR* (February 1348), p. 68; *CCR* (March 1361), p. 162; *CPR* (June 1366), p. 346; and *CPR* (November 1366), p. 368.
178. John Bredeford is associated with TNA PRO JUST 2/33A (1378–1380); *CCR* (February 1383), p. 254; *CPR* (June 1383), p. 300; *CPR* (July 1383), p. 349.
179. Thomas Cole is associated with TNA PRO JUST 2/38 (1378–1388), JUST 2/39 (1387–92), JUST 2/255 (1378–1379). References to his work as JP appear in *CCR* (May 1389), p. 677; *CCR* (July 1391), p. 486; as clerk of the JPs for the county in *CPR* (September 1392), p. 155; and *CPR* (August 1394), p. 472; as undersheriff of Gloucester in *CCR* (July 1392), p. 85; and *CCR* (July 1392), p. 75.
180. Gorski, *Fourteenth-Century Sheriff*, p. 69.
181. William Catour is associated with TNA PRO JUST 2/255 (1394–1395); reference to him as mayor of Reading appears in *CPR* (May 1384), p. 426. Requests for his replacement as coroner survive from *CCR* (1391), p. 223; and *CCR* (November 1395), p. 443. The final request explains that Catour needs replacing because he is dead.
182. William Kellaway, "The Coroner in Medieval London," in *Studies in London History Presented to Philip Edmund Jones*, ed. Albert E.J. Hollaender and Kellaway (London: Hodder Stoughton, 1969), p. 77. Kellaway's research into the careers of medieval London's coroners remarks that "most holders of the coronership and their deputies were men thoroughly acceptable to the City." Many were aldermen, or later became aldermen. Kellaway, p. 85.
183. John of Owthorpe is associated with TNA PRO JUST 2/85 (1381–1393).
184. William is associated with TNA PRO JUST 2/118 (1376–1378), Thomas with JUST 2/188 (1377–1380).

185. Lloyd, "Coroners of Leicestershire," 28. Lloyd provides other examples of mayors who became coroners, or coroners who became mayors, as well as coroners who come from coroner families.
186. Moran, "By the Instigation of the Devil," v. 1, p. 209.
187. *Fleta*, v. 1, p. 40.
188. Gilbert Wace is associated with TNA PRO JUST 2/138 (1391–1396).
189. Gorski, *Fourteenth-Century Sheriff*, p. 176.
190. *CCR* (1377–1381), pp. 74, 149, 165–65, 276, 281, 363.
191. William Retlaw Williams, *The Parliamentary History of the County of Oxford* (Brecknock: Priv. Print. for the author by E. Davies, 1899), p. 23.
192. *CCR* (November 1398), p. 360.
193. *CCR* (November 1383), p. 351; *CCR* (July 1388), p. 516; *CCR* (January 1394), pp. 189; *CCR* (November 1399), p. 21.
194. *CCR* (October 1360), p. 70; *CCR* (October 1378), p. 160; *CCR* (November 1378), p. 162; *CCR* (October 1380), p. 411.
195. W. Mark Ormrod, "The English Government and the Black Death of 1348–49," in his *England in the Fourteenth Century: Proceedings of the 1985 Harlaxton Symposium* (Woodbridge: Boydell, 1986), pp. 177–78.
196. Sutherland, *Eyre of Northamptonshire*, v. 1, pp. 194–95.
197. Sutherland, *Eyre of Northamptonshire*, v. 1, pp. 194–95.
198. G. Wrottesley, *Staffordshire Historical Collections* (London: Harrison and Sons, 1889) v. 10, pt. 1, pp. 52–53. A 1334 petition decries foresters who regularly hindered coroners from carrying out death investigations for those killed in the forest. See "Edward III: February 1334," *PRME*.
199. *CCR* (July 1303), p. 45.
200. Wrottesley, *Staffordshire Historical Collections*, pp. 49, 54.
201. William Hudson and John C. Tingey, eds., *The Records of the City of Norwich*, 2 vols. (Norwich: Jarrold & Sons, 1906), v. 1, p. 205.
202. Alan Crossley and C.R. Elrington, *A History of the County of Oxford* (London: Oxford UP, 1939), v. 4, p. 54.
203. Paul Matthews makes this point quite nicely. He says "[t]he coroner was policeman, pathologist and prosecutor in one." See Matthews, "Involuntary Manslaughter," 190.

2 The Jurors

As Helen Jewell once pronounced, "[g]overnment in the middle ages was very much a local affair."[1] The crown relied heavily on local officials for the efficient running of the state. As a result, communication between center and locality was constant and utterly indispensable. The role of the sheriff, the king's chief financial officer in the county, supplies the best evidence for steady contact. The later medieval sheriff has been described as a "tightly regulated bureaucrat whose chief administrative purpose was to respond to a multiplicity of royal writs."[2] Officials like the sheriff, in turn, administered the locality largely through the hard work and contributions of local inhabitants in the form of juries. Juries existed at all levels of society and for a wide variety of purposes. Juries regulated communal disputes of both a civil and quasi-criminal nature in a number of forums. There were leet courts or sheriff's tourns, hundred and county courts. Urban centers developed local juries to resolve disputes for their own specialized courts focused chiefly on merchant activity, business disputes, and public health regulations: borough, guild, piepowder, and mayoral courts. Juries adjudicated exclusively civil disputes in a wide variety of royal venues, among others: assize courts (or eyre courts before that), King's Bench, and Common Bench. Juries permeated each level of the criminal legal process: inquest, presentment, and trial, but they also took part in the specially commissioned sessions of the peace and trailbastons. When the crown needed to address concerns on an *ad hoc* basis, it also turned to juries as a mechanism for resolution. Sworn inquests were central to the administration of government, and the nature of their charge was without bounds. The crown might task a sworn inquest to investigate anything from corrupt officials to the durability of a town's defenses. The crown entrusted juries also with the responsibility to ascertain the value of lands held by a deceased tenant-in-chief through inquisitions post-mortem. Jury duty was central to the running of the kingdom, so much so that medieval English administration is best characterized as "government-by-jury."[3] The task of empanelling this multitude of juries usually fell to the sheriff and his bailiffs, who were confronted with "seemingly unending demands to have qualified people available to serve."[4]

The crown's confidence in local manpower and the goodwill of the English people was not misguided. While some fraudulent behavior is evident at all levels of the system, most Englishmen embraced a "culture of mutual responsibility."[5] Moreover, England's dispersed governance proffered an unprecedented degree of control over the lives of England's populace. As W. Mark Ormrod argues "[t]he delegation of direct administrative responsibilities to a large number of men in the localities had not only spread the influence of the crown into the provinces; it had also created a highly politicised society with a remarkably detailed knowledge of both local and national affairs."[6] Founding the administration of the kingdom on personal rather than financial investment undeniably paid off, not only in financial terms, but also in a nascent sense of regional pride.

The crown offered no remuneration for jury service or compensation for lost labor. Jury service also generally ranked lowest in terms of perquisites in the hierarchy of officeholding. It offered no special privileges or opportunities, jurors could not easily charge for their services, or find occasions for extortion. Consequently, it should come as no surprise that historians have assessed jury service "as a duty rather than a privilege."[7] Pollock and Maitland long ago described jury service as "oppressive," claiming "[t]he poorer freeholders groaned under a duty which consumed their time and exposed them to the enmity of powerful neighbours."[8] In his analysis of fifteenth-century trial juries and the rules governing their presence in the courtroom, David Seipp produces the most unflattering depiction of medieval juries. Bemoaning jurors as the "unsung heroes of the common law," he maintains that trial jurors "were coerced, belaboured, hungry, thirsty men who did not relish the powers of local self-government that they momentarily held."[9] More generally, James Masschaele opines, "[t]hat medieval people saw jury service as a burden and even a hardship cannot be doubted."[10] Englishmen who worked hard to evade jury service at all costs inflate this negative impression. Not only did trial jurors regularly fail to appear in court in response to court summons, but also the elite repeatedly sought exemptions from jury duty (and other officeholding) from the king. In spite of all this, there is little reason to believe medieval Englishmen held jury duty to be anathema.

Rather, numerous studies draw attention instead to the appeal jury duty held for certain segments of the population. In his study of the Durham halmote jury, Peter Larson rationalizes jury service as a means to control local power structures, concluding that jury service offered "a man an edge in village and estate affairs . . . jurors were information brokers, valuable and dangerous to lord and neighbor alike."[11] Other historians of local government have also highlighted the desirability of these posts, evidenced in large part by the status of the individuals who served and the longevity of their careers as jurors. Anne DeWindt's study of Ramsey (*Hunts.*) observes that jurors were regularly drawn "from among the more prosperous local inhabitants" who served "from one year to the next."[12] Larson arrives at the same conclusion, proposing that jurors operated as an "oligarchy" in Durham's political culture. While more dedicated to affirming the democratic nature of juries, Sherri Olson also stresses the prominence of the elite among local juries, characterizing the typical juror as "the clearest instance of a village notable."[13] Pride in jury participation was not restricted to the village court. Wealthier peasants were also involved in juries at the peace sessions[14] and "local notables" dominated presenting juries.[15] Localities seem to have regarded presentment, in particular, as an opportunity to exert authority over one's community and to identify exactly what constituted offensive behavior. Thus, while presenting juries demonstrated "a strong continuity between jurors . . . from session to session and year to year,"[16] the same cannot be said for trial juries, who had the less onerous task of merely passing judgment—a relatively simple charge given the medieval tendency to acquit. Rational explanations exist also to appreciate those who seemingly evaded jury duty. In reality, exemptions were less about a reluctance to participate in crown service than a desire to control the nature of the service in which one participated.[17] This holds true even at the lowest levels of society. "Peasant choice" explains equally those who failed to respond to crown summonses for trial juries, yet may well have been regular jurors at the village court.[18]

English government worked on a system of *quid pro quo*. From a modern perspective, the English crown seemingly abused the benevolence of its people by exacting their time and energies for unpaid labor. However, the readiness of the English population to participate in government-by-jury suggests just the opposite. English enthusiasm for jury duty is best appreciated by acknowledging that it was a potent "instrument of peasant aggrandizement."[19] Peasant communities understood jury service as a political act. This was their opportunity to mold not only the community in which they resided, but also the realm. Erik Spindler expresses it best when he writes that the jury as an institution "furthered social cohesion and shaped collective understandings of right and wrong."[20] Accordingly, the English embraced the office of juror for very different reasons than the crown promoted it. Their willingness to adapt the office to suit their needs is evident in the fact that jurors often enlarged the office beyond the parameters established by higher authorities. They utilized the courts as they saw fit, "routinely interpret[ing] their jurisdiction according to their own interests, both ignoring offenses they felt were not necessary to present . . . and presenting men and women for misdemeanours over which they had no clear authority."[21] The English concept of jurors as witnesses strengthened juror agency. Because jurors technically were better informed about the nature of a dispute than even royal justices, the court ceded the jury "free rein to decide the case as it pleased."[22] T.A. Green's research on jury discretion is most pertinent here. While it has long been understood that jurors mitigated the severity of the English common law by acquitting those felons facing execution when the jury believed the punishment did not fit the crime, Green's work goes even further to elucidate just how significantly juror values deviated from common law prescription. In particular, he contends that English jurors imposed an "expanded notion of self-defense" in determining verdicts.[23] While the rules of self-defense stipulated an Englishman might defend himself only as a last resort when death was otherwise inescapable, this condition plainly did not accord with communal notions of masculine honor. Rather than allow the law to penalize those who preserve their dignity (and, even more injuriously, reward cowardice), jurors worked around the law by tweaking the details of the story to meet the crown's requirements. Green's findings remind us that there are at least two sides to every story. While the crown envisioned the jury's role as one of royal peacekeeping with the dual mission of augmenting the crown's reputation and filling the king's coffers, jurors had their own agenda and were not willing to subordinate their needs to those of the crown.

The capacity to influence the practice of the law and thus the development of society on a larger scale is one shared by all medieval jurors, to greater and lesser extents, and goes a long way toward illuminating the desirability of the position. Even coroners' jurors shared in this authority. The brashest example of jury prerogative at this level emerged in the nineteenth century when coroners' juries expressed renewed interest in utilizing the deodand to punish negligence. While the deodand eventually fell out of use in the modern era, nineteenth-century coroners' juries reappropriated it in order to address unsafe work conditions, principally in industrial settings, and vehicular accidents. The Sonning railway disaster of 1841, in which jurors confiscated a steam engine as deodand apparently was the last straw.[24] Responding to the concerns of anxious industrialists, the crown ultimately passed the Deodands Abolition Act of 1846, cutting short coroners' juries' innovative response to the dangers of the modern world.[25] While this is a contemporary example, it nonetheless underscores the inventiveness of a coroner's jury when pushed to the limit and its capacity to have a very real impact on a national scale. This example also assists us in appreciating that service on a coroner's jury might be a tempting office.

This chapter explores the composition of the medieval coroners' jury. Beginning first with expectations (both medieval and scholarly), this chapter will explain how coroners' juries fit into the larger schema of England's hierarchy of juries, and address their own unique concerns. Through a close analysis of the composition of coroners' juries in two particular urban centers (York and London), this chapter responds to questions relating to the social status of inquest jurors and the role of medical practitioners in death investigation. London, in particular, gives us an opportunity to imagine the ideal coroner's jury because of its size and the diversity of population. Finally, this chapter hopes to single out those features that made the coroners' juries distinctly medieval.

THE SOCIAL STATUS OF CORONERS' JURORS

Identifying who served on a coroner's jury in the medieval period is not an easy task. Little is known about the process of empanelling a jury, and the extant documentation regarding the jurors themselves is paltry. In practice, the hundred bailiff (or in an urban center, the constable) was responsible for assembling a pool of potential jurors prior to the county coroner's arrival. The coroner had the final word about which of those individuals in fact served on the jury. Ideally, the jury included twelve men from the visne and another four representing neighboring townships. However, there was enormous variation in the practice, especially where representatives of neighboring townships were concerned. Often only twelve jurors attended the inquest and the coroner sought separate approval from the townships for the enrollment. Boroughs typically empanelled more than twelve jurors. London coroners, for example, worked with juries of up to twenty-four men. It is seldom possible to identify who those jurors actually were. Bailiffs recorded lists of potential jurors on scraps of parchment (that is, files), and only some of those made their way into the formal enrollments.[26] The coroners' rolls rarely supply more than a juror's name, although many do not provide even that much information, and with the multitude of occupational by-names that appear in these rolls, it is not clear how formal or widely known those names were. "John the Ploughman" may also have been "John of Doncaster, ploughman" in some other record.[27] Every once in a while, some munificent scrivener will include also the jurors' occupations. This windfall manifests primarily in the records from urban settings, presumably because it was the best method to distinguish between a borough's various "John Smiths." In general, recording details about the jury was the least of the coroner's concerns. He was far more anxious to meet crown expectations that, if he neglected to do so, would result in a fine or reprimand. Failing to record a jury list invited no negative repercussions. As a result, there are many obstacles to unearthing who served on coroners' juries, and our clearest evidence comes from the urban context, which is more ideal than representative.

Nonetheless, identifying the social status of inquest jurors is vital. The medieval English adopted a strategic approach to empanelling juries. They entrusted important decisions to important people. For this reason, Parliament fixed statutory income requirements for jurors of attaint (the Parliamentary form of treason—obviously one of the crown's most pressing concerns) at the highest rate. According to a 1437 statute, jurors of attaint must own property worth an annual value of £20, whereas more generally the crown expected jurors to boast an annual income of only 40*s.* (£2).[28] Given the inclination to match income with priority, an analysis of the social standing of coroners' jurors has much to offer. Not only can it instruct us concerning the worth of the office of inquest juror, but it can also give us a more precise idea of the import of the coroner's jury in the broader system of criminal justice.

The crown likely intended statutory income requirements for presentment and trial jurors only. Because of the legal procedure itself, there was a great need among presentment jurors, at least, for a linguistic aptitude that ineluctably disqualified most peasantry. As M.T. Clanchy explains it,

> jurors were presented with the justices' questions (the 'articles of the eyre' technically) in writing in either Latin or French. They replied orally, probably in English, although their answers were written down as *veredicta* by an enrolling clerk in Latin. When the justices arrived in court, the chief clerk read out the enrolled presentments or *veredicta* in French, mentally translating them from Latin as he went along. On behalf of the jurors, their foreman or spokesman then presented the same answers at the bar in English. Once the presentments, in both their French and English oral versions, were accepted by the court, they were recorded in the justices' plea rolls in Latin. Thus, between the justices' written questions being presented initially to the jurors and the final record of the plea roll, the language in use changed at least five times, although it begins and ends with writings in Latin.[29]

The implications of this process are significant: "the foreman of the jurors, if not his fellows, would need to be able to read French and preferably also Latin. If the oral English statement, which he presented at the bar, deviated in any detail from the written statement, the jurors faced imprisonment."[30] Literacy in both French and Latin required individuals with a degree of education. The English peasantry would not have been adequately proficient in French or Latin to understand the proceedings, let alone possess the necessary literacy to be a foreman. Thankfully, participation on a coroner's inquest jury required little in terms of education. Outside of the courtroom, knowledge of spoken English was sufficient. Only the coroner's clerk needed Latin.

What is more, coroners expecting to empanel juries entirely from those with an annual income of 40*s*. would be hard-pressed to find sufficient numbers of men in a rural community who fit the bill. Yet, even if coroners' jurors were exempt from the normal income requirements, it is clear that Parliament endorsed fully the philosophy that wealth guaranteed honesty. As the Parliament of 1437 articulated it, "the more sufficient that men are of income from lands and tenements, the more unlikely they are to be inclined or be moved to perjure themselves by corruption, brokage, or fear."[31] Affluence ensured not only integrity: there existed also a discrete logic that prosperity broadens one's access to knowledge. Responding to a complaint that sheriffs and their bailiffs regularly pass over the "Rich People" when empanelling jurors, the preamble to a 1293 statute expounds the upper ranks as those "by whom the truth of the matter might be better known."[32] A 1483–1484 chapter of a statute concerning the qualifications of jurors in sheriff's tourns reiterates this ideal. Noting that sheriffs regularly select as jurors "persons of no substance nor having nor dreading God nor worldly shame," leading to a surfeit of wrongful indictments, the statute entreats sheriffs to empanel only those with "lands and tenements of freehold within the same Shires to the yearly value of 20*s*. at the least, or else lands and tenements holding by Custom of manor commonly called Copyhold within the said Shires to the yearly value of 26*s*. 8*d*. over all charges at the least."[33] None of these statutes is especially germane to the coroner's jury. However, the crown's conviction that wealthy jurors were the more trustworthy informants surely applied widely. This conviction is buttressed by the 1189 legal treatise of Ricardus Anglicus, also known as Richard of Mores, once the prior of the monastery at Dunstable. While his *Summa de Ordine Iudiciario* addresses primarily ecclesiastical trials, he had much to say about the requisite qualities of witnesses that seem applicable here. His treatise adopts an authoritative stance. He championed wealthy witnesses on the basis that "the upper classes would be better educated and more conscious of the duty to testify truthfully. The wealthy witness was to be preferred over the poor one since the temptation to swear falsely for money would be less."[34]

Only two medieval statutes speak directly to the composition of the coroners' jury, and both express the same priorities. The first originated in 1300 and states that in inquests, sheriffs and bailiffs must select jurors "such as be next Neighbours, most sufficient, and least suspicious."[35] The statute from 1360 reiterates these obligatory qualities but in a more dramatic fashion. Decrying sheriffs and other officers who appoint either corrupt jurors or those from distant counties "which have no Knowledge of the Deed," sheriffs, coroners, and other "Ministers" are subsequently instructed to draw from "the next People, which shall not be suspect nor procured" in the future.[36] As with many of the quasi-hysterical grievances triggering the creation of statute law, there is no indication whether this behavior was widespread, or springing from an isolated incident. It is also not immediately apparent why a coroner would favor jurors from outside the locality, or even how he would convince them to travel merely to serve on an inquest. Yet, both statutes underline the crown's ideal for coroners' juries: proximity and incorruptibility, and in light of the above discussion, the latter inevitably implies a measure of abundance.

Statute law cracks a window into crown expectations for coroners' jurors; but were these requirements implemented? A complaint voiced in the 1304 Articles of Lincoln implies that coroners had some difficulty applying these rules in practice. Once again referring to the "poor men" as those "who know nothing," and "the better men" as those "who know better the truth," Chapter Nine of the Articles reports that the "better men" frequently defy the coroner's authority.[37] When asked to "go to the book" to be sworn in as jurors, they refused.[38] Again, this anecdote offers no indication as to the scope of the dilemma. Was this attitude an obstacle only for Lincolnshire's coroners, or was the problem more far reaching?

Historians' reactions to both statute law and the records in practice range widely. Early modernists have tended to side with the elite: James Sharpe and J.R. Dickinson recently observed that while "[a]lmost nothing is known of the social status of inquest jurors . . . it seems safe to assume that they were chosen from the 'better sort' of the inhabitants of the parish."[39] Medievalists range more broadly in their conclusions. James Masschaele instead argues in favor of the unfree, noting that "service on a coroner's jury would have been a natural extension of service on a frankpledge jury."[40] In this respect, it is critical to note that villeinage was no bar to jury service: the unfree regularly served on manorial court juries.[41] Thomas A. Green has moved the debate in another direction altogether. Ignoring the question of status, he focuses instead on proximity, seeing coroners' reports as "the testimony of only a few neighbors."[42] R.F. Hunnisett adopts a chronological vision. While initially juries were drawn from representatives of the four vills, he maintains that during the last quarter of the thirteenth century a grouping of twelve freemen supplemented their findings. Eventually participation by the four vills diminished, and the twelve freemen became the jury. By the late fourteenth and fifteenth centuries, juries consisted of twelve to twenty-four men with no explicit status qualifications, drawn from the four neighboring vills.[43] Hunnisett's long experience with the coroners' rolls and the intricacy of his hypothesis makes it appear the most convincing argument; but the coroners' rolls as a collective do not conform to this template.[44] The evidence Hunnisett cites is thin. For example, he puts forward the York county roll of John of Mapples (JUST 2/220) to support his contention that in the thirteenth century "freemen became an essential part of the jury."[45] Yet, when John of Mapples referred to a jury, he regularly described it as being composed of "twelve sworn men" or simply "the twelve" (*xii*). On only one occasion does his formula vary in a meaningful way. In the death of John of Beckingham, he reported an inquest formed from the representatives of the four vills "together with twelve good, sworn men" (*xii hominibus probari jurati*), followed by the names of the jurors.[46] This stock phrase may have become more common toward the end of the medieval period. Lincolnshire coroner John of Leadenham habitually employed this formulaic descriptor in his roll covering 1356–1369.[47] A formulary for a coroner's inquest appearing in *The Boke of Justices of Peas*, published in 1506, uses a similar construction: *probarum et legalium homines de villa*.[48] While this may sound eerily similar to the seventeenth-century phrase "twelve good men and true," in which "good" invariably referred to a man of high standing, there is no rational justification for translating "goodman" as "freeman" in the medieval period.[49] In legal terms, "good" signified "valid at law"; the term "goodman," more colloquially, might also indicate a householder, although one did not have to be "free" to be a householder.[50] A peasant's economic status was a much greater determinant of his communal standing than the nature of the agreement by which he held land.[51] None of this supports the contention that being free was a prerequisite for jury service.

At times, the nature of the inquest may have led coroners to empanel a jury only with freemen.[52] For example, a Cambridgeshire coroner insisted on only "freeholders" (*libere tenentes*) for a massive jury in a high-profile death, going so far as to fine all freeholders who did not respond to the sheriff's summons.[53] Indeed, special circumstances sometimes prompted coroners to empanel jurors with unique qualifications. The 1340 London investigation into the death of Ralph Turk, servant of John Turk the fishmonger, makes this abundantly clear. The first inquest concluded that his death resulted from a violent brawl involving many men and springing from an old quarrel between the fishmongers and the skinners. Jurors blamed John of Oxford as the "chief cause of the felony," but conceded that he did not strike the mortal blow. In the interests of obtaining a clearer picture of the dispute, coroner John of Sherborne ordered two new inquests. The first was to be held in four days' time: he directed the sheriff to empanel only "the best, richest and wisest of men" from the guild of skinners. The second was to be held the following day, with similar instructions for the guild of fishmongers. Given the inability of these two guilds to agree on anything, it is not surprising that their separate inquests fingered different homicide suspects altogether. Perhaps motivated by a desire to sacrifice one of the least experienced members of their ranks, the skinners claimed that Geoffrey Horn, a skinner and servant of Robert of Stodham, struck the victim with a sparth (that is, an axe) on the back of the head so that he died immediately. The fishmongers presented a much wider pool of suspects. They believed that Robert of Stodham, with the assistance of John of Oxford, Robert of Eynsham, and John of Cornwall (all skinners) struck the victim with a pole-axe on the back of the head, killing him instantly.[54]

The London example highlights the versatility of the coroner's inquest. Coroners were willing to adapt the jury to the needs of the inquest. Overall, the great disparity in conclusions among historians confirms that we still have much to learn about the composition of coroners' juries.

LESSONS FROM MICRO-HISTORY: THE CITY OF YORK

Jury lists from the city of York offer the most comprehensive insight into the social status of inquest jurors. Because the city kept copious records of those who purchased the status of freeman, it is possible to correlate jury lists drawn from a city coroner's roll with the *Register of the Freemen of the City of York*,[55] as well as the extant, although admittedly incomplete, poll tax evidence,[56] to discern many jurors' occupations. However, before proceeding any further it is critical to acknowledge the limitations of the evidence. Most perceptibly, the city of York's evidence cannot be understood as a typically English approach. Culturally speaking, England is a land of diversity. While the north has often been stigmatized as being less progressive, England's divide is not just a north-south one. For the medieval period,

England's cultural miscellany is emphasized by the multitude of independent, self-governing liberties and franchises: among others, the Palatinate of Durham, the Palatinate of Lancashire, the Liberty of Ely, the Liberty of the Abbot of Westminster, the Liberty of the Duchy of Lancaster, the Welsh Marcher Lordships, not to mention the various chartered urban liberties.[57] Despite the purportedly "common" nature of common law, regional identity and custom had a colossal impact on the practice of the law. The very fact that medieval Kent's inhabitants embraced partible inheritance (*gavelkind*) instead of primogeniture attests to just how diverse those practices might be. Consequently, no one region can be wholly representative of all of England, especially an urban center.

The *Register of Freemen in the City of York* also suffers from a number of shortcomings. Theoretically, freeman status was imperative to sell goods within the city of York. There were three paths to becoming a freeman: an individual could buy, inherit, or work for it through an apprenticeship.[58] York boasted a "large and broadly based freeman population."[59] For the craftsman, freedom had many perquisites. Only freemen were entitled to hold office; only freemen were eligible for election as mayor or alderman; and being a freeman permitted a craftsman better control over his employees and apprentices.[60] Municipal government also had much to gain. Freemen were the only residents required to pay civic taxes. Freedom brought responsibility, and the city had a "vested interest in the existence of as large a number of responsible members under their authority as was economically practical."[61] Nevertheless, the reality of the market in medieval York was considerably different. Leary of unwanted regulation, many artisans refused to pay for the privilege; and yet, this decision had no impact on their ability to do business. To offer an example: of the 216 masons operating out of late medieval York, only 48 appear in the Freeman's Register.[62] In reality, only the most prosperous, and often those with political aspirations, bothered to pay for the privilege. In terms of the quality of the documentation, the register is not as complete as historians once assumed. There are two principal defects. First, because the register is essentially a record of payments for the franchise, it omits the names of freemen by birth or patrimony who paid no entry fine, even though this was presumably a sizeable segment of York's freemen population.[63] Second, roughly 10% of the enrollments fail to associate the freeman with an occupation.[64] In many instances, the omission may result from the by-name of the freeman: why record Hugh Lorimer's occupation as a lorimer,[65] when his name says it all?

Despite these pitfalls, the coroner's roll for the city of York comprising 1363 to 1378, recorded by city coroners Thomas of Lincoln, Richard of Raisbeck, and Gerard of Burnby,[66] furnishes a valuable overview of one city's approach to empanelling inquest jurors. York's philosophy in empanelling coroners' juries had less to do with finding the most knowledgeable witnesses than in permitting York's aspiring elite a public show of power. The salient feature of York's jurors is the simple fact that many were freemen: it is possible to identify 497 out of the 985 (or 50.45%) jurors in the *Register of the Freemen*. Once again, this figure is probably an underestimate since it cannot account for those men whose freedom came without a price. During the period 1350–1449, an average of ninety-seven individuals paid for the freedom each year.[67] With a city population of somewhere between 11,000 and 15,000, this was still obviously a small, but dominant, minority.[68]

Out of a total number of 985 juror appearances,[69] the *Register of the Freemen* and the city's poll tax evidence permit the identification of 505 jurors (that is, 51%—see Table 2.1).[70]

The slow development of hereditary surnames creates some obstacles in terms of identification. In England, this process was not complete until the sixteenth and seventeenth centuries, and the north lagged well behind the rest of England.[71] Accordingly, it is sometimes a challenge to recognize the same individual from one record to the next. The *Register* and poll tax evidence also adopt different strategies for identification than do the coroners' rolls. The *Register* and poll tax evidence strive for a comprehensive identification: given name + by-name (usually locative) + occupation. Coroners' rolls tend to be records of expedience. Coroners typically identified individuals by their occupations. For example, Robert Mirre ("mirre" is the Middle English term for "physician"), who served on five separate juries, appears nowhere in the *Register* or the poll tax evidence.[72] Yet, both the *Register* and the poll tax evidence list a Robert of Blaxton, *medicus*. In all likelihood, these two are one and the same. The same point can be made for the plethora of individuals with the by-name "cardmaker," "tailor," "spurrier," and "cordwainer."[73] If we assume that those individuals with occupational by-names do not appear in either the *Register* or poll tax evidence because coroners identified them by their occupations and not their place of origin, then we can claim to know 735 of the 985 jurors' occupations (that is, 74.62%)—see Table 2.2.

Careful scrutiny of jurors' occupations sheds light on the appeal of jury service. York's most elite citizens, those who went on to become mayors and aldermen, did not serve on coroners' juries. Much as in other medieval urban centers, the "virtually unassailable mercantile oligarchies" dominated York's municipal government.[74] Craftsmen, not merchants, served as jurors in coroners' inquests and, as Heather Swanson remarks, "there was a recognised social distinction between merchants and craftsmen and one that could operate as a bar to officeholding."[75] York's inquest jurors did not belong to the city's upper crust; although, as freemen, they represent the most prosperous of York's craftsmen. The strong presence of jurors from metalworking and textiles, late medieval York's twin powerhouse industries, highlights their affluence. Death investigation afforded these ambitious, wealthy craftsmen an opportunity to exercise power openly. Coroners' inquests were highly public affairs: the crown required all male residents over the age of twelve to attend.[76] The spectacle of the inquest allowed them to move to the forefront of the community and assume responsibility in a moment of crisis.

Table 2.1 Occupations: Based on Evidence from *Register of Freemen* and Poll Tax Evidence (1363–1378)

Building Crafts (total 26)	**Leather Work (total 118)**	**Medicine (total 8)**	**Metal Work (total 47)**	**Sales (total 23)**	**Textile Crafts (total 177)**	**Victualling (total 61)**	**Miscellaneous (total 26)**
3 carpenters	2 cobblers	4 barbers	1 armorer	2 chapmen	1 boiler	6 bakers	7 bowyers
3 joiners	60 cordwainers	4 spicers	1 bladesmith	17 mariners	4 chaloners	1 brewer	1 fletcher
7 masons	2 curriers		2 cardmakers	4 merchants	8 drapers	15 butchers	6 ostlers
2 moldmakers	8 girdlers		5 cutlers		10 dyers	4 cooks	2 stringers
1 plasterer	1 leather maker		4 furbishers of armor		3 fullers	31 fishmongers	1 bookbinder
1 sawyer	1 parchment maker		4 goldsmiths		5 glovers	4 taverners	1 clerk
2 tilers	12 saddlers		1 ironmonger		1 hatter		8 porters
7 wrights	31 skinners		10 marshals		13 hosiers		
	1 tanner		2 nailers		7 mercers		
			1 pinner		7 pouchmakers		
			2 potters		2 shearmen		
			6 sheath makers		7 shepherds		
			8 spurriers		50 tailors		
					52 weavers		
					7 wool packers		

Table 2.2 Occupations: Based on Evidence from *Register of Freemen*, Poll Tax Evidence, and By-Names (1363–1378)

Building Crafts (total 44)	Leather Work (total 155)	Medicine (total 18)	Metal Work (total 94)	Sales (total 28)	Textile Crafts (total 247)	Victualling (total 80)	Miscellaneous (total 53)
3 carpenters	2 cobblers	6 barbers	1 armorer	7 chapmen	1 boiler	10 bakers	17 bowyers
5 coopers	68 cordwainers	5 physicians	2 arrowsmiths	17 mariners	4 chaloners	2 brewers	11 fletcher
4 joiners	3 curriers	7 spicers	3 bladesmiths	4 merchants	8 drapers	15 butchers	6 ostlers
7 masons	10 girdlers		2 cambsmiths		20 dyers	8 cooks	5 stringers
2 moldmakers	1 leather maker		14 cardmakers		10 fullers	34 fishmongers	1 bookbinder
2 plasterers	12 lorimers		8 cutlers		1 furrier	3 grinders	1 clerk
1 sawyer	1 parchment maker		4 furbishers of armor		12 glovers	1 mustardmaker	9 porters
3 tilers	22 saddlers		5 goldsmiths		2 hatters	1 poulterer	1 washer
2 turners	35 skinners		1 ironmonger		13 hosiers	1 saucemaker	1 waterleader
12 wrights	1 tanner		1 leadbeater		7 mercers	4 taverners	1 “jetour”
			5 locksmiths		9 pouchmakers		
			14 marshals		15 shearmen		
			2 nailers		7 shepherds		
			4 pinners		75 tailors		
			4 potters		55 weavers		
			7 sheath makers		9 wool packers		
			5 smiths				
			11 spurriers				
			1 wiredrawer				

While these craftsmen might never become aldermen, they could still wield power at a time when their communities needed them most.

This observation accords well with the conclusions other historians have drawn regarding the process of indictment. Although those historians are generally discussing presentment rather than coroners' juries, their role in the indictment process was similar. Bernard McLane maintains that "local elites and perhaps the Crown considered presentment jury service to be more prestigious and important than service on trial juries."[77] Trial jurors appeared after all the hard work of the investigation was already complete. They needed only to determine a verdict, and the phrasing of indictments clarified exactly what that verdict should be. Jurors involved in the process of indictment, on the other hand, had a much more onerous task. Presentment jurors had to identify which crimes should be reported to the crown. In many respects, this meant that they were involved in shaping the crown's perceptions of what constitutes a crime and determining how a crime should be prosecuted. For example, when presenting a theft, jurors evaluated whether to classify it as a trespass (punished by a monetary fine) or as a felony (involving loss of life and property).[78] This capacity for discretion conferred on presenting jurors a fearsome degree of power. Juries of indictment functioned as police in the process of social control within their community. As Marjorie McIntosh contends, scolding, eavesdropping, vagrancy, and other social misbehaviors acquired misdemeanor status chiefly because presentment jurors were determined to report them.[79]

In this respect, coroners' jurors also functioned as jurors of indictment, though on a much narrower scale. Not only did they control an open display of royal authority, but they had it within their power to dictate a person's future. The findings of the coroners' jury had great moment. Anyone they suspected of being a felon would soon find himself in prison enduring horrific living conditions. Homicide investigations were not the only channel to authority at their disposal. Deaths by misadventure permitted opportunity for aspersions of negligence. The association of sin with God's wrath meant that deaths by a named disease, such as leprosy or plague, might smear a family's good name; and an honest assessment of a felon's goods and property might impoverish his dependents. York's municipal authorities clearly believed that such weighty responsibilities belonged to those with some social clout. Pollock and Maitland long ago pronounced that "[t]he verdict of the jurors is not just the verdict of twelve men; it is the verdict of a *pays*, a 'country,' a neighbourhood, a community."[80] Given the representative nature of their role, it should come as no surprise that the upper middling ranks preferred to dominate the office.

Not all jurors were equal. While freemen dominated York's inquest juries and likely assumed the role of foreman, there was also a smattering of representatives from the lowest-paid occupations: shearmen, porters, washers, water-leaders, and shepherds. This diversity is best explained by a coroner's resolve to include those with some inside knowledge. For example, in the death of John Clerk, a skinner, in August 1363, the inquest jury included fifteen jurors: a cordwainer, a weaver, a woolpacker, a chapman, a marshal, two pouchmakers, two skinners, four saddlers, and two jurors whose occupations could not be identified.[81] Eight of those jurors were also freemen. Most of them worked in occupations closely associated with skinning. They probably knew the dead, and thus were fitting jurors for the investigation. Occupational connectivity of this sort was typical. While it is only possible to discern the occupations of five of the twelve jurors in the death of John of Bessenay, a mariner, in December 1366, their occupations imply a relationship with the dead: one was a mariner, four were fishmongers.[82] Only two hatters ever appeared as jurors: one of them served on the inquest into the death of Patrick the Hatter of York in May 1366, alongside a pouchmaker, a sheath maker, three cutlers, a tailor, and a stringer.[83] Once again, this insight is critical: York's inquests did not sacrifice efficiency to social standing. The ideal jury was both informed and authoritative: but not all members of the jury needed to embody both qualities.

Many jurors appeared more than once: 608 individuals served in those 985 appearances as jurors. An analysis of multiple appearances tells us that the majority (that is, 393 of them) served only once. Another 129 served twice. But a small group were regular participants on coroners' juries: forty-four served three times, nineteen served four times, twenty served five times, five served six times, and two served seven times. The jurors who appeared most frequently tended to be freemen. Of the two jurors who appeared most often, John Fletcher unfortunately is unidentifiable in the records; but John Dandson was a mariner and also a freeman. Those men who appeared six times each were: William Mareschall, mason and freeman; William Garsdale, hosier and freeman; William of Askham, girdler and freeman; John Tayt, tailor and freeman; and Adam Cardemaker, who is not identifiable in the records. This finding concurs with Carol Loar's conclusion for sixteenth-century Sussex. She remarks that "coroners' jurors often had previous experience on inquests; in some jurisdictions, between 40 and 55 per cent of jurors had served on at least one other case and several had as many as five inquests under their belts in a ten-year period."[84] Because of the gravity of the responsibility, it made sense to empanel jurors with some experience who thus had a better understanding of the needs of the investigation.

The eminent social status of many of York's inquest jurors speaks to a belief that social harmony is best defended through enforcement of the social hierarchy. At its base, "[t]he king's justice embodied a positive and interventionist conception of order, which sought to reveal the natural harmony of a hierarchically ordered society and, where such a harmony did not exist, to impose it."[85] Politics in the urban center functioned expressly on "the deferential belief that the rich should lead and dominate, so that to disobey one's social superior was to commit a sin."[86] Packing an inquest jury with York's social betters was a highly public means of reinforcing that hierarchy by tasking them with the resolution of incidents that threatened communal stability.[87]

DID CLERGYMEN SERVE ON CORONERS' JURIES?

Jury lists drawn from the coroners' rolls boast hundreds of individuals whose by-names indicate that they may well have been members of holy orders. There are countless men with the name "John Clerk" serving on medieval England's coroners' juries.[88] Certainly, some of those John Clerks were craftsmen or farmers sporting a hereditary surname passed down from a clerical ancestor. But we cannot draw this conclusion for all John Clerks. Further, as this chapter has already indicated, occupational by-names were highly useful, and coroners (or bailiffs, or their scriveners) seemed to have preferred occupational by-names to locative or personal ones in general. Variations in the nature of by-names raise further questions. Do the records provide a more reliable guide to a juror's occupation when the rolls describe a juror as John the Clerk (*le Clerk*, or *le Clericus*) rather than John Clerk?[89] Does the definite article make a difference?[90] It is also possible to make the argument that "clerk" was an ambiguous term—some clerks were of an administrative variety, rather than a religious one. For example, John of Staunton, described as a "clerk" (*clericus*) in a London coroner's roll, who served as a juror in the 1340 inquest into the drowning of Henry le Kyng: was he a religious clerk, or a scribe of some sort (or both)?[91] At times, the location of the inquest makes it hard to imagine that the clerks indicated in the record could have been anything other than religious. John Pridy and John Farle, both described as clerks, served on the jury in the accidental death of Edith, daughter of John the Shepherd, a two-year-old child who fell into a ditch and died; the inquest took place at a hospital in Bishopstone (*Wilts*.).[92] In all likelihood, clerks working out of a hospital were, indeed, clergymen. The potential ambiguity with the term "clerk" may help us to feel more confident about other by-names. There is also a multitude of jurors with the by-names "Prest," "Parson," and "Chapelayn," with and without the definite article.[93] Surely, some of these hundreds of jurors were, in fact, actual clergymen.

Admittedly, clergy might also be drawn into the investigative process in other ways. The London coroners' rolls indicate that clergymen sometimes became involved by being the first to stumble across the dead's body. For example, when William Warrok stabbed William of Northampton to death in a street quarrel in 1325 outside of the church of St Mary Magdalene, Henry of Hatfield, a clerk belonging to the church, was the first finder.[94] Similarly, when John of Ireland hanged himself by his shirt from a beam in his London solar in 1322, Walter Michel, a chaplain, was one of the first on the scene. Michel was also well versed in medicine and used his medical knowledge to try to resuscitate John. When this failed, he raised the hue and cry and was later attached as first finder.[95]

Notwithstanding the presence of clergy at coroner's inquests, historians have generally shied away from asking whether the clergy ever served on coroners' juries. Despite the absence of legislation, or crown or papal prohibitions, traditional scholarly belief presumes that clergymen did not serve on juries. In an endeavor to provide substance to this conjecture, Rosemary Pattenden recounts the numerous obstacles blocking the clergy from jury service. The most cogent explanations she puts forward are threefold: 1) clergymen were incapable of meeting property requirements to serve on juries; 2) at Lateran IV in 1215, the church expressly prohibited clergy from participating in judgments of blood; and 3) the church forbade clergy to swear oaths at the instigation of the laity.[96] As this chapter has already made clear, the first argument was not relevant to coroners' juries. As to the latter two points, the church's mandate on blood and oaths was not set in stone. The military careers of numerous English clergymen confirm that some flexibility existed in this respect.[97] What is more pertinent is that *Britton* explicitly recognizes the prospect of clergymen serving as jurors, although in a different setting. *Britton* acknowledges the right of parties in a civil dispute to object to the participation of priests and clerks within holy orders as jurors.[98] Pattenden also furnishes plentiful evidence to establish that clergy served as jurors in both the early modern and modern eras. Indeed, it was not until the Juries Act of 1825 that Parliament firmly supported the exemption of clergy from jury service.[99] Thus, the argument that clergymen did not serve as jurors in the Middle Ages is hard to sustain.

Scholarly assumptions concerning clerical participation in medieval England's juries spring from traditional notions of the separation of church and state. The clergy had their own courts to man. Why would they also involve themselves in the secular courts? Nonetheless, this vision does not take into account the reality of the medieval common law. For much of the Middle Ages, the clergy were the best, and sometimes the only, educated individuals in Europe. In fact, for much of the Middle Ages, the term *clericus* was synonymous with "literate" precisely for that reason. Why would the crown have rejected the assistance of those who might be most useful in the administration of the law? As Ralph Turner reminds us, the bureaucratization of government in the twelfth and thirteenth centuries "made the mingling of clerics in secular matters more common than ever."[100] In particular, clergy filled an essential void as royal justices in the ever-expanding legal system. Their contribution was no small matter. At times as much as a third of the episcopate served as royal justices.[101] Indeed, some of the most famed judges of the English Middle Ages were also clergymen: to name a few, Martin Pateshull, William Raleigh, Walter Map, and Henri de Bracton. A brief perusal of the medieval *List of Sheriffs* reminds us that the clergy also sometimes served as sheriff, a position that not only required an oath to the king, but that also involved them in the adjudication of blood crimes. Hugh Nonant, Bishop of Coventry, was joint sheriff of the counties of Warwick and Leicester in 1189 and 1191, and in the intervening year he assumed the post of sheriff of Staffordshire.[102] Hugh of Wells, Bishop of Lincoln, served as sheriff of Lincolnshire in 1223.[103] In 1270 and 1271, Walter Giffard, the Archbishop of York, was joint sheriff of the counties of Nottingham and

Derby.[104] Finally, Roger de Meyland, Bishop of Coventry and Lichfield, was joint sheriff of Oxfordshire and Berkshire in 1271.[105] The "laicisation of the English civil service" began only during the fourteenth century, such that by the end of the century, "the breakdown of the clerical monopoly was becoming evident even in the royal chancery."[106] Of course, this was only among clerks. It had no impact on the position of chancellor. With the exception of a brief period during the Wars of the Roses, English chancellors, who also acted as secular judges in the king's court of Chancery, belonged to the upper ranks of the church. The opening addresses of chancery petitions act as a powerful reminder of their adjudicators' mixed status. Inevitably, they are addressed to recognize the chancellor's joint achievements, such as: "To the most worshipful and reverent father in God, the archbishop of Canterbury, chancellor of England."[107]

Despite the active participation of clergy in the administration of the common law, the obstacles raised by Pattenden were very real concerns. The church in various manifestations issued repeated bans on the involvement of clergy in judgments of blood: and at least twice during the period English synodal statutes explicitly prohibited clergy from holding the office of sheriff.[108] Yet, the recurring legislation had little impact. Ecclesiastics played a key role as justices of jail delivery, even though it meant issuing sentences of death. Royal administration encouraged clerical participation in upholding the law, not only because clergymen were literate and learned, but also because their benefices provided them with the income necessary to subsidize their administrative offices.[109] If clergy played such an active role as sheriffs and royal justices, why not also as jurors?

All of the above examples are drawn chiefly from the upper ranks of the clergy. Among the parochial clergy, the grounds for excluding clerics from legal actions with such significant impact on communal relations were even slimmer; after all, charity within the parish, understood as "concord with, if not sincere love of, all parishioners and the absence of envy, wrath and spite" was a parish priest's chief priority.[110] In rural England, especially, parish priests had deep ties to the locality. They were "local boys made good," born in the parish or close by.[111] As such, they were very real members of their communities. They were also men of standing, accustomed to guiding their parishioners in issues of morality, and as the York evidence implies, as such they may well have had an interest in serving on a coroner's inquest.

This is a fundamental issue. Because of his pastoral and sacerdotal responsibilities, a parish priest had an "unusual level of knowledge" about the lives of his parishioners.[112] Not only was he privy to his parishioners' moral lapses through the sacrament of confession, he also acted as parish counselor for troubled marriages, dysfunctional families, and breeches in neighborly concord. As the only literate member of his community, he also typically filled the role of village scribe: parish priests regularly drew up wills, prepared charters, and arbitrated business agreements.[113] The parish priest was thus far and away the best informed about personal grudges past and present, hurtful exchanges, minor indiscretions, love triangles and betrayals, disputes over money or loans, personality conflicts, and his parishioners' suicidal or otherwise criminal thoughts. P.J.P. Goldberg has argued elsewhere that the "considerable local knowledge" of a parochial cleric made him an "expert witness" in the provincial ecclesiastical courts.[114] For the purposes of the crown, all of this made him a valuable member of a coroner's jury, too.

More important still, despite Hollywood's fascination with the constraints imposed by the seal of confession, it is important to acknowledge that a medieval priest was not as restricted by the seal as one might think.[115] Lyndwood's *Provinciale*, the collection and commentary of ecclesiastical decrees enacted in England's provincial councils, penned by the fifteenth-century keeper of the Privy Seal, William Lyndwood, makes it clear that canonical authority upheld breaking the confessional seal when it was for the greater good. Lyndwood asked: "what if a confession is made concerning a sin about to be committed, not yet committed? For instance: someone confesses that he wishes to kill a man, or he wishes to commit an evil act, and he says that he cannot resist the temptation. May the priest reveal it?"[116] Select canonists supported disclosing the confession, with the provision that he revealed it only to one who might be of help: surely a coroner, sheriff, or other local authority fell into this category. Lyndwood cited Hostiensis as an authority when he cautioned priests to avoid betraying the confessional by identifying the individual who confessed, but contended that preventing future injury took priority. Lyndwood also addressed overtly the courtroom dilemma, in which a judge commands the breaking of the seal. "When compelled to tell the truth by a judge, a priest is bound to reveal the confession, even if it was received under the confessional seal."[117] There are only two grounds for exception: 1) if the person who made the confession authorized his priest to break the seal, perhaps by calling him as a witness; 2) if the judge acted maliciously or unjustly. In the latter situation, the priest might comfortably respond that he knew nothing from the confession, without fear of perjury, because it will be secretly understood (presumably by God) as "I know nothing through confession to be revealed to you."[118] All of this implies that, in the event of a homicide or suicide, a parish priest could confidently participate as a juror without feeling constrained by his vow.

Clergymen were a practical choice for a coroner's jury also because they played a key role in domestic medicine. The church's repeated prohibitions on clergy studying medicine and participating in surgery have led many historians to assume that their role in the medical profession diminished dramatically after Lateran IV.[119] This was not the case. In England, "[l]earned practitioners (of medicine) were almost all clerics until the later fifteenth century."[120] Indeed, the holistic approach of medieval medicine necessitated clerical involvement. Both medical theory and Christian theology endorsed the ideal that health of body and soul are integrally connected. As canon 22 of Lateran IV reminds us, priests are "physicians of souls"; thus, "physicians of the body called to the bedside of the sick shall before all advise them to call for the physician of souls, so that, spiritual health being restored, bodily health will follow."[121] The geography of medieval English medicine also awarded the clergy a prominent place in medicine. Because formal medicine in England was highly urban in nature, in the countryside, the clergy were often the only individuals with any medical training, however meager. Consequently, "parishioners trusted their clergy to provide sound medical as well as spiritual advice."[122] This *status quo* continued well into the early modern era, indeed, even in defiance of the slow advance of professionalization in the field of medicine. Seeing the clergy as unregulated rivals, early modern London's College of Physicians appointed themselves the "more or less impossible" task of "suppressing the practice of medicine by the clergy."[123]

The medical side of a priest's "cure of souls" made him an ideal juror in two respects: 1) For those sudden deaths best explained by disease or bodily malfunction, the parish priest likely had inside knowledge about the deceased's medical history pertinent to the investigation. Rather than waste time over cause of death, why not ask the one man in town who knew well whether a sickness or medical condition resulted in the subject's death? 2) A priest garnered invaluable experience with death through administering last rites. As a result, he likely understood better than most how the various forms of death present.

JURORS AS WITNESSES

Medieval law conceived of jurors as witnesses, not judges of fact. John Langbein expresses this point clearly when he states, "[t]he medieval jury came to court not to listen but to speak, not to hear evidence but to deliver a verdict formulated in advance."[124] While medieval statute law embraced this perspective, this view has come under fire somewhat as of late with questions revolving around the self-informing nature of the jury. Mike McNair's 1999 study of the origins of the trial jury provides firm evidence for the contention that the crown always intended jurors to be witnesses rather than lay judges. He sees that King Henry II and his advisers made a "conscious choice" to extend the Anglo-Saxon practice of using panels of locals as informants rather than "tightening up the rules of proof by witnesses and documents."[125] McNair's conclusions are buttressed by the research of Anthony Musson and Daniel Klerman, who both argue in favor of a refined view of the "self-informed" nature of the trial jury. As Klerman explains it, "there was testimony 'alongside self-informing.'"[126] We do not have to endorse wholly one model at the expense of the other. Even if some jurors were not self-informing, they had many opportunities to be brought up to speed on the background to a case both before and during the trial. Nonetheless, witness testimony or an impassioned plea by a defendant might still have swayed final verdicts. Witnesses also sometimes presented fresh information discovered after the initial investigation. The existence of witness testimony at court, although rare, does not undermine the essential character of jurors as witnesses themselves. This character is emphasized by the oath sworn by indicting jurors: "Hear this, ye justices, that we will speak the truth about what is asked of us on the king's behalf, nor will we for any reason fail to tell the truth, so help us God, etc."[127] Thus, much like witnesses today, they swore to tell the truth.

Accepting that jurors were witnesses requires us to reorient our understanding of the kinds of people who acted as jurors. While it may seem alien to modern perceptions, medieval officeholders involved in law enforcement regularly participated as jurors. Coroners had an extensive impact in this capacity. The Northamptonshire sessions of the peace for 1295 confirm that coroners Giles Morton and John Buckton served as trial jurors in a total of forty cases in March of that year. In June, Simon Keylmarsh, also a coroner, served as a trial juror on fifty-seven cases alone.[128] Perhaps even more striking, coroners sometimes served on juries to try prisoners whom they had originally indicted.[129] Coroners were not alone in this respect. Many constables and bailiffs served as both presentment and trial jurors.[130] Constables played a key role on local juries: they regularly served as leet jurors.[131] Village reeves also filled this office, and frequently appeared alongside the four men of the vill as trial jurors.[132] In the fifteenth century, justices of the peace, coroners, subsidy collectors, commissions of array and, strangely enough, even blood relations of jail delivery justices, formed a strong presence on trial juries.[133] Certainly, today, a *bone fide* court of law would not select a police detective as a juror in the trial of a man he had apprehended; however, the prosecution doubtless would call him as a witness to explain details of the investigation. It is in this capacity that we need to appreciate those officeholders who doubled as jurors. Who better to put on a jury than someone with a sound knowledge of the law and the process of law enforcement, who may even have participated in the investigation himself, and if not, had good knowledge from his coworkers who had? Even if the constable knew nothing about what had happened, his knowledge of the law and leadership skills would make him a valuable foreman on a trial jury.

Although jury lists rarely included any information about coroners' jurors other than their names, it is possible to detect some few instances in which law enforcement officials served on coroners' juries. Robert Mundesder, one of York's county coroners in the reign of Richard II, regularly included at least one constable on each jury. In fact, for one inquest, he selected three constables to serve on the jury: William Gislay, John Catelyn, and Henry Smyth, all identified as constables in the record, served as jurors in the stabbing death of John Locok at Pontefract in the spring of 1391.[134] Robert Passelewe, another Yorkshire coroner, employed a constable on his jury in the death of Jacob of Reigate in August 1369 at Pontefract.[135] Empanelling constables on a coroner's jury was most likely pragmatic: they were in the right place at the right time, that is, at the scene of the death, while the bailiff was attempting to assemble twelve reputable men. At times, however, law enforcement officers participated as jurors clearly out of self-interest or a desire to see the job done well. For example, when Roger Beler was murdered in February 1326, his own cousin, Ralph Beler of Kettleby, served on the jury. Ralph Beler was a former coroner and sheriff of Leicestershire. Because of his experience in criminal law enforcement, Ralph probably saw himself as being supremely qualified for the job. That several other past or acting coroners also served on the jury attests to the high-profile nature of the homicide and a desire to make sure that the perpetrator was caught.[136]

MEDICAL PRACTITIONERS AS JURORS

Into this vision of the jury as a collection of witnesses falls the role of medical expertise. Today, medical expertise in a criminal investigation derives from two different sources. First, the office of the coroner (or the medical examiner) performs autopsies, analyzes blood samples, carries out toxicological analysis, and so forth. Second, legal representatives can summon as trial witnesses medical experts who have no knowledge about the case at hand, but possess general knowledge that is germane. For example, if the accused in a homicide trial was autistic, his lawyer might hire a specialist in autism to speak to his condition. In the medieval context, securing the participation of medical practitioners as inquest jurors would have permitted them to perform both roles effortlessly.

Once again, Helen Brock and Catherine Crawford's 1994 study of coroners' juries is noteworthy. If surgeons commonly served on juries in seventeenth-century Maryland and used their expertise to guide the investigation, surely colonists were drawing on English practices.[137] At the very least, this experience, in combination with the English studies of Kesselring and Loar,[138] indicates that soon after the close of the Middle Ages, medical practitioners served on coroners' juries as expert witnesses. Significantly, the Anglo-Saxon evidence relays a similar story. There is good reason to believe that medical practitioners often appeared before the Anglo-Saxon courts to testify in personal injury hearings as to the severity of a wound.[139] Compensation rested on prognosis in the short term (will the wound heal? Is he likely to die?) and in the long term (will he ever be able to father children? How will the injury affect his ability to walk/fight/farm?). Only a person with a medical background could offer a reliable prognosis.[140] Medical practitioners also worked closely with the law courts in respect to sick-maintenance. Any individual injured in an assault was eligible for compensation until he could return to work, paid for by the aggressor, and set by the court.[141] It is hard to imagine that medical practitioners played such a key role both before and after the late Middle Ages, but not also during the intervening period.

Medical practitioners were desirable coroner's jurors for myriad reasons. First, to avoid the indignation of a coroner needlessly summoned to the scene of the crime, it made sense to ensure that the body was in fact dead before proceeding any further in the investigative process. This was not necessarily as easy as one might think. With today's technology, we take for granted the ability to recognize signs of death. Yet, until well into the twentieth century, anxiety about vivisepulture (that is, burial alive) was a well-founded concern. The Victorian era represents an extreme example of moral panic over misdiagnosed death, evident in the 1896 foundation of the London Association for the Prevention of Premature Burial and the market for coffins fitted with breathing tubes, alarm bells, and spring-activated flags.[142] This alarm festered despite the fact that the Victorian era's physicians were much more technologically equipped than were their medieval forbears.[143] The medieval English were also less prepared theoretically. As an example, contemporary perspective did not place great priority on modern signs of death, such as the absence of breathing.[144] And while medieval medicine did see pulse as a vital guide to health, without stethoscopes or some other instrument to amplify sound for human hearing, it is not the most trustworthy measure. The medieval moniker for fainting underlines the era's difficulty in distinguishing between unconsciousness and death: fainting was widely known as "little death."[145] Medieval medicine endorsed Galen's radical moisture theory of death, in which a lifeless body was one that was cold and dry. However, depending on when the first finder discovered the corpse and in what conditions, this description may or may not have been apt. The difficulty of establishing whether a person was dead is something that medieval physicians acknowledged and hoped to redress. Jacme d'Agramont, the author of a fourteenth-century guide to plague prevention, remarked "it is certain that many men and women who suffer from the disease are thought to be dead by the common people and many are buried alive."[146] Indeed, the number of criminals who revived after hanging implies that even executioners, whom one would expect to be experts on death, had an imperfect skill at judging the signs.[147] D'Agramont's experience with plague victims led him to suggest two progressive methods of identifying death:

> The first consisted of observing whether a very thin shred of wood, held near the nostrils or the mouth of someone supposedly deceased, moves as a result of the air passing in and out with the breath. The second consisted of seeing whether water in a glass put on the chest near the heart moves as a result of the heartbeat.[148]

But how many English laymen read Jacme d'Agramont's *Regiment de preservació de pestilència*? A Middle English lyric describing the signs of death, surviving in a preacher's handbook, only confirms that d'Agramont's fears must sometimes have been realized:

> When the head trembles, / And the lips grow black / The nose sharpens, / And the sinews stiffen, / The breast pants, / And breath is wanting, / The

> teeth clatter, / And the throat rattles / The soul has left / And the body holds nothing but a clout— / Then will the body be thrown in a hole / And no-one will remember your soul.[149]

Given the challenge of recognizing death, communities in doubt most likely sought the advice of a medical practitioner.

Second, the very nature of their business meant that medical practitioners often were already caught up in the investigation before local authorities even summoned the coroner. Those who survived a near-lethal assault typically sought medical assistance; or, as the records relate, friends and neighbors carried the wounded to a nearby location to seek out medical expertise. The London death of Henry Arnald in 1324 makes this point clear. After a gang beating that left him with injuries on the head, back, knees, and thighs, Henry's friends carried him away "to be medically treated." Regrettably, their assistance came too late: he died soon after.[150] Many medical practitioners who served on juries, or appeared in the records as neighbors or pledges, were there precisely because they had tried to help a dying man. At times, the location of death makes this explicit. In February of 1296/97 when John Motescharp responded to the raising of the hue in the parish of St Aldate's in the city of Oxford, one of the escaping felons shot him in the side with an arrow. It took two nights for the wound slowly to kill him. When he finally passed away, it was in the home of Randalph the Surgeon where he was receiving treatment.[151] Under these circumstances, Randalph the Surgeon was involved in the investigation whether he wanted to participate or not. William of Worksop, a barber, served on the inquest into the death of nine-year-old Thomas, son of Adam Peyntour, of the borough of Nottingham in 1378. The coroner's report relates that William, son of Martin Tankardmaker, feloniously shot Thomas with an arrow shaft in the left eye directly into the brain. He languished for much of the day, and then died.[152] William of Worksop seems to have been a preferred juror for the borough coroners William of Beeston and Richard of Bradmore. They summoned him also in the homicide of Thomas Supter later that same year,[153] to the death by misadventure of John, son of William of Soutwell, in 1380,[154] and again to the homicide of William of Bolton in 1386/87.[155] Medical practitioners also attended many deaths by drowning, probably in the hopes of resuscitation.[156]

Medical practitioners also participated in inquests where the evidence did not accord with local opinion. Walter the Leche served as an inquest juror in the death of Adam Taha, a currier in the borough of Oxford, presumably for this reason. When Adam passed away in September 1343, the jury initially determined his death was from natural causes. However, upon hearing a rumor that a dispute between Adam and Robert the Tableter led to Robert punching Adam in the vicinity of his heart on the Monday prior to Adam's demise, they took a closer look at the body in order to discern whether Robert's attack may have been the cause. Finding no evidence of assault, they ruled out foul play and reverted to their original ruling.[157] Henry Leche participated in the inquest of Richard Boch as one of the nearest neighbors. The roll reports that an argument arose between Richard and Henry Carcere in the spring of 1382 at Alford (*Somt.*). Purportedly, in self-defense, Henry walloped Richard in the head with a rake, inflicting him with a wound an inch and a half in length. Richard was in pain for sixteen days after the event, at which point the priest administered last rites, and he passed away. Jurors determined the wound was not to blame for his death. Rather, he died by the grace of God (that is, a natural death).[158]

The English also expected medical practitioners to participate in an inquest when they possessed relevant information. When a physician and a surgeon failed to testify at the inquest into the death of John Walweyn in 1468/69,[159] Richard Beauchamp complained to the chancellor because, in failing to do their job, they left him vulnerable to an appeal of homicide. His bill states:

> Meekly beseech your good lordship Richard Beauchamp that where there is great variance and trouble upon the death of one John Walweyn of whose death appeal is sued against the said Richard, surmising the same Richard to have poisoned the same John in Herefordshire and it is so that the same John Walweyn died at Oxford of the pestilence and there openly known the cause and sickness wherein he died and there is both the physician, surgeon and diverse other persons which looked to the same John Walweyn in his said sickness knowing the truth [*hole in manuscript*] cause of his death which for great labor and instance made unto them by the parties adversaries to the said Richard Beauchamp restrained to certify the truth thereof. Wherefore please it your said lordship for declaration of the truth in this matter to grant several writs of *sub pena*, one direct to John Clark, Mayor of the said town; another to one Master John Cook, which was physician to the same John Walew-eyn; another writ to one John Barbor, which was surgeon to the same John Walweyn; and another to one William Plumton and Agnes his wife in whose house he lay sick and died commanding them by the same to appear before your said lordship in the Chancery at a certain day there they to be examined in and upon the premises and to declare the truth therein, as right and conscience shall require. And this for the love of God and in way of charity.[160]

Richard Beauchamp's indignation is edifying. He believed medical practitioners with relevant knowledge about an individual's demise had a moral, if not legal, obligation to testify at the inquest. Although he does not explicitly reference the coroner or the inquest in his bill, where else would one "certify the truth" of a death? While Richard's complaint speaks chiefly to fatalities brought on by disease, John Motescharp's death at the home of Randalph the Surgeon above is also applicable here. Richard's bill proposes that any medical practitioner who had recently cared for the dead had an ethical responsibility to come forward and participate in the investigation.

Granted, we should not presume that medical practitioners were always physicians or surgeons. Medieval medical practice was not the specialized profession that it is today. In England, only physicians were university trained: however, their services were costly, they were few in number, and they were frequently unwilling to get their hands dirty. Physicians preferred the theoretical rather than practical side of medicine. Consequently, it was not unusual for a physician to hire a barber to carry out the prescribed cure, further inflating the costs of medical service. In general, English men and women relied first on the medical knowledge of family and neighbors. As a result, "medieval communities had a much greater understanding of the immediacy of wounds and the requirements for cure than we possess in this era of medical specialization."[161] If home remedies failed, they sought the services of the clergy, then midwives, surgeons or barber-surgeons (particularly in urban settings), or apothecaries. Nonetheless, it is critical to recognize that medicine in the medieval context was diffused among a much greater pool of practitioners than today. Faye Getz identifies this characteristic as the most distinctive feature of English medicine: "medieval medicine embraced men and women, serfs and free people, Christians and non-Christians, academics and tradespeople, the wealthy and the poor, the educated and those ignorant of formal learning."[162]

Because medicine in medieval England was rarely a full-time job,[163] most practitioners had to broaden their realm of expertise in order to make a living, leading to an "occupational diversity" that can be somewhat perplexing in the surviving documentation.[164] For example, spicers, pepperers, and grocers often performed the same tasks that we would expect of an apothecary. Guild structures merely add to the confusion. Once again, medieval London's apothecaries did not have their own guild. Rather, they belonged initially to the Guild of Pepperers, then eventually to the Grocers' Company.[165] The same occupational overlap crops up with barbers and chandlers. Wax was a key ingredient in making ointments for medicine. Thus, many chandlers developed their candle-making careers to also include ointments. The association between chandlers and medicine was recognized across England. The municipal governments of Chester, Newcastle, and Norwich awarded chandlers medical privileges.[166] Indeed, the association between barbers and chandlers was so widespread "that the term barber-chandler would be more justifiable than barber-surgeon."[167] There was also much crossover between surgeons and metalworkers. The tools of their profession best explain this alliance. Surgeons engaged in metalworking in order to design functional surgical instruments; however, because the market for surgical goods was insignificant, they turned their skills to profit from the more mundane iron production, such as horseshoes and so forth.[168] Medical expertise was sometimes spread among unexpected professions. In a 1561 complaint by Norwich barbers and physicians regarding unlicensed practitioners, they targeted shoemakers, hatmakers, dornick weavers, smiths, worsted weavers, and women as the most flagrant offenders.[169] Occupational diversity was not restricted to medicine. Many Englishmen had secondary occupations, so much so that King Edward III issued legislation in 1363/64 embodying the ideology of "one craft per person," in the hopes of compelling craftsmen to join guilds.[170] Municipal authorities understood the guilds as policing organizations for the control of trade. Thus, it was in the government's best interest if all craftsmen specialized and joined a guild.[171] Compliance was slow in coming, however. Even in the sixteenth century, it is possible to discover two men admitted to the freedom of York under multiple occupations claiming to be both barbers and stringmakers.[172]

England's occupational diversity in medicine has two meaningful outcomes for this study. First, because medicine was not universally specialized and elitist, it was much easier for coroners to empanel local residents with some degree of medical expertise as jurors than it would be today. Second, even when a coroner's roll munificently records a juror's occupation, that occupation does not necessarily provide any indication of his healthcare experience. A smith might also be a surgeon; a grocer might also be an apothecary. When William the Chandler acted as a pledge for one of the neighbors in the death of Philip le Faitour, who died in London in 1301, was our neighborly chandler called to the scene because of his medical expertise? Or, was he the kind of chandler who worked only in candle making, but just happened to live close by?[173] Inevitably, we will never know the full extent of medical expertise represented by the individuals involved in a coroner's inquest.

Nonetheless, for the city of London, it is feasible to uncover a good number of those jurors who self-identified as medical practitioners, specifically as physicians, surgeons, and barbers, and hence gain a keener appreciation of the regularity with which medical practitioners served on inquest juries. Granted, we must first acknowledge the constraints of London's documentation. London's coroners remarked upon jurors' occupations in a relatively haphazard manner. Of a sixteen-person jury, the coroners were apt to note the occupations for three or four jurors. Regrettably, because the London poll tax evidence has not survived, unearthing the occupations of the remaining jurors is well nigh impossible.[174] Even so, London coroners appear to have been vigilant in documenting when a physician, surgeon, or barber served as a juror, perhaps because of their elite status in London society, or in an effort to prove that they had executed their investigations to the best of their abilities. The coroners' rolls for 1325–1339 include 128 inquests with jury lists. Medical practitioners served as jurors in 42 of those 128 inquests (that is, 33% of the time). Yet, medical practitioners held the office of juror even more frequently than this number implies because multiple medical practitioners sometimes served on the same jury. In fact, fifty-two medical practitioners served on those forty-two inquests. Medical practitioners were also intermittently involved in an inquest as the nearest neighbor or as a pledge, thus confirming their presence at the inquest. It is hard to imagine a medical practitioner present at an inquest remaining silent while the jury alone determined cause of death. Including those individuals raises our rate appreciably: 49 of the 128 inquests, or 38%, included a medical practitioner in some capacity. This figure masks the multiplicity of medical practitioners who may have been involved in one inquest: sixty-nine medical practitioners served in one capacity or another on those forty-nine inquests.[175]

Unquestionably, these figures underrepresent the number of jurors, neighbors, and pledges with medical expertise involved in London's inquests. Not only did coroners fail to record most jurors' occupations, but even when coroners did list them, England's pervasive occupational diversity prevents us from identifying those individuals with substantial training in medicine whose full-time job was not medically relevant. Even so, 38% is a high percentage. Here, we need to recognize that in many inquests, coroners probably did not require the services of a medical practitioner to establish cause of death. The medicalization of death in the modern era makes this proposition difficult to accept: today, death is primarily "a medical problem." Death is so highly medicalized that only physicians can "confirm and explain death."[176] This perception is relevant only to a very modern, Western viewpoint. In medieval England, to the physician belonged the health of the living, not the dead. Coroners and jurors undoubtedly felt secure in their ability to recognize some forms of death on their own. The experienced coroner knew well that the corpse of a murder victim had little in common with that of an individual who had succumbed to disease or old age. Commonsense alone dictated that a woman beaten to death by her husband, for example, should be swathed in bruises. The extant reports of physicians hired by the state to carry out post-mortem examinations in medieval Venice reveal that their confidence was well founded. Little expertise was necessary for documentation: "[i]n many murder cases . . . the cause of death was so apparent and the reportage of the doctor's examination so brief that it is difficult to determine how serious the examination was, or needed to be, in order to prove that a murder had occurred."[177] In the same vein, we need to recognize that post-mortem examinations today are rare. In a survey of current practices in Scotland, Lindsay Prior and Mick Bloor remark that "[m]ost practitioners felt able to find plausible medical reasons for death without post-mortem examination."[178] Perhaps even more startling, they concluded that, in terms of diagnoses at death, "the reasoning of professionals is not essentially very different from everyday reasoning. There is no major break between lay and professional reasoning exhibited here."[179] Autopsies, especially, are today a procedure of last resort: in England and Wales in 2004, only 22.5% of deaths resulted in autopsies.[180] The numbers are even smaller for the United States: in 2007, only 9% of all deaths resulted in autopsies.[181] What is significant for us to recognize here is that, in light of current practice, a participation rate of 38% reveals that medieval coroners were no less conscientious or diligent in post-mortem examinations than are their modern counterparts.

The London records emphasize the civic-mindedness of barbers. Of the sixty-nine medical practitioners serving on those forty-nine inquests, there were three spicers, three leeches (most likely surgeons),[182] and sixty-three barbers. The preponderance of barbers stems from their numbers: studies of fifteenth-century London reveal that "[t]here were more barbers and even barber-surgeons in London . . . than there were physicians and surgeons combined."[183] This finding conforms also to early modern observations. Physicians actively avoided officeholding at every level: "They claimed exemption from all military, policing and jury duties as a right of privilege, while offering little in return in terms of public service."[184] Their aversion to officeholding was so pronounced that Margaret Pelling claims "an aldermanic physician is somehow a contradiction in terms."[185] In many respects, their distaste for public service was a product of an itinerant lifestyle. The careers of physicians involved such mobility that they often defied association with a specific locality. In contrast, through their guilds, barbers and surgeons were tied to an urban environment. More important still, they were astonishingly civic-minded. The numerous barbers and surgeons who exploited officeholding as a springboard for social advancement is a reminder that they did not share in the social respectability routinely conferred on physicians by nature of their university background. In consequence, during the late medieval professionalization of medicine, surgeons consciously forged an alliance with the crown in order to "institutionalize their profession."[186] This fruitful coalition continued well into the modern era. The seventeenth century boasts a whole string of barber-surgeons as sheriffs.[187] There are a few prominent examples also for the medieval period. John Crophill, a literate surgeon whose surviving treatise reveals an extensive knowledge of the sciences of medicine, astrology, and divination, worked principally as bailiff of Wix Priory in Essex.[188] As royal surgeon to King Richard II, William Bradwardine assumed a number of key positions. He was constable of Dryslwyn Castle from 1397 to 1402, and in 1421 he enjoyed a short stint as Marshal of the King's Marshalsea of his Bench.[189] Thomas Morstede, a surgeon, was sheriff in the city of London in 1436; he was also an alderman in 1437, and a prominent member of the fishmonger's company.[190] For those aspiring elites, service in law enforcement offered an opportunity to have a positive impact on communal harmony. As Guido Ruggiero notes in his study of Venetian legal medicine, working side by side with the police allowed doctors to play "a significant role in the replacement of private vengeance with public criminal prosecution."[191] Many barbers and surgeons must have delighted in the opportunity jury service offered to uphold the peace and shape the communities in which they lived.

Jury service might also be an inconvenience, especially when sheriffs called too often upon the same group of people to serve. The clearest evidence for the popularity of barbers as jurors comes from 1525 when London barbers pleaded with city authorities to be released from the responsibility of serving on inquests. Although the mayor and aldermen claimed to "well understand" their grievance, they denied it, explaining that their request was "expressly against the king's laws, also against the liberties of this Cities."[192] The barbers' avid participation in coroners' juries sheds some light on the sixteenth-century barbers' motivation. They were desperate to seek an exemption from jury service because the constant demand for their involvement had evolved into a terrific burden.

Nonetheless, coroners' juries were much better served by the participation of barbers and surgeons than by physicians. Once again, medieval universities strove to graduate physicians who were philosophically minded. Their approach to medicine was highly theoretical, focused primarily on humoral theory and the conception of the body as a microcosm of the universe. In many respects, they functioned more as "dietician, spiritual counsellor and general confidant rather than that of medical practitioner."[193] When they recognized the need for hands-on medical care, they hired surgeons or barbers (that is, craftsmen who worked with their hands) to carry out the task. Barbers and surgeons, on the other hand, had to be jacks-of-all-trade, proficient in surgery, but also in diet modification and herbal remedies. An almost continuous state of war in the Middle Ages meant that barbers and surgeons alike had ample opportunity to learn how to heal the wounds inflicted by weapons that "were highly effective in causing disability and death."[194] Over the course of the era, surgical knowledge in treating wounds from trauma increased exponentially. In the same respect, experience on the battlefield meant surgeons were better able to recognize causes of death, even death by poison, as late medieval warfare often called for dipping weapons in poison before battle.[195] Those without a background in war learned from the surgical texts penned by those who did. The competence of surgical knowledge in dealing with violent injuries is evidenced by the popularity of the illustration entitled "Wound Man" (see Figure. 2.1). The image depicts the variety of injuries a human body might sustain, including blows from clubs, sword and knife cuts, arrow and spear wounds, animal and insect bites, rashes, abscesses, and burns. The illustration dates back to at least the fourteenth century, although probably even earlier than that.[196] Some later depictions include also injuries to internal organs. The value of such a document is to emphasize that surgeons were not only well acquainted with injuries inflicted in violence, but also that wounds of this nature formed the bulk of their surgical labor. At any rate, this experience made barbers and surgeons far more appropriate jurors in death investigations than physicians.

The 1325–1339 evidence from the London coroners' rolls does not appear to be an anomaly. While the surviving documentation for the inquests spanning 1300–1301 and 1322–1325 do not include jury lists, the rate of involvement of medical practitioners as neighbors and pledges is comparable.[197] In the ninety-nine death investigations that include neighbors and pledges, medical practitioners participated in thirty-one (that is, 31% of

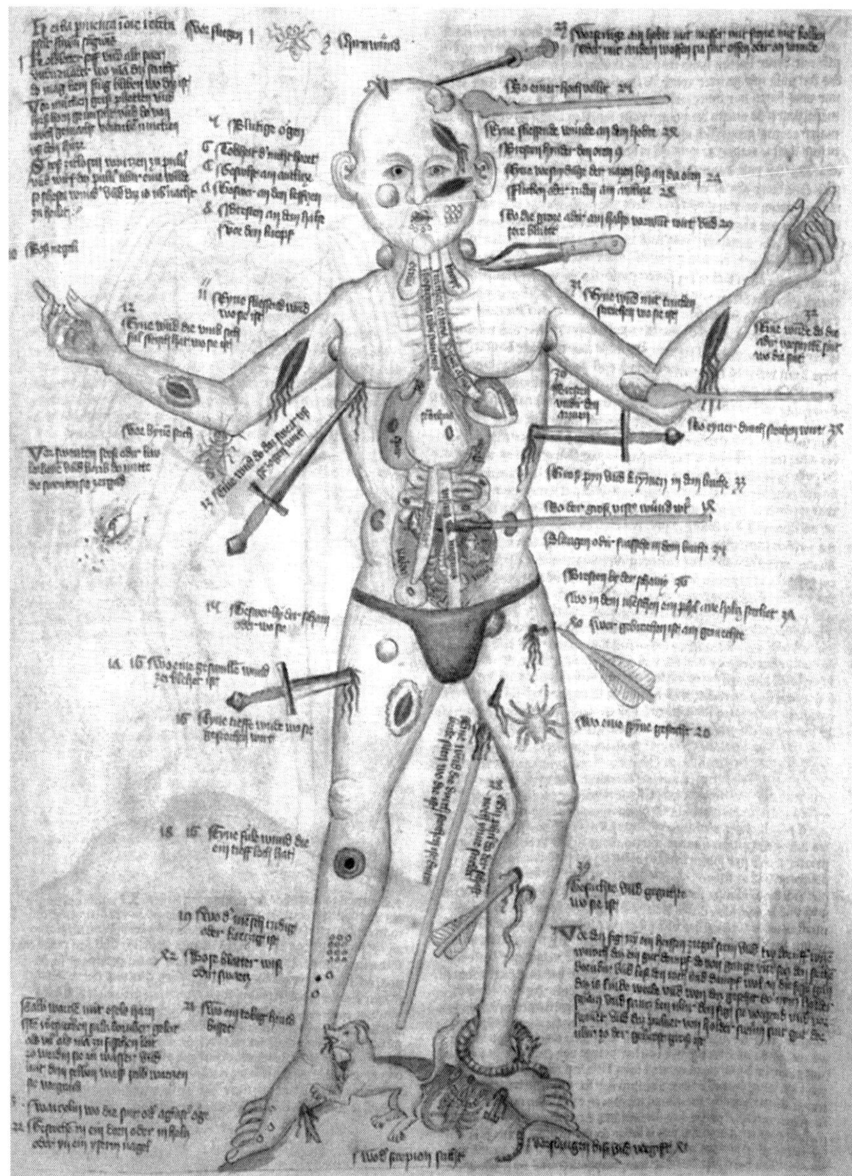

Figure 2.1 "Wound Man," Wellcome Library, London, *ms.* WMS49, *fo.* 35. Ref. no: L0022470.

the total number of inquests). If we consider also those instances where multiple medical practitioners served on an inquest, thirty-six medical practitioners acted as neighbors or pledges in those thirty-one cases. The breakdown in composition of medical practitioners offers somewhat more diversity than the previous sample, although barbers still dominate: of the thirty-six medical practitioners, there were: one spicer, two physicians, four surgeons, and twenty-nine barbers.

How representative are London's figures? London manifestly stands out from all other cities in England because of its population, crown presence, and opportunity for financial growth. As Faye Getz observes:

> The effect of market demand on medical practice was most apparent in medieval London, which in size and wealth dwarfed England's other urban centers. It was to London that the ill came, looking for treatment, drugs, or advice. It was also in London that the medical profession established itself.[198]

London boasted far more medical practitioners of an elite status than any other urban center in England. More important still, professional medicine in medieval England was highly urban.[199] In the countryside, the sick and the diseased turned to family, clergy, and informally trained practitioners, or they travelled to the nearest city. Altogether, this tells us that the participation of professional medical men evident in London's inquest juries cannot be typical; rather, we can interpret it as the ideal. London's coroners' rolls tell us that coroners aspired to have someone with medical experience serving on an inquest jury, and enlisted their services whenever they were available. Because of the wide dissemination of medical knowledge in England, coroners elsewhere would have had little difficulty in finding jurors with some degree of expertise in the field, although we would not necessarily recognize it by the title of their occupation.

Unsurprisingly, the evidence from the city of York suggests that outside London, the participation of medical practitioners on coroners' inquests was not as ideal. Of the eighty-three inquests that appear in the city of York coroner's roll spanning 1363 to 1378, only fifteen of those inquests (or 18%) contained men who are identifiable as medical practitioners.[200] The composition of that group is also distinctive: of the eighteen medical practitioners involved in the fifteen inquests, there were six barbers, five physicians, and seven spicers. Although York's juries still featured a solid involvement of medical practitioners in inquest juries, their participation is noticeably lower than London's. How should this be explained? The justification would seem to reside in numbers. In York, "physicians were relatively thin on the ground," swelling the burden imposed on barbers and surgeons in addressing the daily health needs of residents from the city and its outlying areas.[201] Philip Stell's study of medicine in medieval York uncovered fifteen physicians and seventy-two barbers living in York in the period 1350–1399.[202] For a city of its size, this was a sizeable population; medieval Norwich, in comparison, at about half the size of York, boasted only twenty-three barbers during the same period.[203] However, York's demand for barbers exerted tremendous pressure on this small population of medical practitioners, such that even women were admitted to the barber's craft, one of the few York crafts to make this concession.[204] Moreover, the *Register of Freemen* boasts the names of many barbers who do not appear in the jury lists—implying that their needs were better served working with the living, rather than the dead.

UNIQUELY MEDIEVAL

The disparities between medieval and modern practices of empanelling a jury are easier to detect than their similarities. What passed for normal then, today would lead to a mistrial. Differences in practice relate largely to their distinct roles in the judicial system: while jurors today are expected to listen to a case and pass judgment on the evidence, medieval jurors had to seek out the necessary evidence themselves before they even arrived in court. The unique position of the medieval juror led to some distinctly medieval practices. For example, sheriffs and royal justices tolerated, perhaps even encouraged, overlaps between juries of presentment and trial so that effectively a juror passed judgment on the same individual he had indicted.[205] Daniel Klerman writes that the overlap was so common that "the two juries were hard to distinguish."[206] Indeed, in this respect, a 1352 statute that prohibited presenting jurors from serving on the trial jury might have had the disastrous effect of "barring twelve of the most knowledgeable people . . . from service on the trial jury" if it had been applied in practice.[207] Law enforcement officers also served on trial juries, even when they had directed the investigation leading to the arraignment of the very same defendants. Again, who knew better the details of the investigation and the case against the defendant than the very same men who worked to indict him?

These are not the only medieval deviations in jury composition. On occasion, inquest juries included individuals a modern court would deem entirely inappropriate because of their association with the dead. The inquest into the death of John Syger from May 1381 provides an edifying example. Purportedly, Syger was driving his mare in the meadow of Easington (*Bucks.*) when the mare kicked out with its hind foot and struck him in the belly. He died the following day in the home of Richard Pede (relationship unknown). Joan Syger (presumably John's wife) was the first finder; Richard Pede was her pledge. Richard Pede also served on the coroner's inquest jury.[208] In all likelihood, the county coroner enjoined Pede to become a juror because of his firsthand knowledge of the events leading up to the casualty, as well as a need to meet the twelve-man quota. Yet, how is it possible to conduct an impartial investigation when the fatality occurred in the home of one of the jurymen and that same juror was also a pledge for the dead's wife? What if Richard and Joan were in cahoots? What if they staged the death to look like an accident? No court today would sanction Richard Pede serving on that jury because he was plainly too closely involved.[209]

Sometimes medieval jurors were closely related to the dead. In general, it is not difficult to find jurors bearing the same by-name as the subject of the inquest. With the instability of names for much of the medieval period, this phenomenon is a better indicator of shared occupation or provenance than blood relationship, although, at times, the existence of family ties between the dead and a juror is hard to deny. The inquest into the death of Matilda, wife of Richard Pouk, in 1342 offers such evidence. The jury concluded that Matilda died of natural causes, although upon hearing a rumor that Matilda's husband beat her, the coroner reopened the investigation to search for signs of abuse.[210] Surely, the presence of William de Pouk among the jurors, whose unusual by-name implies a probable relationship with Matilda's husband, accounts, in part, for that rigor. Similarly, when Matilda, wife of William Channtour, slew four-year-old John, son of Richard Rugeman, in a fit of insanity in December of 1380, at least two of the jurors who served at the inquest may have had some relationship to her: Thomas Channtour and Richard Channtour.[211] Obviously members of Matilda's family were far more qualified to judge her mental incapacity than anyone else.

Even more frequently, jurors were also related to each other. In the November 1384 homicide of John Walshman, Milo atte Halle and William atte Halle appear side by side on the jury list.[212] When John Henry was run over by a carriage in December 1365, Richard Benet, William Benet, and John Benet all served as jurors at his inquest.[213] The accidental death of three-year-old John, son of John Hayward, in 1368 exposes a jury stacked with family members: William Kernule, Edmund Kernule junior, and William, son of John Kernule; as well as Richard Passhelewe and his brother William.[214] Admittedly, not all relationships were blood ones: some might have been occupational. In the June 1377 death of Henry Tubbey of Dunchurch (*Warks.*), the jury included two Dudders, two Smiths, two Cooks, and William Burghbach junior as well as William Burghbach senior.[215] At the 1384 inquest into the death of Brother Henry Fryers, who died by falling into a well, his jury included: Richard Parchemyner, Thomas Parchymyner, and Edward Parchemyner.[216] In the death by misadventure of Adam the Cowherd at Oxford in April of 1348, there were four jurors who appear to have been related: Robert Clere, John Clere, Thomas Clere, and Richard Clere.[217] And these examples represent only a small sample of the pool of interrelated jurors. Such close relationship between jurors today would generate fears of partisanship; not so for the medieval courts.[218]

Law enforcement officials in medieval England were resolute to empanel jurors with sound knowledge of the crime, regardless of their association with the dead or the visne. More important still, they were anxious to meet the twelve-person minimum stipulated by the crown and sometimes had to resort to empanelling members of the same family to do so. Nonetheless, there is no suggestion that coroners believed doing so risked the quality of their investigations.[219]

THE PERSONALITY OF THE JURY

The actions of medieval jurors were astonishingly human. The coroners' rolls do not speak from the emotionally detached perspective that one might anticipate of the official record of a death. Medieval England's jurors were judgmental, even disparaging, and did not shy away from expressing their dissatisfaction with an individual's actions. When jurors believed a death occurred needlessly, they said so. For example, when John the Mercer, servant of John of Brooksby, endeavored to cross the river on horse near the mill at Sywaldby (*Leics.*), drowning because he opted to cross at the deepest part of the river, jurors remarked that he brought his death upon himself "out of his own foolishness."[220] In the same way when Juliana, wife of Richard Wodeward, of Bretford (*Warks.*) tumbled into the River Avon in July 1380 and drowned, jurors did not hesitate to condemn her actions by pronouncing she did so through "her own foolishness in her drunken state."[221] Jurors were especially intolerant when one person's careless behavior resulted in another's death. Here, it is imperative to understand that medieval England defined felony as active criminality rather than passive behavior that might lead to criminal ends. Negligence, while certainly reprehensible, was not criminal. Nonetheless, jurors took advantage of the inquest as an opportunity to express quite vocally their contempt for reckless behavior.[222] Parents were the most frequent targets. When the home of John Grocer of Berkshire went up in flames, consuming his four-month-old daughter, jurors blamed the mother: the child was lying in a crib "without the custody of the mother"; "she left the child"; it happened "through the negligence of the mother."[223] The coroners' rolls abound with similar reproaches of the poor parenting skills that led to the pointless deaths of many children.

The willingness of jurors to target negligent behavior is critical because it flies in the face of current historiography. Rab Houston sees the deodand as evidence of the medieval English aversion to confront negligence. He argues that medieval coroners' inquests "strenuously avoided attributing blame to a person, attaching it instead to the object causing death, and the ascription of responsibility was largely concealed behind the language of causation."[224] Only in the time of Blackstone did communities understand this form of forfeiture as punishment for negligent behavior. Rather, he proposes that the deodand served two purposes in medieval England. First, it was an opportunity for the lord to assert his rights. Second, forfeiture of weapons, in particular, removed "a potentially dangerous or disdained object from circulation."[225] With respect to the former, in the medieval period, it would have been the king's rights being asserted, not the lord's. Houston interprets the deodand primarily as an opportunity to assert authority, insisting that its value was "nominal" and thus profit was not a likely motivation for their collection.[226] Yet, the most common deodands were "horses, oxen, carts, boats, mill-wheels and cauldrons," objects of substantial value.[227] Many other deodands were modestly valued. As a collective, however, they represented a good sum, substantial enough to subsidize the rebuilding and sustenance of hospitals and convents across the kingdom.[228] Deodands were an important source of income for the king, allowing him to make a charitable grant or patronize a loyal supporter. As to the latter argument, Houston seems to envision deodands primarily as weaponry—weapons were considered *bane*, also a form of deodand. If we adopt this approach, the most popular weapon involved in a medieval homicide was a knife, often specifically a breadknife.[229] Despite being a "potentially dangerous" object, it was also a useful one. Medieval men typically carried a knife attached to their belts, in large part so that if someone invited them in for a meal they had their own cutlery at hand. Removing knives from a community would have had little impact on violence rates, although it would have made spontaneous dinner invitations much more awkward.

Houston's understanding of the medieval deodand falls wide of the mark. In instances of accidental death, medieval jurors were constrained by the law. Common law provided no option to indict a man for homicide when his sow attacked a child, or when his cart ran over a teenager sleeping in the street. In the absence of *mens rea*, there was no case. But the deodand furnished an opportunity to punish the property's owner. When a pig attacked and killed Alice, daughter of Alan Clerk, of Sheffield in 1370, jurors estimated the value of the pig at 12*d.*—no small sum of money for a fourteenth-century English farmer.[230] On top of the financial loss, the owner's negligence assumed center-stage in the coroner's inquest, a highly public spectacle played out before the entire male population of the four neighboring vills, and everyone knew to whom that pig belonged. Jurors did not need to assign blame by indicting the owner for homicide, especially since they did not believe the crime worthy of the death penalty. The inquest itself was enough to cast aspersion on his character.

Medieval jurors also had capacity for great sympathy, although admittedly there are far fewer instances. Old age elicited the most compassionate language from jurors. For example, when John Broke, a dubber living in Gloucestershire, passed away, jurors observed that for many days before he died he was sick with "old age and debility." He suffered from fever, dysentery, and other "intolerable infirmities," all of which eventually led to his death.[231] Although tentative, juries may have intended such sympathetic descriptions of elderly deaths to head off at the pass any accusations of merciful foul play. Jurors also excused minor infractions when the circumstances merited it. In 1393/94, when John Chapman inappropriately raised the hue and cry after the accidental death of his son in a carting mishap, the enrollment makes allowances for his actions stating that he did so out of sadness and grief (*per tristia et dolore*).[232] On occasion, jurors even took mercy on a felony suspect. Jurors evinced some consideration also in the 1365 self-killing of Leticia, wife of Simon Grindok, of Necton (*Norfolk*). Reportedly, she was suffering from such great sadness that she lacked a sane mind when she journeyed to a nearby forest and stabbed herself in the belly.

The record stands out in commenting that when she confessed her sins and received her last rites, she was indeed contrite.[233] Both stories of reproach and of sympathy remind us that coroners' jurors had the unenviable task of recounting personally meaningful deaths. The inquests revolved around the deaths of individuals who were their friends, neighbors, coworkers, and fellow parishioners.

Although the trial jury might overturn the inquest ruling, the inquest jury's initial judgment was significant. If he had not already fled, the homicide suspect ended up in prison awaiting trial, and the crown confiscated his goods and property.[234] Moreover, trial juries accorded the inquest findings great respect on the premise that jurors from the community where the death took place knew best what had happened and who, if anyone, should be punished. More important still, inquest juries were well aware of their clout and employed the appropriate language in enrollments to signal the gravity of their intentions. In the case of Leticia Grindok above, her indictment is evidence of a jury intent to "soften the verdict."[235] While common law perceived suicide as a felony meriting confiscation of property and an extra-ecclesiastical burial, the coroner's jury hoped to mitigate the severity of the law by presenting a compelling story of a woman whose actions were beyond her control. Jurors might also "harden the verdict" by including "phrases of afforcement," key words or expressions designed to advise the trial jury that capital punishment was indeed the most appropriate penalty for the defendant's actions.[236] Describing a felon as "notorious" or "common," or remarking that he carried out his crime by night (*noctanter*) were popular terms inserted by indicting jurors to signal their intent.[237] Inevitably, this strategy eliminated any need for the trial jury to be self-informing. Trial jurors had only to pay close attention to the wording of the indictment to know whether an acquittal or a conviction was fitting. Conviction rates emphasize the effectiveness of these terms. "Common" felons in the fifteenth century had a conviction against acquittal rate of one to three, compared to a one to eight rate for suspects without this designation.[238] When reading enrollments, it is impossible to mistake the resolve of a coroner's jury intent on conviction. The inquiry into the death of Peter Cornewayle, a London squire found lying dead in Farndon Ward in late November of 1400, incorporated a number of devices to highlight the loathsome nature of the crime. Immediately after the hour of nine, John Warner, a souter, engaged in debate with the said Peter, employing "contumelious words and dishonest threats." This wording is significant: for a man, any aspersion of dishonesty was a sure sign of a disreputable character.[239] The racket arising from their argument alerted the neighbors, who came out of their homes to reproach John. They separated the two and tried to pacify them. After their argument quieted down, John "lay in wait" to assault Peter around vespers that same day, reportedly with "premeditation and aforethought" (*praecogitans et prepens*). Peter was gathered with his neighbors and had no sense that he was about to be attacked, but Warner "maliciously" and "feloniously slew" Peter with his dagger, inflicting a mortal wound in the chest and another nonmortal wound in the humerus. John immediately fled.[240] The medieval English endorsed a masculine ethic that respected the fair fight. John's cowardly and dishonest behavior, described quite verbosely in the enrollment, painted him to be a cold, calculating criminal worthy of the death penalty.[241]

Coroners' jurors clearly had minds of their own and did not hesitate to protect the values of the community. Granted, that their actions seldom brought them into conflict with royal justices is a powerful reminder that "jury nullification" challenged the severity of customary law, not necessarily the beliefs or convictions of England's crown and judiciary.[242] If the York evidence is at all representative, residents viewed service on a coroner's jury as an office with a good degree of influence and respect. Repeated appearances imply that some jurors may even have campaigned to serve in the hopes of fostering their communal prestige through a position of visible authority. Nonetheless, there is no reason to believe that prestige undermined the efficiency of the jury. Bailiffs charged with assembling a jury ensured not only the presence of eyewitnesses whenever possible, but even medical practitioners whose expertise was invaluable to the inquest's findings. Admittedly, judges today would condemn many medieval practices. Not only did medieval justices tolerate overlapping membership between indicting and trial juries, but bailiffs also empanelled law enforcement officers, family members related to the dead and also to each other, as well as individuals whose involvement in the death made them partial witnesses. Nonetheless, there is little reason to believe that law enforcement officials believed their actions endangered the outcome of the trial. Indeed, the placement of these men on juries suggests just the opposite: they empanelled jurors whom they believed most qualified to render a verdict.

NOTES

1. Helen M. Jewell, *English Local Administration in the Middle Ages* (New York: Newton Abbot, David and Charles, 1972), p. 36.
2. Richard Gorski, *The Fourteenth-Century Sheriff: English Local Administration in the Late Middle Ages* (Woodbridge: Boydell, 2003), p. 2.
3. R.B. Goheen, "Peasant Politics? Village Community and the Crown in Fifteenth-Century England," *AHR* 96.1 (1991): 43.
4. James Masschaele, *Jury, State, and Society in Medieval England* (New York: Palgrave Macmillan, 2008), p. 90.
5. Sherri Olson, *A Chronicle of All That Happens: Voices from the Village Court* (Toronto: PIMS, 1996), p. 45.
6. W. Mark Ormrod, "The Politics of Pestilence: Government in England after the Black Death," in *The Black Death in England*, ed. Ormrod and Phillip Lindley (Stamford: Watkins, 1996), p. 167.
7. Masschaele, *Jury, State, and Society*, p. 135.
8. F. Pollock and F.W. Maitland, *A History of English Law before the Time of Edward I*, 2 vols. (Cambridge: Cambridge UP, 1898), v. 2, p. 631.

9. David J. Seipp, "Jurors, Evidences and the Tempest of 1499," in '*The Dearest Birth Right of the People of England': The Jury in the History of the Common Law*, ed. John W. Cairns and Grant McLeod (Oxford: Hart Pub., 2002), pp. 75, 92. Christopher St German specifically addressed the question of whether jurors should be permitted food and drink before making a decision. See T.F.T. Plucknett and J.L. Barton, eds., *St. German's Doctor and Student* (*SS*, v. 91, 1974), pp. 292–93.
10. Masschaele, *Jury, State, and Society*, p. 200.
11. Peter L. Larson, "Village Voice or Village Oligarchy?: The Jurors of the Durham Halmote Court, 1349–1424," *L&HR* 28.3 (2010): 699, 681.
12. Anne Reiber DeWindt, "Local Government in a Small Town: A Medieval Leet Jury and Its Constituents," *Albion* 23.4 (1991): 628.
13. Olson, *Chronicle of All That Happens*, p. 124.
14. Goheen, "Peasant Politics?," 49–62.
15. Bernard W. McLane, "Juror Attitudes toward Local Disorder: The Evidence of the 1328 Lincolnshire Trailbaston Proceedings," in *Twelve Good Men and True: The Criminal Trial in England, 1200–1800*, ed. J.S. Cockburn and Thomas A. Green (Princeton: Princeton UP, 1988), p. 42.
16. Anthony J. Musson, *Public Order and Law Enforcement: The Local Administration of Criminal Justice, 1294–1350* (Woodbridge: Boydell, 1996), pp. 180–81.
17. Scott Waugh, "Reluctant Knights and Jurors: Respites, Exemptions, and Public Obligations in the Reign of Henry III," *Speculum* 58.4 (1983): 967–71.
18. Goheen, "Peasant Politics?," 49–50.
19. Goheen, "Peasant Politics?," 56.
20. Erik D. Spindler, "Youth and Old Age in Late Medieval London," *The London Journal* 36.1 (2011): 12.
21. Shannon McSheffrey, "Jurors, Respectable Masculinity, and Christian Morality: A Comment on Marjorie McIntosh's *Controlling Misbehavior*," *JBS* 37 (1998): 269.
22. Morris S. Arnold, "Law and Fact in the Medieval Jury Trial: Out of Sight, Out of Mind," *AJLH* 18.4 (1974): 271.
23. Thomas A. Green, *Verdict According to Conscience: Perspectives on the English Criminal Trial Jury, 1200–1800* (Chicago: University of Chicago Press, 1985), p. 45.
24. Teresa Sutton, "The Deodand and Responsibility for Death," *Legal History* 18.3 (1997): 46.
25. Elisabeth Cawthon, "New Life for the Deodand: Coroner's Inquests and Occupational Deaths in England, 1830–46," *AJLH* 33.2 (1989): 137–47.
26. Surviving jury lists reveal how this process worked. The lists include the names of more individuals than necessary for a jury: those men chosen for the jury are marked with a pinprick beside their names.
27. This problem is not only an obstacle for historians. In a 1328 arraignment for homicide, the defendant, Adam of Pickering, was accused of having falsely abjured the realm. When Adam denied the accusation, the court sent for the coroner's rolls. The record of the abjuration designated him as Adam of H., rather than Adam of Pickering. Adam stuck firmly to his story. The court then sent a writ requiring the jury to come before the court and determine whether he was, in fact, the same person: the jury declared he was. Adam was hanged. Justices commented that if the defendant had been identified consistently in indictment and the abjuration, this confusion would never have arisen. See Y.B., Hil. term, 2 Edw. III, fos. 21a–21b.
28. 15 Hen. VI, c. 5 (1439) (*SR*, v. 2, pp. 298–98), reiterated in 18 Hen. VI, c. 2 (1439) (*SR*, v. 2, p. 301); and "Statute of Westminster I," 13 Edw. I, c. 38

(1275) (*SR*, v. 1, p. 89). For the purposes of comparison, S.J. Payling employs £5 annually as a loose definition of "gentry" for the early fifteenth century. See his *Political Society in Lancastrian England: The Greater Gentry of Nottinghamshire* (Oxford: Clarendon Press, 1991), p. 3.

29. M.T. Clanchy, *From Memory to Written Record: England 1066–1307*, 3rd ed. (Malden, MA: John Wiley & Sons, 2013), p. 209.
30. Clanchy, *From Memory to Written Record*, p. 209.
31. "Hen. VI: January 1437," *PRME*.
32. "Statute of Persons to be Put in Assises and Juries," 21 Edw. I (1293); *SR*, v. 1, p. 113.
33. 1 Ric. III, c. 4 (1483–1484); *SR*, v.2, p. 479.
34. William Hamilton Bryson, "Witnesses: A Canonist's View," *AJLH* 13.1 (1969): 59.
35. "Articles upon the Charters," 28 Edw. I, c. 9 (1300); *SR*, v.1, p. 139.
36. 34 Edw. III, c. 4 (1360); *SR*, v.1, p. 365.
37. This attitude toward wealth is not exclusive to statute law. As Jenny Kermode has noted, even municipal law frequently utilized terms such as *inferiores*, *mediocres*, *probi homines*, and others in order to distinguish between the privileged and nonprivileged in society. See Jenny Kermode, *Medieval Merchants: York, Beverley and Hull in the Later Middle Ages* (Cambridge: Cambridge UP, 1998), p. 12.
38. F.M. Nichols, ed., "Original Documents Illustrative of the Administration of Criminal Law at the Time of Edward I," *Archaeologia* 40 (1866): 103.
39. James Sharpe and J.R. Dickinson, "Coroners' Inquests in an English County, 1600–1800: A Preliminary Survey," *Northern History* 48.2 (2011): 256.
40. Masschaele, *Jury, State, and Society*, p. 137.
41. Musson, *Public Order and Law Enforcement*, p. 193*n*.
42. Green, *Verdict According to Conscience*, p. 32. Hunnisett has also referred to them as "men of the neighbourhood." See R.F. Hunnisett, *The Medieval Coroner* (Cambridge: Cambridge UP, 1961), p. 21.
43. Hunnisett, *Medieval Coroner*, p. 14.
44. This pattern of change is supported chiefly by the findings for the county of Sussex, Hunnisett's particular area of expertise (at least, for those coroners' rolls that have survived the Middle Ages); but on the whole, there is insufficient evidence to corroborate these changes over time. See particularly R.F. Hunnisett, "Sussex Coroners in the Middle Ages. In 3 parts," *Sussex Archaeological Collections* 95 (1957): 43–44.
45. Hunnisett, *Medieval Coroner*, p. 14.
46. TNA PRO JUST 2/220, m. 1. Even if we could confidently translate "*probari*" as "freemen," only one jury in the entire roll Hunnisett cites as evidence incorporates that descriptor. The communal status of the victim almost certainly determined the status of the jurors: if John of Beckingham was well known in his community, the coroner probably went the extra mile to ensure that so, too, were his jurors.
47. TNA PRO JUST 2/69.
48. Anon., *The Boke of Justices of Peas* 1506 (London: Professional Books Limited, repr. 1972), fo. vii.
49. Charles Trice Martin translates *probi homines* as "good men, an elected body of citizens forming a common council." See his *The Record Interpreter* (1892; Chichester, Sussex: Phillimore & Co. Ltd., repr. 1999), p. 301.
50. *Black's Law Dictionary*,6th ed. (St. Paul, MN: West Publishing, 1990), p. 692, headword "good"; *Oxford English Dictionary* (Oxford: Oxford UP, 2013), www.oed.com/search?searchType=dictionary&q=goodman&_searchBtn=Search : headword "goodman," IIa. Accessed June 2, 2014.

51. Anne and Edwin DeWindt explain that the distinction between "free" and "unfree" was not as simple as it might seem. Indeed, tenure often had little to do with status. Many free men held servile tenements, and unfree men sometimes held free tenements. See Anne Reiber and Edwin Brezette DeWindt, *Royal Justice and the Medieval English Countryside: The Huntingdonshire Eyre of 1286, the Ramsey Abbey Banlieu Court of 1287, and the Assizes of 1287–88* (Toronto: PIMS, 1981), pt. 1, p. 109.
52. Some few enrollments (and here I really do need to emphasize "few") suggest this possibility. Deviating from the formulaic description of "twelve sworn jurors," one Oxfordshire enrollment states instead "twelve free jurors" (*liberi jurati*). See TNA PRO JUST 2/136, m. 1. A Wiltshire indictment mentions the oath of twelve "free jurors" (*liberorum juratorum*). See TNA PRO JUST 2/204, m. 1.
53. TNA PRO JUST 2/42, m. 7.
54. Reginald R. Sharpe, ed., *Calendar of Coroners' Rolls of the City of London A.D. 1300–1378* (London: Richard Clay and Sons, 1913), pp. 266–68.
55. Francis Collins, ed., *Register of the Freemen of the City of York*, v. 1 (Surtees Society, v. 96, 1897).
56. Carolyn C. Fenwick, ed., *The Poll Taxes of 1377, 1379 and 1381: Part 3: Wiltshire-Yorkshire* (Oxford: Oxford UP for the British Academy, 2005).
57. See Helen Cam, *Liberties and Communities in Medieval England: Collected Studies in Local Administration and Topography* (Cambridge: Cambridge UP, 1944); Michael Prestwich, ed., *Liberties and Identities in the Medieval British Isles* (Woodbridge: Boydell, 2008); Matthew L. Holford and Keith J. Stringer, *Border Liberties and Loyalties: North-East England, c. 1200 to c. 1400* (Edinburgh: Edinburgh UP, 2010).
58. Women also occasionally paid for freeman status, although they were in a distinct minority.
59. R.B. Dobson, "Admission to the Freedom of the City of York in the Later Middle Ages," *EHR* 26.1 (1973): 20.
60. Richard Britnell, "Town Life," in *A Social History of England 1200–1500*, ed. Rosemary Horrox and W. Mark Ormrod (Cambridge: Cambridge UP, 2006), p. 175.
61. Dobson, "Admission to the Freedom," 19.
62. Heather Swanson, "Building Craftsmen in Late Medieval York," *BIHR* 63 (1983): 7.
63. Of course, there is some debate on this subject. It has been argued that York was more determined to compel "foreigners" (i.e., those from outside the city) to purchase the freedom, and thus was much less concerned with recruiting freemen from the sons of freemen. See Dobson, "Admission to the Freedom," 14.
64. Dobson, "Admission to the Freedom," 2–8.
65. A "lorimer" is a maker of horse gear.
66. TNA PRO JUST 2/219. This particular roll stands out from others in that the coroners identified specifically the occupations of a minority of jurors.
67. Dobson, "Admission to the Freedom," p. 2.
68. D.M. Palliser offers a useful summary of the various attempts at population estimates for the late medieval city. See his *Tudor York* (Oxford: Oxford UP, 1979), pp. 201–3.
69. There were actually 1,003 jurors; however, eighteen names were unreadable, and thus they have been omitted from this study. This figure does not take into account repeat appearances by the same juror.
70. Many of the jurors whose occupations are not represented in these figures remain unrepresented because their names were too common. For example,

"William of Burton" appears four times in the poll tax records: as a cordwainer (v. 3, p. 146), as a laborer (v. 3, p. 148), as a smith (v. 3, p. 148), and as a mercer (v. 3, p. 151). There is no way to determine which William of Burton served on the death of William de Conton (Compton?), an armorer, who died in June of 1376 (TNA PRO JUST 2/219, m. 12).

71. R.A. McKinley, *A History of British Surnames* (New York: Longman, 1990), p. 22.
72. TNA PRO JUST 2/219, m. 3, homicide of Robert Teghler; m. 3, homicide of Simon of Leeds, cordwainer of York; m. 4, homicide of John Baret, cooper of York; m. 9, death by misadventure of Matilda, wife of Robert of Goldsborough, cartwright; m. 9, homicide of Rachingald Stark.
73. A "cordwainer" made shoes for a living.
74. Heather Swanson, "The Illusion of Economic Structure: Craft Guilds in Late Medieval English Towns," *P&P* 121 (1988): 32.
75. Heather Swanson, "Craftsmen and Industry in Late Medieval York," (Ph.D. Diss., York, 1980), p. 435.
76. This rule was in place throughout most of the medieval period, with the exception of a period of roughly eight years. The Provisions of Westminster in 1259 indicated that it was not necessary for everyone to attend an inquest. See "Provisions of Westminster," 43 Hen. III, c. 24 (1259); *SR*, v. 1, p. 11. However, the Statute of Marlborough in 1267 reinstituted the attendance requirement for all males over the age of twelve. See "Statute of Marlborough," 52 Hen. III, c. 24 (1267); *SR*, v. 1, p. 25.
77. McLane, "Juror Attitudes toward Local Disorder," p. 42.
78. Simon Walker, "Order and Law," in *A Social History of England*, p. 109.
79. Marjorie K. McIntosh, *Controlling Misbehavior in England, 1370–1600* (Cambridge: Cambridge UP, 2002).
80. Pollock and Maitland, *A History of English Law*, v. 2, p. 624.
81. TNA PRO JUST 2/219, m. 1.
82. TNA PRO JUST 2/219, m. 4.
83. TNA PRO JUST 2/219, m. 4. Similarly, when Richard Ithon, a mariner, died in December 1368, the coroners empanelled three mariners and a fishmonger on his jury. TNA PRO JUST 2/219, m. 5.
84. Carol Loar, "Medical Knowledge and the Early Modern English Coroner's Inquest," *SHoM* 23.3 (2010): 484.
85. Walker, "Order and Law," p. 107.
86. S.H. Rigby, "Introduction: Social Structure and Economic Change in Late Medieval England," in Horrox and Ormrod, *A Social History of England*, p. 7.
87. How representative is the York sample? Given the more violent tenor of the medieval north, engendered by the continual state of war and the profusion of cross-border crime, the city's need for stability through hierarchy may have been a greater priority than elsewhere in England. See Cynthia J. Neville, *Violence, Custom and Law: The Anglo-Scottish Border Lands in the Later Middle Ages* (Edinburgh: Edinburgh UP, 1998). However, as the rash of recent research on late medieval social control would seem to imply, the concern for stability and a firm reassertion of the social hierarchy was a pan-English concern. Among others, see: McIntosh, *Controlling Misbehavior*; Judith M. Bennett, "Compulsory Service in Late Medieval England," *P&P* 209.1 (2010): 7–51; Maria G. Muzzarelli, "Reconciling the Privilege of a Few with the Common Good: Sumptuary Laws in Medieval and Early Modern Europe," *JMEMS* 39.3 (2009): 597–617; Miriamne A. Krummel, "Getting Even: Social Control and Uneasy Laughter in *The Play of the Sacrament*," in *Medieval English Comedy*, ed. Sandra M. Hordis and Paul Hardwick (Turnhout: Brepols, 2007), pp. 171–94; Robert C. Palmer, *English Law in the Age of the Black*

Death, 1348–1381: A Transformation of Governance and Law (Chapel Hill, NC: University of North Carolina Press, 2001); Barbara A. Hanawalt, "Good Governance in the Medieval and Early Modern Context," *JBS* 37 (1998): 246–57.

88. For a few examples: John Clerk served on the coroner's jury for the inquest into the death of Richard, son of Robert Brounnyng, in July 1388 at Middlesex (TNA PRO JUST 2/97B, m. 1); another John Clerk appeared as a juror in the inquest into the death of a stranger in December of 1362 at Norfolk (TNA PRO JUST 2/104, m. 7d); John Clerk and Ralph Clerk both served as jurors on the inquest into the death of William Wyroll in August of 1390 at Nottingham (TNA PRO JUST 2/124, m. 2d). There are many other examples.
89. A couple of examples: William le Clerk served as an inquest juror in the death of Lucy Hayhed in the summer of 1366 at Southamptonshire (TNA PRO JUST 2/153, m. 4). John le Clerk was a juror in the death of William Whight in the spring of 1385 at Staffordshire (TNA PRO JUST 2/161, m. 2).
90. In focusing on by-names, I have chosen to follow the lead of Talbot and Hammond, who comfortably designate as medical practitioners men whose names are John the Leech or John Barber. See C.H. Talbot and E.A. Hammond, *The Medical Practitioners in Medieval England* (London: Wellcome Historical Medical Library, 1965).
91. Sharpe, *Calendar of Coroners' Rolls*, p. 251. Nigel Ramsay comments on the difficulty of determining exactly what is meant by the term "clerk" at the end of the medieval period. See his "Scriveners and Notaries as Legal Intermediaries in Later Medieval England," in *Enterprise and Individuals in Fifteenth-Century England*, ed. Jenny Kermode (Gloucester: Sutton, 1991), p. 118.
92. TNA PRO JUST 2/195, m. 14.
93. Richard Prest served as a juror in the death of William Melleward in 1389 at Staffordshire (TNA PRO JUST 2/164, m. 7). John le Preest served as a juror in the homicide of William le Frensh in July of 1349 at Wiltshire (TNA PRO JUST 2/195, m. 5). Nicholas Parson was selected for jury duty in the death of John Vexe in November of 1389 at Southamptonshire (TNA PRO JUST 2/155, m. 16). Robert Chapeleyn served as a juror in the death of John Brerehirst in December of 1395 at Staffordshire (TNA PRO JUST 2/165, m. 3).
94. Sharpe, *Calendar of Coroners' Rolls*, p. 149.
95. Sharpe, *Calendar of Coroners' Rolls*, p. 60.
96. Rosemary Pattenden, "The Exclusion of the Clergy from Criminal Trial Juries: An Historical Perspective," *Ecclesiastical Law Journal* 5.24 (1999): 151–63.
97. See B. McNab, "Obligations of the Church in English Society: Military Arrays of the Clergy 1369–1418," in *Order and Innovation in the Middle Ages: Essays in Honor of Joseph R. Strayer*, ed. W.C. Jordan, *et al.* (Princeton: Princeton UP, 1976), pp. 293–314; Daniel Gerrard, "The Military Activities of Bishops, Abbots and Other Clergy in England c. 900–1200," (Ph.D. Diss., University of Glasgow, 2011).
98. F.M. Nichols, ed., *Britton: The French Text Revised with an English Translation*, 2 vols. (Oxford: Clarendon Press, 1865), v. 1, p. 347.
99. Pattenden, "Exclusion of the Clergy," 159.
100. Ralph V. Turner, "Clerical Judges in English Secular Courts: The Ideal versus the Reality," *Medievalia et Humanistica*, n.s. 3 (1972), 75.
101. Turner, "Clerical Judges," 93*n*.
102. *List of Sheriffs for England and Wales From the Earliest Times to A.D. 1831, Compiled from Documents in the Public Record Office* (London: HMSO, 1898; repr. New York, 1963), pp. 144, 127.
103. *List of Sheriffs*, p. 78.
104. *List of Sheriffs*, p. 102.

105. *List of Sheriffs*, p. 107. Women also sometimes filled the office of sheriff. See Louise Wilkinson, "Women as Sheriffs in Early Thirteenth Century England," in *English Government in the Thirteenth Century*, ed. A. Jobson (Woodbridge: Boydell, 2004), pp. 111–24.
106. Ormrod, "Politics of Pestilence," p. 151.
107. In fact, because chancery petitions are typically undated, the Public Record Office uses those addresses as a means to construct a chronology.
108. The Council of Westminster issued a prohibition in 1175; in 1239, Bishop Robert Grosseteste of Lincoln issued yet another statute. Turner, "Clerical Judges," 78–79.
109. Turner, "Clerical Judges," 75.
110. Daniel Thiery, "Welcome to the Parish. Remove Your Cap and Stop Assaulting Your Neighbor," in *Reputation and Representation in Fifteenth-Century Europe*, ed. Douglas Biggs, Sharon D. Michalove, and Compton Reeves (Leiden: Brill, 2004), pp. 241–42.
111. P.J.P. Goldberg, "'I Know What You Did Last Summer': Knowledge and Power among Parochial Clergy in Later Medieval England," in *Aspects of Power and Authority in the Middle Ages*, ed. Brenda Bolton and Christine E. Meek (Turnhout: Brepols, 2007), p. 195.
112. Goldberg, "I Know What You Did," p. 194.
113. Goldberg, "I Know What You Did," p. 194.
114. Goldberg, "I Know What You Did," pp. 190, 193.
115. The first legislation to defend the seal of confession dates back to the Council of Durham in 1220. See David Wilkins, ed., *Concilia Magnae Brittaniae et Hiberniae*, v. 1 (London: R. Gosling, 1734), pp. 577, 595.
116. William Lyndwood, *Provinciale (seu Constitutiones Angliae)* (Oxford: H. Hall, 1679), p. 334, gloss "q." The translation and punctuation are my own.
117. Lyndwood, *Provinciale*, p. 334, gloss "n."
118. Lyndwood, *Provinciale*, p. 334, gloss "q."
119. The 1131 Council of Rheims forbade priests and monks from attending public lectures on medicine; the 1163 Council of Tours banned clergy from undertaking surgery; finally, the Fourth Lateran Council of 1215 prohibited clergy from the practice of surgery. R. Theodore Beck, *The Cutting Edge: The Early History of the Surgeons of London* (London: Lund Humphries, 1974), pp. 7–8.
120. Faye Getz, *Medicine in the English Middle Ages* (Princeton: Princeton UP, 1998), p. 330.
121. Paul Halsall, ed., "Twelfth Ecumenical Council: Lateran IV 1215," *Internet History Sourcebook* (New York: Fordham University, 1996), www.fordham.edu/halsall/basis/lateran4.asp. Accessed April 3, 2013.
122. Carole Rawcliffe, *Leprosy in Medieval England* (Woodbridge: Boydell, 2006), p. 184.
123. Margaret Pelling, "Knowledge Common and Acquired: The Education of Unlicensed Medical Practitioners in Early Modern London," in *The History of Medical Education in Britain*, ed. Vivian Nutton and Roy Porter (Amsterdam: Rodopi, 1995), p. 253.
124. John H. Langbein, "Historical Foundations of the Law of Evidence: A View from the Ryder Sources," *Columbia Law Review* 96 (1996): 1170.
125. Mike McNair, "Vicinage and the Antecedents of the Jury," *L&HR* 17 (1999): 589.
126. Daniel Klerman, "Was the Jury Ever Self-Informing?," *Southern California Law Review* 77.123 (2004): 127.
127. *Bracton*, v. 2, p. 405.
128. Anthony J. Musson, "Twelve Good Men and True? The Character of Early Fourteenth-Century Juries," *L&HR* 15.1 (1997): 127.

129. Edward Powell, "Jury Trial at Gaol Delivery," in Green and Cockburn, *Twelve Good Men and True*, p. 91.
130. Musson, *Public Order and Law Enforcement*, p. 191.
131. DeWindt, "Local Government," 647–48.
132. Larson, "Village Voice," 685; J.G. Bellamy, *The Criminal Trial in Later Medieval England: Felony before the Courts from Edward I to the Sixteenth Century* (Toronto and Buffalo: University of Toronto Press, 1998), p. 104.
133. Bellamy, *Criminal Trial*, p. 115.
134. TNA PRO JUST 2/250, m. 1.
135. TNA PRO JUST 2/225, m. 14d.
136. Philip Lloyd, "The Coroners of Leicestershire in the Early Fourteenth Century," *Transactions of the Leicestershire Archaeological and Historical Society* 56 (1980–81): 21.
137. See the Introduction. Helen Brock and Catherine Crawford, "Forensic Medicine in Early Colonial Maryland, 1633–83," in *Legal Medicine in History*, ed. Michael Clark and Catherine Crawford (Cambridge: Cambridge UP, 1994), pp. 40–41.
138. See the Introduction.
139. Lisi Oliver, *The Body Legal in Barbarian Law* (Toronto and Buffalo: University of Toronto Press, 2011), p. 42.
140. Mary Richards, "The Body as Text in Early Anglo-Saxon Law," in *Naked Before God: Uncovering the Body in Anglo-Saxon England*, ed. Benjamin C. Withers and Jonathan Wilcox (Morgantown: West Virginia UP, 2003), pp. 97–115.
141. For more on this subject, see Lisi Oliver, "Sick-Maintenance in Anglo-Saxon Law," *The Journal of English and Germanic Philology* 107.3 (2008): 303–26.
142. George K. Behlmer, "Grave Doubts: Victorian Medicine, Moral Panic, and the Signs of Death," *JBS* 42.2 (2003): 206–35.
143. After the 1540 convergence of the barbers and surgeons into one company, the crown regularly granted them permission to perform public autopsies on the corpses of hanged felons. John Stow reported an incident from the year 1587 that is both alarming and amusing at the same time. Apparently, while they were preparing one of the corpses for dissection, the felon revived, causing the company to institute new rules concerning what to do when the felon "shall revive or come to life again, as of late hath been seen." As cited in K.J. Kesselring, "Detecting 'Death Disguised,'" *History Today* 56.4 (2006): 26.
144. Danae Tankard, "Defining Death in Early Tudor England," *Cultural and Social History* 3 (2006): 18.
145. C.M. Woolgar, *The Senses in Late Medieval England* (New Haven: Yale UP, 2006), p. 8.
146. Jon Arrizabalaga, "Medical Causes of Death in Preindustrial Europe: Some Historiographical Considerations," *JHMAS* 54 (1999): 246.
147. For example, a Norwich man named Walter Eye who was hanged in the year 1284 revived after he was taken down and fled to the church. He later received a pardon from the king. See William Hudson and John C. Tingey, eds., *The Records of the City of Norwich*, 2 vols. (Norwich: Jarrold & Sons, 1906–1910), v. 1, p. 214.
148. Arrizabalaga, "Medical Causes of Death," 246.
149. Siegfried Wenzel, ed., *Fasciculus Morum: A Fourteenth-Century Preacher's Handbook* (University Park: Pennsylvania State UP, 1989), p. 721.
150. Sharpe, *Calendar of Coroners' Rolls*, pp. 96–97.
151. TNA PRO JUST 2/128, m. 1.
152. TNA PRO JUST 2/123, m. 1.
153. TNA PRO JUST 2/123, m. 1.

154. TNA PRO JUST 2/123, m. 2.
155. TNA PRO JUST 2/125, m. 6.
156. For example, see the death of Thomas Hickecok, TNA PRO JUST 2/138, m. 1; death of John, son of Thomas le Wewe, of Hornington, TNA PRO JUST 2/130, m. 1d; death of William, son of John Ike Holdere, of Wroxton, TNA PRO JUST 2/130, m. 1; death of Agnes de Gydygrete, TNA PRO JUST 2/155, m. 7d; death of Adam Chapman, TNA PRO JUST 2/183, m. 1; death of Juliana, daughter of Isolde, of Cranbourne, TNA PRO JUST 2/195, m. 1; death of William le Gee, TNA PRO JUST 2/195, m. 6d; death of Thomas Derby, TNA PRO JUST 2/195, m. 17. These are just a few examples.
157. H.E. Salter, ed., *Records of Mediaeval Oxford: Coroners' Inquests, the Walls of Oxford, etc.* (Oxford: Oxford Chronicle Co., Ltd., 1912), p. 28.
158. TNA PRO JUST 2/155, m. 8.
159. The National Archives offer several possible dates for the bill TNA PRO C 1/45/175: 1433–1443, or more likely 1467–1472. However, because the bill identifies John Clark as mayor of Oxford, it is possible to narrow this down to his 1468–1469 term of office.
160. TNA PRO C 1/45/175. For the purposes of accessibility, I modernized the spelling and inserted punctuation.
161. Oliver, *Body Legal*, p. 5. The miracle stories of St Thomas Becket offer a useful example. When Robert, son of Liviva, of Rochester fell into the river while playing with his friends, it was hours before his family found him. Without the assistance or instruction of a medical practitioner, the boy's rescuers had the forethought to hang him upside down by his feet and secure his mouth open with an iron bolt in order to facilitate the expulsion of water from his lungs. When this approach failed, they instead spun him in a trough, hoping to make him vomit. Finally, with the assistance of St Thomas Becket, the boy vomited up the water and was restored to life. See Benedict of Peterborough, *Miracula Sancti Thomae Cantuariensis*, in *Materials for the History of Thomas Becket*, ed. James Craigie Robertson (Rolls Series, no. 67, v. 2, 1876), p. 226. The creativity of this approach (and there are several other examples of this nature among the miracles of St Thomas Becket) tells us that the average person had a good understanding of anatomy and was prepared to address common medical problems.
162. Getz, *Medicine in the English Middle Ages*, p. 5.
163. R. Theodore Beck argues that "until the latter part of the eighteenth century it was virtually impossible for the individual to gain a respectable financial position by surgery alone." See his, *Cutting Edge*, p. 121.
164. Pelling, "Knowledge Common and Acquired, p. 257.
165. Penelope Hunting, *A History of the Society of Apothecaries* (London: The Society of Apothecaries, 1998), pp. 14–15.
166. Robert S. Gottfried, *Doctors and Medicine in Medieval England 1340–1530* (Princeton: Princeton UP, 1986), p. 46. In Norwich, the barbers and chandlers not only marched together behind one banner in the annual *Corpus Christi* procession, they also shared a guild. See Carole Rawcliffe, "Sickness and Health," in *Medieval Norwich*, ed. Rawcliffe and Richard Wilson (London and New York: Hambledon, 2004), p. 322.
167. Philip Stell, "Medical Practice in Medieval York," *BIHR* 90 (1996): 13.
168. Getz, *Medicine in the English Middle Ages*, p. 8.
169. Carole Rawcliffe, "Sickness and Health," in *Medieval Norwich*, ed. Carole Rawcliffe and Richard Wilson (London: Hambledon, 2004), p. 320.
170. "Statute Concerning Diet and Apparel," 37 Edw. III, c. 6 (1363–1364); *SR*, v. 1, pp. 379–80. Swanson, "Illusion of Economic Structure," 29–48.

171. Sylvia Thrupp, *The Merchant Class of Medieval London [1300–1500]* (Chicago: University of Chicago Press, 1948), p. 93.
172. Swanson, "Illusion of Economic Structure," 37.
173. Sharpe, *Calendar of Coroners' Rolls*, pp. 19–20.
174. In this respect, the size of London's population is a distinct problem. I tried to match jurors' names to occupations through the Letter-Books, but there were too many people with the same names to inspire any confidence in the results.
175. These figures are based on Sharpe's *Calendar of Coroners' Rolls* for rolls E, F, G, and H. Please note that when I say "sixty-nine medical practitioners," I am counting appearances, rather than people. Some of those appearances are by the same practitioner.
176. Lindsay Prior, *The Social Organization of Death: Medical Discourse and Social Practices in Belfast* (New York: St Martin's, 1989), pp. 33, 45.
177. Guido Ruggiero, "The Cooperation of Physicians and the State in the Control of Violence in Renaissance Venice," *JHMAS* 33 (1978): 160.
178. Lindsay Prior and Mick Bloor, "Why People Die: Social Representations of Death and Its Causes," *Science as Culture* 3.3 (1993): 366.
179. Prior and Bloor, "Why People Die," 371.
180. Department for Constitutional Affairs, "Coroners Service Reform Briefing Note," (February 2006), p. 6, webarchive.nationalarchives.gov.uk/+/http://www.dca.gov.uk/corbur/reform_coroner_system.pdf. Accessed Dec. 18, 2013.
181. "The Changing Profile of Autopsied Deaths in the United States, 1972–2007," *National Center for Health Statistics Data Brief* (August 2011), www.cdc.gov/nchs/data/databriefs/db67.pdf. Accessed Nov. 27, 2012. These rates represent a significant decline over the course of the twentieth century. See K.G. Shojania and E.C. Burton, "The Vanishing Nonforensic Autopsy," *New England Journal of Medicine* 358.9 (February 28, 2008): 873–75.
182. Beck, *Cutting Edge*, p. 79.
183. Gottfried, *Doctors and Medicine*, p. 22.
184. Margaret Pelling, "Politics, Medicine and Masculinity: Physicians and Office-bearing in Early Modern England," in *The Practice of Reform in Health, Medicine and Science, 1500–2000: Essays for Charles Webster*, ed. Pelling and Scott Mandelbrote (Aldershot: Ashgate, 2005), p. 85.
185. Margaret Pelling, *Medical Conflicts in Early Modern London: Patronage, Physicians and Irregular Practitioners 1550–1640* (Oxford: Clarendon Press, 2003), p. 18.
186. Bryon Grigsby, "The Social Position of the Surgeon in London, 1350–1450," *Essays in Medieval Studies* 13 (1996): 74.
187. Pelling, "Politics, Medicine and Masculinity," pp. 81–106.
188. Peter Murray Jones, "Witnesses to Medieval Medical Practice in the Harley Collection," *Electronic British Library Journal* (2008): 4–6.
189. Talbot and Hammond, *Medical Practitioners in Medieval England*, pp. 387–88.
190. Beck, *Cutting Edge*, p. 81.
191. Ruggiero, "Cooperation of Physicians," 159.
192. Thomas Vicary, *The Anatomie of the Bodie of Man*, pt. 1 (London: Early English Texts Society, 1888), p. 214.
193. Carole Rawcliffe, *Medicine and Society in Later Medieval England* (London: Sandpiper Books, 1995), p. 112.
194. Piers D. Mitchell, *Medicine in the Crusades: Warfare, Wounds and the Medieval Surgeon* (Cambridge: Cambridge UP, 2004), p. 238.
195. Mitchell, *Medicine in the Crusades*, p. 180.

196. Lilla Vekerdy, "Paracelsus's *Great Wound Surgery*," in *Textual Healing: Essays on Medieval and Early Modern Medicine*, ed. Elizabeth Lane Furdell (Leiden: Brill, 2005), p. 84.
197. Sharpe, *Calendar of Coroners' Rolls*, rolls A, B, C, and D.
198. Faye Getz, ed., *Healing and Society in Medieval England: A Middle English Translation of the Pharmaceutical Writings of Gilbert Anglicus* (Madison: University of Wisconsin Press, 1991), p. xxiv.
199. Gottfried, *Doctors and Medicine*, p. 268.
200. TNA PRO JUST 2/219.
201. Rawcliffe, *Medicine and Society*, p. 134.
202. Stell, "Medical Practice in Medieval York," 8.
203. Rawcliffe, "Sickness and Health," p. 321.
204. Stell, "Medical Practice in Medieval York," 11.
205. Bellamy notes that this practice continued into the late Tudor period. See his *Criminal Trial*, p. 28.
206. Klerman, "Was the Jury Ever Self-Informing?," 128.
207. Klerman, "Was the Jury Ever Self-Informing?," 147.
208. Lesley Boatwright, ed., *Inquests and Indictments from Late Fourteenth Century Buckinghamshire* (Buckinghamshire Archaeological Society, v. 29, 1994), p. 45.
209. Here, it is critical to note that Richard Pede's experience is not unique. Among others, the 1351/52 inquest into the death of Alice Elyn of Ulrome (*Yorks.*) presents a similar dilemma. The coroner reported that Alice was lying infirm in bed, huddled close to the fire, at Ulrome in the home of Robert son of Emma (whose relationship to Alice is never identified) when a stray spark ignited the straw from her bed and the home went up in flames. Although Alice survived the fire, she was badly burned and lived only a few days after the incident. Robert, son of Emma, in whose house she died, served on the inquest jury. TNA PRO JUST 2/215, m. 44/1.
210. TNA PRO JUST 2/129, m. 1.
211. TNA PRO JUST 2/155, m. 6.
212. TNA PRO JUST 2/188, m. 4.
213. TNA PRO JUST 2/183, m. 1.
214. TNA PRO JUST 2/104, m. 25. Juries often empanelled the junior and senior members of men bearing the same name in a family (presumably brothers).
215. TNA PRO JUST 2/187, m. 1.
216. TNA PRO JUST 2/133, m. 4.
217. TNA PRO JUST 2/130, m. 1d.
218. Admittedly, because the coroner's inquest jury was made up of individuals drawn from the scene of the death, this greatly narrowed the available number of potential jurors. This is particularly relevant outside the urban environment. Yet, it seems like it should not have been that difficult to find twelve unrelated adult men.
219. This approach may also have been distinctly English. On the Continent, familial relationships were a greater concern for those who assumed the role of witness. In Marseille, for example, legislation prohibited parents, children, spouses, siblings, in-laws, aunts, uncles, nephews, and nieces from testifying on each other's behalf in criminal cases. See Susan Alice McDonough, *Witnesses, Neighbors, and Community in Late Medieval Marseille* (New York: Palgrave Macmillan, 2013), p. 32.
220. TNA PRO JUST 2/52, m. 6.
221. TNA PRO JUST 2/187, m. 2.
222. Sara M. Butler, "Degrees of Culpability: Suicide Verdicts, Mercy, and the Jury in Medieval England," *JMEMS* 36.2 (2006): 263–90.

223. TNA PRO JUST 2/18, m. 45.
224. Rab Houston, *Punishing the Dead?: Suicide, Lordship, and Community in Britain, 1500–1830* (Oxford: Oxford UP, 2010), p. 158.
225. Houston, *Punishing the Dead?*, pp. 158–59.
226. Houston, *Punishing the Dead?*, p. 156.
227. Pollock and Maitland, *A History of English Law*, v. 2, p. 472. To offer some examples: at the inquest into the death of Adam, son of Hugh, of Kercroft in 1365, jurors assessed the offending cart at half a mark (TNA PRO JUST 2/220, m. 8). At the inquest into the death of Alice of Bartleby in February of 1366/67, jurors assessed a cauldron at 6*d*. (TNA PRO JUST 2/222, m. 3d). In August of 1367, jurors at the inquest of Joanna, wife of Thomas Tailor, valued the cart and four horses that trampled her to death at £4 6*s*. 8*d*. (TNA PRO JUST 2/220, m. 6).
228. TNA PRO SC 8/15/736, 1334 petition from the Prior of the Hospital of St John outside the New Gate in Dublin, requesting grant of the deodands from his Irish lands to rebuild his church and granges after they were destroyed by the Scots, and to support the resident brothers, poor and sick; TNA PRO SC 8/172/8568, 1330 petition from the converted Jews of King's House of London, complaining that although the king had granted them all deodands in all of England's eyres to support rebuilding their chapel and buildings, as well as to provide for their sustenance, late chancellor, Henry de Bornhassh, had absconded with 200 marks from the eyre of Northampton; SC 8/88/4351, 1320 petition from the Prior and Convent of St Katherine near Waterford (Ireland), requesting the king to grant them the deodands for all of Ireland, as his father had done by letters patent.
229. Barbara A. Hanawalt observed that 41.7% of homicides in the coroners' rolls involved knives. See her *Crime and Conflict in English Communities, 1300–1348* (Cambridge, MA: Harvard UP, 1979), pp. 100, 302.
230. TNA PRO JUST 2/224, m. 6.
231. TNA PRO JUST 2/40, m. 4.
232. TNA PRO JUST 2/98, m. 4.
233. TNA PRO JUST 2/104, m. 44.
234. Theoretically, the king confiscated a felon's landed property for only a year and a day. However, moveable goods were permanently forfeit, and if the felon had fled at any point in the process, the landed property was also permanently forfeit. See K.J. Kesselring, "Felony Forfeiture in England, c. 1170–1870," *JLH* 30.3 (2009): 201–26.
235. This is Alexander Murray's description. See his *Suicide in the Middle Ages*, 2 vols. (Oxford: Oxford UP, 1998), v. 1, p. 384.
236. This is Bellamy's expression. See his *Criminal Trial*, p. 29. Communication between juries is a central argument of Bellamy's study, and he includes conviction rates to support this hypothesis.
237. England was not alone in its abhorrence of "notorious" crimes. In fact, drawing on Roman precedent, most European law courts were eager to see notorious crimes punished more harshly. See Sarah Rubin Blanshei, "Crime and Law Enforcement in Medieval Bologna," *Journal of Social History* 16.1 (1982): 125; Trevor Dean, *Crime in Medieval Europe 1200–1550* (Edinburgh: Pearson, 2001), p. 11.
238. Bellamy, *Criminal Trial*, p. 30.
239. Derek G. Neal, *The Masculine Self in Late Medieval England* (Chicago: University of Chicago Press, 2008), pp. 43–55.
240. TNA PRO KB 9/185, m. 1.
241. The subject of "premeditation" and what that term or others (such as "malice aforethought") meant in the medieval mindset is a subject that has been

discussed at great length and does not need to be revisited here. Please see: J.M. Kaye, "The Early History of Murder and Manslaughter. 2 pts," *Law Quarterly Review* 83.3 (1967): 365–95, and 83.4 (1967): 569–601; Thomas A. Green, *Verdict According to Conscience: Perspectives on the English Criminal Trial Jury, 1200–1800* (Chicago: University of Chicago Press, 1985), Chapter Two; Bellamy, *The Criminal Trial*, pp. 57–69.

242. Bellamy contends that "jury nullification" is a term without much meaning in this period, primarily because a consensus existed between layman and lawman alike that conviction rates should be low. See Bellamy, *Criminal Trial*, p. 14.

3 The Process of Investigation

Inquest records normally report the findings of coroners and their juries, not the process of discovery. This unevenness in documentation generates some complications with respect to this study. When enrollments do include particulars about the investigation, should we suppose the process was representative of a typical investigation? Or, was the coroner making note of a course of action that was exceptional? In general, this study treats the bountiful insight of those less plentiful, well-crafted coroners' enrollments as a windfall, presuming that any variation is the product of the documentation rather than the process. Inevitably, this approach risks normalizing the abnormal. Yet, at its worst, this strategy privileges the actions of the most diligent coroners, furnishing us with a sense of medieval detective work at its best. In attempting to reconstruct the typical death investigation, it is difficult to divorce ourselves entirely from modern expectations: nonetheless, as this chapter will impress, the medieval death investigator shared many concerns with his modern counterpart. For example: when a death was sudden and unnatural, scene integrity was also a priority in medieval inquests. Although coroners were aware that they were not the first to arrive at the scene of a death, they certainly wanted the body and its surroundings untouched as if they were. Coroners and their jurors astutely exploited all available evidence: the body, the scene itself, weapons (if applicable), and witness testimony wherever it was to be found.

Not only did medieval coroners share similar concerns with modern investigators, but their records also signal comparable pitfalls. Modern studies of death certification remind us that records of this nature must be approached with a suitable degree of vigilance. In determining cause of death, coroners and their juries engaged in the process of "assigning meaning to death."[1] Death, no matter what the pronouncement, is never free of subtext. In their study of the history of death certification, George Alter and Ann Carmichael note that "[a]s physicians became the agents of the state in reporting causes of death, they often had to balance the public's interests against the reputations of patients and families who could be stigmatized by certain diagnoses."[2] While Alter and Carmichael associate this development with the modern era, the sentiment rings true for many medieval enrollments. The most obvious instance in which external concerns might sway the verdict of a coroner's jury is in a case of suicide, described in the medieval context as *felo de se* ("felony of self"). The medieval church equated suicide with apostasy. Thus, all self-killers, much like Judas, were sinners of the worst kind. Not only was a suicide prohibited from church burial, but local tradition also prescribed desecration of the body and burial at the crossroads out of fears that the killer, who died before his time, might rise from the dead to harass the living.[3] While the family of the dead might have preferred a formal declaration of death by misadventure to avoid smearing the family's honor, the coroner had other interests to negotiate. Between them, the coroner and his jury had to cooperate in the forging of an enrollment that produced the best possible compromise between family honor and resources, communal safety, and safeguarding the king's profits. Suicide is the most clear-cut example of a death encumbered with social connotations. Yet, even natural death presented the coroner and his jury with similar problems. Medieval medicine held that diseases had both natural and divine origins. While physicians might explain the plague naturally as humors polluted by a miasma, they endorsed also the supernatural interpretation, which focused instead on the corrupt morality of the afflicted, chosen by God to suffer during life as well as after. Isidore of Seville affirms this in his *Canon of Medicine*: plague "arises from corrupt air, and by penetrating into the viscera settles there. Even though this disease often springs up from air-borne potencies, nevertheless it can never come about without the will of Almighty God."[4] As a divine reprimand for sin, medieval medicine coupled each disease with a corresponding sin. Bubonic plague was a punishment for usury, leprosy for lechery.[5] A coroner faced with a foul-smelling corpse riddled with buboes knew that he had a plague death on his hands: but he and his jury might have elected instead to play down the nature of the disease in the official documentation out of compassion for the family.

Conscious manipulation to avoid scandal is only one concern in analyzing coroners' reports. Determining cause of death inevitably means "fitting accounts of individual death into a cultural framework."[6] Certainly, religious interpretation and medical insight are both critical facets of that cultural framework. Social perceptions of death also play a considerable role. Today, science dominates our comprehension of death, dictating that death certificates shine the spotlight on pathology apart from social conditions (such as poverty or poor housing) or even health behaviors (such as cigarette smoking or poor diet). This was not the case in the Middle Ages.[7] Thus, medieval coroners' reports drew conclusions that do not fit with the modern conceptual framework of death. For example, when Stephen Gagnebald of Norfolkshire suddenly fell dead at the age of ninety in 1360, his enrollment confidently declared joint causes of death: poverty and old age.[8] A modern certificate for a similar death undoubtedly would read much differently:

1. Immediate cause of death: myocardial infarcation (*heart attack*)
2. Intermediate cause of death: myocardial degeneration of heart muscles
3. Underlying cause of death: inanition (*starvation*)

While the modern certification presents a more accurate story of physical death, it tells us little about the life that led up to this final moment. For the social historian, this discrepancy in perception between eras is a boon. The record of Stephen's death furnishes a wealth of information for the historian hoping to illuminate contemporary knowledge of the impact and distribution of poverty. Conversely, for the medical historian hoping to track rates of disease, this approach is an impenetrable barrier. All of this needs to be taken into consideration when approaching the medieval records.

Coroners and their juries had very set objectives when initiating an investigation. Unearthing the evidence to support those goals, however, was not always as easy as one hoped. The inquest relied heavily on two distinct forms of evidence. Physical evidence, that is the body and the visne (the location where the death occurred), assumed pride of place in the investigation. Examination of the body, in particular, spoke volumes to coroners and their jurors about the nature of the death. While the scholarship has often scoffed at the rudimentary quality of the medieval post-mortem examination, the documentation reveals that they adopted a proto-scientific approach to the process. Testimonial evidence of various kinds also played a critical role: witness depositions, confessions, even dying declarations. Procedurally, it is important to recognize that when death investigation ground to a halt because of insufficient evidence, the solution was not necessarily to give up. Sometimes jurors requested the inquest be adjourned while they gathered more information. At times, coroners looked farther afield by seeking out the testimony of a broader range of informants. Inevitably, not all deaths were treated equally. The scanty documentation in deaths of a noncontroversial nature strongly imply that both coroners and communities were much less concerned to perform a thorough investigation when they believed they already knew what had happened.

GOALS OF THE INVESTIGATION

A survey of the most complete enrollments show us that medieval England's death investigators ideally hoped to uncover the following information:

a) Name, age, residence, and occupation of the dead.
b) Name, residence, and occupation of the perpetrator (if applicable).
c) A jury list, including the names of the four nearest vills.
d) Nature of the death, including a chronology of events (and in the case of a felony, the motive, if discernible), as well as all participants.
e) Date, estimated time, and location of death. Date and location of inquest.
f) If a homicide or suicide: precise location of the wounds on the body as well as their dimensions (length, width, depth); identification of the weapon used to create those wounds; assessment of the value of the weapon.

g) Chronology of death, including date of demise and conditions (for example; after an assault, did the victim die immediately, or languish for some time before the death? Did he receive last rites?)
h) If there was a perpetrator: what happened to him after the crime (Did he flee? If so, where? Was he arrested and imprisoned, and if so, in which prison?)
i) Financials:
    1) If there was a perpetrator, an assessment of the value of the goods and properties of the perpetrator; plus a statement as to who was responsible for those properties.
    2) If it was a death by misadventure, was a deodand involved? If so, how much was it worth? And, who was responsible for making sure that money was paid to the king?
    3) A list of any amercements for infringement of process (undervaluing goods and chattels; failing to appear; failing to raise the hue and cry, etc.).
j) List of the names of:
    1) coroner(s) (and any other law enforcement officials involved).
    2) first finder (and did he raise the hue and cry?).
    3) four nearest neighbors.
    4) pledges for first finder and nearest neighbors.
    5) witnesses (if there were any), as well as a verdict on whether those witnesses should be suspected for involvement.
    6) accomplices (including anyone who might have harbored the felon).

Again, this is a composite drawn from the most complete enrollments, and thus it represents the ideal from the historian's perspective, if not the coroner's. The vast majority of enrollments were not this meticulous or even close to it. For example, only the most industrious of coroners reported the age of the dead, and ages tended to be estimations at best ("he was twenty years or more"). In general, medieval methods of time measurement were far less precise than they are today. Coroners noted dates in terms of their proximity to feast days: that is, "the Tuesday closest following the Decollation of Saint John the Baptist." Years tended to be recorded in relation to the reigning monarch: "the forty-third year of the reign of King Edward the Third since the Conquest." Communities measured hours in a wide variety of ways. Most popularly they adhered to the Christian prayer schedule: matins (sunrise), prime (first hour of daylight), terce (third hour), sext (sixth hour), vespers (end of the day), compline (bedtime), vigils (during the night). Some enrollments judged according to the position of the sun in the sky: dawn, noon, twilight, sunset, night. In urban contexts curfew was a useful measure of time; in both urban and rural settings cockcrow (such as, *ante galli cantum*) was a popular gauge. This approach to measuring time reminds us that the medieval world was far less compulsive about exactitude than we are today. In fact, J.B. Post goes so far as to suggest that clerks working for the medieval courts had a "contempt for precision."[9] He writes

> [a]bove all, it is important to remember that in the great majority of cases the specific details did not matter to the writer: the court was sitting to decide whether or not an individual then present should be hanged, amerced, or set free, and if that could be done satisfactorily without establishing all his aliases or his true place of residence, then so it was.[10]

This approach to documentation is evident also in descriptions of unknown perpetrators in homicide inquests. Investigators today take this information to heart, recording a full physical description (estimated height, weight, hair color, eye color, distinguishing features, and so forth) and in high-profile cases even employing a forensic artist to sketch a portrait based on the testimony of eyewitnesses. Medieval coroners were much more lax in their approach. Occasionally, they identified a suspect according to gender, age ("unknown young man"), occupation ("a certain boatman, name unknown") or distinguishing features ("a certain unknown woman carrying a child in her arms"). Yet, in general, they were quite comfortable referring to a homicide suspect in the vaguest terms imaginable, as an "unknown evil-doer," or an "unknown man." Once again, this lack of meticulousness results from the purpose of the documentation. The law did not instruct the coroner to append a physical description of the perpetrator to his enrollment of a crime, nor would such an addition in the coroners' rolls have achieved any specific goal. Rather, it was appropriate to reserve physical descriptions of accused felons for public proclamations in the marketplace. Although there are no surviving written records of public proclamations, James Masschaele has stumbled across two pertinent notations in which officials mandated marketplace announcements in the hopes of turning up evidence concerning a crime or locating a criminal. William Greenfield, the Archbishop of York from 1306 to 1315, ordered public decrees in a number of churches and markets around Lancashire, eager to unearth information about a cleric accused of theft.[11] A 1325 Cambridge borough roll notes payment to a town crier for publication of a recent theft of oxen in order to procure more information that might lead to an arrest.[12] Without doubt, the marketplace was the more logical venue to disseminate a physical description of a perpetrator than in an enrollment buried in a coroner's roll.

All of this reminds us that we should not model our expectations of the records for death investigation on modern precedents. Medieval documentation fulfilled different purposes and their expectations for precision varied widely from ours. More important still, the completeness of the documentation has little bearing on the competency of the investigation.

RULES OF EVIDENCE

In accidental deaths or deaths by disease, the coroner's inquest produced a verdict that brought the investigation to its conclusion: while the coroner might mandate the filling of a well or the confiscation of a pig, no further legal action was required beyond the inquest. Homicide investigations, which formed the vast majority of the cases in the coroners' rolls, were of a different variety altogether. Inquests relating to homicide produced an indictment; the resulting trial was subject to England's rules of evidence. Thus, in order to assess the rigor of medieval homicide investigation, it is critical first to understand what kind of evidence the crown considered sufficient to indict a man for homicide.

A formal law of evidence did not emerge in English common law until relatively recently. Its origins can be located in the eighteenth century, although even a rough date of universal implementation is still up for debate.[13] Nevertheless, it would be misleading to argue that the medieval English did not endorse, if less formally, rules of evidence to guide them in their deliberations. *Bracton* pinpoints two particular forms of evidence. First, *Bracton* underscores the centrality of material evidence by addressing the thief caught with the proceeds of the theft on his body, what the English call the "hand-having thief."[14] In terms of homicide, if the perpetrator had stolen goods from his victim, or he was found "still holding the gory knife," the coroner and his jurors presumed his guilt.[15] Second, the great emphasis placed on interviews throughout the legal treatises reveals the critical role played by testimony. Obviously, testimony can assume multiple forms. *Bracton* allows for the possibility of the perpetrator's testimony through a confession of guilt. Yet the distinct repugnance exuded by the treatise toward approvers leaves the impression that *Bracton* believed only a desperate liar would pursue this route.[16] More commonly, *Bracton* and other legal commentators looked elsewhere for testimony, implementing the Biblically inspired two-witness rule.[17] The *Mirror* expresses  the centrality of two witnesses to convict as a fact: "according to the word of God, two proper witnesses are sufficient," although regrettably nowhere does the treatise elaborate on the criteria for weeding out the improper witnesses from the proper ones.[18] There is good reason to believe that *Bracton* and the *Mirror* were referring specifically to eyewitnesses. The legal treatise commonly attributed to England's Chief Justiciar Ranulf de Glanvill—while it predates the coroner, it did not predate law enforcement—speaks to the importance of interviewing the "suitable witness," that is, one "who heard and saw the facts."[19] Regrettably, the English legal tradition tells us little else. Without any further elaboration, it is difficult to discern how they defined a proper witness in terms of status, education, occupation, gender, etc., or if any other kinds of evidence were necessarily admissible.

While English authorities were less than forthcoming concerning evidentiary requirements, Continental and canon law had much to say on the subject. Both legal systems approved as well the two-witness rule, chiefly because so many scriptural passages support this model. Biblical inspiration, in general, was responsible for much of the thirteenth century's procedural innovations within the two systems of law. For example, while it was the rediscovery of Roman law that prompted legal thinkers to promote a judicial process that included a court summons and a timely judgment, their reasoning was founded not on Roman, but on Biblical precedent. This is the process modeled by the trial of the first transgressor. Johannes Monachus explained that, "God could not condemn Adam without a trial because even God must presume that Adam was innocent until proven guilty."[20] Lawyers on the Continent adopted a much more stringent approach to evidentiary forms. Suitable proofs might take the form of: 1) the free confession of guilt by the accused, 2) the sworn testimony of two credible eyewitnesses, 3) evidence in two "authentic" documents, or 4) a combination of written and oral proofs.[21] Gratian expanded the idea even further to incorporate public notoriety. The *Decretum* maintained that full proof might constitute one witness (thus, a half-proof) together with the community's general belief in the perpetrator's guilt (another half-proof; jointly the two half-proofs constitute one full proof).[22] The *ius commune* also construed witnesses in a very narrow perspective. They must testify to events that they had experienced with the five senses, an elaborate formula for stipulating firsthand knowledge. [23]

If England shared the Continent's esteem for Biblical precedent, and both sanctioned the two-witness rule because of it, is it fair to assume that English law shared other aspects of the *ius commune*'s law of evidence? Again, it is hard to ignore the fact that many of England's royal justices, at least in the formative period, were trained in both the *ius commune* and canon law and may have brought their expectations of the law to England's criminal justice system. Did the English judiciary also insist that a defendant might only be convicted with proof "as clear as the light of day"?[24] Did the English embrace the canonical maxim "it is better to let the guilty go unpunished than to punish the innocent"?[25] Indeed, the fifteenth-century Lord Chief Justice of England and Wales, John Fortescue, also the author of a well-known legal treatise, echoed this thought. In extolling the virtues of England's criminal justice system, he wrote, "I should . . . prefer twenty guilty men to escape death through mercy, than one innocent to be condemned unjustly."[26] Admittedly, in the absence of evidence either way, it is hard to draw any firm conclusions, but the Continental sources provide a useful baseline for our expectations. It is critical to acknowledge, however, that the medieval rules of evidence generally were more stringent than modern expectations. As Richard Fraher argues, "[t]o the modern western mind, proof beyond a reasonable doubt is readily seen as a product of inferences drawn from circumstantial evidence."[27] To offer an example: a man is seen entering a room where another man is later found stabbed to death. After an interval, he is seen leaving that room, knife in hand. In all likelihood, a modern jury sitting in judgment upon this case would convict him, believing that enough circumstantial evidence existed to connect him to the crime. However, a medieval jury would be forced to admit that there was not enough solid proof to connect the dots.

All of these queries bring us back to the role of the jury. Once again, the work of Sir John Fortescue offers some insight. His praise for the English jury was founded on the scriptural two-witness rule. If the Bible recommended two witnesses, then how much better must it be that the English required twelve?[28] Here we need to remind ourselves that not all witnesses are equal. While Biblical authors had eyewitnesses in mind, medieval jurors rarely possessed such intimate knowledge of the deed. Moreover, while they swore to tell the truth, their oath did not guarantee the factual truth modern testimony implies. As Richard Firth Green reminds us, "trowthe" in medieval England meant many things: loyalty, good faith, even honor. Thus, when a juror swore to tell the truth, he was referring less to an "approximation of the 'facts,'" than to "an 'ethical truth' based in social consensus."[29]

A greater awareness of the medieval perception of truth is critical to our understanding of the medieval jury and its role in the legal process. Legal historians have long recognized that juries mitigated the severity of the common law by embracing legal fiction. As Milsom so eloquently put it, "jurors made unacceptable rules produce acceptable results by adjusting the facts."[30] Similarly, Thomas A. Green argues that jurors "remained free to say the 'truth' as they knew it."[31] Both Milsom and Green see deliberate prevarication in order to enforce a communal morality at odds with the king's law. However, Firth Green contends that historians are focusing on the wrong truth: medieval law endorsed a "trial of the trouthe of the man [that is, his honor] not the truth of the accusations made against him."[32] In terms of homicide, medieval jurors effectively discerned the honorable from the dishonorable killing. Rather than sentencing all killers to death as the common law would lead us to expect, medieval jurors believed that only dishonorable killers should bear the full weight of the law: honorable killers should be acquitted. Firth Green expresses the sentiment best when he writes of the "(no doubt apocryphal) Australian jury that is said to have found a local sheep-stealer 'not guilty, so long as he returns the sheep.'"[33]

What impact does any of this have on the way we see the coroner's inquest? All of this reminds us that coroners' juries did abide by rules of evidence, even if we are not entirely clear on the extent of those rules. Both physical and testimonial evidence played a large part in the investigative process. However, as historians, we need to be aware that the "truth" recorded in the coroners' enrollments may sometimes reflect an ethical rather than a factual truth.

PHYSICAL EVIDENCE: A) THE DEATH SCENE

Today, if foul play is suspected, maintaining the integrity of the scene of death is a fundamental aspect of any death investigation. Police officers immediately cordon off the area from public traffic, detectives and technicians don latex gloves before disturbing the physical environment, and technicians are cautious in removing and preserving pertinent material evidence in paper bags for laboratory analysis.[34] Not surprisingly, the medieval coroner did not share all the same concerns. Medieval English trials did not include an examination of material evidence[35]—this was pertinent *only* to coroners' juries. Thus, coroners had no responsibility to preserve physical evidence, and without the use of modern technologies there were plainly fewer apprehensions about contaminating the scene. Nonetheless, the coroners' rolls do evince a distinct need to safeguard the site where the body was discovered, as well as the body of the dead, untouched, if on a much more basic scale.

The corpse was the chief priority. After ascertaining that the individual was indeed dead, the law prohibited the first finder and others present at the scene from moving the body of an individual whose death was sudden and unnatural. Medieval Englishmen and women took this mandate seriously. In 1293, two sudden deaths transpired simultaneously at Bury St Edmunds: a boy of twelve drowned, and a man was crushed to death by a heavy weight while lighting a lamp at church. When locals set off to summon the coroner, they were told that he was away on holiday and by law only a coroner might convene an inquest. The residents had no choice but to leave the bodies where they had been discovered, awaiting the coroner's return. In due course, the stench from the putrefying corpses became so overpowering that the families of the deceased turned to the abbot for a solution, claiming the smell was making them sick.[36] The importance of leaving the body intact in anticipation of the coroner's arrival is a constant refrain in the miracle stories of St Thomas de Cantilupe. Explaining the English process of death investigation for the benefits of the judges in Rome, the writer of the miraculous tale of a five-year-old child brought back to life explains:

> no one must move the body of the slain or drowned person from the place in which it was first found without calling in the king's officer in charge of the investigation of such events for, in the kingdom of England, such matter bore upon the rights of the crown. This was the case even when the king's officer lived so far away that he might not come before three months had passed. Should anyone do otherwise, he would commit an extremely grave offence.[37]

The death of Walter of Maulden emphasizes just how strictly individuals complied with this requirement. When Walter was mortally injured in an altercation with the local miller after being accused of stealing a bushel of flour, his wife and sister-in-law gathered up the injured Walter and bore him away to a friend's home. Later that night, realizing that he was not going to recover from his injuries, they carted him back to the place they had found him. He was still alive the next day when his sister came to visit him at the scene of the altercation, but he died soon after.[38]

Some of these stories might lead us to believe that coroners had little appreciation of the need for prompt investigation. This is certainly not the case. There are no surviving examples of coroners taking three months to visit the scene of death, as the above excerpt suggests. In urban centers, the coroner typically arrived the day the death occurred. Death investigations in rural areas moved more slowly. In her statistical analysis of the coroners' rolls, Barbara Hanawalt reports that in the countryside, coroners arrived usually within three days of a death.[39] A study of coroners' inquests in Hampshire and Wiltshire offers a worst-case scenario. The average interval between death and investigation was seven days or less, "short enough to ensure that evidence was still new in witnesses' minds and the corpse fresh enough to decide cause of death."[40] What is important about all of the above examples is the careful attention paid to crown mandates: when residents were told to leave the body *in situ*, they did as they were ordered, even when it was highly disagreeable for them to do so and even when it meant abandoning a dying man.

Coroners and juries placed great faith in the body as a guide in the absence of witness testimony. On its own, a corpse has much to offer. The corpse can indicate the nature of the death itself: was it a natural death? Death by misadventure? Homicide? Suicide? Trauma to the body, in particular, signals whether an individual died by homicide or suicide, deaths that present in similar ways and are notoriously difficult to distinguish. Signs of struggle or defense wounds (broken fingernails, scratches, bruising on the forearms, slash wounds on the hands) have the coroner and his jury asking entirely different questions than they would otherwise. Given the centrality of the body itself as evidence, it was crucial to prevent any careless post-mortem bruising that might lead the jury to draw the wrong conclusion. The major threat to bodily integrity sprang from the need to disrobe the corpse. For many medieval men and women their clothing represented some of their few possessions and accordingly they were used to pay mortuary fees to the local parish priest.[41] Because the clothes themselves held value, it was in the family's best interest to remove them as soon as possible and thus eliminate the opportunity for theft.[42] Legal tradition did not indicate precisely who was responsible for undressing the corpse prior to post-mortem examination, but a 1329 amercement of a Northamptonshire township for the mismanagement of a body confirms that this took place before the coroner's arrival.[43] The legal record recounts how "a man was found dead in the fields of a town and that the body had been stripped and that it had lain there so long that the eyes had been torn out by crows and other birds. The entire township was therefore declared to be in mercy."[44] Two immediate observations can be gleaned from this enrollment. First, the crown did not hesitate to punish those who risked the efficiency of an investigation by failing to preserve the corpse. While the body was to remain in place, it was of little value to a homicide investigation if picked over by birds. Granted, this imparts only a hazy sense of the usual process. It is still unclear whether the crown expected communities to assign a guard to ward off birds and other predators, or create a protective tent of sorts over the corpse. In all likelihood, communities instituted a "wake" or "night watch" over the body of the dead, as was the normal process for funeral customs.[45] In the case above, the coroner may have taken so long to arrive that those responsible for the wake grew lax in their responsibility. Second, locals stripped the body before the coroner even arrived. If this was the usual practice, one can only presume that great care was taken to avoid inadvertent bruising that might lead the investigation astray.

Concern for the integrity of the body, in large part, is why so many enrollments supplied such a detailed narrative of the body's travels. For example, when Agnes, wife of John Driver, of Little Baddow was found dead, the jury composed an elaborate narrative of the events leading up to her death to explain why her body had been removed from the scene of violence. Apparently, she and her husband struggled first in a field known locally as Westfield at Little Coggeshall (*Essex*). There, he beat her around the head and neck and treated her so violently that he imagined she had died. "Believing her to be dead," he threw her body into a well—presumably one that had fallen into disuse. She remained immersed in water up to her neck for the next four days, at which point one of her neighbors discovered her and fished her out of the well. He carried her to the house of a friend, where she languished for another six days before dying.[46] Such an elaborate account makes it clear why her body had been separated from the initial crime scene. It also signaled to the coroner that there were, in fact, two crime scenes to investigate (Westfield and the well), even though the victim did not die in either place.[47]

Bracton's directives for scene analysis offer especial insight into death investigations involving homicides. As discussed in Chapter One, *Bracton* stresses the importance of discovering and following cart tracks, hoof marks, and footprints, or other material evidence that might alert jurors to the whereabouts of the fleeing perpetrator.[48] That jurors followed this directive is evident in the 1271 record of the death of a stranger in the woods close to Roxton (*Beds.*). When a stranger's body turned up with a four-inch gash above the left ear, deep enough to expel his brains, the jury explicitly remarked that not only did they know nothing about who he was or where he had come from, but they could not find any tracks (*vestigia*) showing how he had arrived in the woods.[49] A London enrollment from 1300 illustrates a coroner questioning jurors to determine whether the scene had been altered in any way. In November of 1300, John de Bois of Suffolkshire was standing at the intersection of two streets in Cheapside when a piece of wood fastened to a solar directly above him came loose and collapsed upon his head, inflicting a mortal wound. He lingered for two more days after the incident before passing away. Upon arrival, the first question the coroner reportedly asked was if "any man or woman had touched or moved the piece of wood," presumably hoping to get a better sense of the trajectory.[50] The inquest into the death of another unknown man in May 1332 confirms that jurors examined the location with an eye to reconstructing the events preceding the death. Jurors swore before the Northamptonshire coroner that they did not know the name of the victim or who had killed him, but they were confident that he had not been killed in the location where he was found. Rather, the felon must have carried the victim to the fields of Tiffield where he lay after he was already dead. Regrettably, they offer no indication as to what led them to this conclusion, but it is not hard to imagine that modern practices like blood splatter analysis in its most rudimentary form already played some part in the analysis of a crime scene.[51]

How did communities preserve the physical evidence from tampering by curious onlookers until the coroner arrived? There is no extant evidence to signify that local authorities barricaded the scene from public entry in any way prior to the arrival of the coroner. Of course, the absence of evidence proves little. Why would anyone bother to write down something so mundane? If the early modern evidence is any indication, this must have been one of the more challenging aspects of the investigation. Carol Loar's examination of sixteenth- and seventeenth-century coroners' inquests highlights that villagers regarded death investigation as a spectacle. She remarks upon two inquests in particular where swarms of residents inhibited the progress of the investigation with their curiosity: "the crowd that had gathered had to be 'forced back' so that the physician, coroner and jury could do their work."[52] Granted, it is significant that the coroners' reports themselves did not make this statement. This comment derives instead from the memoir of Abraham Jennings, a physician who served as foreman of a coroner's inquest in 1664.[53] Did the crowds wait for the coroner's arrival before gathering? Or, were they a threat to the crime scene from the moment the body was discovered?

Although not for trial purposes, coroners did confiscate weapons used in homicides. The medieval crown considered weapons used in a homicide forfeit to the crown. Thus, enrollments regularly insert an assessment of the weapon's value into the narrative of the text, but in the most awkward manner imaginable: "and the said Henry Rolves with a sword worth 12*d*. feloniously wounded Ralph in the right part of his face."[54] It is not clear what became of the weapons. Theoretically, they belonged to the king, although as the record implies relatively early on deodands were commuted into money payments.[55] Thus, coroners probably collected weapons only to pass them over to the escheator for sale. Nonetheless, an examination of weaponry played a key part in the investigative process. Jurors endeavored to match weapons to wounds. A Northamptonshire coroner targeted the homicide suspect in the death of John Baker of Pilsgate specifically by tying the wound to the corresponding weapon. When the county coroner arrived to view the body, he discovered that the locals had buried it before his arrival. He immediately mandated that it be disinterred. Upon examination of the corpse, he noticed a lesion on John's head, which he deemed had been inflicted by an axe. During the inquest itself, discussion with jurors revealed that John had been beating his wife Emma, causing her to raise the hue. Her brother appeared to assist her, conveniently bearing an axe. Apparently, with her consent, he struck John with the axe, killing him instantly.[56]

Coroners may have also searched the dead's belongings, although it is not possible to discover whether this was standard practice or only when suspicion led them to believe they might learn more about a death in the process. In those instances where a search turned up nothing, it is hard to imagine anyone would have considered the search noteworthy. The surviving evidence highlights examinations of this nature usually when the dead person was also a felon. Since the coroner was responsible for assessing the value of the homicide's goods, his clothing and belongings were directly relevant to the record. For example, a London enrollment from 1338 notes that when the body of John the Brewer was discovered in the parish of St Bride, the coroner and the sheriffs rummaged through his clothes, finding 160 florins and a seal—precisely the items purportedly stolen from two Florentine merchants earlier that day. The coroner was well aware that the Florentine merchants had spent much of the day hunting John the Brewer—indeed, their hunt is what prompted him to take a closer look at the victim's clothing.[57]

PHYSICAL EVIDENCE: B) THE BODY

In the absence of eyewitnesses, the body assumes a privileged role. Textbooks in forensic pathology today underline the central place of the corpse as proof. An analysis of the traumata of the body allows the coroner "to speak for the dead," a slogan that holds great meaning for modern coroners.[58] In homicide inquests in particular, the body is "the text of victimization," guiding the jurors through the process of investigation.[59] The external examination of the corpse played a fundamental part in the medieval inquest in verifying witness testimony and reconstructing the events leading up to a death. For example, homicide indictments commonly included a telling phrase: "The corpse was viewed on which appeared the wound but no other hurt." When jurors reported that Christina Morel died in 1300 after throwing herself in front of her husband's attacker, who proceeded to kick her repeatedly in the stomach, the inquest concluded only after viewing her body to confirm that her belly "appeared blue and inflamed."[60] Coroners' rolls are full of gruesome, disturbing details of the physical condition of the dead, more than enough to corroborate that medieval coroners performed a genuine physical examination. The composers of some enrollments were at pains to underscore that the inquest incorporated a view of the body.[61] Others commonly testify that the coroner "saw and felt" (*vidit et palpavit*) the body.[62] The need to record the dimensions of injuries guaranteed a hands-on approach to the post-mortem examination. How could jurors have known John Sheffeld's wound in his right side was five inches deep and two inches wide unless someone had actually measured it? And, could they have confidently pronounced Richard Waldogne, a Northamptonshire dyer, responsible for his death if they had not also compared the wound to the dimensions of his dagger?[63] Death in all its grisly and horrifying reality confronted coroners and their jurors on a daily basis. Thomas Pylevyn was eviscerated.[64] Geoffrey Fuk was beaten so badly that a vein burst in his head and he bled to death.[65] Thomas Stevenson of Cropston (*Leics.*) died after a year of lying in bed when his bedsores became infected and putrefied.[66]A sow had eaten much of the chest and nose of two-year-old John, son of Thomas Selede, before the coroner and jurors examined his body.[67] Given the wide array of ghastliness coroners and their jurors regularly addressed, there is no reason to believe that they were squeamish or shied away from contact with a corpse.

External examination did not involve mere poking and prodding at the body. In some cases, coroners and their jurors had to go to great lengths to ensure that they had learned everything possible from the corpse. The 1342 death of Matilda, wife of Richard Pouk, of Oxfordshire is a prime example of a more comprehensive inspection. Upon initial examination, the jury determined that Matilda died of natural causes. She was elderly and had been suffering with various illnesses for some time prior to her demise. After learning of a rumor that her husband regularly beat her, jurors began to question their original conclusion. Resolute to uncover any bruising that might expose signs of abuse, the coroner rolled Matilda's naked body over and over in the presence of the jurors, but they found no wounds or bruising in the head or members to indicate that the death was anything other than natural.[68]

Some corpses presented extraordinary challenges in terms of the physical examination. In cases of infanticide, for example, jurors documented whether the child had undergone the rite of baptism.[69] A coroner's roll for the borough of Oxford explains that an untied umbilical cord is a telltale sign of an unbaptized child.[70] Physical evidence of this nature clearly speaks to motive: a mother who never intended to keep her child would not make an effort to have him baptized. A conscientious investigation should consider this kind of evidence. The deaths of prisoners also entailed a more complex physical examination. When an individual died in prison, the crown charged coroners with holding a "true inquest" to determine specifically whether "his death was hastened by the harsh keeping of his gaolers, or by pain unlawfully inflicted on him."[71] Living conditions in medieval England's prisons complicated the post-mortem examination. Because the crown expected prisoners to pay for their meals, most prisoners were malnourished and many died from starvation. Impoverished prisoners incapable of paying the *sewet*, a traditional fee to be released from irons, might also die with wounds of an unusual nature.[72] Perhaps most significant to a jury, carrying out an inquest in prison exposed coroners and jurors to the possibility of contagion. In fact, the short duration of medieval trials has been explained by the fears of justices of jail delivery wishing to minimize their contact with prisoners in order to avoid catching the infamous "jail fever."[73] Coroners and inquest jurors did not merely share the same room with dead prisoners, they had to undress them and inspect their bodies for signs of fatal abuse. Yet, even when prisoners died from bubonic plague, the enrollments indicate that jurors still carried out the requisite physical examination.[74]

The physical examination sometimes required investigators to comment on injuries that were only partly external. It was common for jurors to remark on head injuries that "reached to the brain"; chest injuries described as extending "halfway through the body"; a stomach wound that reached "to the bowels" or "penetrated the intestines." Coroners were not ordering autopsies. Yet, it is striking just how frequently inquest post-mortems spoke to internal injuries. For example, when a bull gored William Grys, rector of the church of Ibworth (*Hants.*), to death in 1383/84, jurors concluded with confidence that the bull had broken three bones in the left part of his body.[75] Purportedly, when Alice Soustan fell from the top step of her front stairwell while exiting the house in 1393, she fractured three ribs on her left side, from which she died.[76] At the inquest of Richard the Brewer, jurors deduced that he ruptured his bowels and diaphragm when he stumbled drunkenly and toppled from the steps leading to a friend's home while lugging a bag of malt.[77] Comments relating to internal injuries provide sound evidence for genuine physical examination. Bruising or swelling only hint at the possibility of broken bones. The most decisive visible evidence is the protrusion of a bone penetrating the skin, yet jurors usually remarked when this happened and none of the above cases make mention of it. In most of the above situations, the presence of crepitus, miniscule fragments of broken bone rubbing together beneath the surface of the skin, most likely guided jurors in their conclusions. How else might they have spoken confidently of broken bones? The evidence of the coroners' rolls exposes the inadequacy of the term "view" for the physical examination: such sound conclusions did not derive from a mere visual inspection of the body.

Jurors surely needed little assistance in identifying something as common as broken ribs. Were they as capable of recognizing on their own Richard the Brewer's ruptured bowels and diaphragm? In many instances, the jury's diagnosis is too elaborate for twelve laymen working independently of a medical practitioner to have produced. Plague deaths provide some of the best evidence for the covert workings of a medical practitioner at the post-mortem examination. The coroners' rolls record at least four individuals whose deaths were caused by the "true pestilence."[78] Academic medicine in the medieval period employed the adjectives *true*, *very*, and *certain* "to specify the nature of the sickness, their opposites denoting conditions caused by putrefied humours."[79] Thus, for example a "true flegmon" describes an excess of blood; an "untrue flegmon," corrupt blood. In the instance of "true pestilence," the qualifier is intended to underscore that this is not just any pestilence, but indeed the bubonic plague.[80] What is significant about the usage of the phrase "true pestilence" is that only a learned physician would describe the plague in this manner. While academic and surgical texts made frequent usage of the adjectives *true* and *untrue* in their discussions of sickness, popular remedy books did not.[81] A medical practitioner, and specifically one who could read, must have supplied the coroner with the wording for this cause of death.

PHYSICAL EVIDENCE: C) CRUENTATION?

Recent studies explain that the body played an exceptional role in the investigative process because of the divine properties attributed to blood by the medieval world.[82] In his avant-garde 1998 study of murder reporting, Malcolm Gaskill remarks, "[i]n modern murder trials forensic evidence speaks for the dead; in early modern England, the dead had to speak for themselves."[83] Here, Gaskill refers explicitly to cruentation, in which the corpse bled to signify the presence of its murderer. Gaskill uncovers a number of late sixteenth- and seventeenth-century inquests in which coroners and their juries utilized corpse touching to elicit cruentation as a tool of investigation. A 1572 Cheshire inquest into the death of Roger Crockett metamorphosed into a spectacle worthy of the circus after the victim's wife prompted the coroner to convene the local inhabitants to

> stand by, and be present about the corps, that all the people according to the opinion of Aristotle and the common experiment, might behold and see whether the body would expell excrements and fall to bleed afreshe in the sight of them all.[84]

Gaskill unearths enough examples to contend that not only did coroners and magistrates command the performance of the ordeal, but they also accepted the validity of these "fictionalized narratives" as proof in homicide investigations.[85]

The medieval documentation is not as fruitful. This study uncovered no evidence to indicate that the medieval English also availed themselves of this investigative strategy.[86] Of course, given how few coroners' rolls survive and how much of the investigation typically is omitted from the formal record, this finding is not conclusive. Given the usefulness of cruentation, it is hard to imagine that the English did not occasionally turn to corpse touching. Outside of the coroners' rolls, there is some evidence to substantiate English familiarity with the convention. Matthew Paris's account of the death of King Henry II at Chinon furnishes a model example of cruentation. When Richard arrived to view the body, "blood suddenly poured from the dead king's nostrils; as if his spirit revolted at the arrival of the man who was thought to be the cause of his death, so that it seemed his very blood cried out to God."[87] The canonization trial of St Thomas de Cantilupe, bishop of Hereford, produces an additional example. Before Thomas's death, a disagreement with John Peckham, the Archbishop of Canterbury, led to Thomas's excommunication. He died in Italy in 1282, while attempting to persuade the pope to lift the sentence. A witness in the canonization process in 1307 observed that when Thomas's bones were passing through Canterbury on the way to Hereford, the urn in which they were placed began to bleed, clearly identifying Peckham as the one responsible for his death.[88]

It is central to understand the place of cruentation in medieval theology and science. Gaskill sees cruentation as a deliberate deception. Referencing the above excerpt, he writes, "[m]agical experiments were attributed to Aristotle to lend scientific standing to quack cures."[89] Gaskill's conclusion neglects the simple fact that cruentation fit easily into the theological and scientific mindsets of the medieval era. Popularly, cruentation belonged to the category of *iudicium Dei* (that is, judicial ordeals), tests designed to determine an accused felon's guilt by seeking judgment from God. For the medieval period, the more familiar ordeals were those of cold water (in which the innocent sank while the guilty floated) and hot iron (if the accused's hand was found to be free of infection three days after walking nine paces with a piece of scalding hot iron, then God declared his/her innocence). Cruentation, also known as the ordeal of the bier, worked on much the same principles. While the church revoked its support for judicial ordeals at the Fourth Lateran Council (1215), popular belief in their efficacy did not wane, as evidenced by the continuation of the practice of judicial combat. Theological support for cruentation was founded on another premise altogether. Medieval theologians considered blood to be the "seat of life," the vessel containing the human soul.[90] Cruentation is easily understood as the soul speaking after the body has lost the capacity. This conviction led some philosophically minded physicians to decry preventative bloodletting, noting that "in draining blood the phlebotomist drained the patient's soul."[91]

Cruentation also has a long history as part of the scholastic tradition: discourses on the nature of the practice appear in the Prose Salernitan Questions, as well as in treatises by Albert the Great and Roger Marston.[92] The examination of Giles of Rome by the Faculty of Theology at Paris in 1290, recorded in Question 25 of Giles's *Quodlibet V*, provides useful insight into the practice. In order to answer the query posed before him, Giles first had to refute popular hypotheses with which he disagreed. As a result, his work offers a valuable summary of the current conflicting scientific explanations for cruentation. First, Giles addressed Avicenna's rule of attraction, in which "like attracts like." Thus, "because a trace of the victim's blood had been left on a knife the returning murderer was still holding or on his clothes, the blood remaining in the corpse was drawn out of the wound by attraction when the killer approached sufficiently close."[93] Giles easily dismissed this theory because he claimed it should function in the reverse: that is, the victim's corpse should attract the blood on the person of the killer, and not the other way round.

Second, Giles proposed a mechanistic explanation centered on motion and contact between subject and object. In this case,

> the explanation ran that in the violence of the act certain material spirits or vapors were generated in both the murderer and the victim. Parts of these spirits or vapors were exchanged through the eyes on the occasion of a mutual glance at the instant of the murder, so that when murderer and corpse were brought together again, the parts sought to return to the source whence they came, following a presumed rule that a part seeks to go back to the whole. The resultant commotion in the matter of the dead body then led to the emanation of a certain quantity of blood.[94]

Giles also rejected this rationale on the basis that this process is not one that is normally observable in nature, and thus while it seems like a logical approach, there is insufficient evidence to uphold the theory.

After rejecting popular conjectures for understanding the process of cruentation, Giles proposed three alternative perspectives that he saw as more likely explanations. First, in line with the *iudicium Dei*, God was so horrified by the nature of the crime that he made sure it was punished by intervening directly to indicate the murderer's guilt. Second, if not God, then demons were at work, "manipulating material objects so to procure, by the natural procedures of material action and local motion, an apparently wondrous effect."[95] Or, third, cruentation may be a matter of chance.

What is critical to recognize about Giles's multifaceted response is that cruentation can in no way be dismissed as mere superstition. A good deal of scientific thought had gone into explaining the process. Indeed, Steven Marrone holds up cruentation as a harbinger of the seventeenth-century's Scientific Revolution.[96] Thus, even if medieval coroners' inquests did embrace corpse touching as an investigative strategy, this is evidence of progress, not irrationality.[97]

TESTIMONIAL EVIDENCE: A) WITNESSES

The 1236 inquest into the death of a London man identified only as "Roger" provides valuable insight into the process of investigation:

> In the same year etc., on the feast of St. John the Apostle [27 December 1236], a man named Roger was found by night in Candlewick Street so badly beaten and ill-treated that he could not speak. Richard Tyllebrigge, Elias son of William Goday, William Utlaghe, Richard son of Richard Nog', and Robert of Berkhampstead, watchmen, found him thus in the street and carried him to the house of Thomas le Pipere, where he died very early next morning of that beating. Afterwards the watchmen went from their ward to that of Roger Blund, then alderman, because they

> believed the dead man to belong to that ward, to see if they could learn the truth about how the affair had happened. The watchmen of that ward, asked if they knew anything about the above-named John said that he was their companion in keeping watch that night, and as they were all going together to keep watch they chanced to meet a man carrying an unlighted lantern, whom they pursued as far as opposite Consel's shop. There they found a number of unknown men standing in the street, armed with swords and other weapons, who, when they attempted to arrest them, assaulted them, and so beat Roger that he died. The other members of the watch they badly wounded, and then fled. Asked then whether they recognized any of the malefactors or suspect anyone, the watch said that they suspected William le Large, 'coureru', who fled for the deed and could never afterwards be found. Gerard of St. Edmunds, one of the watchmen who was wounded by the malefactors, comes, and asked if he suspects anyone, says that he knows nothing more than has been said above. The mayor and aldermen, asked whom they suspect of the said death and wounds, say that they suspect the same Walter le Large and no one else, because the others were unknown. Therefore he is to be put in exigent and outlawed according etc. His chattels are worth 2*s*., for which the sheriffs are to answer. He was in frankpledge. Therefore [his pledges] are in mercy.[98]

This enrollment stands out from most inquest records because it presents a systematic narrative of the investigative process. In doing so, it reinforces a number of key points. First, it confirms the error of presuming that the coroner (in this case, the mayor filled that role) always headed up the investigation because the crown charged him with documenting the results. Here, it is worth remembering that medieval communities typically policed themselves. Policing in the village community took place at two distinct levels. All men over the age of twelve were required to belong to a tithing group tasked with keeping the peace.[99] This system functioned on the basis of mutual accountability. If one member of a tithing engaged in criminal activity, the others were amerced at the next eyre if they failed to arrest him.[100] After the 1230s, all vills added a secondary level of security by appointing a night watch, as indicated above. Henry Summerson has described the medieval vill as "a neighbourhood of voluntary spies."[101] This system had its perquisites. If your neighbor's actions might result in you paying a fine, it made sense to know what your neighbor was up to, and to prevent him from dabbling in any criminal activities. What is significant is that none of this required organization by a crown official to resolve what assuredly they believed was an internal problem. This does not imply a lack of cooperation with the coroner. Rather, a community's self-sufficiency instead reveals that the investigation into a sudden or unnatural death was well under way before the coroner arrived on the scene. Here, it is worth returning to the point made earlier in this chapter that outside urban centers coroners regularly took up to three days to journey to the site of investigation. This interval was highly productive in terms of the investigation. It provided neighbors "ample time to shake their heads, speak of strangers in the neighbourhood, exchange information about old hatreds and feuds, and build consensus for a story of events."[102] This is not to suggest that juries used this time to fabricate evidence. In fact, the process was geared to prevent deception. The crown stipulated widespread attendance at inquests on the premise that "the entire male population [over the age of twelve] of four vills would find it much harder to unite either to tell a falsehood or to stick to it once told."[103] The delay in process until the arrival of the coroner instead allowed neighbors to sift through preliminary evidence to construct an overall picture of what had happened so that they were better prepared to answer the coroner's questions.

Second, despite the great importance attached to the mid-sixteenth-century legislation requiring coroners to document interviews of witnesses and suspects, we need to recognize that the innovation represented in this statute is one in record taking, not in process.[104] Not only were medieval jurors themselves witnesses, even if only of a hearsay variety, but interviewing witnesses was a foundational part of the work performed by coroners and their jurors. Again, the crown mandated all male residents over the age of twelve living in the four vills closest to the visne to attend the inquest. The very purpose of this gathering was to furnish the coroner and his jury with the necessary information to complete their investigation. Relevant witnesses (first finder, nearest neighbors, any eyewitnesses) were mainperned at the inquest to appear also at the formal indictment of the accused—if there existed any gaps in the official record, they were available for questioning at that time. Typically, the scholarly tradition has focused its attention chiefly on the presence of trial witnesses. Research establishes that witnesses participated intermittently in the trial process, often only to show support for an indictment by their presence in the courtroom.[105] Witness testimony during the trial, however, was necessarily abbreviated. Medieval justice moved at breakneck speed: royal justices endured a grueling schedule to deliver a jail of its prisoners in a day or two at the most. Thus, unlike modern trials that might extend for weeks or months at a time, medieval trials lasted somewhere between fifteen minutes and half an hour.[106] Given the time constraints, the scholarly spotlight on witnesses must shift from the trial to the coroner's inquest. Testimony at the coroner's inquest made the presence of witnesses at any future date redundant. Why make men and women miss work and travel to the assize to give depositions that they had already presented at the inquest, especially when the coroner or the sheriff might speak for them? Hearsay, when it came from a source of authority, had no stigma in the medieval courtroom; and with the openness of the coroner's investigation, its findings would have been public knowledge anyway.[107]

While oral interviews with residents from the visne laid the essential groundwork for every coroner's investigation, most enrollments do not afford this impression. In fact, the portrait painted by the coroners' rolls is quite the opposite. They steer clear of identifying precise individuals and illuminating how they assisted in the investigation.[108] Instead, manifold enrollments depict the inquest as a simple exchange between coroners and their juries. Enrollments generally incorporate the following formula: upon meeting his jurors, the coroner "diligently inquired concerning the death"; in response, "the jurors on their oath say. . . ." Others adhere to this question-and-answer structure, but fail to state who was asking the questions. Instead they focus entirely on the jury as a collection of witnesses: "when asked if . . . they say. . . ." This paradigm is a simplified construction of the actual exchange: it is hard to imagine that any jury spoke consistently in one voice, without any dissent or variance, and had concluded the investigation before the coroner even arrived, which in urban areas was often later that same day. The format of many coroners' rolls does not reflect the process as it happened.

Why, then, did the coroners' scriveners create and perpetuate such a misleading representation of the criminal process? Frugality is the obvious response. The overriding sense offered by the bulk of the coroners' rolls is that coroners instructed their scriveners not to squander parchment. Enrollments are brief and often mechanical, frequently including only what the crown deemed necessary. Rather than waste parchment, scriveners etched out errors or corrected with inter-linear insertions. At times, they so condensed the enrollments that the cramped, miniscule writing make the records almost illegible without the assistance of modern technology. For the sake of expedience and parchment, scriveners needed to draft a comprehensible summary of the proceedings that filled only a few lines. The question-and-answer structure itself was most likely chosen because of its popularity. It is still unclear exactly how a medieval scrivener received his education.[109] If he had spent any time in a university environment, he would have been well acquainted with the Socratic method, endorsed by the Scholastic movement of the Twelfth-Century Renaissance. The use of dialogue between individuals who held opposing opinions was a well-known genre that dominated philosophical and theological studies. Scriveners might also have been familiar with this format from the presentments of grand juries and diocesan visitations. In both scenarios, local representatives responded to fixed lists of questions—in terms of presentment jurors, those fixed questions are referred to as articles of the eyre. Regardless of where this structure originated, even if it did not truthfully reflect the process of investigation, it was a useful framework to arrange the record of a coroner's inquest and alert the reader of those rolls to the pressing concerns of the investigation.

When enrollments mention testimonial evidence, they do so in generic terms, creating the impression that the evidence derives from communal, rather than individual, sources of knowledge. The aversion to naming names holds true even with respect to eyewitnesses. Although coroners were meant to list everyone present at the homicide, they rarely did so. By and large, the only locals whose names turn up in enrollments, other than the central actors and jurors, are the first finder, every so often the four nearest neighbors and their pledges, and it is meaningful that the coroners' reports seldom clarify how their inside knowledge helped to solve the crime. When a homicide transpired in a crowded location, rather than specify who was present at the scene, jurors report that there was a multitude of onlookers, but they did not know their names. Or, the crowd was so vast that jurors could not remember who was there.[110] Thomas Green explains that coroners purposely excluded the names of witnesses out of concern for their well-being, a contention that makes a good deal of sense in the context of the medieval English village.[111] Some deponents may even have pleaded for anonymity in exchange for information, fearing reprisals for their forthrightness. Because coroners read their rolls aloud at presentments to ensure continuity between the coroner's indictments and those of the grand jury, witnesses had good reason to avoid having their names persistently associated with solving a case that might then set in motion a private vendetta. Wealthy defendants who could afford to sue a plaint of conspiracy were the most worrisome. The Year Books confirm that jurors of indictment were frequent targets of actions of conspiracy.[112] Other witnesses feared being identified in the coroners' reports because they did not want to fall under suspicion themselves. Their consternation was legitimate. Coroners' reports typically question whether the jury suspected the first finder or anyone else present of involvement. In fact, first finders and bystanders on occasion took flight after the crime, anxious that their presence alone somehow implicated them.[113]

While the rolls consistently failed to identify eyewitnesses, their presence casts a long shadow over the coroners' reports. The comprehensiveness of some homicide narratives, in particular, indicates that the evidence must have come from witnesses rather than being pieced together purely through physical evidence and/or hearsay. The coroner's account of the 1370 death of Egidius Vers de Oucheon, a barker in the city of Leicester, reveals an instance of eyewitnesses hovering in the background, yet never reported. The record commences with the domestic spat that set Egidius's homicide in motion. John Draper of Leicester was at home with his wife when dissension arose between the two. As the clamor of their disagreement escalated, Egidius, who was one of their neighbors, decided to step in. The medieval English typically took a much more public approach to marriage than we do today. Medieval communities not only worked hard to initiate a marriage, they kept marriages together by supervising their domestic disputes.[114] Thus, upon hearing such great dissent and strife between them, Egidius burst into their home in the hope of bringing peace. This was not to be the case. Irate at the intrusion, John Draper drew his knife from its sheath and struck Egidius in the chest, stabbing him so forcefully that the knife plunged all the way to his heart. The wound was mortal. John Draper fled but was eventually captured and imprisoned.[115] Some segments of this narrative may have been reconstructed from circumstantial evidence; but how would they have know Egidius entered the house in order to play peacemaker unless someone witnessed him doing so? Did John confess after his arrest? Was his wife the source of the information, or would her account have been sufficiently credible on its own given that she was also a participant in the altercation? As with most enrollments, we are left with more questions than answers, but the jury must have had informants in order to assemble the comprehensive narrative that appears in the coroner's report.

Deliberate omission of this sort is the most common tactic adopted by coroners and jurors to mask witness identities even when their testimony acted as the foundation for the investigation. A similar situation crops up in the death of Philip Port of Oxford in 1305. Around dusk on a Sunday in March, John of Bardon appeared at Philip's door. The two retired to a tavern for a drink. Later that evening, John was the first to make his way home from the tavern. Upon Philip's return to his chamber, five unknown clerks brutally attacked and killed him. They fled instantly after the attack.[116] The enrollment fails to name any witnesses. The physical evidence showed clear signs of assault. Philip was "wounded in the front of his head from one ear to another, so that all his brain was scattered outside; and he had another wound across his face to within the teeth, four inches long and one inch wide, and his right hand was cut off and lay beside him." But how did the jury conclude based on the physical evidence alone that five unknown clerics were involved and, in fact, the entire attack had been masterminded by John of Bardon? There must have been witnesses or, at the very least, rumors of ill will between the two; but none of this made its way into the coroner's report.

Coroners' records make liberal usage of the term "rumor" (*fama*). English law considered public fame acceptable grounds for accusation, providing it was widely known, rather than founded on "a single report."[117] At times, the purpose of citing rumor may have been to conceal witness identities. This strategy was especially useful when informants came forward with controversial evidence that might incite the jury to reverse its preliminary verdict. Rumor provided a convenient explanation for considering new evidence or theories without revealing the source. The death of Agnes, daughter of Reginald Stobmot, of Sutterton (*Lincs.*) in 1353 provides an example of a jury that went to great lengths to ascertain the cause of death in light of recent information. When Agnes died, her inquest declared that her death was the product of natural causes. After the view, the coroner ordered her body buried in the parish cemetery. The enrollment reports that sometime after her interment, "scandal broke out." The record does not reveal the character of that scandal, nor does it indicate who was responsible for alerting the coroner to this gossip. However, it must have been virulent enough to warrant consideration: the coroner ordered Agnes's body to be disinterred and reassembled his jury to examine Agnes's body once again. Only after this second inquest was the jury able to declare confidently that Agnes did indeed die naturally and from no other cause.[118]

Coroners' reports sometimes implemented passive constructions as a tactic to avoid singling out informants. In the death of Alice, wife of Robert, of Portsmouth in 1339, the jury was prepared to proceed against her husband when "information was given to the Coroner" that Robert's son, also named Robert, had in fact been arrested on suspicion of his stepmother's homicide and was being held at Newgate. The sheriff summoned a new panel of jurors the following day for a second enquiry in light of this fresh information. The second jury implicated both father and son, but ultimately held the father responsible. While the son struck Alice with his hand, the father beat her with a "wombedstaff" across the neck. The physical examination concluded that the father's blow, which had broken her neck, was in fact the fatal blow.[119]

Was the aversion to identifying witnesses always deliberate? At times, the evasiveness of the enrollments seems to spring from the narrative style that was so typical of coroner's reports. The inquest into the suicide of Hugh Parker in December 1400 makes this point explicit. Jurors remarked that before he hanged himself from a beam in the local tannery, he told his wife, Joanna, that he was going to check on the horses in the field.[120] Nowhere in the enrollment do jurors indicate that they interviewed his wife during the investigation, but they must have. In this example, they were not trying to hide the witness's identity. Rather, jurors were significantly more concerned to piece together what happened to create a comprehensive narrative than to present evidence of an investigation well done. In general, this inference holds true: enrollments do not provide a systematic account of the process of discovery. Instead, they focus on delivering the findings of that investigation. From the historian's perspective, this approach presents innumerable obstacles. To name a few, coroners' reports

a) Rarely identify how the coroner and his jury discovered the perpetrator's identity
b) Omit any explanation of what kind of evidence formed the base of the investigation
c) Offer no opportunity to discover whether jurors regularly evaluated the accuracy of witnesses' statements, although the fact that they rejected the findings of some "rumors" after reexamining the body of the dead demonstrates the existence of an evaluation process
d) Fail to identify who led the investigation, whether the coroner or a juror assumed that role, and who among those jurors played a greater role

In this respect, legal tradition is a useful complement to the sources of law in practice to help fill in some of those gaps. *Bracton* addresses "c" particularly well. First, the treatise highlights the dangers of rumor: "For uproar and public outcry are at times made of many things which in truth have no foundation, and thus the idle talk of the people is not to be heeded."[121]

In essence, what *Bracton* is saying is that sometimes smoke is just smoke, there is no fire. Given the importance of *fama* and reputation in medieval European society, this statement is key. While rumor might be sufficient to initiate an investigation, it was not enough on its own to lead to a conviction. Second, *Bracton* warns that witness depositions might sometimes be motivated out of a desire for revenge. In this instance, it was up to the king's representative to discern the truth. The treatises states:

> the judge, if he is wise, ought first to inquire . . . from what man or men the twelve jurors have learned what they put forward in their *veredictum* concerning the indicted man; having heard their answer thereon he may readily decide if any deceit or wickedness lies behind it. For perhaps one or a majority of the jurors will say that they learned the matter put forward in their *veredictum* from one of their fellow jurors, and he under interrogation will perhaps say that he learned it from such a one, and so by question and answer the judge may descend from person to person to some low and worthless fellow, one in whom no trust must in any way be reposed. Let the judge so inquire into matters of this kind that his glory and the renown of his name may increase and that it not be said 'Jesus is crucified and Barrabas delivered.' For by such inquiries, if they are carefully and discreetly made, many scandalous things may be discovered. It sometimes happens that a lord accuses his tenant, or causes him to be indicted and a crime imputed to him, through a greedy desire to secure his land in demesne, or one neighbour accuses another through hatred and the like.[122]

Here, *Bracton* is obviously referring to a judge dealing with a jury of presentment. Surely the same advice was applicable also to a coroner hearing testimony from an inquest jury. Third, *Bracton* explains that variance in records may sometimes be explained by an appealer's apprehension, and "fear provides an excuse for his lack of knowledge."[123] Altogether, these indices imply that *Bracton*, and most likely England's royal officers of the law, understood that testimony could not always be accepted at face value. Rather, it was critical to evaluate what might have motivated a witness to offer testimony in the first place.

Bracton's fears of the "low and worthless fellow, one in whom no trust must in any way be reposed" might lead one to believe that the court only considered testimony from those deemed "oathworthy"—a restrictive approach that could act contrary to the best interests of the process of death investigation. This was not necessarily the case. The chronicle evidence implies a more measured and cautious approach. The French Chronicle, a thirteenth-century London chronicle, so called because it was written in Norman French, confirms that local authorities did not dismiss valuable information because the informant was less than ideal. The scandalous death of Laurence Duket, a death that shocked all of London, provides an instructive example. In July of 1284, Duket, a London goldsmith, fought and badly wounded a town clerk named Ralph Crepyn in a marketplace quarrel at Cheapside. Fearing the repercussions if Ralph did not survive the assault, Laurence fled to the church of St Mary le Bow and claimed sanctuary. The next morning, Duket's body was found hanging by a rope in the steeple of the church. Given the evidence, the coroner's inquest declared *felo de se*. Duket's body was treated to a suicide's burial. His corpse was dragged by the feet through the streets of London and thrown into a ditch outside the city. It was only after the inquest itself that a witness came forward to testify about what had really happened. A boy, whose age is unknown, thought to have been a street beggar or maybe even one of Duket's servants, was also present in the church and witnessed the entire affair. He claimed that a group of men entered the church by night. They hunted down Duket and strangled him. In order to mislead the inquest jurors, they tied a cord to the mullion of one of the windows and hanged him there to make it look like a suicide. The boy's testimony was critical. Not only did it warrant the reopening of the case, but it led to many arrests, some quite high profile, and sixteen executions, including the public burning of Alice atte Bowe, Ralph's mistress and purportedly the mastermind behind the entire operation. The clerk, Ralph Crepyn, who survived the altercation with Duket, was imprisoned for some time after the event; so, too, was Jordan Godchep, the presiding sheriff, thought to have concealed information concerning the homicide out of his friendship with Alice. Local authorities also ordered the retrieval of Duket's body: he was afforded a Christian burial. The church itself was placed under interdict. The doors and windows were filled with thorns until the bishop arrived to purify the environments.[124]

Admittedly, we have no idea exactly what happened in the death of Laurence Duket. His murder and the subsequent plethora of executions are so deeply immersed in scandal that it is hard to draw the line between truth and gossip. For our purposes, what is significant about Duket's death is that the testimony of a child was sufficient to reopen the investigation. The records imply that the executions and exposure of corruption in the sheriff's office hinged on this boy's testimony: this may or may not have been true. Indeed, the boy's evidence may have resonated with other voices, tipping the balance from private opinion to public fame. However, it is significant that the child's age did not prevent the local authorities from looking more closely into the matter and overturning their previous verdict.

TESTIMONIAL EVIDENCE: B) CONFESSIONS

In criminal investigations, some of the most instructive evidence came from the defendants themselves. Medieval law venerated confessions as the "queen" of proofs.[125] Continental Europeans were so enamored of the confession as the ultimate evidence that they reintroduced the Roman practice of torture precisely to encourage an accused felon to confess. England's *Placita Corone*, an anonymous treatise on law and legal procedure from the second half of the thirteenth century, is useful in understanding the place of the confession in English law. Described by Alan Harding as "a handbook for accused felons, telling them how to resist the verbal trickery of judges," the treatise makes it clear that confession was a necessary element of the inquisitorial process.[126] It pronounces boldly "that a man will never be hanged so long as he does not admit his guilt by his own mouth."[127] In reality, voluntary confessions were rare. Generally, defendants fled the scene of the crime and were never heard from again. Those few homicide suspects who suffered the indignity of arrest and imprisonment did not regularly confess because little was to be gained from doing so. Medieval law did not endorse gradations in punishment. Death was the sole penalty for a felony, and medieval law provided no mechanism of plea bargaining for a lesser sentence. The only alternative was to turn king's approver, or what the *Placita Corone* refers to as becoming "the king's child."[128] An approver not only admitted his own guilt to a crime but also incriminated his accomplices both past and present. In doing so, he negotiated with the crown for perpetual imprisonment or abjuration of the realm, providing the courts validated each and every one of his appeals with convictions. For career felons, turning approver was an attractive choice. The process of justice halted temporarily while authorities rounded up and tried the appellees, conceivably offering the approver occasion to apply for a pardon or to escape from prison. For those with good reason to believe a conviction was forthcoming, becoming an approver was a last ditch attempt to avoid the gallows. Felons might also have turned approver to upgrade their circumstances in prison. Jailers housed those strongly suspected of felony under harsh conditions, providing little nourishment and lodging them "in the foulest part of the gaol," with the intent to persuade the felon to finger "his erstwhile associates"; turning king's evidence led to an immediate improvement in prison lifestyle.[129]

From the crown's perspective, promoting the procedure was in the best interests of both the crown and the kingdom. At the time when the crown introduced it, English law relied heavily on victims to initiate criminal proceedings. Thus, turning approver "offered the means of prosecuting crimes which otherwise might have gone undetected," fattening the crown's purse and curbing disorder.[130] The pressure applied to encourage turning king's evidence is a measure of the crown's zeal for approvers. Officially, the English disdained the Continent's use of torture to extract confessions; unofficially, English authorities showed little restraint. Anthony Musson's study of approvers articulates the nature of the treatment they received in prison:

> Four men claimed they were hung up by their hands and feet and forced to turn approver by the constable of Worcester castle. Norwich approver, John Bond, withdrew his appeal and testified in court that he had been kept naked in gaol without food or drink for three nights and tortured by

the sheriff and constables so that he did not know what he was saying. Similarly, at his trial, John, son of Agnes Cloucham, withdrew his appeal and said that he was not *compos mentis* when he made it (presumably on account of some torture).[131]

Turning king's evidence was not without risks. While the Crown was content to exploit a felon's acquaintance with the underworld, it was hesitant to allow a confessed criminal back on the streets. Subsequently, even those approvers whose appellees were duly convicted ultimately were convicted themselves.[132] Approvers' appeals were the least trustworthy of all forms of confessions. Desperate to save their skins, approvers might implicate total innocents. Some approvers, frantic to prolong their lives by sending sheriffs on wild goose chases, fabricated appeals against people who did not even exist.[133] Crown expectations heightened the potential for bogus accusations. The crown expected approvers to appeal multiple accomplices. Some approvers identified as many as thirty or forty former associates; William Rose of Hampshire in 1389 named fifty-four.[134] The unreliability of approvers' appeals was widely known. Thus, apart from an approver's own confession, little was to be gained in a coroner's investigation from the multitude of an approver's appeals.

Admissions of guilt by defendants arose expressly in two other scenarios: abjurers' confessions and pleas of self-defense. In the former, the crown conceded immunity to a felon granted sanctuary in a church for up to forty days, at which point the felon had three options: 1) depart and undergo the consequences of his actions, 2) confess to the coroner and abjure the realm, or 3) refuse to leave and be starved out of the church.[135] The crown conferred on coroners the responsibility to oversee the sanctuary process. They attended and documented confessions; they assigned abjurers a port from which to leave the kingdom. For felons of all kinds, sanctuary was a popular option. The irresistible benefit of sanctuary was time: to apply for a pardon, for tempers to cool, for new evidence to crop up, for reluctant witnesses to come forward.[136] While some recipients of the privilege may have hoped for a safe place to plot their escape, the likelihood was remote. Implacable villagers and townsfolk kept vigilant watch over all exits to prevent any possibility of escape. Those sanctuarymen who set foot outside the bounds of the church risked summary execution. Historical tradition extols sanctuary as an example of the merciful nature of the church intent to civilize the kingdom. Yet, while certainly not as callous as capital punishment, sanctuary was punitive in terms of its consequences: loss of property and exile from England.[137] In a largely cashless society where affluence was measured in land and goods, abjuration guaranteed a life of destitution and ostracism, even for those who failed to leave the realm as law and conscience dictated.[138]

In terms of crime detection, occasionally coroners got more than they had bargained for with an abjuror's confession. In unburdening his conscience prior to departing the kingdom every so often an abjuror offered up an unexpected confession, incidentally solving a case long cold. For example, when Hugh Lucas of Thruxton (*Northants.*) claimed sanctuary after escaping authorities in 1321, the constable and tithingmen who pursued him believed him to be a thief. His confession revealed that he had also killed a man four years earlier.[139] Abjuration created further complications: abjurors also sometimes confessed to crimes they did not commit. Gervase Rosser tells the story of a woman who

> was so desperate to get away from her husband that she went to the church, accused herself of an invented felony, and swore to go into exile. When, as she left, her husband attempted to restrain her, a supporter of the woman held him back, allowing her to make her escape.[140]

Pleas of self-defense were not straightforward examples of confessions. Rather, in cases of self-defense, the coroners' rolls exude a distinct reluctance to divulge the source of their information, although it is not clear whether this hesitance stemmed from a compulsion to protect witnesses or to defend the integrity of the investigation. Nonetheless, the ubiquity of dialogue in enrollments of excusable homicides exposes how the defendants themselves participated in shaping the narrative. The characteristically narrative format of many coroners' accounts made the insertion of dialogue relatively effortless. A case of self-defense from a Leicestershire coroner's roll exhibits how dialogue not only signals the contribution of the accused, it also constructs a much more compelling case for pardoning. In August of 1367, Henry Bailiff; John, son of Juliana; and Alice, wife of the said John, were gathered together in a field at Stanton-under-Bardon (*Leics.*) when a dispute ensued over a loan that had not been repaid. Ostensibly, Henry had borrowed money from John and Alice but had failed to repay it at the appointed time. Perhaps hoping to disgrace him into settling his debts, Alice boldly declared, "you have 12*d.* that belong to us." Her pronouncement merely provoked Henry's ire. Flying into a rage, he shouted, "I curse you!" before brandishing his axe. Sensing Henry's intentions toward his wife were not honorable, John swung into action. Purportedly, John declared loudly that "Henry wishes to kill my wife" before taking up his knife and stabbing Henry with it. Henry died on the spot, not even living long enough for last rites.[141]

Because England maintained such rigid standards of self-defense, coroners' enrollments often went overboard in the attempt to fulfill the requirements of the law. As Naomi Hurnard observes, the result can be somewhat ludicrous:

> [i]t may be judged that too many slayers in self-defense pulled stakes from fences and poles from carts, bolted into *culs de sac* or tried and failed to climb walls, were brought up against dykes or rivers, found swords unexpectedly but conveniently to hand or made random knife thrusts that just happened to hit vital spots.[142]

In the case of John and Alice, an overblown account is exactly what they needed. Technically, Henry's homicide did not meet the conditions for self-defense. Alice's life was in danger, not John's. While the courts were content to uphold the fiction of unity of person in property disputes, husband and wife were two persons at law when it came to self-defense. This is where the dialogue comes into play. Henry's own words imply much about his personality to those who did not know him: he does not repay his debts, he curses those he has wronged, and he is impulsive and violent. These traits instantly depict him as the kind of individual one wants to blame for a death. The dialogue also sheds light on John's state of mind. We know that John firmly believed his wife's life was in danger because that is precisely what he said. This account substantiates the jury's findings. Although the parish church of Stanton had since granted John sanctuary, an act that the court might interpret as an admission of guilt, the jury believed that the bid for sanctuary should not color the outcome of the trial. The jury declared that John killed Henry in self-defense. Here, it is important to appreciate the value of the coroner's indictment. When a trial lasts only fifteen minutes and its jury was constituted hastily, trial jurors needed guidance to decide which way to cast their vote. The coroner's enrollment acted as a valuable tool of communication between juries. If a man's neighbors, men who knew him best, believed they should acquit, then it was probably the most appropriate verdict.[143]

The inclusion of dialogue in this account was calculated. Not only does it add context, but it also permits the accused to mount his own defense. Convincing pleas of self-defense were some of the most difficult to construct. As John and Henry's quarrel above attests, the addition of dialogue went a long way toward building a case for excusable homicide. Thus, it is not surprising that fragments of conversation between the central actors commonly made their way into enrollments alleging self-defense. A Leicestershire report once again highlights how dialogue contextualizes the narrative by speaking to motive and personality. At home one evening in August 1403, John Couper senior overheard his neighbor, Richard Wenlok, beating his wife. He did what any conscientious neighbor would do. He entered their home and asked Richard, "why are you beating your wife?" In response, Richard redirected his anger at John. Seeing that his life was in imminent danger, John had no choice but to defend himself by striking Richard on the head, instantly killing him.[144] John's actions in endeavoring to bring peace to his neighbors were commendable. In fact, a man's honor and respectability was very much founded on the need to govern one's neighbors' morality in the interests of communal peace and harmony.[145] If a jury convicted John for his actions, in essence they would be eschewing English masculinity.

Cases of self-defense establish just how creative and persistent jurors might be in rationalizing some deaths. Occasionally, one encounters an instance of self-defense that was not just over the top; it is hard to imagine that it ever occurred. The death of William Boney in September 1392 falls into this category. According to the enrollment, William turned up at the home of Robert Bower at Croxton (*Leics.*) while Robert's wife, Margery, was lying in childbirth. William wished to sleep with her against her will, and so Margery raised the hue on William, shrieking "Villein, get out of my home!" But William would not leave. As he continued to struggle with her, Margery grasped that she had no other choice but to defend herself. She picked up a staff and struck William on the head, inflicting a fatal wound. William languished for three days before passing away.[146]

So much of this story is implausible. First, it is hard to envisage anyone trying to rape a woman in labor. Second, if Margery was actually laboring in childbirth, where were all the other women? Childbirth in medieval England was a very female-centered process. Not only a midwife attended a woman in childbirth, but also other women from the community. Indeed, the medieval English conceived of childbirth as an opportunity for women's social advancement. The English placed great emphasis on inviting the right women to this momentous occasion.[147] The story could not have happened as reported. This enrollment attests to the difficulty of creating a compelling story of self-defense for a woman in an instance of rape. A popular medieval *exemplum* in which a woman accused a man of rape before a royal justice highlights the problem:

> The judge commanded the man to pay her a sum of money in compensation for the loss of her virginity. After he paid her and she left the court, the judge told the man to follow her and forcibly take the silver from her. He was unable to do so, so hard did she defend herself, and he returned to the court. The judge called the woman back in, took back the silver, and said she had lied: 'if she had preserved the treasure of her virginity as she did the money, it would never have been taken from her."[148]

Because the medieval discourse of sexuality attributed to women a passive role, there was a thin line between rape and consensual sex.[149] An aggressive woman was a contradiction in terms: a woman like Margery defied expectations of femininity. Even more damning, the medieval English rarely convicted rapists because they did not see death as a fitting punishment for the crime.[150] With all of this stacked against her, it is unlikely that a jury would acquit Margery without some embellishment. The coroner's report tells us that Margery's account, when taken together with her reputation and social standing, had convinced the jury of her innocence. In order to induce the trial jury to acquit, they needed to provide an unassailable defense. Who could convict a woman defending herself while in labor?

While felons' confessions usually fell into one of these three categories, it was also possible for the occasional felon on his deathbed to unburden a guilty conscience. A Bedfordshire inquest offers a useful example. Roger of Benfield and at least thirteen companions came to the house of Simon Read at dusk one evening in August of 1267. Upon entering the home, they immediately attacked Simon; his daughter, Matilda; and his son, John. With an arrow lodged deeply in his forearm, John became convinced that their lives were at stake. He grabbed an axe and struck Roger on the head in self-defense. Witnessing the attack on Roger, his companions instantly deserted him. Roger lived until the next day. Before he died, he confessed in the presence of the coroner that he and his accomplices had come to the house expressly to kill Simon and his entire family, conveniently corroborating John's story of self-defense.[151]

TESTIMONIAL EVIDENCE: C) DYING DECLARATIONS

When dealing with a potentially fatal assault today, manuals on crime scene investigation instruct police officers to speak to the victim in the hopes of obtaining a dying declaration. No one knows better what happened in an assault than the victim himself. Medieval coroners and their juries also adopted this approach whenever possible. This idea fit in particularly well with medieval theories of repentance: "the idea was normal in the Middle Ages that what a man did and said at the moment of death was crucial to his destiny; that a thoughtless man might escape the fire by a deathbed repentance."[152] This philosophy guaranteed the honesty of a dying declaration. Only a heretic or an apostate would use his last breaths to sin through perjury. Death was slow in coming to many victims of assault, allowing ample opportunity for them to tell their side of the story, even if only to their nursemaids. The coroners' rolls are scrupulous in recording whether the victim lived long enough to be given last rites. The reason for this was procedural. Coroners appended this detail to explain why some enrollments included no mention of the first finder: first finders discovered corpses, not dying men.[153] For the purposes of this book, this notation is advantageous in pinpointing an investigation founded chiefly on the testimony of the victim himself. *The Mirror of Justices* emphasizes the importance of obtaining a dying declaration, instructing coroners to comment whether the victim had the "power of speaking before his death."[154] Occasionally an enrollment acknowledges the centrality of the victim's dying declaration in unraveling the mystery of his fatal wound. For example, William, son of William Vescy, of Saxton (*Yorks.*) lived just long enough after an assault in May 1345 to confess his sins, dying before the priest had a chance to administer last rites. In his confession, he blamed unknown men for robbing and attacking him.[155] On at least one occasion, the victim's health was sufficiently stable for the coroner to assemble a police line-up of sorts. In November 1269, unknown thieves descended upon the vill of Roxton to wreak havoc. They first broke into the home of Ralph Bovetoun, carrying away all his goods. They then moved on to the next house, slaying Maud del Forde and mortally injuring Alice Pressade. Finally, they entered the home of John Cobbler, where they immediately killed him, wounded his wife and daughter, and slew his servant. Before she passed away, Azeline, John Cobbler's wife, implicated Richard of Neville, former servant of the prior of Newnham and one of the men who supervised the collection of tithes the previous autumn, as well as four glovers from the town of Bedford. The coroner ordered the arrest of all five men. However, he was doubtful whether the man they had arrested was indeed the Richard of Neville that Azeline had described. Thus, he escorted her to the prison at Bedford so she could identify him herself.[156]

When the dead could not speak for themselves, family members occasionally spoke for them. English women played an especially active role appealing assaults and homicides committed against their families. Indeed, women brought nearly two-thirds of all homicide appeals in the thirteenth century.[157] While common law notionally limited a woman's appeals to physical attacks upon her person and the homicide of her husband providing he died in her arms, in reality royal justices rarely quashed defensible cases that fell outside these parameters.[158] Enrollments of appeals are highly instructive. They are far and away the most meticulous enrollments in terms of detail. Further, the comprehensiveness of some appeals points to the possibility that wives profited from their encounters with the coroner to receive legal advice concerning the correct presentation of the case. After all, in a rural setting, the coroner might be the closest thing to legal counsel. A 1480 jury challenge drawn from the Year Books substantiates that coroners did sometimes hire themselves out as legal consultants. Premised on the sheriff's partiality, the plaintiff spoke to potential replacements for the sheriff. Typically, in these situations one of the coroners stepped in to empanel a new jury. However, the plaintiff warned the court that, of the two available coroners, one had been retained as his counsel (*est retenu de counsel*), and thus was equally as partial as the sheriff.[159]

Appeals had "notoriously difficult pleading requirements," and justices seemed content to quash appeals for trifling details.[160] J.B. Post observes an instance when a judge invalidated a woman's appeal because she failed to state which door a man used when entering a house to attack her.[161] Given the obstacles, a wife intent to pursue her husband's attackers in court needed some assistance in framing her appeal. The coroner's view of wounds played a key role in this respect. The beating of John of Britville of Great Barford (*Beds.*) illustrates how helpful interaction with the coroner might be for a wife intent on building an ironclad appeal. After a violent altercation with Simon, son of Roger de Cainhoe, one evening in October 1271, John of Britville's wife, Emma, at once raised the hue. Ralph of Goldington, the coroner, arrived at Great Barford the next day to consult with John and view his wounds. Emma was present at the time. Before the coroner, Emma pledged that "if John should recover from his wounds, he would sue in prison at the next county court against Simon as against a felon. And that Simon committed the said felonies against him Emma offered to prove or deraign in all ways according to the award of the king's court." Several weeks later Emma appeared before the Bedfordshire county court to present her appeal.

The formal statement furnishes the model testimony, including every detail a coroner might have ever wanted. She declared:

> When she and her husband were walking together in the king's highway in Great Barford between Jordan Cappe's house and that formerly of John of Blunham at vespers on 10 Oct., Simon came there and pursued and assaulted her husband, and struck him on the top of the head on the left side between the crown and the ear with a sword of iron and steel, giving him a great wound 5 inches long, 3 inches wide and as deep as the brain, whence 13 pieces of bone issued. Simon struck him again with the sword on the little finger, called the auricular finger, of the left hand on the inside of the hand, cutting the sinews of the finger and thus maiming him; and he struck him on the next finger, called the leech (*medicus*) finger, breaking its bones, and so he was maimed in both fingers. His malice did not stop there, but he again struck John many bloodless blows with the plat (*flat*) of the sword on the right side of his head, so that the whole of his head was excoriated and swollen and he lost his hearing on the left side. Simon also robbed John of a cordwain (*a Spanish leather*) purse worth 6*d*., with 8*s*. of new money inside it.[162]

The only detail missing from the ideal coroner's report was the value of the weapon. While the details about the wound presumably come from the coroner's assessment at the view, how is it that Emma knew to include these details in her appeal? While professional pleaders were common in civil cases, this was not true of criminal appeals.[163] Without some coaching by the coroner, however informally, it is hard to imagine that Emma could have constructed the perfect appeal.

PROCEDURE:
A) CONFRONTING THE WALL

Occasionally an investigation into cause of death hit a wall. In this situation, a coroner had two options. Sometimes coroners gave up and reported that the jury did not know what had happened. Other times, coroners pursued information through other means. The London death of Gilbert of Aldenham provides a good example. The initial inquest provided a barebones outline of a homicide. On Easter Monday in 1325, Gilbert and "certain companions" came to the house of William Wynter in Holborn where it was suspected that he was harboring Thomas of Aldenham. Against William's will, they searched the house looking for Thomas in order to arrest him. The illicit search provoked a quarrel between Gilbert and William, in which William struck Gilbert across the head with a sickle, killing him at once. Although the record does not explain why, the coroner, Stephen of Abingdon, was unsatisfied with this account. In the hopes of obtaining more detail, he adjourned the inquest until the following Monday, ordering the sheriff to summon "a similar jury of the neighbourhood of Holborn where the felony was committed." With time and new faces on the jury, the second inquest filled in many of the gaps in the previous account. In the new version of the story, all three companions are named. The story also exonerates William. Rather, Gilbert struck the first blow, throwing William to the ground. Fearing retaliation, one of Gilbert's companions, Richard Bukkeskyn, drew a knife intending to strike William, but in the confusion he struck and killed Gilbert.[164] G. Rowland, a Bedfordshire coroner, also ordered a second inquest in the 1270 death of Bertram Polet of Willington. The first inquest drew its jurors from the townships of Willington and Cople. They concluded that evildoers had slain Bertram, but they knew little else. In the second inquest, Rowland broadened the jury-base considerably, summoning jurors not only from Willington and Cople, but also Moggerhanger, Northill, Blunham, Beeston, Cardington, and Sandy. Nonetheless, the second inquest was not much more productive. Jurors listed potential witnesses, noting that two servants were thought to have been looking for fodder in the visne immediately prior to Bertram's death. They also suspected several shepherds of having witnessed the felony. The shepherds were required to find pledges. Otherwise, the story remained the same.[165]

Sometimes the jurors stood out as the voice of reason demanding supplementary information. The men who served on inquests often did so as a means to assert authority within their communities and garner the respect of their peers. Thus, inquest jurors were not shrinking violets. A coroner's irritation when his jury refused to conclude an investigation, even though he felt further questioning was unnecessary, demonstrates just that. The 1272 inquest into the death of an unknown woman could well have remained unresolved if jurors did not insist on learning more. Although they had not yet located them, jurors claimed that Thomas Sayle of Risely and Ellen Seward of Melchbourne (*Beds.*) "know the truth concerning this affair better than anyone else." They refused to reach a verdict without them.[166] The death of the cordwainer Thomas of St Albans in 1326 produced an equally insistent jury. Initially, they reported that Thomas was standing in his shop one June afternoon when he saw two goldsmiths, Thomas of Walpole and James of Shoreditch, drawing near his shop with swords and bucklers in hand. Perceiving danger, St Albans moved to the offensive: he knocked Walpole to the ground with a staff. In response, James drew his sword and stabbed St Albans repeatedly: first in the head, then the right side and left arm. St Albans died just before sunset in his shop later that day. Once again, the coroner's roll fails to explain what part of the narrative made jurors wary, but they requested a day to make further inquiry into the homicide. The revised account reveals that they had the wrong man. In fact, James of Shoreditch was not there at all. Rather it was Walpole and William of Stormoth. St Albans did cast the first blow by knocking Walpole to the ground; but this act merely prompted Walpole to stand up, burnish his sword, and stab St Albans in the head. William of Stormoth followed up by inflicting the two subsequent wounds.[167]

PROCEDURE:
B) WAS THE INVESTIGATION ALL MALE?

Undeniably, medieval death investigation was an exceedingly male process. The coroner was male; so, too, were the sheriff and his bailiffs, as well as the town constable (when applicable); the jury was composed of twelve sworn men; nearest neighbors and pledges were usually male; and only men over the age of twelve were required to attend the inquest. Among the cohort of "expert witnesses" whose services might be called upon to attend the inquest, once again, they, too, were men: wardens, watchmen, tithingmen, medical professionals, clergy. Yet, it is noteworthy that, although the crown barred women from participating in the administration of the law, multiple courts of law recognized their expertise in women's health and sexuality and encouraged them to act as witnesses in a variety of venues. The English church courts were the first to employ "wise women" as chief investigators in annulment suits alleging impotence.[168] Because the church courts granted annulments on the grounds of impotence or frigidity, providing the couple had never consummated the union, the church required solid proof that the husband's physical impairment was real. Canonists, in particular, were convinced that couples desirous of a divorce would collude to hoodwink authorities by faking allegations of impotence. Accordingly, the church employed women, most likely prostitutes, but possibly also midwives, to test men's virility.[169] The English church also acknowledged women as a voice of authority in matrimonial litigation. In examining matrimonial suits from fourteenth-century England, Frederick Pederson observes that of the 565 witnesses, 389 were men, and 175 were women.[170] As a ratio, these figures reflect 1:2.22 female to male witnesses, revealing a much greater female participation rate than in any other legal process ecclesiastical or royal. Charles Donahue, Jr., contends that women appeared so frequently as witnesses in cases of marital litigation because their testimony was thought to be especially appropriate.[171] The common law courts also exploited the proficiency of women in a range of circumstances. The crown regularly called upon women to perform a physical inspection of those who "pleaded the belly." When a woman entered this plea before the court it was because officials were preparing to hang her for felony, but she hoped to delay her execution by asserting that she was pregnant. To determine whether she was, in fact, pregnant *and* quick with child, the crown mandated a physical assessment.[172] Royal justices also enlisted the services of women to inspect pregnant widows whose husbands had recently died. If the child stood to inherit his property, once again the court required proof that she was indeed pregnant and pregnant enough that the child definitively belonged to her dead husband.[173] Requests of this nature were so common that a writ existed specifically for this purpose. The writ *de ventre inspiciendo* compelled a sheriff to seek out the services of local women to perform the necessary inspection. *Fleta* explains that the sheriff employs "lawful and discreet women" to inspect the woman by handling her about the belly and breasts in order to ascertain whether she was indeed pregnant.[174] In criminal law, women's participation as jurors was restricted to two specific scenarios. First, when a woman cried rape, not only did she turn to local authorities, such as the coroner, to witness signs of physical violence, but also local women examined her to testify that her virginity was no longer intact.[175] Second, women also contributed to infanticide investigations. When a community stumbled across the corpse of a newborn, the sheriff instructed local women to feel the breasts and bellies of those whom they suspected might have recently given birth.[176]

All these scenarios attest a distinct recognition that women possessed expertise that was exclusive to their sex. It is not hard to imagine situations in death investigations necessitating a woman's counsel. A good number of the disputes discussed in this monograph have related in one way or another to marital spats. If a coroner and his jury had good reason to believe a troubled marriage laid the groundwork for a homicide, who better to ask than the couple's female friends and family? Not only did the medieval English consider wives to be experts in matrimony, wives were also thought to be renowned gossips. Thus, they were probably better in touch with a community's questionable activities, enough to know whether an extramarital dalliance might be to blame. In the event where the dead was a woman, the local community may also have felt it most appropriate, in terms of modesty, to seek out another woman to disrobe the corpse and carry out the physical examination. Indeed, while death investigation was primarily a male activity, death itself was typically female. Women were responsible for preparing the dead for burial. They washed the dead, they wrapped the body in a winding sheet, or shroud, and when it was a woman who had died, they processed alongside the body to the churchyard.[177] Given the prominent role women played in funeral preparations, women were the logical choice for handling the dead throughout the investigative process.

Women's medical know-how also made them ideal witnesses in death investigation. Because of the domestic nature of most medieval medicine, women played an invaluable role in home medical care. Indeed, the English recognized a woman's proficiency in this realm sufficiently to exploit it as a selling feature. Books of home remedies advertised precisely on these grounds, knowing that consumers had greater confidence if they knew a recipe came recommended by a woman.[178] Because of domestic medicine, women were better prepared to identify the signs and symptoms of a disease than most laymen. The association between women and medicine went far beyond traditional ideas of women as nurturing beings. Women also assumed an official role in medicine. Not only were women midwives and nurses, but there are also numerous examples of women working in a wide range of medical professions. Historians have uncovered evidence of female barbers active in Canterbury, Bristol, London, and York;[179] there are a significant number of references also to women working as physicians across England;[180] women may even occasionally have acted as surgeons.[181]

Unfortunately, even if women did play a role in death investigation, the records would not reveal it. As women, they could not play any "official" role in the investigation, and thus coroners had no need to document their participation.

Yet, the documents do support the participation of women in other roles. Women played a key role as first finders. In fact, 32% of first finders were the mothers or wives of the dead.[182] Women initiated nearly two-thirds of all homicide appeals.[183] Women probably played a central role as witnesses also, but as this chapter suggests, the narrative format of coroners' rolls makes it difficult to discover exactly who the witnesses were in most cases. Women also occasionally acted as the nearest neighbor. William Alisaundre, one of Norfolk's county coroners, attached Annabil Hukester as one of the four nearest neighbors in the death of Sara, wife of William, of Grimston, when she was attacked and slain by strangers whom she had put up for the night at South Lynn (*Norfolk*) in November of 1363.[184] He also attached Emma Julyon as nearest neighbor in the death of Godfrey Skeppere the year before.[185] At the death of Matilda Ran of Cleye, aged seventy, in November of 1361, he not only attached two women as nearest neighbors (Agnes Barker and Alice of Brounfeld), but one of their pledges was also a woman (Agnes Beverage.)[186] Was Alisaundre unusual in seeking women to fulfill these roles? Women do not function as nearest neighbors or pledges in other coroners' enrollments. However, it is critical to note that coroners only sometimes included the names of the nearest neighbors and their pledges. What may be more unusual about Alisaundre's actions was the degree of comprehensiveness of his documentation. Regrettably, there is no way of knowing whether this was a common, yet undocumented, approach, or an aberration.

PROCEDURE:
C) DEATH INVESTIGATION AS A DEMOCRACY

The coroner's oath for medieval London contains an inspiring promise that he "shall do equal justice . . . to all manner of people, as well poor as rich, denizens as well as strangers."[187] Nonetheless, when faced with such a rigidly hierarchical society, the democratic premise of this pledge is not compelling. Quite simply, it is hard to imagine that coroners held all dead to be equal. Granted, noble impunity is a given. The nobility is largely absent from most criminal records, in large part because Parliament was considered a more appropriate venue to try men with such close ties to the crown, and whose criminal actions might easily be categorized as treason.[188] Further, as tenants-in-chief, their homicides were of personal interest to the crown, and more likely the result of a private warfare than being in the wrong place at the wrong time. Yet, even if we peel away this upper layer from the hierarchy, historians still reject the plausibility of equality in justice. W. Mark

Ormrod expresses it most succinctly when he states that "the high level of corruption that operated at all levels within the legal system meant that justice had always been weighted against the interests of the poor."[189] In view of this reluctance, it is necessary to acknowledge that the poorest segment of society is well represented among the dead. To illustrate this point: on Friday, June 24, 1321/22 at Weston (*Northants.*), jurors held an inquest into the death of a beggar (*mendicant*) who was "poor and greatly debilitated."[190] Another beggar woman, reportedly a stranger to the community whose name jurors did not know, died at Covenham Saint Bartholomew (*Lincs.*) in June 1379. Jurors commented that the woman was staying in the home of Robert Barsot where she hanged herself with a halter during the night.[191] In the spring of 1377, an unknown child aged roughly two days was found in a field referred to locally as "Shepcotefeld" (*Berks.*). Jurors reported that no one knew the child or how he died.[192] An enrollment from 1393/94 reports the death of Christian of Hessle, a beggar woman who drowned at Wrangle (*Lincs.*) after suffering from an attack of paralysis.[193]

The paucity of detail in many of these records implies that coroners and their jurors did not overexert themselves in their investigations—yet admittedly, many inquest records share this brevity and sparse detail. One explanation is that locals were not interested in reaching the bottom of the investigation when an outsider or vagrant died. It is equally plausible that the dead's marginal status left jurors with little guidance. Not knowing much about the dead's background or associations, they may have been at a loss as to where to begin. In this respect, Christian of Hessle's inquest is significant. How did the coroner and his jury discover her name? Christian may have communicated with locals before her death, who later relayed her name to the coroner. This detail may also point to the thoroughness of the investigation. By the mid-thirteenth century, the English crown required vagrants to carry certificates of good character. A physical examination of the body might have unearthed documentation of this nature.[194] Overall, the poorest segment of society was not as well represented among the perpetrators of crime. This is best explained by the "developing doctrine" of "required and forbidden 'additions.'" The crown declared an indictment void if it described the defendant as a "vagabond" or other variant of the term as an addition.[195]

If the quality of the investigation was tied to the social status of the dead, it is striking that the deaths of prisoners, one segment of the population that would seem to evoke little sympathy from jurors, are surprisingly well documented. Naturally, part of the coroner's mission with prison deaths was to document whether the jailer's behavior was in any way responsible. Yet, the enrollments often include a description of the circumstances leading up to each death, implying a higher degree of supervision in prisons than previously imagined, as well as confirmation that a legitimate investigation had indeed taken place. For example, when Hugh Cartwright died at Leicester jail in 1398/99, jurors noted that he languished with an illness for six weeks before he finally passed away.[196] Similarly, John Sewale of Coggeshall was ill for a month at Colchester prison before his illness got the better of him.[197] The death of Thomas Franke of Minstead of New Forest is positively effusive. Thomas was imprisoned at Winchester castle in the custody of William Slouthe. Apparently, one day in 1385, Thomas sought permission from William to get water from the nearby River Itchen. At the river's edge, he bent down to drink, but because his body was so debilitated, he fell into the river and drowned; his body was born away by the current.[198]

It is hard to deny that coroners viewed some deaths with more seriousness than they viewed others. This is most perceptible in terms of categories of death. While accidental deaths comprise a substantial fraction of the coroners' rolls, even when a coroner included jury lists, he was far less likely to include them for deaths by misadventure than for homicides.[199] The documentation constructs a powerful impression that some coroners investigated homicides, but merely reported deaths by misadventure, without even bothering to assemble a jury. What do we make of this? Some coroners may have dispensed with the usual process because the nature of the death was so obvious a jury had nothing more to offer an investigation. Or, those coroners may have believed that including a jury list was superfluous in deaths of a noncontroversial nature; that is, where there was little possibility that the integrity of the investigation would be questioned. The latter hypothesis fits best with the documentation of John Mapples, one of Yorkshire's county coroners in the 1360s. Mapples was meticulous in recording the names of jurors in cases of homicide, but when it came to accidental deaths, he neglected to include jury lists. Nonetheless, it is clear that he was working with a jury: he makes repeated references to juries of twelve men, even if he does not mention their names.[200] Undoubtedly, while this approach to deaths by misadventure is disconcerting, one can always hope that those coroners who adopted this investigative strategy did so only when accidents took place in a public setting with copious witnesses.

Medieval coroners and their juries shared most of the same evidentiary concerns as do their modern counterparts. The body took priority in the investigation, and communities respected the need for integrity of body and scene of death. In terms of criminal deaths, the major distinction between medieval and modern trials lay with material evidence. Weapons and other material objects, including deodands involved in deaths by misadventure, assumed center-stage only at the inquest itself. Even if the inquest determined homicide as cause of death, the escheator had sold all material evidence for the crown's profit long before the trial even began. While English sensibilities barred coroners from performing autopsies, nonetheless their physical examinations were thorough. The ability to detect internal injuries such as broken bones and burst diaphragms reminds us that there was more to the post-mortem examination than poking and prodding, and medical practitioners must sometimes have conducted the examination. Beyond the body, the investigation relied closely on oral interviews, from a wide variety of subjects: neighbors, family, friends, witnesses, suspects, even the dead themselves. Of course, some depositions were more trustworthy than others. Approvers and sanctuarymen sometimes fabricated allegations and accomplices to gain time. Coroners also showed compassion by protecting their sources of information. In documenting the investigative experience, the rolls mask informant identities in the interests of avoiding a cycle of violence. Not all deaths were necessary equal. Certainly, the documentation suggests that investigations into deaths by misadventure were much less rigorous than those for homicides. Yet, in general, the coroners' rolls suggest that the ideal medieval investigation was comprehensive and thorough—coroners and jurors used all means within their powers to extract the necessary information to reach a valid conclusion.

NOTES

1. Jon Arrizabalaga, "Medical Causes of Death in Preindustrial Europe: Some Historiographical Considerations," *JHMAS* 54 (1999): 242.
2. George C. Alter and Ann G. Carmichael, "Classifying the Dead: Towards a History of the Registration of Causes of Death," *JHMAS* 54 (1999): 116.
3. For a fuller discussion of folkloric concerns relating to suicide, see Sara M. Butler, "Cultures of Suicide? Regionalism and Suicide Verdicts in Medieval England," *The Historian* 69.3 (2007): 427–49; Robert Halliday, "The Roadside Burial of Suicides: An East Anglian Study," *Folklore* 121 (2010): 81–93.
4. Isidore of Seville, *Canon of Medicine*, as cited in Faith Wallis, ed., *Medieval Medicine: A Reader* (Toronto: University of Toronto Press, 2010), p. 8.
5. Bryon Grigsby, *Pestilence in Medieval and Early Modern English Literature* (New York: Routledge, 2004), pp. 1, 52.
6. Lindsay Prior and Mick Bloor, "Why People Die: Social Representations of Death and Its Causes," *Science as Culture* 3.3 (1993): 351.
7. Prior and Bloor, "Why People Die," 368–70.
8. TNA PRO JUST 2/102, m. 1.
9. J.B. Post, "Crime in Later Medieval England: Some Historiographical Limitations," *C&C* 2.2 (1987): 215.
10. Post, "Crime in Later Medieval England," 215.
11. James Masschaele, "Space of the Marketplace in Medieval England," *Speculum* 77.2 (2002): 394–95. For May 14, 1315, the archbishop's register notes, "[m]andate to the official of the archdeacon of Richmond to inquire 'super condicionibus, conversacione et vita,' of William, son of John de Tryvels (also Trevels), accused of theft in a secular court, and in Ripon prison." This is followed by a mandate for July 29 of the same year that states "[p]roclamation that anyone wishing to oppose his purgation was to appear on Saturday before Michaelmas (Sept. 27), in Ripon church. Proclamation to be made in the churches and markets, especially in the deanery of Aymundernesse." See William Brown and A. Hamilton Thompson, eds., *The Register of William Greenfield Lord Archbishop of York 1306–1315*, 4 vols. (Surtees Society, 1931–1940), v. 4, p. 231.
12. Masschaele, "Space of the Marketplace," 395.
13. John H. Langbein, "Historical Foundations of the Law of Evidence: A View from the Ryder Sources," *Columbia Law Review* 96 (1996): 1170.

14. Henri de Bracton, *De Legibus et Consuetudinibus Angliae*, ed. George Woodbine, ed. and trans. Samuel E. Thorne, 4 vols. (*SS*, 1968–1976), v. 2, p. 429.
15. F. Pollock and F.W. Maitland, *A History of English Law before the Time of Edward I*, 2 vols. (Cambridge: Cambridge UP, 1898), v. 2, p. 579. As *Fleta* puts it: "if he has been taken over [the body of] the slain man with his knife fresh with blood (in which case no other proof is needful)." See H.G. Richardson and G.O. Sayles, eds., *Fleta*, 3 vols. (*SS*, 1953–1983), v. 2, p. 79.
16. *Bracton*, v. 2, pp. 429–30.
17. LaMar Hill, "The Two-Witness Rule in English Treason Trials: Some Comments on the Emergence of Procedural Law," *AJLH* 12.2 (1968): 96.
18. F.W. Maitland and W.J. Whittaker, eds., *The Mirror of Justices* (*SS*, v. 7, 1895), p. 116.
19. G.D.G. Hall, ed., *The Treatise on the Laws and Customs of the Realm of England Commonly Called Glanvill* (Oxford: Clarendon, 1993), p. 24.
20. As cited in Kenneth Pennington, "Innocent until Proven Guilty: The Origins of a Legal Maxim," *The Jurist* 63 (2003): 115.
21. James A. Brundage, "Full and Partial Proofs in Classical Canonical Procedure," *The Jurist* 67 (2007): 60.
22. Brundage, "Full and Partial Proofs," 62.
23. Richard Fraher, "Conviction According to Conscience: The Medieval Jurists Debate Concerning Judicial Discretion and the Law of Proof," *L&HR* 7.1 (1989): 34.
24. Fraher, "Conviction According to Conscience," 24.
25. Fraher, "Conviction According to Conscience," 24.
26. John Fortescue, *De Laudibus Legum Angliae*, ed. S.B. Chrimes, 2nd ed. (Cambridge: Cambridge UP, 2011), p. 65.
27. Fraher, "Conviction According to Conscience," 23.
28. Fortescue, *De Laudibus Legum Angliae*, p. 101.
29. Andrea Frisch, *The Invention of the Eyewitness: Witnessing and Testimony in Early Modern France* (Chapel Hill: North Carolina Studies in the Romance Languages and Literatures, 2004), p. 38.
30. S.F.C. Milsom, *Historical Foundations of the Common Law*, 2nd ed. (London: Butterworths, 1981), p. 422.
31. Thomas A. Green, *Verdict According to Conscience: Perspectives on the English Criminal Trial Jury 1200–1800* (Chicago: University of Chicago Press, 1985), p. 52.
32. Richard Firth Green, *A Crisis of Truth: Literature and Law in Ricardian England* (Philadelphia: University of Pennsylvania Press, 1999), p. 13.
33. Firth Green, *Crisis of Truth*, p. 133.
34. Television crime shows perpetuate the popular misconception that technicians use plastic bags for evidence preservation, but the breathability of paper bags makes them a better choice for long-term preservation.
35. The only exception is in instances of hand-having thieves—that is, when a thief was caught with the stolen goods on his person—or, when a murderer was caught in the act. See Pollock and Maitland, *A History of English Law*, v. 2, p. 579.
36. Helen M. Cam, *Liberties and Communities in Medieval England* (Cambridge: Cambridge UP, 1944), p. 189.
37. *AS*, p. 610. Translation is drawn from Valerie I.J. Flint, "The Saint and the Operation of the Law: Reflections upon the Miracles of St Thomas Cantilupe," in *Belief and Culture in the Middle Ages: Studies Presented to Henry Mayr-Harting*, ed. Richard Gameson and Henrietta Leyser (Oxford: Oxford UP, 2001), p. 344.

38. TNA PRO JUST 2/1, m. 1.
39. Barbara A. Hanawalt, "The Voices and Audiences of Social History Records," *Social Science History* 15.2 (1991): 164.
40. Carrie Smith and Brian Barraclough, "Suicide in Hampshire and Wiltshire 1327–1399," *History of Psychiatry* 6 (1995): 106.
41. Margaret Harvey, "Some Comments on Northern Mortuary Customs in the Later Middle Ages," *Journal of Ecclesiastical History* 59.2 (2008): 272–80.
42. The value of clothing is emphasized by the inquest into the 1322 death of Lucy Faukes. Jurors fingered Richard the Shearman and Christina, his wife, for her homicide. Apparently, they quarreled with her in the hopes of obtaining a pretext for killing her and stealing her clothes. See Reginald R. Sharpe, ed., *Calendar of Coroners' Rolls of the City of London, A.D. 1300–1378* (London: R. Clay & Sons, Limited, 1913), pp. 68–69.
43. Hanawalt argues that it was the coroners' responsibility to strip the body, but she does not offer evidence to explain why she believes this to be the case. See her "Voices and Audiences," 162.
44. Donald W. Sutherland, ed., *The Eyre of Northamptonshire, 3–4 Edward III (1329–30)*, v. 1 (*SS*, v. 97, 1983), p. 209.
45. Christopher Daniell, *Death and Burial in Medieval England 1066–1550* (London and New York: Routledge, 1997), p. 38.
46. TNA PRO JUST 2/35, m. 12.
47. The record of Agnes's death is not unusual. Enrollments regularly traced a body's movements, and when the body had been contaminated, the coroner's report took note. For example, when the first finder came across the body of a stranger at Beaconsfield (*Bucks.*) in 1362, the report of his death noted specifically that the body had been partially torn by dogs; the dogs were not blamed for the death, however. Rather, local jurors examined the body closely to see if there might be more to the story. They surmised that he was the victim of a knifing. Only after he had died from the knife wounds did the dogs encounter his body. TNA PRO JUST 2/12, m. 2.
48. *Bracton*, v. 2, p. 343.
49. TNA PRO JUST 2/2, m. 1.
50. Sharpe, *Calendar of Coroners' Rolls*, pp. 4–5. Sharpe has interpreted this question as an attempt to determine whether the wood should be deodand because "in order that a thing causing death should become 'deodand' it was necessary that it should be *moving*" (p. 4*n*.). Whether the piece of wood moved was not at issue—after all, it fell from the solar and struck John in the head. Nor does it seem likely that the question was intended to determine if anyone should be blamed for the death: that question was asked quite specifically a few lines later. Rather, it seems clear that the coroner was intent to discover if the piece of wood was still in the same location as when it fell from the solar.
51. TNA PRO JUST 2/111, m. 12. The 1270 death of Gilbert the Shepherd of Kinswick suggests a similar conclusion. See TNA PRO JUST 2/1, m. 7d. Coroners were not only anxious to find the body untouched, but they also hoped to find a pristine scene of death in which evidence of this nature was preserved untouched from bystanders.
52. Carol Loar, "Medical Knowledge and the Early Modern English Coroner's Inquest," *SHoM* 23.3 (2010): 484.
53. See Abraham Jennings, *Digit Dei, Or an Horrid Murther Strangely Detected* (London, 1664). Available through *Early English Books Online*.
54. TNA PRO JUST 2/102, m. 13.
55. Teresa Sutton, "The Nature of the Early Law of Deodand," *Cambrian Law Review* 30.9 (1999): 16.

56. TNA PRO JUST 2/107, m. 1.
57. Sharpe, *Calendar of Coroners' Rolls*, pp. 204–05.
58. Joseph Pugliese, "*Super visum corporis*: Visuality, Race, Narrativity and the Body of Forensic Pathology," *Law and Literature* 14.2 (2002): 369.
59. Mary Richards, "The Body as Text in Early Anglo-Saxon Law," in *Naked Before God: Uncovering the Body in Anglo-Saxon England*, ed. Benjamin C. Withers and Jonathan Wilcox (Morgantown: West Virginia UP, 2003), p. 114.
60. Sharpe, *Calendar of Coroners' Rolls*, p. 3.
61. For example, in the 1370s roll of Wiltshire county coroner, John of Keevil, the phrase "*super visus corporis ipsius* [name of the dead]" is inserted interlinear in almost every enrollment, as if to emphasize that the coroner did actually view the body. See TNA PRO JUST 2/200.
62. For example, see the death of Agnes wife of John Driver of Little Baddow, TNA PRO JUST 2/35, m. 12.
63. TNA PRO JUST 2/118, m. 5.
64. TNA PRO JUST 2/102, m. 13d.
65. TNA PRO JUST 2/104, m. 52.
66. TNA PRO JUST 2/61, m. 9/7.
67. TNA PRO JUST 2/105, m. 2d.
68. TNA PRO JUST 2/129, m. 1.
69. For an example of a child who died unbaptized, see TNA PRO JUST 2/194, m. 5d.
70. TNA PRO JUST 2/129, m. 3.
71. F.M. Nichols, ed., *Britton: The French Text Revised with an English Translation* (Oxford: Clarendon Press, 1865), v. 1, p. 45.
72. Jonathan Rose, "Feodo de Compedibus Vocato le Sewet: The Medieval Prison 'Oeconomy,'" in *Law in the City: Proceedings of the Seventeenth British Legal History Conference*, ed. Paul Brand, Andrew Lewis, and Paul Mitchell (London: Four Courts Press, 2005), pp. 72–94.
73. See J.G. Bellamy, *The Criminal Trial in Later Medieval England: Felony before the Courts from Edward I to the Sixteenth Century* (Toronto and Buffalo: University of Toronto Press, 1998), p. 13
74. For example, all seven of the Southwark prison deaths in TNA PRO KB 9/265, m. 33 depict jurors pronouncing that the prisoners died of plague (and other illnesses) and no other cause.
75. TNA PRO JUST 2/155, m. 10d.
76. TNA PRO JUST 2/146, m. 5.
77. Sharpe, *Calendar of Coroners' Rolls*, p. 12. When Richard Rede of Great Horwood (*Bucks.*) lost his footing and fell from his cart while loading hurdles, the record notes only that he broke something internally: *Ita quod infra corpus ipsius frangebatur*. Lesley Boatwright, ed., *Inquests and Indictments from Late Fourteenth Century Buckinghamshire* (Buckinghamshire Archaeological Society, v. 29, 1994), p. 3.
78. Nicholas of Essendon at the Coventry jail in 1388, TNA PRO JUST 2/189, m. 2; Richard Mey in 1388/89, JUST 2/189, m. 2d; Joanna, daughter of Adam Shotewell, also at Coventry, in 1391/92, JUST 2/191, m. 3; Peter Cornwall, squire, in London in November of 1400, KB 9/185, m. 1.
79. Juhani Norri, *Names of Sicknesses in English, 1400–1550: An Exploration of the Lexical Field* (Helsinki: Suomalainen Tiedeakatemia, 1992), p. 227.
80. Email communication with Juhani Norri, October 31, 2012.
81. Norri, *Names of Sicknesses, passim*.
82. For a good summary, see Bettina Bildhauer, "Blood in Medieval Cultures," *History Compass* 4 (2006): 1–11.

83. Malcolm Gaskill, "Reporting Murder: Fiction in the Archives in Early Modern England," *Social History* 23.1 (1998): 25.
84. Cheshire Record Office, Chester, DDX 196, fo. 10, as cited in Gaskill, 9. This case is described in greater depth in Steve Hindle, "'Bleeding Afreshe'?: The Affray and Murder at Nantwich, 19 December 1572," in *The Extraordinary and the Everyday in Early Modern England: Essays in Celebration of the Work of Bernard Capp* (Houndmills and Basingstoke: Palgrave Macmillan, 2010), pp. 224–45.
85. Gaskill, "Reporting Murder," 28.
86. Outside of England, corpse touching occasionally appeared in court records. Claude Gauvard, *"De Grace Especial": Crime, Etat et Société à la Fin du Moyen Age* (Paris: Publications de la Sorbonne, 1991), v. 1, pp. 179–89. The ordeal also materializes in some medieval works of literature. In the *Nibelungenlied*, when Siegfried was laid to rest on his bier, Hagen was summoned to prove his innocence by drawing near the corpse, at which point the "wounds flowed anew," proclaiming his guilt. The *Nibelungenlied* also asserts that it was a common practice, declaring "it is a great marvel and frequently happens today that whenever a blood-guilty murderer is seen beside the corpse the wounds begin to bleed." *The Nibelungenlied*, trans. A.T. Hatto (London: Penguin, 1965; rev. 1969), p. 137. Arthurian literature incorporates cruentation as a stage-device on more than one occasion. For example, see Chrétien de Troyes's "The Knight with the Lion," in his *Arthurian Romances*, ed. William W. Kibler (London: Penguin, 1991; rev. 2004), p. 309. Hartmann Von Aue's *Iwein* furnishes the most potent statement about the practice: "[o]ne thing has often been told to us as true: if a slain man is borne past his murderer, no matter how long ago his wounds were incurred, he will start bleeding again." Frank Tobin, Kim Vivian, and Richard H. Lawson, trans. and ed., *Arthurian Romances, Tales and Lyric Poetry: The Complete Works of Hartmann Von Aue* (Philadelphia: Pennsylvania State UP, 2001), p. 251.
87. Robert P. Brittain, "Cruentation in Legal Medicine and in Literature," *MH* 9.1 (1965): 85.
88. Alain Boureau, "La preuve par le cadavre qui saigne au XIIIe siècle: Entre expérience commune et savoir scolastique," *Micrologus* 7 (1999): 254. The English literary tradition associated with cruentation is early modern. William Shakespeare, *Richard III*, ed. David Bevington (New York: Bantam Books, 1951; rev. 1980), p. 13; Anon., *Arden of Faversham*, in *Drama of the English Renaissance, I: The Tudor Period*, ed. Russell A. Fraser and Norman Rabkin (New York: Macmillan, 1976), pp. 436–37. Sir Walter's Scott's novel, *The Fair Maid of Perth*, although written in the nineteenth century, is set in the fourteenth century and includes an ordeal of the bier. See Walter Scott, *The Fair Maid of Perth*, ed. Andrew Hook and Donald MacKenzie (Edinburgh: Edinburgh UP, 1999), Chapter Twenty-Three.
89. Malcolm Gaskill, *Crime and Mentalities in Early Modern England* (Cambridge: Cambridge UP, 2000), p. 227.
90. Caroline Walker Bynum, *Wonderful Blood: Theology and Practice in Late Medieval Northern Germany and Beyond* (Philadelphia: University of Pennsylvania Press, 2007), p. 162.
91. Shigehisa Kuriyama, "Interpreting the History of Bloodletting," *JHMAS* 50.1 (1995): 17. In the sixteenth century, cruentation also became a subject of interest in the works of a number of physicians. See Antonius Blancus, *Tractatus de Indiciis Homicidii* (Venice: Lugduni Beringi, 1547); Andreas Libarius of Halle, *De Cruentatione Cadaverum* (Magdeburg: Hendel, 1594). Both of these are cited in Brittain, "Cruentation," 82–88.

92. Boureau, "La preuve par le cadavre qui saigne," 250–52.
93. Steven P. Marrone, "Magic and the Physical World in Thirteenth-Century Scholasticism," *Early Science and Medicine* 14 (2009): 182.
94. Marrone, "Magic and the Physical World," 183–84.
95. Marrone, "Magic and the Physical World," 184–85.
96. Marrone, "Magic and the Physical World," 158–85.
97. The closest the coroners' rolls come to embracing superstition is in the death of Alan Man of Grimsby (*Lincs.*) in 1392/93. Alan had been suffering with an abscess (*unum felonem*) under his right knee that greatly irritated him, as well as another abscess (*unum apostem*) on his left side, for two years and more. He had been in such pain for the final five weeks of his life that he believed he was cursed. Eventually the abscess on his left side burst, killing him immediately. See TNA PRO JUST 2/93, m. 3. Alan's conviction that he had been cursed certainly falls into the category of superstition. However, the fact that the jury declared his death to be from natural causes, rather than initiating a witch-hunt, is good evidence that they rejected his hypothesis.
98. Helena M. Chew and Martin Weinbaum, eds. *The London Eyre of 1244* (London: London Record Society, 1970), p. 45.
99. Anne and Edwin DeWindt argue that membership in a tithing group was a marker of unfree status. The Huntingdonshire eyre of 1286–1288 makes occasional note that a man did not belong to a tithing group *quia liber* (because he is free). Anne Reiber DeWindt and Edward Brezette DeWindt, *Royal Justice and the Medieval English Countryside: The Huntingdonshire Eyre of 1286, the Ramsey Abbey Banlieu Court of 1287, and the Assizes of 1287–88* (Toronto: PIMS, 1981), pt. 1, p. 109.
100. H. Summerson, "The Structure of Law Enforcement in Thirteenth Century England," *AJLH* 23.313 (1979): 316.
101. Summerson, "Structure of Law Enforcement," 317.
102. Hanawalt, "Voices and Audiences," 164.
103. Summerson, "Structure of Law Enforcement," 322.
104. James Sharpe and J.R. Dickinson, "Coroners' Inquests in an English County, 1600–1800: A Preliminary Survey," *Northern History* 48.2 (2011): 254. Fortescue wrote that witnesses were permitted to offer testimony in criminal cases "in the presence of twelve trustworthy men of the neighbourhood in which the fact of question occurred." Surely, here he was referring to the coroner's inquest. See Fortescue, *De Laudibus Legum Angliae*, p. 67.
105. Anthony J. Musson, *Public Order and Law Enforcement: The Local Administration of Criminal Justice, 1294–1350* (Woodbridge: Boydell, 1996), p. 205. Bellamy argues that conviction was unlikely if the victim or his kinfolk did not appear at the trial. See his *Criminal Trial*, p. 103.
106. R.B. Pugh, "The Duration of Criminal Trials in Medieval England," in *Law, Litigants and the Legal Profession*, ed. E.W. Ives and A.H. Manchester (London: Royal Historical Society, 1983), p. 108.
107. Hearsay was not excluded as evidence until the mid-eighteenth century. See Barbara J. Shapiro, *A Culture of Fact: England, 1550–1720* (Ithaca: Cornell UP, 2000), p. 15.
108. Carrie Smith has made the same observation, noting that "it is impossible to establish, in most cases, whether there were any witnesses to the fatal incidents described in coroners' inquests." See her "Medieval Coroners' Rolls: Legal Fiction or Historical Fact," in *Courts, Counties and the Capital in the Later Middle Ages*, ed. Diana E.S. Dunn (New York: St Martin's Press, 1996), p. 110.
109. While "scriveners" were craftsmen who belonged to a guild (such as the London Company of Scriveners), Nigel Ramsay contends that their background was in fact clerical. See his "Scriveners and Notaries as Legal Intermediaries in

Later Medieval England," in *Enterprise and Individuals in Fifteenth-Century England*, ed. Jenny Kermode (Gloucester: Sutton, 1991), pp. 118–31.

110. Jurors opted for this strategy when testifying about the death of John of Glenham, an apprentice of King's Bench. John was assaulted and killed in a London tavern while it was teeming with patrons. When the jurors were asked who was present at the homicide, they identified only the principle actors by name. They described the rest as simply "many apprentices of the court," stating explicitly that they did not know their names. Sharpe, *Calendar of Coroners' Rolls*, p. 135.
111. Green, *Verdict According to Conscience*, p. 32.
112. Bellamy, *Criminal Trial*, pp. 34–35.
113. Naomi D. Hurnard, *The King's Pardon for Homicide before AD 1307* (Oxford: Oxford UP, 1969), p. 136. Even today, many people are reluctant witnesses, and work to avoid becoming involved in the process. See Michael Lyman, *Criminal Investigation: The Art and the Science*, 6th ed. (Upper Saddle River, NJ: Pearson, 2011), p. 28.
114. Sara M. Butler, *The Language of Abuse: Marital Violence in Later Medieval England* (Leiden: Brill, 2007), Chapter Five.
115. TNA PRO JUST 2/53, m. 3.
116. H.E. Salter, ed., *Records of Mediaeval Oxford: Coroners' Inquests, the Walls of Oxford, etc.* (Oxford: Oxford Chronicle Co., Ltd., 1912), p. 13.
117. Ian Forrest, "Defamation, Heresy and Late Medieval Social Life," in *Image, Text and Church, 1380–1600: Essays for Margaret Aston*, ed. Linda Clark, Maureen Jurkowski, and Colin Richmond (Toronto: PIMS, 2009), p. 149. Rumor was an acceptable means of accusation within limits: statutes passed in 1275 and 1276 not only prohibited the spreading of rumors relating to the king or the nobility, they also raged against barrators who wasted the court's time with unnecessary litigation provoked by baseless rumors. See *SR*, v. 1, pp. 35, 44. For a discussion of late medieval concerns about *fama*, see Sandy Bardsley, "Sin, Speech, and Scolding in Late Medieval England," in *Fama: The Politics of Talk and Reputation in Medieval Europe*, ed. Thelma Fenster and Daniel Lord Smail (Ithaca: Cornell UP, 2003), pp. 145–64.
118. TNA PRO JUST 2/67, m. 10d.
119. Sharpe, *Calendar of Coroners' Rolls*, pp. 245–47.
120. TNA PRO JUST 2/60, m. 4d.
121. *Bracton*, v. 2, p. 404.
122. *Bracton*, v. 2, p. 404.
123. *Bracton*, v. 2, p. 396.
124. This story appears in several versions. See H.T. Riley, ed., *Chronicles of the Mayors and Sheriffs of London: 1188–1274* (London: Trübner, 1863), pp. 240–41; R.R. Sharpe, *London and the Kingdom: A History Derived Mainly from the Archives at Guildhall in the Custody of the Corporation of the City of London* (London: Longmans, Green, & Co., 1895), v. 1, p. 119; Charles Trice Martin, ed., *Registrum Epistolarum Fratris Johannis Peckham Archiepiscopi Cantuariensis* (Princeton: Princeton UP, 1885), pt. 3, pp. l-lii; and William Stubbs, ed., *Chronicles of the Reigns of Edward I and Edward II: Annales londonienses and Annales paulini edited from mss. in the British Museum and in the Archiepiscopal Library at Lambeth* (London: Longman, 1882), pp. 92–93.
125. Edward Peters, *Torture* (New York: Basil Blackwell, 1996), p. 40.
126. Alan Harding, *A Social History of English Law* (Gloucester, MA: Peter Smith, 1973), p. 78.
127. J.M. Kaye, ed., *Placita Corone, or La Corone Pledee Devant Justices* (*SS*, supplementary series, v. 4, 1966), p. 22.
128. Kaye, *Placita Corone*, p. 24.

129. Bellamy, *Criminal Trial*, p. 41.
130. Anthony J. Musson, "Turning King's Evidence: The Prosecution of Crime in Late Medieval England," *Oxford Journal of Legal Studies* 19.3 (1999): 474.
131. Musson, "Turning King's Evidence," 470.
132. Musson, "Turning King's Evidence," 477.
133. Y.B., Pasch. term, 25 Edw. 3, fo. 85b.
134. Musson, "Turning King's Evidence," 472.
135. None of this applies to permanent sanctuaries. For more on that subject, see Shannon McSheffrey, "Sanctuary and the Legal Topography of Pre-Reformation London," *L&HR* 27.3 (2009): 483–514.
136. Gervase Rosser, "Sanctuary and Social Negotiation in Medieval England," in *The Cloister and the World: Essays in Medieval History in Honour of Barbara Harvey*, ed. J. Blair and B. Golding (Oxford: Clarendon Press, 1996), pp. 57–79.
137. William. C. Jordan, "A Fresh Look at Medieval Sanctuary," in *Law and the Illicit in Medieval Europe*, ed. Ruth Mazo Karras, Joel Kaye, and E. Ann Matter (Philadelphia: University of Pennsylvania Press, 2008), p. 31.
138. William R. Jones, "Sanctuary, Exile, and Law: The Fugitive and Public Authority in Medieval England and Modern America," in *Essays on English Law and the American Experience*, ed. Elisabeth A. Cawthon (College Station: Texas A&M UP, 1994), p. 25. K.J. Kesselring recounts a number of cases of abjurors who failed to leave the realm. See her "Abjuration and Its Demise: The Changing Face of Royal Justice in the Tudor Period," *Canadian Journal of History* 34.3 (1999): 348; Jessica Freeman, "And He Abjured the Realm of England, Never to Return," in *Freedom of Movement in the Middle Ages: Proceedings of the 2003 Harlaxton Symposium*, ed. Peregrine Horden (Donington: Shaun Tyas, 2007), pp. 287–304.
139. TNA PRO JUST 2/106, m. 10.
140. Rosser, "Sanctuary and Social Negotiation," p. 68.
141. TNA PRO JUST 2/52, m. 9.
142. Hurnard, *King's Pardon*, p. 267.
143. Hanawalt has argued that jurors throughout England knew the "formulas for the various excusable homicides that would work to convince the justices and ultimately the king that a pardon was in order." See Hanawalt, "Voices and Audiences," 171.
144. TNA PRO JUST 2/61, m. 2.
145. Shannon McSheffrey, "Men and Masculinity in Late Medieval London Civic Culture: Governance, Patriarchy, and Reputation," in *Conflicted Identities and Multiple Masculinities: Men in the Medieval West*, ed. Jacqueline Murray (New York: Taylor and Francis, 1999), pp. 243–78.
146. TNA PRO JUST 2/57, m. 14.
147. For a discussion of English childbirth practices, see Gail McMurray Gibson, "Scene and Obscene: Seeing and Performing Late Medieval Childbirth," *JMEMS* 29.1 (1999): 7–24.
148. Cited in Ruth Mazo Karras, *Sexuality in Medieval Europe: Doing unto Others* (New York: Routledge, 2005), p. 51.
149. This is the premise behind Karras's book, *Sexuality in Medieval Europe*.
150. Karen Jones, *Gender and Petty Crime in Late Medieval England: The Local Courts in Kent, 1460–1560* (Woodbridge: Boydell, 2006), pp. 78–9.
151. TNA PRO JUST 2/46, m. 2.
152. Rosalind and Christopher Brooke, *Popular Religion in the Middle Ages: Western Europe 1000–1300* (London: Thames and Hudson, 1984), p. 108.
153. Sutherland, *Eyre of Northamptonshire*, v. 1, p. 205. This point is also noted in a coroner's roll. The 1332 enrollment of the death of Richard Millward of

Little Houghton (*Northants.*) states: "there was no first finder because he had the rights of the church" (*Nullus inventor quia habuit jura ecclesiastica*). See TNA PRO JUST 2/111, m. 12.

154. *Mirror of Justices*, p. 31.
155. TNA PRO JUST 2/212, m. 14. When John of Hammerton was attacked in London in 1325, his health held out long enough to flee to the nearest church and sound the bell as a hue and cry. While he died in the process, his actions signaled the felonious nature of his death. Sharpe, *Calendar of Coroners' Rolls*, pp. 112–13. The importance of the dying declaration explains also why records often note that the victim lingered "speechless" for some time before his death, plainly indicating that no evidence could be gleaned from that source. For example, see the death of Gerard Andreu de Garbiak, in Sharpe, *Calendar of Coroners' Rolls*, pp. 78–80.
156. TNA PRO JUST 2/46, m. 3.
157. Daniel Klerman, "Women Prosecutors in Thirteenth-Century England," *Yale Journal of Law* 14.2 (2002): 271.
158. Patricia R. Orr, "*Non Potest Appellum Facere:* Criminal Charges Women Could Not—but Did—Bring in Thirteenth-Century English Royal Courts of Justice," in *The Final Argument: The Imprint of Violence on Society in Medieval and Early Modern Europe*, ed. Donald J. Kagay and L.J. Andrew Villalon (Woodbridge: Boydell, 1998), p. 157. The stipulation that a man die in his wife's arms does not seem to have been enforced in the later Middle Ages. See Susanne Jenks, "*occidit . . . inter brachia sua*: Change in a Woman's Appeal of Murder of her Husband," *Legal History* 21.2 (2000): 119–122.
159. Y.B. Pasch., 20 Edw. IV, fo. 2b.
160. Daniel R. Ernst, "The Moribund Appeal of Death: Compensating Survivors and Controlling Jurors in Early Modern England," *AJLH* 28 (1984): 170.
161. Post, "Crime in Later Medieval England," 214.
162. R.F. Hunnisett, ed., *Bedfordshire Coroners' Rolls* (Bedfordshire Historical Record Society, v. 41, 1960), pp. 18–19.
163. Klerman, "Women Prosecutors," 282.
164. Sharpe, *Calendar of Coroners' Rolls*, pp. 118–19.
165. TNA PRO JUST 2/1, mm. 1–2. Another Bedfordshire coroner, Robert le Crevequer, also questioned his inquest jury's verdict in the 1275 death of Thomas Cook at Flitton. An inquest of the four neighboring townships reported that Thomas and Ralph Otny quarreled before his death. Ralph struck Thomas once, but the blow did not lead to Thomas's death. When the coroner convened a second inquest before the whole county with a jury of twelve men, the jury concluded just the opposite. In fact, Ralph Otny's blow did lead to Thomas's death. TNA PRO JUST 2/4, m. 12.
166. TNA PRO JUST 2/1, m. 3.
167. Sharpe, *Calendar of Coroners' Rolls*, pp. 158–60.
168. Jacqueline Murray, "On the Origins and Role of 'Wise Women' in Causes of Annulment on the Grounds of Male Impotence," *Journal of Medieval History* 16.3 (1990): 235–49.
169. For a further discussion of annulments on these grounds, please see my *Divorce in Medieval England: From One to Two Persons in Law* (New York: Routledge, 2013), Chapter One.
170. Frederik Pedersen, "Demography in the Archives: Social and Geographical Factors in Fourteenth-Century York Cause Paper Marriage Litigation," *C&C* 10 (1995): 420.
171. Charles Donahue, Jr., "Female Plaintiffs in Marriage Cases in the Court of York in the Later Middle Ages: What Can We Learn from the Numbers?" in

Wife and Widow in Medieval England, ed. Sue Sheridan Walker (Ann Arbor: University of Michigan Press, 1993), p. 130.

172. Although his evidence is drawn from a later era, the best discussion of this subject is James C. Oldham, "On Pleading the Belly: A History of the Jury of Matrons," *Criminal Justice History* 6 (1985): 1–64.
173. Thomas R. Forbes, "A Jury of Matrons," *MH* 32 (1988): 23–24.
174. *Fleta*, v. 1, p. 31.
175. See Hiram Kümper, "Learned Men and Skillful Matrons: Medical Expertise and the Forensics of Rape in the Middle Ages," in *Medicine and the Law in the Middle Ages*, ed. Wendy J. Turner and Sara M. Butler (Leiden: Brill, 2014), pp. 88–108.
176. Sara M. Butler, "A Case of Indifference? Child Murder in Later Medieval England," *Journal of Women's History* 19.4 (2004): 59–82. Alice Ridyng's confession before the episcopal court of the diocese of Lincoln highlights the process. After an illicit affair with a local chaplain resulted in an unwanted pregnancy, Alice gave birth in secret and suffocated the child, burying him in a dung heap. But her secretive behavior had not gone unnoticed. Soon after the birth, the "women and honest wives of Windsor and Eton took her and inspected her belly and her breasts by which they knew for certain that she had given birth." She confessed to everything, even bringing the authorities to the site where she had buried her son. See M. Bowker, ed., *An Episcopal Court Book for the Diocese of Lincoln 1514–1520* (Lincoln Record Society, v. 61, 1967), pp. 53–54.
177. Katherine L. French, *The Good Women of the Parish: Gender and Religion after the Black Death* (Philadelphia: University of Pennsylvania Press, 2008), pp. 71–72.
178. Peter Murray Jones, "Medical Literacies and Medical Culture in Early Modern England" in *Medical Writing in Early Modern English*, ed. Irma Taavitsainen and Päivi Pahta (Cambridge: Cambridge UP, 2011), p. 36. It is fair to say that the idea "mother knows best" still plays a critical role today as rhetoric in television advertising for cold and flu medication (among others).
179. Robert S. Gottfried, *Doctors and Medicine in Medieval England 1340–1530* (Princeton: Princeton UP, 1986), p. 88; Philip Stell, "Medical Practice in Medieval York," *BIHR* 90 (1996): 11.
180. C.H. Talbot and E.A. Hammond's register of medieval medical practitioners includes references to a *medica* named Agnes, from Stanground (*Hunts.*) in 1270 (p. 10); a physician named Christiana at Jarrow in 1313 (p. 28); a leech named Joanna working out of Westminster in 1408 (p. 100); a leech named Margery of Hales in Worcester between the years 1300–1306 (pp. 209–10); and Pernell, wife of Thomas de Rasyn, who worked as a physician in Sidmouth (*Devon*) around 1350 (p. 241). See Talbot and Hammond, *The Medical Practitioners in Medieval England: A Biographical Register* (London: Wellcome Historical Medical Library, 1965).
181. Katherine "la surgiene," daughter of Thomas the Surgeon, and sister of William the Surgeon, is mentioned in a quitclaim dating to 1286. Talbot and Hammond, *Medical Practitioners in Medieval England*, p. 200.
182. Hanawalt, "Voices and Audiences," 162.
183. Klerman, "Women Prosecutors," 271.
184. TNA PRO JUST 2/102, m. 6.
185. TNA PRO JUST 2/102, m. 9.
186. TNA PRO JUST 2/102, m. 12d.
187. See Chapter One.
188. This would seem to have held true across Europe. See Trevor Dean, *Crime in Medieval Europe 1200–1550* (Edinburgh: Longman, 2001), pp. 31–34.

189. W. Mark Ormrod, "The Politics of Pestilence: Government in England after the Black Death," in *The Black Death in England*, ed. Ormrod and Phillip Lindley (Stamford: Watkins, 1996), pp. 158–59.
190. TNA PRO JUST 2/109, m. 9d.
191. TNA PRO JUST 2/82, m. 8.
192. TNA PRO JUST 2/9, m. 1d.
193. TNA PRO JUST 2/92, m. 4.
194. M.T. Clanchy, *From Memory to Written Record: England 1066–1307*, 3rd ed. (Malden, MA: John Wiley & Sons, 2013), p. 50.
195. David J. Seipp, "Crime in the Year Books," in *Law Reporting in Britain*, ed. Chantal Stebbings (London and Rio Grande, OH: Hambledon, 1995), p. 21.
196. TNA PRO JUST 2/61, m. 17/1.
197. TNA PRO JUST 2/33A, m. 11.
198. TNA PRO JUST 2/155, m. 11d.
199. To offer some examples: John Mundy, an Oxfordshire coroner from the 1340s, although far from scrupulous in his reporting of jury lists, was inclined to exclude them altogether for deaths by misadventure, but not for homicides. See TNA PRO JUST 2/130. Similarly, Thomas of Greenhill and John of Worksop, coroners for the county of Nottingham in the 1360s, seldom recorded jury lists for accidental deaths. See TNA PRO JUST 2/121.
200. For example, see the death of Walter Shepherd of Newbald (*Yorks.*) in TNA PRO JUST 2/220, m. 9.

4 The Medical Dimension of a Coroner's Inquest

The function of the jury in the English legal system, in large part, is what makes common law unique. English jurors fulfilled much the same role as justices elsewhere in the West: and yet, they shared none of the same instruction and/or experience as Continental justices, nor did they benefit in the elevated social status that went with the appointment. Despite the centrality of the position to English common law, traditional scholarship has persistently undervalued the contributions of these simple laymen by seeing them as mere "judges of fact." Barbara Shapiro sums up this viewpoint: "[j]urors were assumed to have the qualities of mind necessary to make judgments of matters of fact. They were intelligent enough to consider whether the 'fact' [i.e., the act or deed] had actually occurred and who had been responsible for it."[1] In this respect, the common law perceived "facts" primarily as "direct sensory products: what neighbours saw, heard, or smelled. Neither judgment nor inference was thought to be required."[2] This emphasis on fact has its advantages: concern with "factual matters" reduces the opportunity for "judicial discretion."[3] From this vantage point, even though an English juror bore the same weight of responsibility as a Continental justice, he needed none of the same instruction because the law expected him only to observe, not to think.

To the dismay of many jurors throughout the centuries, the reality of jury service bears little similarity to this theoretical construct. Medieval coroners' juries constantly confronted complex decisions with meaningful ramifications. As Chapter Three suggests, juries sometimes completed much of the heavy lifting of the investigation before the coroner even arrived. In fact, the greatest ethical challenge of death investigation took place upon discovery of a fatality. The coroner's inquest was reactive. It was not up to the coroner to decide which deaths necessitated investigation. His work commenced only after local representatives sent for him.[4] The discretion of the community to determine when it was most appropriate to call for the services of the coroner remind us of the formidable authority wielded by local law enforcement and those who regularly served on coroners' juries. Traditional historiography privileges the presenting jury as a mechanism for social control; but how much more powerful is it to conceal a homicide by pronouncing the body, in fact, dead from natural causes, and thus determining an inquest to be unnecessary?

This chapter seeks to examine the taxing side of being an inquest juror, beginning with the overarching question: why these deaths? How did English communities decide when to alert the coroner? What criteria did they employ to designate a death as unnatural and thus in need of an inquest? This query is especially pertinent given the presence of deaths by disease within the coroners' rolls. Why did some deaths of this nature merit an inquest, but not others? Inquest jurors encountered many other queries with answers that were not that straightforward. When an assault occurred prior to a fatality, how did jurors know whether the assault actually caused the death? This becomes even more complicated when applied to abortion by assault, that is, an attack on a pregnant woman resulting in a miscarriage: exactly how much force was necessary to produce an abortion? Given that common law classified abortion as homicide, the jury's verdict was meaningful. Finally, not all accused felons deserved to be held accountable for their actions. Because of their intimate knowledge of the perpetrator, coroners' juries were in the unique position to create a persuasive argument for an insanity defense. Yet, how did they decide when a person was insane enough to be excused from culpability for his actions?

As this corpus of examples makes clear, the most challenging investigations were decidedly medical in nature. While Chapter Two examines the composition of the inquest jury in order to document the role of medical practitioners in the inquest process, this chapter looks instead to the nature of the verdicts themselves, in the hopes of explaining what factors guided jurors in their medically relevant decisions.

UNNATURAL DEATH

The crown expected coroners to hold inquests into any sudden or unnatural deaths. But how did the medieval English define "unnatural"? Certainly, if one adopted a wholly clinical perspective, one could argue that death *is* the body's natural response to being stabbed, or struck with an axe, or drowned, or strangled, and thus homicide is a natural form of death. Despite the centrality of "unnaturalness" to the coroner's office, it is striking that British law has never defined what it means by "unnatural." Sir John Jervis's textbook for coroners, entitled *The Office and Duties of Coroners*, published first in 1829, was the first to brood over the meaning of unnatural death in its 1957 revised edition. The definition furnished by the text comprised the following parameters:

1) Violent death with and without human intervention
2) A peculiar death
3) One that is not natural

4) A death from homicide, drowning, poisoning, or accidental injury
5) An unexpected, exceptional, or extraordinary death
6) A death that cannot be satisfactorily explained by medical science
7) A suspicious death
8) A death that is not due to disease or old age[5]

While many of these components overlap or lack specificity (for example, what precisely is the difference between a "peculiar" death and a "suspicious" one?), these guidelines offer considerable insight into Western perceptions of (un)naturalness. In terms of gaining an appreciation for why some deaths made the cut for coroners' inquests while others did not, the most significant component is plainly the last. As Lindsay Prior concludes, Western civilization perceives human agency to be one of the pivotal criteria in determining an unnatural death. Thus, old age and disease "naturalize" death "by eliminating human agency. . . . Where disease exists, motives, will, purpose and agency are held to be absent."[6] Of course, this view of (un)naturalness then problematizes accidental death by adding yet another dimension: a death by misadventure is one that may include human agency but excludes intention.[7] The essence of the Western view of (un)natural death turns on the presence or absence of human agency and intent: "[t]he deletion of human agency naturalises death, and the deletion of intent morally neutralises it."[8]

J.D.J. Havard argues for a different perception of death in the medieval Western worldview. He believes the medieval world defined the (un)naturalness of a fatality by employing two distinct models. First, encouraged by his copious reading of the English Year Books, he maintains that the medieval English embraced a highly legalistic view of death. Natural death was a physical death. Unnatural death was civil death, experienced in outlawry or upon taking holy orders, in which the individual, while physically alive, was dead to the world of the living.[9] Second, and most pertinent to the function of the coroners, he contends that the medieval world placed great weight on the presence or absence of violence. A natural death was nonviolent. An unnatural one was violent.[10] While this perception does not conflict with Prior's hypothesis, it clearly places the emphasis on different criteria.

Discerning what the medieval English considered a natural death as opposed to an unnatural one is central to our understanding of why the coroners' rolls include those particular deaths to the exclusion of many others. Granted, we must concede that medieval authorities did not always concur on how to define (un)naturalness. This variance is highly instructive in terms of delineating a broader consensus. A decidedly brief 1329 amercement magnifies this dissension. Reportedly, the township of Brackley (*Northants.*) buried the body of Robert the Barker after he died of hunger. Because he was interred without view of the coroner, the crown ordered the township amerced.[11] The township's choice not to convene an inquest reveals a disjuncture in classifications. What the locality regarded as natural death, the crown deemed unnatural and thus in need of investigation. Some divergence in opinion is evident also in deaths by exposure. An enrollment from December 1397 describes the demise of Robert Hayward of Saxelbye, at Saxelbye (*Leics.*). The jury remarks that he was old, debilitated, and poor; moreover, he did not have sufficient clothing, and thus passed away from debility and cold.[12] The medieval period was no stranger to begging and poverty. Yet, fatalities like Robert's are few and far between in the coroners' rolls. The only feasible explanation for their underrepresentation is that most communities did not believe death through exposure met the crown's standards for unnatural death. Deaths relating to hunger, poverty, and homelessness all share a common feature. These are passive deaths: no one person's actions can be held accountable. Nonetheless, the confusion about whether those deaths were, in fact, unnatural is understandable. *The Mirror of Justices* would argue that these deaths were felonious: "[o]ne can kill another by blow, famine, or other torment." The treatise categorizes as homicide deaths where "cripples, children, and others who cannot walk are cast and left in desert places, or in such spots that if they do not die of hunger it is no thanks to those who put them there."[13] What the records demonstrate, however, is that the larger English populace did not share this perception. On the whole, medieval jurors punished active criminality: they did not consider negligence to be felonious, even if it was a neglect of one's Christian duty to charity.[14] This principle holds true even in terms of deaths by misadventure: the crown needed a culprit whose actions, however involuntary, were blameworthy. When the crown could not hold an individual responsible, it laid blame instead on an object: the deodand. Yet, blaming the object in many respects was a legal fiction: it was a means of holding the object's owner accountable in a death that was not criminal. This inherent need to find fault in someone or something helps us to understand better the parameters of (un)natural death. Natural deaths were passive deaths.

The only glaring exception to this rule would seem to be in two fourteenth-century enrollments of deaths by *peine forte et dure*. For those accused felons who refused to submit to trial by jury, justices ordered them returned to prison to submit to the practice of *peine forte et dure*, which involved not only a starvation diet, but also the placing of weights upon the accused felon's chest, all in the hopes of prompting a confession.[15] Usually, the coroners' rolls omitted any comment about whether a death by *peine forte et dure* was natural or otherwise. Rather, they concluded that the punishment imposed on the felon had caused his death. Two coroners for the city of Lincoln offered a markedly different assessment. When John Assell died at the castle of Lincoln during the process of *peine forte et dure* in November 1386, Nicholas de Werk's enrollment determined that his was a natural death.[16] Similarly, John of Owlthorpe reported that John Howden, who passed away in August 1392 at the castle jail at Lincoln from *peine forte et dure*, also experienced a natural death.[17] While death surely is a natural response to having one's lungs crushed, nothing else about this process seems natural. These verdicts most likely reflect the coroners' concern to exonerate Lincoln's jailers from accusations of the use of unauthorized force. In this case, "natural death" is best interpreted as a statement that the jailers had done nothing reprehensible.

If disease naturalizes death, then one might reasonably ask, why did coroners record so many deaths by disease? A plausible explanation would seem to be that some communities were oblivious and erroneously summoned the coroners to all deaths, rather than merely those that best met the crown's criteria of unnatural or sudden. Yet, as Katharine Park observes, medieval Europe was beset by infirmity: "[t]he high death rates indicate rates of illness that were truly staggering."[18] The coroners' rolls do not replicate the enormity of these rates. The records do not include enough deaths by disease to account for a coroner who imprudently incorporated everything. Instead, three explanations move to the forefront to explain the significance of disease fatalities in the coroners' rolls:

1) Many deaths by disease appear primarily to exonerate those who were otherwise vulnerable to accusations of homicide. The enrollment of Richard Chapell's death in 1345 makes this point overtly. Richard Chapell and his brother, Alan of Scargill, came to blows at the local smithy after having consumed too much alcohol, such that Alan pursued Richard when he left for home, piercing him through the chest with an arrow. Since that time, Richard's wound had mended sufficiently that he returned to work at the smithy: but not long after his recovery, he succumbed to an acute (unnamed) sickness and passed away. After deliberation, the jury declared cause of death to be the illness, not the injury.[19] When death followed closely on the tail of an assault, the enrollments went to great lengths to draw attention to the thoroughness of the investigation. This is somewhat unexpected given that coroners' rolls often record only what is obligatory. If the jury suspected the assault was irrelevant, why include it at all? A conscientious coroner incorporated details of the quarrel because he wished to state freely that he and his jurors were aware of the altercation and had taken it into consideration when determining cause of death, preventing any future protests that might incite doubt among trial jurors. Also, because coroners were present at the view of wounds, a coroner who neglected to mention an assault prior to the victim's demise might look like he was hiding something. Given the persistent unease regarding the moral integrity of the coroners, a diligent coroner would want to document this deliberation in order to defend his honor. Deaths such as these only appeared in the coroners' rolls, then, as an emphatic statement of their naturalness.

2) Deaths by disease had implications for the confiscation of property as deodands. Many sickly individuals died, not from the disease, but by misadventure resulting from their weakened condition. When a child died by falling accidentally into a well, the coroner ordered that well stopped

up to prevent future mishaps. Should the same rule apply when an epileptic fell into a well while his body was seizing uncontrollably?[20] The child's experience confirmed that the water supply was poorly situated and thus might lead to further accidents. The epileptic's death, however, proved nothing of the sort. If the individual had not been experiencing a seizure, he would not have fallen into the well at all. This distinction was significant, and thus legal practice altered the consequences. While a child's death resulted in a crown mandate to fill the well, an epileptic's death, if it occurred during a seizure, was deemed an exception to the rule. While a wide variety of illnesses might stand in for epilepsy in this model, the example of epilepsy is particularly apt. The coroners' rolls would lead us to believe that epileptics were notorious for having seizures at inconvenient moments, causing them to fall into wells, springs, from ladders, from trees, under carts. In all of these cases, the normal "rules" of deodands did not apply.[21] Nevertheless, coroners needed to report the deaths in order to dictate proper procedure.

3) Some deaths by disease were intended to signal the onset of an epidemic. With such a high death toll during plague outbreaks, the presence of disease fatalities among the coroners' reports makes sense only if these were the first deaths in a vill or township since the preceding outbreak. This explanation fits also with the character of the enrollments. Jurors were at pains to establish that these deaths were, in fact, plague related. For example, the inquest into the 1382 death of John atte Wike (*Wilts.*) incorporated a statement by jurors reporting that he was overcome by the "sickness of pestilence, having diverse buboes (*bubbos*) around his body and purpulles (*porples*) [that is, swollen and inflamed lymph nodes]."[22] Jurors in the death of Agnes Lawe (*Glos.*) in November 1384 reported that she died from the "sickness of plague called *bocche*."[23] "Botche" was the common name for bubonic plague in England.[24] In light of the sparse detail found in most coroners' enrollments, these descriptions are positively effusive. The 1396 death of John Caskere, former servant of William Rene of Hardwick (*Oxon.*), is equally impressive in the sketch of the disease's symptoms. In this case, the jurors' verdict had greater moment: a recent altercation with William Hobbes cast suspicion that the death, in reality, might have been a homicide. With force and arms, John assaulted William in late September 1395. In self-defense, William struck John on the head with his cutlass, inflicting a wound three inches in length. Since the altercation, his wound had healed. He passed away the following August. The jury confidently declared his death resulted from plague, not the head wound. The presence of botches and other "mortal signs" on his body provided definitive evidence.[25] The phrase "mortal signs" or variations of it may also have been a euphemism for buboes: Gilbert Wace, county coroner for Oxford in December 1392, remarked specifically that Nicholas Randulph of Cowley had "signs of death" on his body, that is "splotches" (*splottes*) contracted during an outbreak of plague. What is interesting also about this case is that the coroner

inquired specifically if he had been adequately ministered to during his infirmity, hinting at some sort of communal responsibility to care for plague victims, despite received wisdom that abandonment and flight were the most common medieval responses.[26] The jurors replied that he had; thus, it was a natural death.[27]

Local representatives confronted with plague deaths after a prolonged absence of the disease summoned the coroner for a specific purpose: to offer an official verdict that might signal publicly the beginning of a new outbreak. After the initial epidemic, communities learned to be highly conscious of future epidemics. The psychological impact was tremendous, turning the English into "a nation of hypochondriacs."[28] As Leif Søndergaard emphasizes,

> [p]eople who lived in a town that was attacked by the Black Death felt that they were first of all victims. They felt that they suffered from the effects of a powerful force beyond their reach. . . . People needed not only explanations for the causes of the disease but even more practical measures that could be taken in order to prevent contagion with the plague, not only on the official town or state level, but also on a personal level.[29]

This is not to imply that the crown hoped to monitor the spread of disease through the office of the coroner.[30] There exist no royal communications to this effect. Nor were coroners and their juries sufficiently meticulous in enrollments to have fulfilled this function. Rather, community authorities themselves hoped to exploit the spectacle of the coroner's inquest to issue a public warning that another outbreak had begun. Knowledge is a powerful weapon in fighting disease. After the initial epidemic of bubonic plague in the 1340s, plague manuals proliferated throughout Europe, offering advice on how to prevent infection. Because medical authorities alleged plague was spread by miasma (poisoned air), treatises recommended cleansing air in the home as the first line of defense by burning herbs such as wormwood, mugwort, laurel, juniper, and marjoram.[31] Leading a Christian lifestyle, avoiding fornication, and adhering to a moderate diet were other popular disease-fighting strategies. Using the public spectacle of a coroner's inquest as a means to urge local residents to take precautions made sense. Moreover, what frightened people most about epidemic disease was the lack of control they had over its spread. Knowledge offered a measure of control, permitting residents to pursue whatever disease prevention they believed necessary, curbing the natural human tendency toward widespread public panic. Here, it is critical to note that this usage of the coroner's inquest was not a deviation from normal practices. Communities well understood the didactic nature of the inquest. Hanawalt has argued this was apparent especially in terms of accidental death:

> After hearing a range of graphic stories about poorly constructed scaffolding, the dangers of wells and latrines, the hazards of carting, and the

> disaster awaiting those who sat on the tree limbs they were sawing off, workmen learned how to take more care at their jobs. The stories do not condemn these workmen for their folly, but by recounting their accidental deaths the tellers instilled caution in others.[32]

The spectacle of the inquest, attended by the entire male population of the four nearest vills, and surely many curious women and children as well, provided the ideal opportunity for a teaching moment.

If communities sometimes exploited plague deaths as an occasion to spread word of an impending epidemic, it should come as no surprise that their enrollments reveal traces of the guidance of a medical professional—that is, an expert whose medical judgment was valued widely. Thomas Clerk served on the inquest jury assigned to the death of Nicholas Randulph. If he was indeed a cleric, he may have been the medical expert behind the enrollment. The contribution of medical practitioners in crafting these plague descriptions is emphasized by medieval England's general silence on the medical aspects of the Black Death.[33] The only description of plague symptoms extant from medieval England derives from Geoffrey le Baker's *Chronicle*. Baker was a secular cleric working out of Swinbroke in Oxford during the 1340s. With a solid educational background, his confident use of precise medical terminology is not extraordinary. He wrote:

> Some were tormented by boils (*apostemata*) which broke out suddenly in various parts of the body, and were so hard and dry that when they were lanced hardly any liquid flowed out. Many [people] escaped from this, by lancing [the boils] or by long suffering. Others had little black pustules (*pustulos*) scattered over the skin of the whole body, very few of whom, that is scarcely any, recovered life and health.[34]

What is significant about Baker's description, from the English perspective, is that he expands his vocabulary of symptoms beyond the more common "boil" (*aposteme*). The coroners' rolls contain a plethora of deaths from *apostema*; but the mention of pustules tells us that this was not your ordinary abscess. Similarly, the accounts above drawn from the coroners' rolls steered clear of the more general term, employing instead those symptoms that speak directly to bubonic plague as it is described in the medical treatises: *bubbos*, *porples*, and *botches*. The complexity of these descriptions implies the shadowy presence of a medical practitioner. Jurors were determined also to highlight that this was not just a pestilence. Historians have argued that when medieval sources employed the term "pestilence," it implied a fatal sickness. Jurors used these qualifiers to report that this was not just any pestilence, it was indeed bubonic plague. Indeed, prolonged experience with the disease undoubtedly made all jurors uncomfortably familiar with the vocabulary of symptoms. The presence of a medical practitioner, however, is evidenced in those deaths from the "true pestilence," mentioned in Chapter Three.[35] Only academic physicians employed this particular descriptor explicitly to distinguish bubonic plague from other fatal diseases. If local authorities hoped to warn communities of an impending rash of disease, surely they would employ the services of a medical practitioner to make this point.

Altogether, the coroners' rolls confirm both Prior's and Havard's theories of unnatural death. As Prior suggests, death by disease was inherently natural. It was principally when one's diseased condition led to a death by misadventure, or when violence was thought to have caused one's condition that the communities and coroners alike felt an inquest was necessary. Communal authorities also appreciated the didactic qualities of the inquest, and on occasion used it to their advantage to advertise impending epidemics. This does not suggest that they, in any way, believed plague death was unnatural. Rather, localities recognized the value of a public spectacle and subordinated it to their own needs when they believed the situation warranted it. Havard's notion that unnatural death involved violence also has merit. Coroners' juries preferred to see unnatural death as active; that is, someone or something was to blame.

CAUSE OF DEATH

The greatest obstacle an inquest jury faced in the investigative process was identifying cause of death. A corpse with a knife protruding from the heart supplied incontrovertible evidence of a felony, although jurors might still be torn between a homicide and a suicide, depending on the angle of entry and presence of defensive injuries; but victims were rarely considerate enough to die in such an unambiguous fashion. Accordingly, both statute law and the legal treatises proffer practical instruction for the coroner inexperienced in recognizing the signs of a homicide. The most perplexing deaths were those where jurors knew well that an assault had occurred—and even had witnesses to attest to it—but they had reason to believe the assault was not fatal. How did coroners and their jurors establish a firm causal connection between wounding and death? This was not a simple process, especially in the absence of post-mortem dissections. Moreover, contemporary medical theory may have actually impeded their ability to recognize causation. The medieval world's tenuous grasp on the dangers of infection is overt in these accounts. Galenic medicine espoused a precarious approach to infectivity. Medieval physicians deemed infection a vital part of the healing process. Thus, it was only when a "wound did not become infected and if it showed signs of healing normally [that] the surgeon had grounds for alarm." When this happened, surgeons deliberately contaminated the wound, doing more harm than good.[36] The underlying lesson here is that medieval jurors would not have routinely connected a fever or other illness with infection springing from an earlier injury. For example, on August 1, 1345, in the village of

Rowthorn (*Derbys.*), John Houles and Richard Doget engaged publicly in a drunken brawl. During the exchange, Richard drew his knife and struck John in the head, meting out a wound that was half an inch long and half an inch deep. Since that time, jurors observed that John's wound healed; but his health began to decline the Monday after the Assumption of Mary (August 15), and he eventually succumbed to an acute (unnamed) sickness on August 23. Today, we realize that such a short interlude between incident and death is insufficient to exclude the possibility of infection or blood poisoning; medieval jurors believed otherwise. Because of the interval between the two events, jurors felt secure in pronouncing the sickness, not the assault, the cause of his death.[37]

Time was of the essence with respect to an inquest's verdict. The inquest into the death of Richard the Smith of Litton (*Derbys.*) corroborates this supposition. Jurors recount that Richard was together with William the Tailor and John, son of Robert Bakester, at the tavern around the hour when they should have been in bed. In their state of drunkenness, a dispute erupted between the three men, and Richard was wounded on the head with a sword; the other two were also gravely injured. Since that time, Richard's head injury had healed enough for him to return to work at the smithy. Accordingly, when he fell ill and died less than two weeks later, the jury was convinced that his illness was unrelated to the head wound.[38] As Richard the Smith's demise illustrates, time was not the only element: the victim's behavior was also crucial. Jurors held it to be significant that Richard had returned to work after his injury. A man at death's door does not slave away at the smithy over a sweltering fire. Jurors at the Northamptonshire eyre of 1329 made this connection explicit: they accused a coroner who glossed over the year between a woman's beating and her death of taking bribes. In their minds, the passage of time clearly negated the possibility of a causal relationship.[39] This perception resonates also with the needs of the law. Common law required that an appeal of felony be made within a year and a day of the crime.[40]

In terms of jurors' perceptions, the wound's dimensions had a considerable impact. John Houles's head wound was only half an inch long and half an inch deep.[41] Surely, such a minor injury was not life threatening? This is not to suggest that the medieval English were unaware of the dangers of brain injuries: even in early medieval law, head wounds took top priority as "the most universally and extensively regulated wounds."[42] Across Europe, law codes compensated for injuries to the skull according to damage to the inner and outer *tabula*, as well as injuries that exposed the brain, implying a sound knowledge of human anatomy.[43] The coroners' rolls also demonstrate some understanding of the impact of brain health on bodily function. For example, some jurors understood that paralysis might be tied to a brain's proper functioning.[44] Nonetheless, the majority of enrollments concerning head wounds emphasize penetration and the size of the wound.

With the twenty-first century's incisive appreciation of neural performance, we know that head injuries of any size can be fatal. Trauma to the brain, even without penetration (such as Shaken Baby Syndrome), can be lethal, causing internal hemorrhaging or swelling, as well as twisting of the brain stem. In fact, closed head injuries often produce far more extensive neurological damage than those involving penetration, including paralysis, cognitive dysfunction, and persistent vegetative states. The repeated references in coroners' rolls confirm that jurors recognized the likelihood of a causal connection in assaults involving head injuries. Yet, the ease with which they dismissed wounds when they were visibly unimpressive implies that head wounds were probably some of the most misleading for coroners' juries to diagnose. The death of Nicholas Mandeville substantiates this perception. In 1301 in Northamptonshire, when Richard Mandeville and his brother, Nicholas, were playing the game "a duck on the rock,"[45] one of Richard's throws went askew: a stone struck Nicholas's head causing a small wound (*parvam plagam*). Three days later, while Nicholas slept, paralysis set in; he died soon after.[46] Jurors were at pains to emphasize that the wound was trivial, even if there was no other apparent source of the paralysis. In the end, the jury's decision was meaningless. Richard confessed before a coroner that he was a murderer and a thief, and abjured the realm.

Because many of these deaths fall into the pattern of assault rationalized as illness, it is imperative to acknowledge that jurors sometimes drew the reverse conclusion. Jurors questioned their initial verdict in the death of seventeen-year-old John, son of Reginald Curteys, of Chieveley (*Berks.*) after hearing that Henry Trumpe of Weston had beaten him with a small rod the Saturday before. Their preliminary investigation concluded that he had succumbed to the flux (dysentery), from which he had been suffering for a year. With this new information in hand, they called for a deeper inquiry.[47] Jurors in the death of Peter the Bailiff of Stilton (*Hunts.*) made a similar call. In February of 1268, Hugh and Giles, both servants of the Prior of Bushmead, quarreled for possession of the prior's barn. Hugh threw Giles out of the barn and refused to let him enter. Incapable of performing his duties, the next day Giles went to the bailiff and asked for his assistance in the matter. Peter and Giles approached the door to the barn and Peter tried to enter. Hugh immediately attacked, stabbing him in the back with a knife. Although Peter survived the assault, the following Sunday he became ill (with an unspecified sickness) and died. Jurors overlooked the illness and declared that the wound was responsible for his death.[48]

When assessing the link between assault and death, there is good reason to believe that coroners took their lead from a medical practitioner. First, English jurists would have come to appreciate the value of medical expertise in their observations of canon law procedure, if not also the Continental law courts. Canon law addressed the need for medical expertise specifically. William Duranti's *Speculum iudiciale*, the "classic proceduralist handbook" for canon law and civil law from the 1270s until the early modern era, addressed this scenario explicitly.[49] In Book Four, he offered up the following advice:

> Person A wounded Person B, who died after he was overcome by a fever. A was accused concerning the death, but he himself asserted that B died from the fever, and many lay witnesses (*laici testes*) were brought in to say that: but a few physicians (*medici*) said that the wound was the cause of the fever. I say, it is better that the few physicians should be believed, since they have a better understanding of the matter.[50]

The *Decretales* of Pope Gregory IX also underscored the need for testimony from medical professionals in such a situation, stating, "if a man wounds another who subsequently dies, he is not guilty of homicide if in the judgment of skilled practitioners the wound would not of itself have been fatal."[51] While common law was jurisdictionally separate from canon law, the two coexisted in medieval England, and Oxford's doctors of law played a critical role as consultants for English royal justices. As a result, English judges were well acquainted with the principles and conceptual structures of canon law. Indeed, in their endeavors to delineate the procedural distinctions between the two systems of justice, the Year Book reports include over two hundred references by England's learned justices to the "law of the Holy Church" in the period 1300–1600.[52] To emphasize further the fallacy of a law based on custom, interaction between canon law and civil law inspired numerous common law developments during the medieval and early modern period. With respect to criminal law, in particular, canon law instigated England's "gradual rationalization of the law of evidence, the development of standards of judicial objectivity and impartiality . . . [and] the rehabilitative theories of penal law."[53] English justices would certainly have been familiar with canon law's definitive textbook on procedural law, and may well have found these instructions useful.

Second, semiology, or the "art of reading signs" was a "difficult-to-learn doctrine." It was also widely held to be the crucial distinction between the educated physician and "the crowd of unlearned practitioners."[54] And yet, reading the body's signs was exactly what a coroner was required to do at the mandatory view of wounds after an assault. The crown expected the victim to seek out the coroner and other local authorities directly after the altercation in order to evaluate the severity of his injuries and, in particular, to give law enforcement officials some indication of whether a homicide investigation was pending. Indeed, a statute issued during the time of Edward I commanded that the appealed parties be arrested immediately, and "kept until it be known perfectly, whether he that is hurt shall recover or not."[55] Across Continental Europe, this was the primary responsibility of court-appointed physicians and surgeons. Admittedly, English law does not require the services of a medical practitioner—in fact, the statute does not even mention the possibility of intervention by a medical practitioner. Nor are the records of actual views helpful in this respect. When documentation from a view survives (and most did not—coroners were not obliged to document the experience), they are usually vague in nature. For example, John Aventerous's attack on Hugh Butcher at Colchester in 1311 led to a view of Hugh's wounds before "the Coroner with the neighbours" who declared "that there was no imminent peril of death."[56] There is no way of knowing whether one of those neighbors was, in fact, a medical practitioner. Nonetheless, because prognosis required distinctly medical training, it is hard to imagine that sheriffs and coroners did not occasionally seek out the advice of a medical practitioner. In this respect, the Catalonian experience with the view of wounds is instructive. As Michael McVaugh explains, for many views of wounds, medical practitioners were unnecessary. After all, it did not take an expert to verify that the victim was bleeding, or even close to death. The Catalonian court required a surgeon "only when survival was still a possibility."[57] Out of simple pragmatism, the English may well have adopted a similar approach.

If the sheriff was uncertain whether a victim of an assault was going to live, the most rational solution was to seek the advice of a medical practitioner. Medical professionals were uniquely qualified to speak to prognosis. Uroscopy, which has come to be understood as the *sine qua non* of medieval medicine, expressed in the iconic image of the physician with urine flask in hand, was not only a critical diagnostic tool, but it also led to the development of invaluable prognostic formulae based on color, texture, and presence of sediments in the urine. Any learned medical practitioner worth his salt knew well that "[u]rine which is pure and has a cloud floating on top like a mist signifies impending death," regardless of any other physical symptoms.[58] Medical texts also included a wide variety of "iatromathematica," that is "divination devices," for the less obvious medical cases.[59] Physicians and surgeons were capable of predicting death by employing *lunaria*, a method of divination based on the day of the moon when the patient fell ill. A medical practitioner might also calculate the patient's odds using the *Sphere of Apuleius*. This practice involves

> a circle bisected horizontally, with numbers inscribed in the upper and lower halves. One takes the numerical value of the patient's name, and divides by the day of the lunar month on which he fell ill; if the remainder is in the upper half of the sphere, he will live; if in the lower, he will die. Some spheres have four or six segments, to accommodate predictions of the speed of his recovery or demise.[60]

A physician's training in prognosis was motivated in part by self-interest. As McVaugh once noted, "it was particularly important for practitioners to be able to identify the signs of imminent death in a patient . . . it enabled them to dissociate themselves more or less honorably from the case."[61] Accusations of malpractice were a perennial anxiety for the medieval medical practitioner, a fact that discouraged most physicians from tending to the needs of a dying patient, no matter what the cost.[62] Given all these factors, a learned medical practitioner was the most qualified individual to determine whether an assault might indeed be fatal. With such powerful tools at the disposal of a medical practitioner, it seems logical that a sheriff would seek his advice.

Common law did not require a medical practitioner to participate in the view of wounds; nor did it prohibit law enforcement authorities from participation, and some sheriffs and coroners did enlist the services of a medical practitioner. This is confirmed by the 1298 London inquest into the assault of John of Stoneham, servant to the Earl of Lincoln:

> on the Friday evening before Michaelmas, John de Stonham and William de Dodington, servants of the above Earl, entered the house of John le Keu in Westsmethfeld to drink, and a certain Stephen, servant of Brother William de Ringeland, drank with them in turns, and words having arisen between them, Stephen struck John on the jaw with his hand, whereupon John le Keu turned them out of the house. Immediately Stephen followed John de Stonham with two knives in his hands to kill him, and seeing this, William knocked him down opposite the house of Richard ate Hole, while John fled towards the monastery church. Nevertheless Stephen pursued John to a bridge called Kaytifbreg, so that John in fear of his life drew a knife and struck Stephen in the left side, while they were in the kennel, and then fled into the church. Afterwards Stephen with a certain Walter de la . . . and other unknown persons of the household of the Hospital of Clerekenwell followed John to the High Altar in the church, dragged him out and took him to the house of Stephen de Weresdal, chief tithingman, to keep him till the morrow; and since Stephen was in danger of death from the blow, the tithingman asked Brother William de Ringeland to lend him the shackles of the Hospital to keep John safely. The jurors also said that these people put John de Stonham's feet higher than his head. Next day Roger de Appelby, Undersheriff of Middlesex, came and carried him off to Neugate, as Stephen's life was despaired of, until he could have sure information on the point from the physicians (*medici*). He remained in prison for three days, and was afterwards mainprised to stand his trial against anyone who should accuse him.[63]

The victim's association with the Earl of Lincoln may explain the undersheriff's decision to seek out the advice of physicians. Out of concern for his servant, the earl may have paid for a physician's services. Yet, the record offers no indication of the earl's involvement. Nor does it suggest that anything out of the ordinary was taking place in the decision to consult a physician. The inevitable conclusion is that sometimes it made sense to consult with a physician.

Even if local authorities did not deem the services of a medical practitioner necessary, the defendant (or an authority on his behalf) may have demanded it. If the accused believed a proper medical examination would exonerate him, then he might insist upon it. Defendants did not usually sit idly by waiting to be convicted. In a case of mayhem from 1354 sued before King's Bench, the defendant interrupted court proceedings to request that the judges examine the plaintiff's wound in order to establish whether the assault had inflicted permanent damage that might fall into the crown's definition of mayhem. English law defined mayhem quite specifically. According to *Bracton*, mayhem is when

> one is rendered incapable of fighting, especially by him whom he is appealing, as where bones protrude from his head or a large splinter of bone projects, as was said, or a bone is broken in some part of his body, or a foot or hand, or part of a foot or hand, or other member is cut off, or where sinews and limb are crippled by the wound dealt, or fingers become crooked, or an eye has been gouged out, or some other thing done to a man's body whereby he is rendered less able and effective in defending himself.[64]

The focus of the court's analysis, then, was not on disfigurement or even permanent injury, but on the ability to fight in battle. Yet, a public viewing of the wound put the court no further ahead. Justices observed that the wound was so fresh they could not discern the long-term impact. Justices of the bench thus ordered the sheriff to find "medical surgeons of the best of London" to make the pronouncement on their behalf. However, they made it clear to the defendant that if the medical men pronounced mayhem, the court would side with their judgment.[65]

Views of wounds are relevant also to death investigation. If a medical practitioner participated in the view, even if the coroner was unable to empanel a medical practitioner on his jury, he already had the benefit of an expert's prognosis to guide the investigation. Significantly, royal justices placed great value on the outcome of the view. In a 1481 appeal of homicide, justices concluded that if the victim had already been buried, the coroner could indict the accused on the evidence of the view alone, skipping the inquest altogether.[66] On at least one occasion, coroners pursuing a homicide investigation summoned the medical practitioner who had examined the victim before he died, to give an assessment of the victim's injuries. Reportedly, William of Buford, a baker in the city of Oxford, was standing in his doorway after curfew one evening when two clerks, John of Belgrave and John of Cliffe, arrived at his home and beat him. William survived for seventeen days after the assault, during which time he was examined by Master Roger, a surgeon, who later testified before the coroner that "there was no despair of the life of the said William from the said wounds." What is most striking about this testimony is how little impact it had on the findings of the coroner's jury, which concluded that the attack was fatal. They excused John for the gaping wound he inflicted on William's left shoulder with a sword, six inches long and two inches deep. Yet, they determined that the smaller wound on his left side, only one inch long, half an inch wide, and two inches deep, made by John of Belgrave's dagger, was in fact mortal.[67]

Master Roger's example stands out from others because he did not serve on the inquest jury. Rather, the coroner summoned him because he knew that Roger had evidence pertinent to the investigation. In all likelihood, it is not the coroner's actions here that are extraordinary, but rather the detail of the record. More typically, when medical practitioners attended an inquest, the coroners' rolls record their presence as either serving on a coroner's jury, or as a neighbor or pledge. For that reason, the record permits no insight into how the medical practitioner's expertise shaped the jury's final verdict, although it is hard to imagine an expert in anatomy standing silently by while others passed judgment on medical issues. The records are not silent when discussing the criteria jurors employed to correlate an assault with a subsequent death. In the London death of Robert le Braceour in June of 1301, the account tells us that Robert, an unruly servant who departed from his master's home without permission, encountered Robert de Amias while they were both inebriated. The other Robert beat him into unconsciousness. Robert le Braceour spent a comatose night on the street, returning to his master's home just before dawn. His disorderly behavior so upset his master that he denied Robert entry into the house. Thus, Robert moved on to the home of a friend and lingered there until the following Thursday. Jurors were content to pin the blame for Robert's death on his ungovernability. Despite the "bruised and excoriated" appearance of the corpse, the jury expressly stated that "he was not nearer death nor farther from life by reason of the beating, but that he died from the illness he contracted by passing the night in the street, and not from any felony." William the Surgeon is listed as a pledge for one of the neighbors.[68] In a death from August of the same year, Henry the Surgeon served as a pledge in the death of John Kyngessone of London. Purportedly, John was sitting with Thomas Willeday in the house of Henry de Keilles outside Aldresgate when a quarrel erupted between the two. Thomas unsheathed his knife and stabbed John in the right arm. Soon after, John proceeded to his master's house, but when met with a locked door, he and his fellow servants slept in a nearby field where they were mistaken for robbers by the village watch, who beat John and his companion. John languished until the following Monday when he expired, reportedly "from the effects of the beating at daybreak." The coroners explicitly asked the jurors "if the said John Kyngessone was brought nearer death and further from life by the wound on his arm." They replied in the negative. They then asked "if the aforesaid watchmen were guilty of the death." The jury responded with "yes." The corpse confirmed their suspicions: "a great part of which appeared blue and bruised."[69]

The phrasing of the coroners' inquiry is highly instructive. Not only does it furnish deeper insight into the guiding principles behind a jury's declaration of guilt, but it also mirrors the interrogation of defendants at trial. When an inquest jury accused Cecily, wife of Jollan, of Durham of poisoning her husband, she swore before justices "that she never gave any poisonous drink to her husband Alan or did anything by which he was nearer to death and further from life, so help her God and these holy things." Cecily repeated this oath six times before the jury was prepared to accept her explanation.[70] The broad scope of this query provided much room for speculation. Any injury, surely, could be argued to bring an individual closer to death than to life, even if it did not, in fact, lead to the victim's death. While the above cases display examples of responsible juries determined to live up to the spirit of the law, it is not hard to imagine that others took advantage of the situation to harass individuals when the evidence was insufficient to support a connection between death and a prior assault.

Fatal assaults provided the additional challenge of ruling which injury was the mortal one. This is significant for two reasons. First, jurors held responsible (as principal) only whoever cast the fatal blow. All others were mere accessories to the crime, and the principal's trial determined their fates. Only if trial jurors convicted the principal might the accessories also be convicted. If the principal fled, the crown ordered the accessories mainprised until authorities located and tried the principal. Second, the law confiscated only those weapons involved in homicide. The clerk of the crown claimed *banes* worth 12*d*. or less; those with a greater value were forfeit to the king.[71] Thus, jurors needed to determine which weapon to confiscate. Inquest records regularly comment on which wound was the mortal one.[72] The obligation to discern the mortal wound provided ample room for manipulation. Chiefly, it afforded jurors the opportunity to craft a particularly damning enrollment. When Matilda, daughter of John de Sheyles, feloniously slew a fifteen-year-old child (whose name jurors did not know) in 1365, jurors at the inquest determined the child had ten wounds, all of which were mortal.[73] With such a punitive record, it is hard to imagine Matilda's trial jury pronouncing an acquittal. Appeals also molded this requirement to implicate more than one person as a principal in a homicide. When a woman known only as Elienor, wife of T.C., appealed her husband's death in King's Bench against sixteen people, she identified Richard W. as the principal, but tried to single out also three others as being particularly blameworthy. While Richard had actually cast the blow that killed her husband, another man struck him in the chest with an arrow "from which he would have died if he had not already died from the first blow." A third man struck him with an arrow in the ribs, "by which he would have died, if he had escaped the other wounds." In the end, her argument was successful for those she deemed principals; however, because one of the principals was outlawed, the other twelve who were indicted with presence, force, and aid were mainprised because it was not clear which principal they had abetted.[74] This requirement was useful also in constructing the ideal case of self-defense. The 1266 inquisition into the death of Michael, son of Roesia Aboveton, provided Arnald le Knyth with an ironclad defense. Jurors reported that when an argument arose between the two drunken men, Michael was the first to resort to physical violence. He attacked Arnald with a scythe, even though Arnald was "walking peaceably down the street, telling him to wait a little that he might drink to him." He struck Arnald "almost mortally"—and then announced that he would strike him again. "Seeing that Michael meant to kill him," Arnald struck him on the head with a hatchet that just happened to be in his hand, killing him instantly. Not surprisingly, the jury determined that Arnald's actions were in self-defense.[75]

ABORTION BY ASSAULT

The difficulty of establishing a link between assault and death was magnified in allegations of abortion, defined broadly under medieval law to include also assaults on pregnant women resulting in a miscarriage. English law regarded abortion as a homicide; however, as the legal treatises relate, the era's expanded definition of abortion generated a whole host of complications for death investigators. *Bracton* enunciates clearly the first challenge. The treatise declares "[i]f one strikes a pregnant woman or gives her poison in order to procure an abortion, if the foetus is already formed or quickened, especially if it is quickened, he commits homicide."[76] Medieval medicine defined the quickening as the first fetal movements (usually around the end of the first trimester), signaling not only human formation but also ensoulment. Both common and canon law considered any attempt to extract the fetus prior to this time as contraception, undoubtedly a sinful act, but not a felony. In order to declare an abortion homicide, the jury thus had to assess how far along the woman had been in her pregnancy before the incident. The treatise *Britton* reveals an additional challenge. Despite being derived from *Bracton*, *Britton* does not adopt the same approach as its forerunner. In fact, the treatise rejects abortion as a felony altogether, stating, "[f]or an infant killed within her womb, she may not bring any appeal, no one being bound to answer an appeal of felony, where the plaintiff cannot set forth the name of the person against whom the felony was committed."[77] The common law courts do not reflect *Britton*'s stance on abortion. Yet, the treatise hints at a seemingly long-standing concern. *Britton* implies that because the fetus was not a distinct legal entity (that is, a person with a name), the law could not recognize it as a victim. The very same line of reasoning influenced the court's judgment in *Roe v. Wade*. The value in *Britton*'s perspective is to provide insight into jurors' mentality. It was entirely possible that jurors felt uncomfortable passing sentence in a case where a legitimate (that is, *breathing*, *named*) victim did not exist. This anxiety is reflected in the courtroom musings of a 1348 indictment for homicide. Justices declared that "no man is held to answer to an appeal of felony where the plaintiff does not name the name of the dead man." One justice followed the statement with a question:

"if one kills an infant in his mother's womb," should he suffer the death penalty? The response: "I believe that he would not, because the killed is not named, nor was he ever in existence."[78]

Here, it is critical to acknowledge that the realm of obstetrics in the medieval world was largely "women's business."[79] Granted, this perception has come under fire somewhat in recent years. In her path-breaking 2008 study, Monica Green questions the premise by asking the critical question: if women had a monopoly on women's medicine, why were men writing and reading so much about obstetrics? As she emphasizes, "most written knowledge about women's bodies is to be found in texts composed *by* male physicians and surgeons, *for* male physicians and surgeons . . . and incorporated into volumes *owned by* male medical practitioners or other male literates."[80] The medical manuscript of fifteenth-century English surgeon Thomas Fayreford is key to deciphering this argument for the English context. Fayreford's text reveals that female ailments were his specialty, leading Peter Murray Jones to conclude that "Fayreford's expertise in gynaecological matters belies the once prevalent idea that male medieval doctors did not meddle in female complaints."[81] Nonetheless, in the English context, male medical practitioners faced sizeable obstacles infiltrating obstetrics. There were few medical practitioners with elite training. England had no medical school to speak of until Oxford and Cambridge began granting medical degrees in the fourteenth century, and the number of graduates was consistently small.[82] As a result, not only were the options for elite medicine limited, but few could afford professional care.[83] In the absence of reliable contraception, childbirth was a normal part of everyday life. If a family was going to drain its life savings on medical care, surely it would be for a medical emergency rather than for childbirth. Taking all of these factors into consideration, we need to concede that women's medicine in late medieval England was still largely women's business.

This finding is relevant for appeals of abortion by assault. An all-male jury convened to assess distinctly gynecological matters may have felt that such a crucial decision, in which the life of the defendant lay in their hands, was beyond their knowledge or experience. Again, this does not suggest that medieval men were entirely uninformed on the subject of pregnancy. As husbands and fathers at a time when most women spent the majority of their childbearing years pregnant or nursing, many men might have claimed a measure of knowledge through simple observation. Would an all-male jury have had enough confidence in their familiarity with women's bodies to condemn a man or woman to death? Given the complexity of the issue, this kind of poise and self-belief may have evaded most jurors. The significance of the quickening, in particular, to a successful suit of abortion may have presented some worries. Many medieval men may have been ill-informed about the various stages of pregnancy and thus unaware at what point a woman should be able to sense fetal movement. Moreover, the observance of fetal movement is a very subjective experience. A jury had to rely almost exclusively on the testimony of the plaintiff. In a world where women's voices carried little weight in courts of law, some jurors may have been reluctant to stake a man's life on the word of a woman. If the disgraceful history of rape in the Western courts can teach us anything, it is that when a man's word is pitted against a woman's, rarely is she capable of swaying a jury in her favor.[84]

The medical dimensions of abortion by assault may have presented some obstacles to even the most diligent of jurors. The crux of the issue was to demonstrate competently the causal connection between a beating and a subsequent miscarriage. As we saw with assault in general, this was no easy task. The investigation was even more challenging when the evidence was primarily internal. Even today, with higher levels of education and a more comprehensive knowledge of female anatomy, most men and women would be hard-pressed to determine the level of violence required to produce a miscarriage. A woman who could provide evidence of bruising or bleeding in the abdominal region had the best hope of convincing a jury that the assault was indeed a homicide. The 1368 inquest into the death of Joanna, daughter of John, of Chesterfield illustrates this point. The coroner's report notes that an argument broke out between John's wife, also named Joanna, and Agnes, wife of John Spicer. During the altercation, Agnes punched Joanna in the stomach "so that the child died." The record does not clarify how Joanna knew the child had died, but she may have been far enough along in the pregnancy that she could make a convincing argument for the absence of regular fetal movement. Blows to her stomach presumably left bruises that the jury was able to assess in drawing their conclusion. Crucially, childbirth occurred soon after the assault: six days later, Joanna gave birth to a stillborn girl. Local authorities arrested Agnes and imprisoned her to await judgment.[85] The death of Joanna, daughter of John Boteler, in the town of Leicester provides another relatively uncomplicated instance of abortion by assault. When Robert, son of Robert Hikelyng, attacked Boteler's pregnant wife, also named Joanna, in August of 1403, the jurors reported that he did so with a pitchfork, striking her on the back and the stomach (although the account does not describe the nature of the physical evidence, an attack with a pitchfork must have caused substantial scraping and bruising). The incident induced early labor. Joanna experienced a difficult and protracted labor: after four days, she finally gave birth to a stillborn girl. The jury determined that the child had died because of the force and violence of the assault. While Robert had already fled, the jury treated him as a felon. He was outlawed and his goods assessed at 40*s*.[86]

Occasionally, the corpse itself afforded evidence of violent attack. Before the London eyre of 1244, Isabel, wife of Serlo, of London alleged her baby was born "with its head crushed and its left arm broken in two places and its whole body blackened" as the result of an assault.[87] The court found the evidence compelling. The mayor ordered the defendant to defend himself thirty-six-handed, that is, with eighteen compurgators (character witnesses) chosen from one side of the Walbrook and eighteen from the other.[88] Although the record offers no conclusion to this case, the reader is left with a powerful impression that the defendant's future was bleak. Similarly, the 1415 inquisition into the attack on Elizabeth, wife of John Cokkes, reveals jurors uncertain of whom to blame, but strongly convinced of a connection between assault and abortion. Elizabeth was so ill treated "by her legs so that she was delivered of 2 children then in her womb 5 weeks before her time, to the great despair of her life, by which assault the back of one child and the legs or limbs of the other were broken so that they died immediately after their birth."[89]

Allegations of abortion presented jurors with many of the same obstacles as those of fatal assault. Chiefly, jurors had difficulty establishing a relationship between a beating and the abortion. The jury indicting Stephen Tulbuche of London was confident that Stephen had beaten and ill treated Alice, wife of Geoffrey, of St Albans, but it could not prove a causal connection: "it was not from that cause that she miscarried."[90] Jurors followed a similar approach also in the appeal against William Ammory. The plaintiff alleged that he broke into the home of Emma of Whitewell, threw her down, and beat her so violently that she gave birth to a stillborn child and was confined to her bed for a period of seven weeks after the incident; and yet, the jury chose to acquit.[91] It is possible that bed rest was good evidence in a case of assault, but not necessarily enough to convict William of homicide. At the very least, it seems clear that neither jurors nor plaintiffs were prepared to argue that a woman miscarried from a simple slap or jab to the belly. Once again, the element of time played a critical part in the assessment. When faced with allegations of abortion by assault, Maud, wife of Walter Buk, and her daughter centered their defense on the issue of time. Both denied whole-heartedly that they had beaten Sarah, wife of Aubyn the Porter, in June of 1238. Yet, they argued that even if they had beaten her, the interlude between the alleged beating and the birth was implausible. Sarah asserted that the attack brought on an early birth fifteen weeks after the incident. The child was born living, but survived three days, just long enough to be baptized. Jurors sided with the defendants. They declared that Maud and Stanota never beat Sarah, nor did she give birth before her time.[92]

The predominance of women in women's medicine has led Carol Loar to assume that women regularly participated in the coroner's proceedings in early modern England. Quite rightly, she points out that the nature of the coroner's inquest lent itself to women's participation: "the investigation of homicides and suicides seems often to have involved the entire community. Anyone with relevant information could and did participate in the process even if, as in the case of women, their roles as formal witnesses were seriously circumscribed."[93] While opportunity does not prove involvement, the confidence with which they preceded in many of these judgments implies that jurors were drawing on some form of expertise, and women were the recognized experts.

INSANITY

Not all felons were answerable for their actions. On this issue, the legal treatises were in firm agreement. *Bracton*'s account of the felony of suicide reveals a wide reach in terms of application. The treatise asks,

> And [what] of the deranged, delirious and the mentally retarded? or if one labouring under a high fever drowns himself or kills himself? *Quaere* whether such a one commits felony *de se*. It is submitted that he does not, nor do such persons forfeit their inheritance or their chattels, since they are without sense and reason and can no more commit an *injuria* or a felony than a brute animal, since they are not far removed from brutes. . . . That a madman is not liable is true, unless he acts under pretense of madness while enjoying lucid intervals.[94]

As the above excerpt hints, *Bracton* identified categories of the insane, distinguishing between those born mentally disabled (*idiotis*), the mentally incapacitated (*mente captis*), and the insane (*furiosis*) who may or may not experience lucid intervals.[95] *Bracton* defines the insane as "he [who] knows not how to understand or has no understanding at all."[96] Although the treatises furnish little guidance in how to differentiate between the mentally incapacitated and the insane (presumably, *mente captis* implied permanent madness, while *furiosis* was only temporary), this categorization is largely consistent across the board. The only deviation from the established path appears in *The Mirror of Justices*, which remarks,

> Then as to fools let us distinguish, for all fools can be adjudged homicides except natural fools and children within the age of seven years; for there can be no crime or sin without a corrupt will, and there can be no corruption of will where there is no discretion and an innocent conscience, save in the case of raging fools.[97]

While somewhat vague in their terminology, the legal treatises nonetheless display an established sense of what it meant to be *non compos mentis* as well as recognition of a moderate range of existing mental incapacities. Moreover, their chief criterion resonates with modern conceptions of mental incapacity. Moral discretion, that is, the ability to recognize the difference between right and wrong, takes top billing. Given the intricacy of assessing an individual's mental health, one might expect some instruction in terms of the signs or symptoms of mental instability; however, the legal treatises concerned themselves primarily with safeguarding inheritances, not homicidal insanity.[98] The crown left coroners and jurors largely to their own devices to determine when they should invoke mercy.

Nonetheless, the civil records afford plentiful insight into contemporary perceptions of how to recognize mental incompetence. The interrogation of

Emma, widow of Edmund, of Beeston in July 1382 by royal justices assigned to evaluate whether she was an "idiot" strays somewhat from *Bracton*'s established categories, reporting that Emma had not always been an idiot, "but during four years and more, having been suddenly deprived [of her senses] by the snares of evil spirits. . . . She has no lucid intervals, but always remains in the same condition."[99] However, her examination provides a strong sense of the guiding factors in pronouncing an individual unfit:

> The said Emma, being caused to appear before them, was asked whence she came and said that she did not know. Being asked in what town she was, she said that she was at Ely. Being asked what day that Friday was, she said she did not know. Being asked how many days there were in a week, she said seven, but could not name them. Being asked how many husbands she had had in her time she said three, giving the name of one only and not knowing the names of the others. Being asked whether she had ever had issue by them, she said that she had had a husband with a son (*ad filium*), but did not know his name. Being asked how many shillings there were in forty pence, she said she did not know. Being asked whether she would rather have twenty silver groats (*grossos*) than forty pence, she said they were of the same value. They examined her in all other ways which they thought best and found that she was not of sound mind, having neither sense nor memory nor sufficient intelligence to manage herself, her lands or her goods. As appeared by inspection she had the face and countenance of an idiot.[100]

While the purpose of this test was to evaluate whether Emma's condition necessitated guardianship of her properties, the nature of the questions themselves stress that royal officials identified mental capacity with several salient features: basic common sense and math skills, awareness of one's surroundings, and memory as it relates to one's family and personal history. It is striking also that they appraised her "face and countenance." If Emma had been an "idiot from birth," one might be inclined to suggest they were referring to the facial features regularly associated with Down's syndrome. Emma may also have suffered a stroke, affecting not only her mind but also her appearance.[101] Her examination confirms that royal officials had a good sense of how to recognize and define mental incapacity. An early sixteenth-century law dictionary suggests continuity in this approach to the mentally disabled. Under the headword "idiot," it states:

> Idiot is he that is a fool naturally from his birth, and knows not how to account or number xx pence, nor cannot name his father or mother, nor of what age himself is or such like easy and common matters: so that it appears he hath no manner of understanding of reason, nor government of himself, what is for his profit or disprofits etc. But if he have so much knowledge that he can read, or learn to read by instruction &

> information of others or can measure an Ell of cloth, or name the days in the week, or beget a child, son or daughter, or such like, whereby it may appear that he hath some light of reason: then such a one is no Idiot naturally.[102]

Admittedly, both above examples are better tests of mental incompetence than insanity—that is, the kind of mental incapacity that a coroner and his jury were more likely to encounter in death investigation. Here, it is critical to note that "no rational method exists to this day to discriminate insanity from crime."[103] Of course, jurors in modern courtrooms do have a defined sense of clearly identifiable evidence of mental instability, largely popularized by Hollywood. Modern hallmarks of homicidal insanity include delusional or paranoid behavior, morbid impulses, and lack of remorse.[104] But we need to acknowledge that how a society distinguishes crime from insanity is dependent upon time and place. Michael MacDonald's study of insanity in seventeenth-century England, for example, observes that jurors recognized insanity by the inability to name one's mother and father, taking no pleasure in one's family, and failing to acknowledge one's immediate superiors. In the American 1960s, these characteristics were more fitting to depict adolescence than madness. Graziella Magherini and Vittorio Biotti make a similar observation in their examination of medico-legal declarations of insanity in Florence between the 1300s and 1600s. The court's classification of mental illness was highly subjective. Criteria included not only scandalizing one's family and offending public decency, but also the wasteful expenditure of one's (or one's family's) property.[105] As a result, Magherini and Biotti conclude that "the line between mental illness, antisocial behavior, and delinquency . . . was not at all a clear one."[106] Sylvia Huot's analysis of medieval French culture contends that madness was defined in large part by the "failure to respect the categories of difference—class, gender, lineage—that define the individual subject," tying rebellion to insanity.[107] How did the medieval English define madness?

The medieval English understood mental incapacity as an illness. *Britton* makes this connection explicit in its references to those "who become insane by any sickness," presumably incorporating also *Bracton*'s self-killers laboring under a high fever.[108] Enrollments in the coroners' rolls furnish an even stronger argument for viewing mental incapacity as a bodily dysfunction. When Mathew Arundel tumbled into a well and drowned at Shipton (*Glos.*) in September 1357, he was "greatly vexed by the infirmity of fury."[109] Isabel, wife of William Sherman, of Lincolnshire was suffering from "an illness called frenzy" when she slew her stepson, Thomas, in the mid-fourteenth century. So, too, was Emma le Bere at the time she slit the throats of her husband and three children in June 1316.[110] Much like *Bracton*, jurors also regularly associated insane acts with feverish states.[111] The term "feverish" appears so recurrently that it would seem to be synonymous with "frenzied" or "furious." At times, poor health is thought to have driven the diseased mad. The 1382/83 coroner's report recounts how William, son of John, of Barnwell lay sick with an acute fever for three weeks before "entering into a frenzy." He rose from his bed in the middle of the night and stumbled against a rock because of the debility of his body, killing himself.[112] A 1321 Year Book also made this connection. When a woman named only as Joan drowned herself in the Thames out of her madness, the Year Book explained that "because of her illness," her chattels would be given in alms for her soul.[113] The Year Books acted as texts to instruct how best to plead. Accordingly, the conception of madness as illness was firmly ingrained in the legal mindset.

Seeing madness as illness would seem to have been a distinctly English approach. In his study of the courts of the Crown of Aragon, for example, Michael McVaugh observes that "there is very little to show that people thought of mental disorder as a medical problem." As a result, "the determination of mental incompetence was not reserved to physicians."[114] Admittedly, despite the English's overt recognition that mental dysfunction sprang from ill health, they, too, did not consider the evaluation of the mentally ill to be the preserve of the medical practitioner.[115] Writing about the origins of the insanity defense, Thomas Maeder provides the key. He writes, "[t]hroughout most of history there have been no specific criteria for exculpatory insanity; none, after all, were necessary in a relatively small community where everyone knew the offender."[116] If a jury's evaluation relied primarily on inexplicable changes in personal behavior, then certainly no medical examination was necessary to reach this verdict. Indeed, those who were most familiar with the insane were best qualified to make this judgment. Joel Eigen adds another significant dimension to the debate. Drawing on evidence from Victorian trials, he observes the widespread perception that "[n]o one needs a skilled practitioner to decode the verbal pandemonium and behavioral histrionics of the deranged."[117] This observation concurs with the medieval evidence. The characteristics of the insane inscribed in the English records draw attention to the distinctively manic character of medieval madness. Wandering aimlessly or rushing madly about, ranting, delirium, impulsiveness, and suicidal tendencies all appear to have been identifiable traits of the medieval insane.[118] The disorderly and disruptive nature of the insane is an underlying theme running throughout the records, although only one case actually labels the insane as such. John Eme of Gedney is portrayed as both a lunatic and a "disturber of the peace." In John Eme's case, it is entirely possible that jurors had little idea how else to classify his inane actions. With ax and knife in hand, he appeared at the home of Robert Eme. In a moment reminiscent of Stephen King's *The Shining*, John hacked through the wall of the house with the ax. Once inside, he struck and killed a dog and then attacked a neighbor who attempted to restrain him. John injured himself in the process and died soon after.[119] The singularly manic face of medieval madness is emphasized by a 1285 inquisition into the death of Brother Walter del Hospital by another clerk, Richard, son of Peter le Pessoner. Jurors offered the following account:

> On Wednesday after St. Wilfrid 13 Edward I [17 October 1285] after dinner, Brother Walter lay asleep on his bed in his chamber at Beverley, and Richard the clerk, whom he much loved, lay very sick in the same chamber. And being by the sickness rendered frantic and mad, Richard rose from his bed, and by the instigation of the devil smote Walter on the head as he slept, first with a form, and afterwards with a trestle, so that the brains came out. He then went to the men in the court and the kitchen with blood and brains on his hands. And when they asked him what he had done, he said, laughing: "I have killed my dear master, brother Walter: come and see where he lies slain; he will never speak another word." And he brought them to the slain man saying: Do I not say true, he is slain? So being mad he was taken and imprisoned, and still persists in his madness.

The manic side of madness is emphasized also by the vocabulary. Of the 115 individuals described by the coroners' rolls as having been mentally incapacitated, thirty-two perpetrators were "furious," "in a fury," or "gripped by fury"; thirteen were "frenetic," "frenzied," or "having frenzy"; another twenty-three were out of their senses (*extra sensum*). All of these terms speak to a manic state of mind and appear almost interchangeable. Given that medieval juries privileged the manic side of madness, did they actually need a medical practitioner to interpret such a colorful spectacle?

As the death of Brother Walter above reveals, the focus on the manic side of madness produced a distinct association between madness and the devil. Inquest jurors attributed madness to diabolical incitement in 21 of the 115 cases (18.3%). This correlation is not markedly English. It extends far back in Western heritage, and both the church and medical authorities acknowledged the connection between the devil and mental dysfunction.[120] Significantly, only coroners' juries show this obsession with the devil. Jurors of presentment rarely blamed the devil for an individual's manic behavior.[121] Why would coroners' juries be more inclined to blame the devil? Fellow villagers and neighbors were those jurors most intimately affected by the actions of the homicidally insane. Certainly, the trauma they felt at a madman's behavior may well have left them confused and frightened. As we see today in cases of suicide, family and friends frequently experience an overriding sense of the incomprehensibility of the act, that it was somehow unpredictable and out of character, and thus not preventable. A common explanation today for these unexplainable acts is to suppose an imbalance in brain chemistry. Without science, the medieval world turned instead to the devil. Thus, the records underscore the iniquitous and diabolical features of the death: the secretive nature of the crime, noting that it took place by night, when the defendant was all alone (an almost impossible feat for the medieval period),[122] when the defendant was "taken by demons"[123] or acting under the "instigation of the devil."[124] In some instances, the act itself was of such an extreme nature, surely jurors had no idea how else to explain the death. In 1374/75, with diabolical instigation, John atte Bek of Stoke (*Lincs.*) attacked Robert, son of Richard the Iremonger, striking him repeatedly with an axe, and inflicting twenty mortal wounds (nine in the head, eleven in the body).[125] How else does one explain such uncontrollable rage?

Keeping with the seriousness of the allegations, there is no impression that determinations of diabolical temptation were made lightly. For example, in 1361, when Agnes of Gayton (*Lincs.*) hanged herself by a rope in her home on the eve of Palm Sunday, jurors noted that she did so "not having stable faith, and vexed by a demon, not having memory of, nor faith in, the Lord Jesus Christ nor in the sacrament of the church."[126] Given that royal records of felony tend to be somewhat pithy, this description is positively verbose, indicating that jurors evaluated her behavior as inexplicable otherwise. Allegations of diabolical intervention may also mask a degree of compassion, giving jurors an easy "out" in those cases where they wished to exonerate a suicide. In one particularly tragic case, a daughter happened upon her mother trying to drown herself in the River Severn, and jumped in to save her life. While the mother survived the attempt, the daughter lost her own life trying to rescue her. With the guilt Alice, wife of John, son of John, of Greenhill (*Salop.*) must have felt, the most compassionate way a jury of her fellow villagers could have recorded the case was to note that the death of her daughter occurred while she was acting under the temptation of the devil.[127]

The presence of diabolical instigation as an explanation for aberrant behavior in the coroner's rolls is significant because it speaks to current debates in the history of insanity. Joel Eigen's recent work explores the difficult transition in modern Britain's courts in representations of insanity. For much of British history, the courts entertained insanity pleas only when there was an "impairment of the cognitive faculties—*knowing* the nature of one's acts, *knowing* the difference between right and wrong." The willingness of the courts to expand beyond this conception of madness, Eigen believes, should be credited to nineteenth-century medical practitioners who pressed the courts to think also about "loss of control" as an acceptable variant of madness.[128] Medieval common law, as *Bracton* suggests, also prioritized cognitive impairment. Nonetheless, the law in practice reveals a broader appreciation for mental illness, even if only at the level of coroners' juries. Diabolical instigation is the ultimate expression of "loss of control." A parallel can also be drawn between modern medicine's explanation for particular manifestations of impulsive behavior. Victorian medical practitioners sometimes imputed homicidal expression to epilepsy. As Eigen remarks, the elision between epilepsy and insanity is an easy one. "When the prisoner evinced no cognitive error, a mental convulsion equivalent to an epileptic spasm could address the issue of volition."[129] Thus, it is striking that the medieval coroner's rolls occasionally (although not often) couple epilepsy and mental illness to comprehend homicidal tendencies. The coroner's jury remarked that twenty-four-year-old John, son of Randalph Rykkes, was both out of his mind and suffering from epilepsy when he rose from his bed in the Octave of Easter 1367, dashed to the village of Thursford (*Norfolk*), and dove into a well.[130]

The medieval evidence undermines the innovation Eigen attributes to the nineteenth-century profession. In general, medieval jurors understood mental incapacity in a much more refined and thoughtful manner than has often been imagined. Jurors employed a wide variety of terms for the insane.[131] While the vocabulary of manic madness dominated, some of the terms jurors employed emphasize chiefly senselessness. Insanity (*insania*) appears eight times; dementia (*demens* or *amens*) appears sixteen times. "Lunatic" or "lunacy," which indicates temporary insanity (usually madness tied to the lunar cycle) is employed in only four instances. The language of the legal treatises also appears in the records. Ten individuals are reported as having been *non compos mentis*. Two cases, in particular, make it clear that jurors were heedful of the legal reasoning behind the insanity defense when drawing their conclusions. In 1365, when William, son of Thomas de Below (*Yorks.*) the elder, took his own life by drowning himself in a well, jurors reported he was suffering with "a sickness called frenzy" so that "he had no discretion between good and evil."[132] Similarly, when Alice, wife of Reginald, of Tibthorpe (*Yorks.*) strangled her daughter, Agnes, she had been vexed with the illness of dementia so that "she was lacking all sense and human reason" for some time before the act. She, too, had "no sense of discretion between good and evil."[133] Jurors also demonstrate an awareness of the categories of insanity spelled out in the English legal treatises. *Bracton*, *Britton*, and *Fleta* all emphasize that accountability was tied to the chronology of the illness. The treatises differentiate between the defendant who was born senseless and one who became senseless later in life (distinguished usually by the terms "idiot" versus "lunatic"); and in the case of those who became senseless, whether that was a permanent state, or one broken up by lucid intervals.[134] Obviously, a crime carried out during a moment of lucidity carried a different weight than the actions of a madman. Presumably, jurors had these directives in mind when they took it upon themselves to probe into the onset and duration of the defendant's insanity. Most often, the records lack the kind of meticulousness preferred today. For example, Richard of Burton of Riccall (*Yorks.*), was *non compos mentis* for "a long time" before he hanged himself in 1370.[135] Occasionally one finds a more precise chronology and a jury intent to describe a defendant who evidently was not acting during a moment of lucidity. A London case from 1300 observed that Isabella, wife of Robert, of Pampisford had suffered from "frenzy" for two years before she hanged herself in the solar.[136] John Jugg junior of Garthorpe (*Leics.*) was "furious," "out of his mind," and "under the influence of the devil" for two days before and after he struck and killed his wife, Hawise, in November 1378.[137] Particulars concerning the duration of a defendant's insanity were not included only to build an argument for a pardon. Rather, these details were necessary in order to classify the nature of the offense (that is, whether it was a simple or excusable homicide). Cases like these illustrate a jury's keen awareness of the responsibility set before them and the determination to live up to the expectations of the law.

Only eleven of the 115 mentally incapacitated individuals in the coroners' rolls merited the description of being simple (*fatuus*, *stultus*). This category presents the utmost potential for misunderstanding. It is necessary to examine closely the context in order to establish whether jurors believed the individual was a "fool," or he was merely carrying out a "foolish" act. For example, the above figure does not include Henry Carter, whom a Leicestershire jury described as having killed himself "out of his own foolishness," by removing a rock from a pile and causing the pile to topple down upon himself.[138] Rather, the eleven cases represent only the definitively simple folk, classified distinctively as a fool. At times, the enrollments are very precise. In the 1368 death of Catherine, daughter of Nicholas atte Assh, the jury remarked that she was a fool by nature (*a natura*). Only fourteen years old, the enrollment recounts how she fell into a well and drowned.[139] The rolls characterize a surprising number of young children as being simple-minded.[140] Here, it is important to point out that the coroners' rolls are no strangers to child death. In terms of death by misadventure, children dominate. And yet, only a few of them are depicted in this manner, which tells us that jurors were not equating childish innocence with idiocy. Moreover, the coroners' rolls do not create the firm division between simple-mindedness and insanity embraced by *Bracton* and the other legal treatises. Myriad enrollments portray individuals as suffering from both illnesses. The enrollment reports that Alice Balthweye was both an "idiot" and "out of her senses" when she fell into the River Derwent and drowned in November 1381.[141] When Alice wife of Walter Elsy slew her four-year-old daughter, Joanna, at Saxthorp (*Norfolk*) in 1363, the record observes that for the five years preceding the homicide, she had been "foolish" (*fatua*), "furious," and "demented" (*amens*).[142] Perhaps the oddest representation is that of an unknown man who slew a woman named Katherine with a staff at Staffordshire in 1404/05. The inquest jury characterized him as being a "fool by diabolical instigation" (*diabolica infatuus instigatus*).[143]

What stands out most about jurors' descriptions of mental illness is this tendency to employ multiple terms simultaneously. Indeed, coroners' enrollments describe 36 of the 115 mentally incapacitated individuals (or 31%) as suffering from more than one mental illness at a time. John of Appleton (*Yorks.*) was "furious" and "out of his mind" when he drowned himself in the River Ouse in December 1355;[144] John Roper of Norfolkshire was "frenzied, feverish, and furious" when he struck a man in the head with a short sword, killing him instantly, in 1377/78.[145] This coupling of diseases does not demonstrate either a lack of consensus or a deficient understanding of mental illness. Rather, it is a product of their medical worldview. Medieval medicine embraced a pluralistic view of disease.[146] As Jon Arrizabalaga observes, "[b]efore the laboratory it was accepted that patients suffered from 'mixed' diseases, and that the 'morbid matter' freely moved within the body, which implied that any disease could change its seat, and even be transformed into another one."[147] Citing joint causes for a death was standard practice up until 1948, when the World Health Organization announced that death investigators now had to record only the principal cause of death.[148] This conception of disease is substantiated by the coroners' rolls. Jurors regularly reported that the diseased passed away from joint causes, even when the issue at hand was unrelated to mental health. Jurors attributed Matilda Gaylard's death in September 1404 to debilitation, being "vexed with many various sicknesses."[149] Joanna Burforde, who died in June 1385, suffered from "diverse intrusive sicknesses, which the jurors did not recognize."[150] The demise of Reginald, son of Thomas Ladde, of Alresford was explained as resulting from both the ague and a blood sickness (*morbo sanguine*).[151] Here, it is important to recognize that the distinction between disease, symptom, and sign is a modern innovation.[152] Subjects who manifested multiple symptoms, from the medieval perspective, were obviously afflicted simultaneously by different illnesses. These enrollments thus represent the best possible means of describing the broad scope of a victim's symptoms. For example, in the case of Alice, wife of Walter Elsy, above, described as "foolish, furious and without sense," jurors conceived that she was suffering from three distinct illnesses.[153] How do you describe the behavior of a person who deviates between such radical extremes? Surely, if she suffered from several different mental illnesses, her behavior made much more sense. Thus, jurors who reported a death caused by two distinct forms of mental illness respected the categories of illness, but realized that in some extreme cases, an individual suffered from multiple illnesses all at once.

Jurors' recognition of degrees of insanity emphasizes their capacity to assess distinctions in mental incapacity and to judge accordingly. At times, jurors were content to declare a defendant both insane and legally competent.[154] This phenomenon applied strictly to cases of suicide. To offer a couple of examples: the jury determined that Adam Cose, a chaplain, was demented (*amens*) and furious when he "of his own will and voluntarily" stabbed himself with his knife in February 1378/79. And yet, they declared his death a felony.[155] Eighty-year-old John Austyn of Southery (*Norfolk*) was insane when he voluntarily drowned himself at dawn in the spring of 1370; jurors also declared his actions a suicide (*felo de se*).[156] This seeming contradiction in inquest verdicts is not evidence of an ill informed or clueless jury. Rather, it previews a modern trend in the history of the insanity defense. In 1883, the English Parliament passed the Trial of Lunatics Act, permitting jurors to return a verdict of guilty while recognizing a defendant's mental instability: if convicted, the individual was held in prison as a criminal lunatic.[157] More recently, American justice has adopted a similar approach. In 1975, the state of Michigan took the lead in enacting "guilty but mentally ill" (GBMI) provisions, setting an example that at least twenty states have since emulated.[158] A verdict of GBMI is intended to acknowledge those situations when a defendant's mental illness played a role in a crime without entirely causing it. Thus, such a judgment would have been particularly apt for medieval judgments of suicide. Suicide was a crime with many religious, folkloric, economic, and social implications. Certainly, for the medieval juror, a verdict of guilty but insane presented a compromise between the many conflicting emotions jurors dealt with when faced with a self-killing.

What is perhaps most surprising about jurors' interpretation of mental incapacity is that they sometimes applied this terminology to identify temporary mental dysfunction caused by inebriation.[160] Historical tradition usually attributes recognition of this connection to Frankfurt jurist Johann Fichard. In 1538, he claimed that the madman was most similar to the drunkard, and that in "both cases the mind-beclouding condition should mitigate the punishment, if any punishment at all were appropriate."[159] Nonetheless, the medieval English conceded that alcohol produced significant mental impairment. When Elena, wife of Geoffrey le Hordere, of Wiltshire left the tavern with her husband one evening, jurors commented that she was both *non compos mentis* and drunk. She drowned soon after when she fell into a nearby dike filled with water where she had intended to wash her feet.[160] Similarly, when Ralph Deblet stumbled on a cartload of wood, injuring himself in the head and eventually dying, jurors noted that he "was so drunk that he did not know what he was doing."[161] Jurors made this point most clearly in the death of John Couper. He was so drunk and impotent that "he could not govern himself" and so fell into a well and drowned.[162]

Inquest records also provide abundant insight into the treatment of the mentally ill. Emphasizing once against the aggressive nature of mental illness, the coroners' rolls highlight that many criminally insane presented a danger to themselves and others and needed to be restrained. Robert, son of Elena, of Normanby, who killed both his son and daughter while furious and out of his mind, had to be tied before he could be escorted to prison.[163] Regrettably, despite efforts to control the insane, several madmen escaped their restraints, only to lash out violently against the first person with whom they came into contact. Thomas Laxman of Fleet, who reportedly had been vexed with dementia for quite some time, broke his chains and pounced upon his sleeping custodian with a hammer, striking him in the head and killing him instantly.[164] Roger Wry of Wainfleet (*Lincs.*) chewed through the ropes tying his hands. Spying Thomas Attehill in the street, Roger struck him with a staff to the head; Thomas died ten days later.[165] Those who did not escape often turned their anger inward, harming themselves. A graphic case of prison death recounts the tale of John Raven, imprisoned at the castle of Lincoln for having struck and wounded a man while furious. The injuries inflicted to his feet from thrashing about while in chains caused his feet to putrefy so that they emitted a great stench, eventually leading to his "natural death."[166] Other madmen were destructive. When John Maynard got up from his bed, smashed the shutter of his window in order to exit through it, then drowned soon after in a brook, the inquest observed that it was as if he was furious (*quasi furebund*).[167]

Perpetual imprisonment was not generally understood as the solution to monitoring the criminal actions of the mentally insane. This is recognized in a 1270 inquiry into the welfare of Richard Blofot of Chediston, a long-time prisoner of the jail at Norwich.

> On behalf of Richard of Cheddestan, taken and held in our prison at Norwich, it has been stated to us that when he, more than six years ago, was suffering from a frenzied seizure and in that frenzy killed his wife and two children, our then Sheriff of Norfolk, who had heard tell of this deed, took Richard and confined him in the aforesaid prison, where he is wretchedly detained. We therefore, wishing to know the truth of the aforesaid matter, depute you to enquire on oath of the knights, and other trustworthy and law-abiding men of the county from whom the truth may best be got, whether the aforesaid Richard, under the influence of the aforesaid frenzy, acted thus or otherwise, and if otherwise how and in what fashion, and whether the aforesaid Richard is restored to his former soundness of mind, or whether it would be dangerous if he were released from the prison on the ground that he was ill. And therefore we instruct you that on a given time and place to be arranged by you for this purpose you instruct our Sheriff of the aforesaid county that at a time and place which you will make known to him he shall cause to appear before you such knights and other trustworthy and law-abiding men as are needed for getting at the truth of these matters. In witness whereof we have had these letters patent drawn up. In my presence at Westminster on the 25th day of July in the fourth year of our reign.

Here is the sheriff's response:

> The Sheriff of Norfolk [states that] Richard Blofot, in custody for the death of his wife and two slain children, the reason for his arrest, appeared and says that he is not guilty thereof; and for this places himself upon his country. The jurors say on their oath that the aforesaid Richard, together with his wife, came from Reepham market; and when the same Richard had come near a certain marl-pit full of water he was seized with a frenzy and cast himself into it, wishing to drown there. But, they say, his wife with much difficulty dragged him from the aforesaid marl-pit before he drowned. Later Richard was taken to his home with his wife and children and behaved peacefully. And while his aforesaid wife was away from his home in search of necessaries the aforesaid

> Richard was seized with frenzy and killed his two children. And when his wife returned and found her aforesaid children dead, she cried out in grief and tried to hold him, but was killed by Richard in the grip of the aforesaid frenzy. And when the neighbours, summoned by the noise made by Richard and his aforesaid wife, reached the house they found the same Richard trying to hang himself from a roof-beam, and they held him and prevented him from doing so. And they say clearly that the aforesaid Richard in the grip of a frenzied sickness did all the aforesaid harm, and that he is continually frenzied.
>
> The same Richard is well enough; but it cannot safely be said that he is so restored to soundness of mind that there would not be danger in setting him free, especially when the heat of summer is increasing, lest worse befall.[168]

Both letters offer plentiful insight into medieval interpretations of madness. Not only did they consider insanity an illness, but its principal manifestation is one of unrestrained violence toward others and toward one's self. The centrality of humoral theory in which madness springs from heated blood, making the prospect of release in the heat of summer somewhat daunting, tells us that whoever offered this assessment was well informed concerning the fundamentals of Galenic medicine. More important still, Richard Blofot's case is a good example of the decision to treat the insane humanely. In February of 1277, the king issued a mandate to the sheriff of Norfolk to release Richard into the hands of four of his friends, "who shall keep him securely so that damage or peril shall not arise from him to anyone."[169]

Jurors serving on medieval inquests were no mere "judges of fact." From the moment a death was discovered, jurors were called upon to make decisions on highly technical issues, legally, ethically, and medically speaking. With little guidance from the crown, jurors and local authorities had to determine when a death was, in fact, unnatural and in need of an inquest—a task that was not as self-evident as the crown seemed to believe. Most of the greatest challenges were medically relevant. When an assault precipitated a death, jurors employed all the tools at their disposal to verify a causal connection between the two. Their approach was rational and coherent: they took into account the length of time between death and incident, the nature of the injury (or injuries), and the behavior of the victim. While it is easy to criticize from the vantage point of modern medical knowledge and technology, at the very least, their approach demonstrates 1) a good familiarity with the era's medical advances, and 2) the existence of a standard protocol for death investigation. The difficulty experienced by jurors in establishing a causal connection between assault and death, or abortion and death, is understandable given the era's medical knowledge.

More than any other aspect of death investigation, fatalities involving the mentally ill reveal the capacity of coroners' juries to meet the challenges of the job with both acumen and aplomb. The legal treatises had a great deal to say about the nature of mental incapacity and, by extension, how the courts should tailor their sentences to the variant of mental dysfunction. Medieval jurors were not only acutely aware of the categories of mental illness included in the treatises, as well as their implications for judgment, but the descriptions of mental affliction in the coroners' rolls also suggest a significantly more nuanced classification in line with contemporary theories of disease. Jurors developed also their own jurisprudence of mental incapacity. While the legal treatises instructed readers to excuse the crimes of the mentally ill, with the exception of those who acted during lucid intervals, jurors did not see all mental afflictions as equal. Their willingness to designate some accused felons as both insane and guilty is instructive. Jurors submitted the accused to an evaluation process of their own design, in which they determined just how insane one had to be in order to be excused from homicide.

NOTES

1. Barbara J. Shapiro, *A Culture of Fact: England, 1550–1720* (Ithaca: Cornell UP, 2000), p. 24.
2. Joel Eigen, "Sense and Sensibility: Fateful Splitting in the Victorian Insanity Trial," in *Domestic and International Trials. Trials in History*, ed. Rose Anne Melikan, 2 vols. (Manchester: Manchester UP, 2003), v. 2, p. 22.
3. Eric Barber, "Judicial Discretion, Sentencing Guidelines and Lessons from Medieval England, 1066–1215," *Western New England Law Review* 27.1 (2005): 34.
4. There was a great deal of resentment when coroners overstepped their boundaries and held inquests into deaths that local authorities deemed unnecessary. This seldom happened, but there are occasional records of coroners who "forcibly held an inquest" into a death. For example, see the inquest into the death of John Smyth in September of 1440. William Hudson and John C. Tingey, eds., *The Records of the City of Norwich* (Norwich: Jarrold & Sons, 1906), v. 1, p. 326.
5. John Jervis, *The Office and Duties of Coroners*, 9th ed. (London, 1957), as cited in Lindsay Prior, "The Good, the Bad and the Unnatural: A Study of Coroners' Decisions in Northern Ireland," *Sociological Review* 33.1 (1985): 69. Now in its thirteenth edition, Jervis's text is still the most popular manual for death investigators in the Western world. See Paul Matthews, ed., *Jervis on Coroners*, 13th ed. (London: Sweet & Maxwell, Ltd., 2013).
6. Prior, "The Good, the Bad and the Unnatural," 83.
7. Prior, "The Good, thc Bad and the Unnatural," 83–84.
8. Prior, "The Good, the Bad and the Unnatural," 85.
9. J.D.J. Havard, *The Detection of Secret Homicide: A Study of the Medico-Legal System of Investigation of Sudden and Unexplained Deaths* (London: Macmillan, 1960), p. 41. Because of the rules of coverture, one might also argue that a wife fell into this category; however, the Year Books reveal that medieval jurists were uncertain whether a wife shared in a monk's civil death. See Sara M. Butler, "Discourse on the Nature of Coverture in the Later Medieval Courtroom," in *Married Women and the Law: Coverture in England and the Common Law World*, ed. K.J. Kesselring and Tim Stretton (Montreal: McGill-Queen's UP, 2013), pp. 24–44.

10. Havard, *Detection of Secret Homicide*, p. 41.
11. Donald W. Sutherland, *The Eyre of Northamptonshire, 3–4 Edward III (1329–30)*, v. 1 (*SS*, v. 97, 1983), p. 199.
12. TNA PRO JUST 2/61, m. 15/3.
13. F.W. Maitland and W.J. Whittaker, eds., *The Mirror of Justices* (*SS*, v. 7, 1895), p. 23.
14. The only exception to the rule was with the offence of treason. It was considered treason merely to "imagine" or "compass" killing the king. 25 Edw. III, *Stat.* 5, c. 2 (1351–52); *SR*, v. 1, p. 322.
15. For more on *peine forte et dure*, see Henry T. Summerson, "The Early Development of the *Peine Forte et Dure*," in *Law, Litigants, and the Legal Profession*, ed. E.W. Ives and A.H. Manchester (London: Royal Historical Society, 1983), pp. 116–25.
16. TNA PRO JUST 2/80, m. 2.
17. TNA PRO JUST 2/85, m. 2d.
18. Katharine Park, "Medicine and Society in Medieval Europe, 500–1500," *Medicine in Society: Historical Essays*, ed. Andrew Wear (Cambridge: Cambridge UP, 1992), p. 61.
19. TNA PRO JUST 2/25, m. 7d (1345). Even if jurors believed there was no correlation between a wounding and a subsequent death, the enrollment needed to address the assault. This is stressed by a Bedfordshire appeal from a wife who refused to accept that the attack on her husband was not fatal. When a disagreement escalated into a physical quarrel between William the Red and John of Goldington one September evening in 1267 at Goldington Green, purportedly William cast the first blow. He slashed John across the face with an axe, leaving him no alternative but to defend himself. John struck William with a sparthe axe on the head directly between the crown and the nape of his neck. The wound was four inches in length and in depth went right to the bone. However, since that time, both their wounds had healed and the two were reconciled. After the period of recovery, much like Richard the Smith above, William returned to work. In fact, he was so recuperated he worked in the fields, he went to markets, he attended wrestling matches. Almost a year later, William sickened with the ague and died suddenly. The jury concluded that William died not from the wound, but from infirmity. Nonetheless, William's wife, Margaret, raised the hue on John, accusing him of homicide. The jury declared that Margaret's hue was motivated by spite. TNA PRO JUST 2/46, m. 2.
20. Sutherland, *Eyre of Northamptonshire*, v. 1, p. 185a.
21. Of course, there were no formal rules of deodand. Jurors seem to have applied their own guidelines leading to some standardization in practices. As Anna Pervukhin explains, those rules articulated by treatise writers were often an attempt to bring organization to chaos, rather than identify set rules applied in practice. See her "Deodands: A Study in the Creation of Common Law Rules," *AJLH* 47.3 (2005): 237–56.
22. TNA PRO JUST 2 /203, m. 2.
23. TNA PRO JUST 2/38, m. 16.
24. See Charles Creighton, *A History of Epidemics in Britain from A.D. 664 to the Extinction of Plague*, 2 vols. (Cambridge: Cambridge UP, 1891), v. 1, p. 208.
25. TNA PRO JUST 2/139, m. 1d.
26. There is an abundance of literature on the Black Death. A useful summary of the state of the field appears in Paul Slack, *Plague: A Very Short Introduction* (Oxford: Oxford UP, 2012). In terms of abandonment by medical practitioners, see Samuel K. Cohn, Jr., *The Black Death Transformed: Disease and Culture in Early Renaissance Europe* (London: Hodder Arnold, 2003); Shona Kelly Wray presents a more positive image of medieval doctors. See

her, "Boccaccio and the Doctors: Medicine and Compassion in the Face of the Plague," *Journal of Medieval History* 30.3 (2004): 301–22, and also her "Tracking Families and Flight in Bologna during the Black Death," *Medieval Prosopography* 25 (2004): 145–60.

27. TNA PRO JUST 2/138, m. 1.
28. Carole Rawcliffe, "Sickness and Health," in *Medieval Norwich*, ed. Rawcliffe and Richard Wilson (London and New York: Hambledon, 2004), p. 319.
29. Leif Søndergaard, "Imagining Plague: The Black Death in Medieval Mentalities," in *Living with the Black Death*, ed. Søndergaard and Lars Bisgaard (Odense: UP of South Denmark, 2009), p. 227.
30. Admittedly, the crown has exploited the coroner's inquest for this purpose in the colonial world. See Khaled Fahmy, "The Anatomy of Justice: Forensic Medicine and Criminal Law in Nineteenth-Century Egypt," *Islamic Law and Society* 6.2 (1999): 231.
31. Søndergaard, "Imagining Plague," p. 229.
32. Barbara A. Hanawalt, "The Voices and Audiences of Social History Records," *Social Science History* 15.2 (1991): 169.
33. John Theilmann and Frances Cate, "A Plague of Plagues: The Problem of Plague Diagnosis in Medieval England," *Journal of Interdisciplinary History* 37.3 (2007): 392.
34. Edward M. Thompson, ed., *Chronicon Galfridi le Baker de Swynebroke* (Oxford: Clarendon Press, 1899), p. 100.
35. Nicholas of Essendon in 1388, TNA PRO JUST 2/189, m. 2; Richard Mey in 1388/89, TNA PRO JUST 2/189, m. 2d; Joanna, daughter of Adam Shotewell, in 1391, TNA PRO JUST 2/191, m. 3; Peter Cornwall, squire, in 1400, TNA PRO KB 9/185, m. 1.
36. R. Theodore Beck, *The Cutting Edge: Early History of the Surgeons of London* (London: Lund Humphries, 1974), p. 12. Whether a wound should be left to fester or be disinfected was a subject of great controversy among late medieval physicians. See Carole Rawcliffe, *Medicine and Society in Later Medieval England* (London: Sandpiper Books, 1995), p. 74.
37. TNA PRO JUST 2/25, m. 6d.
38. TNA PRO JUST 2/25, m. 7.
39. Sutherland, *Eyre of Northamptonshire*, v. 1, p. 183.
40. F.M. Nichols, ed., *Britton: The French Text Revised with an English Translation* (Oxford: Clarendon Press, 1865), v. 1, p. 12.
41. Death investigation in medieval Manosque adopted a similarly flawed approach. When a young Jewish man named Barba was killed during a game in June 1262 after being hit in the ribs with a paddle, witnesses all agreed that "the blow received by Barba was not very significant, as it was given by an object light in weight." His death was thought instead to have been bad luck. See Joseph Shatzmiller, *Médecine et Justice en Provence Médiévale: Documents de Manosque, 1262–1348* (Aix-en-Provence: Publications de l'Université de Provence, 1989), p. 57.
42. Lisi Oliver, *The Body Legal in Barbarian Law* (Toronto and Buffalo: University of Toronto Press, 2011), p. 74.
43. Oliver, *Body Legal*, p. 87.
44. When John, son of Edward Tailor, of Retford (*Notts.*) was struck by an infirmity of the head, he suddenly found himself unable to stand. He fell to his death from the bridge where he was standing. TNA PRO JUST 2/127, m. 1.
45. See "plat," in R.E. Latham, ed., *Revised Medieval Latin Word-List from British and Irish Sources with Supplement* (London: The British Academy, 1965; rev. 1995), p. 355.
46. TNA PRO JUST 2/107, m. 1.

47. TNA PRO JUST 2/17, m. 8.
48. TNA PRO JUST 2/ 46, m. 2.
49. Richard M. Fraher, "Conviction According to Conscience: The Medieval Jurists' Debate Concerning Judicial Discretion and the Law of Proof," *L&HR* 7.1 (1989): 25.
50. Guillelmus Durandus, *Speculum iuris* (Venice, 1576), bk. 4, pt. 4, *De homicidio*, fo. 491. As cited in Joanna Carraway Vitiello, "Forensic Evidence, Lay Witnesses and Medical Expertise in the Criminal Courts of Late Medieval Italy," in *Medicine and the Law in the Middle Ages*, ed. Wendy J. Turner and Sara M. Butler (Leiden: Brill, 2014), p. 133.
51. *Decretalium Gregorii IX*, IX.v.xii, cap. 18, as cited in Michael McVaugh, *Medicine before the Plague: Practitioners and Their Patients in the Crown of Aragon 1285–1345* (Cambridge: Cambridge UP, 1993), p. 208.
52. David J. Seipp, "The Reception of Canon Law and Civil Law in the Common Law Courts before 1600," *Oxford Journal of Legal Studies* 13.1 (1993): 391.
53. William W. Bassett, "Canon Law and the Common Law," *Hastings Law Journal* 29 (1977–1978): 1412.
54. Silvia De Renzi, "Medical Expertise, Bodies, and the Law in Early Modern Courts," *Isis* 98.2 (2007): 316. Faith Wallis also makes this point. See Faith Wallis, *Medieval Medicine: A Reader* (Toronto: University of Toronto Press, 2010), p. 361.
55. "Office of the Coroner," 4 Edw. I (1275–1276); *SR*, v. 1, pp. 40–41.
56. Isaac Herbert Jeayes, ed. and trans., *Court Rolls of the Borough of Colchester* (Colchester: Town Council of the Borough of Colchester, 1921), v. 1, p. 42.
57. McVaugh, *Medicine before the Plague*, p. 217.
58. Faith Wallis, "Signs and Senses: Diagnosis and Prognosis in Medieval Pulse and Urine Texts," *SHoM* 13.2 (2000): 273.
59. Wallis, "Signs and Senses," 274.
60. Wallis, "Signs and Senses," 274.
61. McVaugh, *Medicine before the Plague*, pp. 143–44.
62. Rawcliffe, "Sickness and Health," p. 302. Michael McVaugh discusses surgeons' fears of bad outcomes in light of the pressure of the marketplace in his "Cataracts and Hernias: Aspects of Surgical Practice in the Fourteenth Century," *MH* 45 (2001): 335–37. Fears of malpractice allegations are what led to the 1435 insistence of London surgeons to hold joint consultations when a patient seemed close to death. See Rawcliffe, *Medicine and Society*, p. 71.
63. A.H. Thomas, ed., *Calendar of Early Mayor's Court Rolls of the City of London. A.D. 1298–1307* (Cambridge: Cambridge UP, 1924), pp. 22–23. Similarly, a 1321 case from the London eyre reports an instance of a coroner ordering the imprisonment of an individual after a view of wounds because the victim's life "was despaired of." See Helen M. Cam, ed., *Year Books of Edward II*, v. 26, pt. 2 (*SS*, v. 86, 1969), pp. 162–63.
64. Henri de Bracton, *De Legibus et Consuetudinibus Angliae*, ed. George Woodbrine, ed. and trans. Samuel E. Thorne, 4 vols. (*SS*, 1968–1976), v. 2, pp. 409–10.
65. Y.B., term uncertain, 28 Edw. III, fo. 145b. A brief summary appears in Y.B., Trin., 28 Edw. III, fo. 18b probably refers to the same case. An exceptionally brief reference to another appeal of mayhem from 1505 implies that seeking the advice of surgeons may have been a normal part of the process. When an assault left the plaintiff wounded in his shoulder, the court deliberated how best to resolve the case, through inspection of the court, or surgical consult. See Y.B., Mich., 21 Hen. VII, fo. 336.
66. Y.B., Mich., 21 Edw. IV, fos. 70b–71a.

67. H.E. Salter, ed., *Records of Mediaeval Oxford: Coroners' Inquests, the Walls of Oxford, etc.* (Oxford: Oxford Chronicle Co., Ltd., 1912), p. 10. The enrollment plants no clues to reveal why the jury dismissed Master Roger's assessment. Yet, even today's courts do not accept forensic evidence without question. It, too, is submitted to a critical assessment. Modern common law applies the *Daubert* standard to all forensic evidence. The judge must assess forensic evidence according to the following criteria: 1) falsifiability, 2) peer review and publication of the expert, 3) known or potential rate of error with the technology, and 4) the general acceptance of the methodology in the scientific community. For an extensive discussion of the *Daubert* standard, see Sayed Sikandar Shah Haneef, "Forensic Evidence: A Comparative Analysis of the General Position in Common Law and Sharī'ah," *Islamic Studies* 46.2 (2007): 204. While the jury in this instance provided no explanation for why they rejected Master Roger's evaluation, at the very least, their reaction implies the existence of an assessment process, even if not as established or codified as the *Daubert* standard. They may have had reason to question his credentials and thus his credibility.
68. Reginald R. Sharpe, ed., *Calendar of Coroners' Rolls of the City of London, A.D. 1300–1378* (London: R. Clay & Sons, Limited, 1913), pp. 23–24.
69. Sharpe, *Calendar of Coroners' Rolls*, pp. 27–28.
70. Martin Weinbaum, ed., *The London Eyre of 1276* (London: London Record Society, 1976), pp. 56–57.
71. Sutherland, *Northumberland Eyre*, p. 184.
72. To offer an example: the investigation into the death of Elias, son of William del Park, of Stevington recounts an assault that took place within the Tower of London in 1324. Elias worked with his brother, John, in the Tower. The two quarreled and eventually came to blows. Pressed against the Tower wall with death imminent, John drew his knife and plunged it into his brother's breast, "inflicting a mortal wound an inch and a half long and penetrating to the heart, whereof he immediately died." Sharpe, *Calendar of Coroners' Rolls*, pp. 102–03. Not all enrollments specifically include the phrase "mortal wound"; yet, even without the phrase, the point is clear. When Christina of Menstrie was stabbed in the shoulder blade with a knife, jurors reported only that it caused "a wound an inch broad and six inches deep, of which wound she then and there died." Sharpe, *Calendar of Coroners' Rolls*, pp. 7–8.
73. TNA PRO JUST 2/184, m. 1.
74. Y.B., term uncertain, 40 Edw. 3, fo. 245a.
75. *CIM*, v. 1, p. 568.
76. *Bracton*, v. 2, p. 341. This definition of abortion extends well back into antiquity and was endorsed across Europe: as Oliver notes, "[m]ost barbarian laws . . . address the issue of attacking a pregnant woman, killing either the woman or the fetus, or both." See her *Body Legal*, p. 195.
77. *Britton*, v. 1, p. 114.
78. Y.B., term uncertain, 22 Edw. III, fo. 106b. Justices do note that none of this applies to the indictment for the death of an unknown man.
79. Monica H. Green, "Women's Medical Practice and Health Care in Medieval Europe," *Signs: Journal of Women in Culture and Society* 14 (1988): 434.
80. Monica H. Green, *Making Women's Medicine Masculine: The Rise of Male Authority in Pre-Modern Gynaecology* (Oxford: Oxford UP, 2008), p. 19.
81. Peter Murray Jones, "Witnesses to Medieval Medical Practice in the Harley Collection," *Electronic British Library Journal* (2008): 3.
82. Faye Getz, *Medicine in the English Middle Ages* (Princeton: Princeton UP, 1998), p. 17. Carole Rawcliffe notes: "Only forty individuals are known either

to have read or taught medicine at Oxford during the fourteenth century and fifty-four during the fifteenth, while a mere fifty-nine graduated in it from Cambridge between 1300 and 1499." See her *Medicine and Society*, p. 108.

83. Carole Rawcliffe, "The Profits of Practice: The Wealth and Status of Medical Men in Later Medieval England," *SHoM* 1.1 (1988): 66.
84. For a discussion of rape in the medieval context, see John M. Carter, *Rape in Medieval England: An Historical and Sociological Study* (Lanham, MD: University Press of America, 1985).
85. TNA PRO JUST 2/116, m. 3.
86. TNA PRO JUST 2/60, m. 11.
87. Helena M. Chew and Martin Weinbaum, eds., *London Eyre of 1244* (London: London Record Society, 1970), pp. 62–63.
88. This is an exceptionally high number of compurgators demanded by the court. Although there were no set rules to the number of compurgators a defendant might be required to bring forward in his defense, usually the courts asked for between six and twelve. Thus, at thirty-six, the court was making it very difficult for the accused to purge himself of the accusation.
89. *CIM*, v. 7, p. 296.
90. Chew and Weinbaum, *London Eyre of 1244*, p. 36.
91. A. H. Thomas, ed., *Calendar of Plea and Memoranda Rolls, Preserved among the Archives of the Corporation of the City of London at the Guildhall, Rolls A1a–A9, A.D. 1323–1364* (Cambridge: Cambridge UP, 1926), pp. 253–54.
92. Chew and Weinbaum, *London Eyre of 1244*, p. 50.
93. Carol Loar, "Medical Knowledge and the Early Modern English Coroner's Inquests," *SHoM* 23.3 (2010): 487.
94. *Bracton*, v. 2, p. 424.
95. *Bracton*, v. 4, p. 177.
96. *Bracton*, v. 3, p. 308.
97. *Mirror of Justices*, p. 138.
98. In general, the crown showed great concern for protecting the property of the insane and were conscientious in their efforts to make sure they suffered little abuse in this respect. See Margaret McGlynn, "Idiots, Lunatics and the Royal Prerogative in Early Tudor England," *JLH* 26.1 (2005): 1–20.
99. *CIM*, v. 4, p. 125.
100. *CIM*, v. 4, pp. 127–28.
101. Many thanks to Katherine D. Watson for this interpretation.
102. The spelling has been modernized. John Rastell, *An Exposition of Certain Difficult and Obscure Words and Terms of the Laws of this Realm* (London: John Rastell, 1579; Clark, New Jersey: Lawbook Exchange, repr. 2003), pp. 134–35. Although the cited edition is from 1579, it is substantively the same as the 1527 French edition, with the exception that Rastell's son added a facing English translation.
103. Janet Colaizzi, *Homicidal Insanity, 1800–1985* (Tuscaloosa: University of Alabama Press, 1989), p. 6.
104. Colaizzi, "Introduction."
105. Graziella Magherini and Vittorio Biotti, "Madness in Florence in the 14th–18th Centuries: Judicial Inquiry and Medical Diagnosis, Care, and Custody," *International Journal of Law and Psychiatry* 21.4 (1998): 359–61.
106. Magherini and Biotti, "Madness in Florence," 368.
107. Sylvia Huot, *Madness in Medieval French Literature: Identities Found and Lost* (Oxford: Oxford UP, 2003), p. 24.
108. *Britton*, v. 2, p. 20.
109. TNA PRO JUST 2/34, mm. 18–19.
110. TNA PRO JUST 2/69, m. 7d; TNA PRO JUST 2/6, m. 2.

111. In 1282, when John of Fleet, a cleric, slew Robert de Hallyhok and wounded Margery Peris, the enrollment reports that he was first lying infirm with a fever that "grew into the sickness of frenzy." TNA PRO JUST 2/107, m. 6.
112. TNA PRO JUST 2/106, m. 9. A 1410 coroner's roll from Middlesex provides a comparable situation: Henry Porter was suffering from a "violent infirmity that developed into a frenzy." His insanity prompted him to race to the River Thames where he drowned. See TNA PRO KB 9/201/4, m. 58.
113. In Helen M. Cam, ed., *Year Books of Edward II*, v. 26, pt. 1 (*SS*, v. 85, 1968), p. 93.
114. McVaugh, *Medicine before the Plague*, p. 232.
115. Although jury lists are admittedly problematic in terms of a guide, they do not indicate any identifiable correlation between mental illness and medical practitioners serving on juries.
116. Thomas Maeder, *Crime and Insanity: The Origins and Evolution of the Insanity Defense* (New York: Harper & Row, 1985), p. 3.
117. Joel Eigen, "Lesion of the Will: Medical Resolve and Criminal Responsibility in Victorian Insanity Trials," *Law and Society Review* 33.2 (1999): 430. The scorn of nineteenth-century psychiatrist John Haslam reflects this belief. He remarked "to constitute madness, the minds of ignorant people expect a display of continued violence, and they are not satisfied that a person can be pronounced in that state, without they see him exhibit the pranks of a baboon, or hear him roar and bellow like a beast." See John Haslam, *Observations on Madness and Melancholy* (London: J. Barrow, 1809), pp. 77–78, as cited in Andrew Scull, "The Domestication of Madness," *MH* 27.3 (1983): 237.
118. The coroner in Alice, wife of Henry, of Warwick's inquest said it best when he characterized her as having been in a "wild state" in February 1339 when she ran to the port of Dovegate and threw herself into the River Thames. Sharpe, *Calendar of Coroners' Rolls*, p. 249. Nakedness was a sure sign of insanity. When John de Balnea hanged himself in a "fit of madness," jurors reported that he first took off his clothes and ran naked through the local park. *CIM*, v. 1, pp. 603–04.
119. TNA PRO JUST 2/82, m. 11.
120. Kristen Uszkalo contends that "one of the most consistent expressions of demon possession in Western Christian tradition is the powerful display of rage. Swearing, cursing, and raging against God, often accompanied by frightening facial contortions, extreme gestures, uncharacteristic ejaculations, and wild physical behavior, all bespoke a foreign entity having displaced the subject's personality." See her "Rage Possession: A Cognitive Science Approach to Early English Demon Possession," in *Bodies of Knowledge: Cultural Interpretations of Illness and Medicine in Medieval Europe*, ed. Sally Crawford and Christina Lee (Oxford: Archaeopress, 2010), p. 5.
121. This is the premise behind my "Local Concerns: Suicide and Jury Behavior in Medieval England," *History Compass* 4.5 (2006): 820–35.
122. TNA PRO JUST 2/64, m. 4.
123. TNA PRO JUST 1/683, m. 62d.
124. TNA PRO JUST 2/57, m. 12.
125. TNA PRO JUST 2/72, m. 4d.
126. TNA PRO JUST 2/67, m. 23.
127. TNA PRO JUST 2/146, m. 5d.
128. Joel Eigen, "Diagnosing Homicidal Mania: Forensic Psychiatry and the Purposeless Murder," *MH* 54.4 (2010): 456.
129. Eigen, "Diagnosing Homicidal Mania," 456.
130. TNA PRO JUST 2/104, m. 47. A Leicestershire jury in January 1401/02 characterized John Norfolk as both lunatic and epileptic. Shut up in his room,

presumably for his own safety, he became thirsty. He rose from his bed and broke open the shutters. From the window, he jumped to the ground below and proceeded to the local well known as "Stokewell" for a drink. There, the illness overcame him. He accidently fell into the well and drowned. TNA PRO JUST 2/61, m. 7.

131. The names of illnesses employed by coroners' juries do not necessarily reflect the subtleties of their perceptions. Basil Clarke's seminal history of mental illness published in 1975 helps to explain the problem. He observes that the number of phrases used to indicate mental illness "indicate an ability to recognize firmly enough such states, an ability which was more stable than the ways of expressing it. Doubtless in individual cases the choice of phrase meant something very specific to the witness or official employing it, and the record being in Latin dulls distinctions, but certainly no close consistency seems discernible in the vocabulary, though some phrases are more frequent than others. The lack of firmness was doubtless partly due to the infrequency of such cases, and there seems no instance where a medical appraisal was available and taken into account." Clarke's assessment seems quite apt. Jurors were not frequently called upon to evaluate the mental health of their neighbors; nor do we have any means of learning what English terms they actually used to describe the various states of mind that were then translated into Latin by the coroner's scribe. Nonetheless, the variety of terms and their usage strongly implies that this vocabulary had meaning, and that jurors did not equate all forms of mental illness. Basil F.L. Clarke, *Mental Disorder in Earlier Britain: Exploratory Studies* (Cardiff: University of Wales' Press, 1975), p. 61.
132. TNA PRO JUST 2/221, m. 3.
133. TNA PRO KB 27 / 335, m. 17d.
134. *Britton*, v. 2. p. 20; H. G. Richardson and G.O. Sayles, eds., *Fleta*, (*SS*, v. 72, 1953), p. 21; *Bracton*, v. 2, p. 424.
135. TNA PRO JUST 2/217, m. 41.
136. Sharpe, *Calendar of Coroners' Rolls*, pp. 36–37.
137. TNA PRO JUST 2/57, m. 12.
138. TNA PRO JUST 2/52, m. 5.
139. TNA PRO JUST 2/104, m. 25.
140. Jurors report that four-year-old John de Chandlham at South Lynn (*Norfolk*), who drowned in a fountain in 1378, was a "lesser fool." TNA PRO JUST 2/105, m. 1. Felicia, daughter of William Huberd (*Oxon.*), who also drowned in 1392/93, was only two years old at the time, but jurors also identify her as simple. TNA PRO JUST 2/140, m. 2.
141. TNA PRO JUST 2/31, m. 7.
142. TNA PRO JUST 2/102, m. 10.
143. TNA PRO JUST 2/162, m. 5. At the very least, the coroners' rolls imply that the medieval English did not prevent *idiota* from leading normal lives. When John Foltidboundan, reported as having persistent foolishness (*continua fatuitate detenta*), drowned in 1386, his son, John Steyn, was the first finder, implying that marriage and fatherhood were within the realm of possibility even for the simple-minded. TNA PRO JUST 2/61, m. 14/1.
144. TNA PRO JUST 2/215, m. 4d.
145. TNA PRO JUST 2/105, m. 1d.
146. Jon Arrizabalaga, "Medical Causes of Death in Preindustrial Europe: Some Historiographical Considerations," *JHMAS* 54 (1999): 244.
147. Arrizabalaga, "Medical Causes of Death," 249.
148. Lindsay Prior and Mick Bloor, "Why People Die: Social Representations of Death and its Causes," *Science as Culture* 3.3 (1993): 361.

149. TNA PRO JUST 2/61, m. 2.
150. TNA PRO JUST 2/96, m. 6.
151. TNA PRO JUST 2/106, m. 7.
152. Juhani Norri, *Names of Sicknesses in English, 1400–1550: An Exploration of the Lexical Field* (Helsinki: Suomalainen Tiedeakatemia, 1992), p. 101.
153. The combination of symptoms suggests that she may well have been bipolar.
154. This enigma is one that I have addressed elsewhere at some length in studies on self-killings. See Sara M. Butler, "Degrees of Culpability: Suicide Verdicts, Mercy, and the Jury in Medieval England," *JMEMS* 36.2 (2006): 271–72.
155. TNA PRO JUST 2/119B, m. 2.
156. TNA PRO JUST 2/ 104, m. 34.
157. See Stephen White, "The Insanity Defense in England and Wales since 1843," *Annals of the American Academy of Political and Social Science* 477 (1985): 43–57.
158. See C.A. Palmer and M. Hazelrigg, "The Guilty but Mentally Ill Verdict: A Review and Conceptual Analysis of Intent and Impact," *Journal of the American Academy of Psychiatry and the Law* 28.1 (2000): 47–54.
159. See H.C. Erik Midelfort, *A History of Madness in Sixteenth-Century Germany* (Stanford: Stanford UP, 1999), p. 196.
160. TNA PRO JUST 2/194, m. 3d.
161. *CIM*, v. 1, p. 611.
162. TNA PRO KB 9/195/1, m. 11.
163. TNA PRO JUST 2/214, m. 2. His pardon can be found in *CPR*, *Edward III*, v. vii, p. 210.
164. TNA PRO JUST 2/67, m. 31.
165. TNA PRO JUST 2/67, m. 38.
166. TNA PRO JUST 2/67, m. 49.
167. TNA PRO JUST 2/139, m. 2. Similarly, John Mundevylle was also *quasi furebund* when he escaped from his home by breaking through the walls in 1397. He went to a brook and drowned himself. TNA PRO JUST 2/139, m. 2.
168. TNA PRO C 145/34/59; as cited in Nigel Walker, *Crime and Insanity in England: Volume One: The Historical Perspective* (Edinburgh: Edinburgh UP, 1968), pp. 20–22. The sheriff's response is printed also in *CIM*, v. 1, pp. 589–90.
169. *CCR*, for 1277, p. 371.

5 Health and Healthcare in the Coroners' Rolls

Much historiographical debate has dwelt on the question of just how effective, if at all, medieval medicine was. Given the propensity of herbal remedies to incorporate bizarre ingredients such as animal droppings, quaintly named herbs, and snake venom (distasteful to modern sensibilities and dubious in their medicinal properties); to dictate the method of gathering herbs according to the astrological calendar; to incorporate prayers in nonsensical Latin; and the often total absence of instructions for dosage, it is no wonder that questions have arisen concerning medical efficacy.[1] Nonetheless, conclusions regarding the value of medieval medical practice range widely. John Riddle, for example, claims that the problem lies with historians' linear view of history: "[m]odern scholars have been unwilling to believe that medieval people could have been so well informed,"[2] when in fact, medieval pharmacological knowledge evinces a high degree of proficiency.[3] Even the charms and nonsensical prayers achieved a degree of therapeutic success. In such a highly ritualistic society, what might seem superfluous, even ridiculous, to us, was comforting and authoritative.[4] Carole Rawcliffe likewise extols the virtues of medieval surgery. In addressing the competency of field surgeons, she states "[i]t is a testimony to the skill of the medieval surgeon that so many badly wounded individuals actually lived to fight again."[5] On the other end of the historiographical spectrum, the vision is bleak. Vivian Nutton presents an astonishingly gruesome outlook on medieval surgery:

> One cannot neglect the torments of those left for years with a suppurating wound after being cut for bladder-stone or the almost inevitable recurrence of an inguinal hernia. One can only shudder at the agonies of patients forcibly held (or chained) down while the surgeon plied the knife or the red-hot cautery, whose pain was only slightly dulled by draughts of opiated wine or by the soporific sponge.[6] . . . Surgery had its drawbacks as much as physic, and it was very much a treatment of last resort.[7]

The literature of the period is to blame for inspiring much of this negativity. Despite his readiness to undertake a pilgrimage to Canterbury, Chaucer's "Doctour of Physik" is a poor specimen of Christianity: he cares only for gold and fine clothes, and his practice aims for profit at the expense of good healthcare.[8] Langland's *Piers Plowman*, which is replete with derogatory aspersions of contemporary medical practice and its practitioners, fearlessly equates doctors with witches: "his pharmaceuticals are no more effective than her superstitious charms."[9] Dante is equally hostile to medical practice. He happily consigns the physician to Hell in what Pasquale Accardo refers to as "The Circle of Malpractice."[10]

This uninhibited pessimism has forced some historians on the defensive. In a recent publication, Lisi Oliver refutes the modern, Tarantino-esque inclination to construe "medieval" as "backward." She offers a stirring defense of early medieval medicine, asserting that "the Germanic peoples possessed knowledge of functional anatomy far beyond the average perceptions of my own contemporaries."[11] Surely, the average Tom, Dick, or Mary today knows nothing of synovial fluid, secreted from the synovial membrane surrounding the knees and elbows, thickening into a fluid that oils the joints. Yet, Alfred of Wessex's law code dictates various compensations for wounds that cause an eruption of *liðseaw* (synovia).[12] Oliver's confidence in barbarian medical expertise prompts her to conclude that "[t]he Germanic territories provide a model for such communal health practices."[13]

Nonetheless, the arguments emanating from both ends of the spectrum share the same flaw: the absence of evidence relating to medicine in practice. The sources are chiefly prescriptive: medical treatises, literature, and legislation comprise the corpus of evidence from which most English medical historians draw. Granted, several prominent English medical practitioners penned treatises purportedly based on their own patient care. For the later medieval period, John Arderne and Thomas Fayreford stand out as shining examples.[14] Yet, the lingering question is always: how representative were these men as medical practitioners? The vast majority of medical practitioners did not write treatises and, most likely, were not even literate.

Legal records offer a lens through which to view medicine in practice. Admittedly, it is not the ideal lens. Medical practice in the legal setting often represents instances of medicine gone awry, particularly in the coroners' rolls. Moreover, because the records gloss over the constitution of the jury, treating it as one collective voice, it is not always easy to identify the source of medical knowledge, that is, whether it represents learned or popular culture. Yet, coroners and their juries together functioned in a medical capacity when diagnosing cause of death. An analysis of their forays into the realm of medicine has much to offer in terms of enhancing our knowledge of medicine in practice, and complementing the perceptions molded by the prescriptive literature.

If the legal materials are burgeoning with medical insights, why have English historians normally shied away from using them for medical historical purposes?[15] Some English medical historians have drawn on legal practice, primarily in the area of malpractice, generally sued as breach of contract.[16] However, their findings rely on a small corpus of printed legal materials and, as a brief perusal of the note 16 below will confirm, the findings have been published in journals intended for a somewhat exclusive audience—it is hard to imagine that a journal entitled *Clinical Orthopaedics and Related Research* is read much outside medical circles.[17] Medicine at law is a subject that stands at the intersection of two very exclusive disciplines. Both medical history and legal history require a mastery of distinct skill sets in terms of Latin and paleography. The respective historiographies also communicate in their own distinctly jargon-ridden languages. Not surprisingly, many have found the prospect of tackling medicine in law too daunting. This chapter aims to shed light on how rewarding such a venture might be.[18]

A PRELIMINARY DEBATE

Realistically, how much can the coroners' rolls tell us about the medical practices of coroners and their jurors? Historical studies of the office have stressed the carelessness and imprecision of coroners' verdicts. The preponderance of verdicts describing a death "by visitation of God" (*ex visitatione Dei*) remains a touchstone for those wishing to draw attention to the inadequacy of early death investigation. This expression is best understood as "a whitewashing phrase,"[19] a "wonderfully flexible category"[20] that the historiography has interpreted in a multiplicity of ways. Was it merely a euphemism for natural death,[21] or was it "an exculpatory formula regularly invoked by coroners over the centuries for deaths in prison"?[22] Still others stress the term's expediency for masking a growing disinclination to cast blame on the dead in suicides; or, as a ruling of last resort when faced with the broad-reaching implications of pronouncing death by insanity.[23] Medical ineptitude, in particular, has dominated the debate for some time. The most unflattering portrayal comes from Thomas Wakley, a medical coroner who wrote in the 1840s: "case after case was reported in which the most favoured verdict of 'visitation of God' was returned when the real cause of death had not been ascertained owing to inadequate medical evidence and insufficient knowledge on the part of the coroner."[24] Thankfully, Lindsay Prior's observations of coroners' inquests have helped to narrow the definition in a constructive fashion. Drawing on its usage by modern northern Irish coroners, he sees it as a catch-all phrase for those deaths where human agency was absent, but so, too, was disease.[25] The significance of this descriptor comes from its popularity as a cause of death. Drawing on the superfluity of cases of death by "visitation of God," seventeenth-century jurist Matthew Hale considered it a category of death unto itself.[26]

Despite the fact that the Middle Ages are stereotyped as a blindly religious era, deaths "by visitation of God" were much rarer in the medieval inquests than they were in the early modern era. Jurors ascribed death to God in approximately seventeen instances in the coroners' rolls. As a cause of death, the phrase dates to at least the thirteenth century. *The Mirror of Justices* links the expression to deaths by misadventure, speaking of "cases where the person died from drowning or falling or other visitation of God."[27] In general, the medieval evidence reflects few of the early modern features. First, there is no standard vocabulary. What later became distinctly *ex visitatione Dei* surfaces in the medieval evidence in a wide range of phrasings: *ex gracia dei*, *in gracia dei*, *ex gracia domina*, *sola grace dei*, *per graciam dei*, *per dispositionem divina*. The Nottinghamshire coroner's roll of Lawrence Chaworth and John Power accounts for nine of those seventeen instances in which jurors ascribed death to God: the phrase *ex gracia dei* was obviously one of their preferred formulaic descriptors. Second, in the medieval coroners' rolls, "visitation of God" is unmistakably an expression to describe death by disease. Coroners typically inserted the phrase after first articulating more precisely the cause of death. Of those named illnesses, jurors visited by God died from flux,[28] epilepsy,[29] *le felon* (an abscess),[30] quinsy,[31] and bubonic plague.[32] At least one coroner explicitly equated death by disease with visitation of God, stating Thomas, servant of William, of Riddings (*Derbys.*) died "by divine disposition, namely by plague."[33] One of the few cases where it seemed most fitting to employ the softening descriptor was in the death of John, son of Joanna, of Toft. In 1373, when he was just four weeks old, he contracted an illness and died *ex gracia dei*—surely, his mother preferred to think there was a higher purpose to the death of her young son.[34] Finally, there is no particular association with death in prison. Only John Mettley, who reportedly died of an unspecified infirmity in November 1393, passed away by visitation of God while imprisoned.[35]

What does the general absence of the phrase tell us about the death reports of the medieval coroner and his jury? Typically, jurors involved in medieval inquests did not share the same concerns as their early modern counterparts. The early modern evidence implies a hesitance to name the actual cause of death for a variety of reasons:[36] shame over prison conditions; anxiety in complying with the requirements of the law, especially in terms of suicide; or even simple ignorance, medically speaking. With respect to the former, medieval enrollments signal no obvious discomfiture with poor prison conditions, even if they perhaps should have. The story of prison life told by the coroners' rolls is both tragic and alarming—implying that they made little effort to hide the truth. Disease was rife in jail. Many prisoners died from pestilence,[37] flux,[38] quinsy,[39] *lentfevre* (a slowly developing fever),[40] and ague.[41] Living conditions in prison facilitated the spread of disease. In the death of John Martyn at Leicester prison in December of 1403, the coroner commented that he fell ill from the cold temperatures and bad air in the prison.[42] Prisoners regularly died from cold and poverty; others died from thirst.[43] When Walter Aveneye passed away in Reading Gaol in 1377/78, the coroner's roll stated expressly that he died for want of food, but that the jurors did not know who was supposed to feed him.[44] At times, the coroner remarked only that death came from natural causes, asserting firmly that it was not a product of malicious custody in jail.[45] Incarceration in medieval England operated on the principle that prisoners should pay for their amenities: food, drink, heat, and bedding all came at a price. While prison wardens habitually released impoverished prisoners on Sundays to beg, the perfunctory enrollments of prison death through starvation reveal that the system was not terribly effective. Yet, the enrollments evinced no embarrassment over the deaths produced by these horrific living conditions. Even the numerous fatalities resulting from *peine forte et dure*, England's unique form of torture for those accused felons who refused to submit to trial by jury, evoked no sense of disgrace. To encourage compliance with the law, justices of jail delivery ordered weights placed on the chest of the defendant in the hopes that the pain incurred might elicit willingness to submit to trial by jury. Felons who chose this approach usually did so for monetary reasons. When a prisoner died by *peine forte et dure*, his goods and chattels were safe from royal forfeiture.[46] Deaths of this nature were not uncommon, and jurors did not shy away from reporting them.[47] In fact, enrollments typically place the blame for this inhumane treatment squarely on the shoulders of the defendant: "for his disobedience" in refusing to submit to the process of the common law, "he would have his penance" (*penitencia*, the Latin term for *peine forte et dure*).[48]

Medieval jurors were sometimes hesitant in complying with the requirements of law, but they did not need to resort to such a woolly phrase as "visitation of God" in order to defy the crown's mandates. Historians of suicide have already explored the solution to this problem at great length. Given that death by drowning was the method of choice for most medieval self-killers, it would have been easy enough for jurors to pronounce instead "death by misadventure." As P.E. Hair declared in 1971, "it is possible that since the sixteenth century the incidence [of suicide] has remained fairly consistent, and that what has changed markedly is the incidence of concealment."[49] Recent studies continue to emphasize the inquest jury's reluctance to blame the dead. Alexander Murray claims that "records of 'suicide' clearly deriv[e] from the jurors' agreement to rob the gallows of a man they believe innocent of the kind of murder *they* thought he should be hanged for, for instance, of a notorious local bully."[50] Of course, this hypothesis is founded chiefly on conjecture: in reality, there is no evidence to substantiate the assumption that jurors preferred to declare a death by misadventure rather than suicide. Nonetheless, the approach fits in well with typically medieval jury behavior. Medieval jurors were already consciously altering homicide indictments to meet the law's rigorous standards of self-defense. Transforming a suicide by drowning into a death by misadventure is not that different.

While coroners' juries did not contentedly resort to God as an explanation for death, it is striking that they were more comfortable blaming the devil. The corpus of self-killers driven mad through temptation of the devil, discussed at length in the previous chapter, reveals the ease with which neighbors blamed bizarre behavior on the supernatural. What is critical to recognize here is that diabolical possession was not a folkloric creation, but a familiar medical theory endorsed by scholars of great renown, such as Hildegard of Bingen[51] and Bernard de Gordon,[52] and reinforced regularly by miracle stories repeated and endorsed by church authorities. Naturally, diabolical pathology was a diagnosis of last resort. Nonetheless, from this vantage point, when a jury could find no other rational explanation for the uncharacteristic behavior of a (self-)killer, pointing a finger at the devil was a reasonable, and even scholarly, explanation.

But the question still remains: do the coroners' rolls point to incompetence in assessing cause of death? Assumptions of ineptitude make sense if we continue to believe that medical practitioners played no role in the inquest, and if we disregard the general dissemination of medical knowledge throughout the ranks of medieval England's populace. However, ignoring the reality of medieval life does not seem the most productive strategy. A closer analysis of the inquest in practice demonstrates a wide range of medical competencies. In some cases, the coroner and his jury proved to be wholly inept in determining cause of death—and they had little trouble admitting to this. Some enrollments declare that the jury did not know who or what was responsible for the dead's state. In those instances, they adopted three distinct approaches to "whitewashing" their ignorance: 1) they pronounced cause of death to be a "sudden death." Sabina le Moy, found dead one night in November 1346, died a "sudden death," having no lesions on her body.[53] 2) They determined the individual had died a "natural death." When Walter the Baxter of Wellingborough was found dead in December 1348, jurors mentioned only that he died a natural death.[54] 3) They admitted that they had no idea what led to the person's death. Surprisingly, such an overt admission of incompetence was not uncommon. Granted, the fatalities that produced this verdict were either those without eyewitnesses, or truly baffling deaths. In July 1379, when Agnes, wife of John, of Saxby of Melton (*Leics.*) went to her home where she had left her daughter, Isabella, sleeping in the crib, she found her dead, although her body exhibited no wounds, no obvious cause of death. Jurors concluded that they did not know how she had died, but they did not suspect anyone of her death.[55] In the end, the vagueness of these phrases achieves much the same goal as verdicts of "visitation by God." For the purposes of an historical study, however, the reasoning behind the verdict is less open to interpretation. We also cannot fault a jury for not understanding the causes of some natural deaths: after all, modern medicine does much the same thing when pronouncing Sudden Infant Death Syndrome as cause of death.

Admittedly, all of this implies some degree of ineffectiveness in terms of death investigation. Those instances in which jurors produced highly unsophisticated descriptions of death also form a distinct impression of medical incompetence. For example, Agnes Cowherde of the parish of Kingsclere (*Southants.*) died through misadventure. While she was walking from the home of William Burnolf toward her own domicile, she accidently fell to the ground through the "debility of her body" and died suddenly.[56] Surely, a medical practitioner would insist on a better description than "debility of the body"? What caused that debility? Old age? Disease? Drunkenness? Similarly, jurors described a cleric found late one evening as "half-dead" (*semimortuus*). He languished for three days before his demise, although the jurors had no idea what precipitated his death.[57] It is hard to imagine that "half-dead" was a legitimate medical diagnosis. The death of Isabel the Brewster of Trimley (*Suffolk*) in 1356/57 also falls squarely into the category of inexpert causes of death. She went to the dwelling of Robert Mulling for a beer one evening, and when returning home, she tripped on a basket in the street and tumbled to the ground. In falling, she "broke" her stomach so that her viscera spilled out, dying soon after. At the inquest, the jury deduced that she suffered from an illness that repelled her viscera, causing them to exit through the wound.[58]

One might also interpret the many English men and women who died from "sickness" (without any attempt to identify the nature of the illness) as evidence of ineffectiveness. Mathew of Wales passed away from a "natural infirmity" in September of 1355, coincidentally, immediately after being struck on the head with a stone by John of Wales.[59] When Robert, son of Thomas the Tailor, of Woodstock died in Oxford's city prison in the spring of 1343, jurors reported multiple (unnamed) sicknesses as the cause.[60] The clumsiest example of a death verdict surfaces in the enrollment of the 1368 death of John Spryng of Springthorpe, found dead in the king's prison at Burgh St Peter (*Norfolk*). Jurors arrived at the conclusion that he died from "mortality."[61] It is hard not to experience some frustration with the coroner and his jury in recording such vague causes of death. And yet, this is definitively not evidence of incompetence on behalf of the coroner and his jury. It was not, in fact, the medieval coroner's responsibility to identify the exact nature of the illness leading to a person's death. Rather, it was sufficient for the purposes of the investigation to resolve that sickness and not homicide was to blame.[62] We cannot condemn the coroner for failing to do more than his job required.

Even if it was not their responsibility, many other coroners and jurors exhibited at least a tenuous grasp of contemporary medical knowledge. For example, the enrollments bring to light some familiarity with medieval contagion theory. From the time of the Greeks, medical theory advocated "one great universal cause of epidemical disease": poisoned, foul-smelling air, what they referred to as *miasma*.[63] According to this theoretical position, epidemic disease is a product of environmental conditions: polluted air influenced a body's humoral balance, making one vulnerable to infection. One proponent of this ideology, the Sienese Mariano di Ser Jacopa, contended that plague derived from "malign vapours emanating from lakes and bogs"; others argued that earthquakes released these noxious vapors.[64] Malaria, which draws its name from "bad air," is the quintessential expression of miasma theory, and eventually gave birth to the sanitation movement of the modern era. Miasma theory was so deeply entrenched in the medical mindset for hundreds of years that Louis Pasteur's discovery of germ theory had little immediate impact on the sway miasma theory had over medicine. Epidemiologists had great difficulty laying siege to the "citadel of Miasma."[65] Remnants of this theoretical outlook still pervade the modern era in parental admonitions to children of the necessity to play outside and get some "fresh air."

Miasma theory crops up in numerous accounts of natural deaths among the coroners' enrollments. John Martyn at Leicester prison died in 1403: his enrollment concludes that he contracted an illness from the bad air in the jail.[66] The antithesis, good air, was the prescription for better health: John Hamelton junior fell ill with an infirmity in 1398/99. To combat his illness, he sampled all the approved remedies: first, he heard mass. Next, he went into a country field specifically to take some air; unfortunately, because of the debility of his body, while there he fell into a river and drowned.[67] While the coroners' rolls fail to include the term "miasma" (in Latin, *halit*),[68] they furnish a good number of investigations revolving around individuals who died through exposure to corrupt air. Many involved fatalities brought on suddenly while in wells or pits. In September 1337, John of Maldon, a porter, was hired to clean an empty well. In descending into it, he "was overcome by the foul air and immediately died."[69] Since the advent of germ theory, much ridicule has been heaped on adherents of the outdated miasma theory. Yet, jurors were not wrong in attributing these deaths to bad air, even if they did not entirely understand what made that air "bad." Hydrogen sulfide, which occurs naturally in wells, can accumulate in low-lying spaces like a well bottom, producing an oxygen-deficient environment. Descending into such a toxic atmosphere would result in rapid asphyxiation. Depending on the soil type or nearby geological factors, radon gas, methane, sulfur dioxide, even carbon monoxide, are all other possible culprits.[70] Some jurors seem to have understood the problem: when William atte Mersche at Sutton Mandeville (*Wilts.*) died suddenly in May 1341, while digging a trench in the enclosure of John le Deye, jurors pronounced that he died from "a defect of air."[71] When Roger Heliboth descended into a well at Oxford 1389/90, he fell from the bucket holding him to the well bottom. Jurors reported that he suffocated from a total absence of air.[72] More generally, juries blamed moisture levels in the air for these deaths. The enrollments are replete with cautionary tales of the dangers of moist air. In October 1382, John Edenson of East Markham (*Notts.*) of his own volition went into the well of Roger Gildham on a rope to retrieve a pike. While down there, he encountered an evil vapor (*malum vapore*) called "le Dampe," from which he suddenly died.[73] Wells were not always to blame: John Colier died in July 1392 after descending into a coal pit, where he was exposed to an evil wind (*malignum ventum*) called "Dampe."[74]

However unusual it may seem to the modern reader, the focus on moist air may also spring from humoral theory. Humoral theory sees good health as the proper balance of bodily fluids, that is, humors, namely blood, phlegm, yellow bile, and black bile. Imbalance leads to infirmity, and can be cured best by alterations in diet and activity levels (for deficiency), as well as purgation in various forms (for excess: bloodletting, enema, vomiting, etc.). The four humors are defined also by their qualities such as warm, cold, moist, and dry, which in turn are intimately connected with individual temperaments. The ideal personality derives from a balance of the four humors: when one humor dominates, it produces a temperament identified with a surfeit of that humor (see Table 5.1). Thus, because of the humoral focus on wet and dry qualities, a sudden, overwhelming exposure to wet air produces an overly phlegmatic disposition that is fatal. The English manuscript of John of Burgundy's 1365 medical treatise makes it clear that wet air is one of the various causes of plague.[75]

The coroners' rolls do not explicitly reference the humors, or humoral theory; however, as the above cases suggest, jurors seem to have been aware of humoral theory, if only in a rudimentary form, and articulated their health concerns accordingly. This is true also in a number of cases that emphasize the choleric impact of heat. A Bedfordshire investigation from May 1273 recounts the fatality of Geoffrey the Woodward, who had been ill with the "hot sickness" for nine days prior to his death. The infirmity eventually drove him into a frenzy. Around the hour of prime, he walked into his courtyard and stood by the well. He was so ill and debilitated that he fell into the well and drowned.[76] A Lincolnshire death from 1393/94 warns of the dangers of overly heating one's body: Christian of Hessle, a vagabond, was in the vill of Wrangle (*Lincs.*) at the kilnhouse of the abbot of Waltham when she unexpectedly sickened with the palsy. The illness caused her to collapse and drown in the well. The coroner's roll notes that the heat of the kilnhouse provoked the illness.[77] The heat of summer regularly drove John the Chapman of Taunton into a frenzy: a 1286 inquisition comments that "he was afflicted with frenzy at times in summer in the three preceding years" before he drowned himself at Tone (*Somt.*).[78] None of this is concrete evidence of a solid understanding of humoral theory, but it does at least point to an awareness of the connection between heat and a choleric temperament, as well as the dangers of inundating an individual with one particular humor.

What is important about these deaths is the attempt by jurors to explain them according to the medical theory of the time. Jurors could have taken

Table 5.1 The Four Humors

Humor	Qualities	Temperament	Characteristics
blood	warm and moist	sanguine	hopeful
phlegm	cold and moist	phlegmatic	calm
yellow bile	warm and dry	choleric	easily angered
black bile	cold and dry	melancholic	despondent

the easy way out by blaming God, as coroners did throughout the early modern and modern eras. They could also have justified them merely as "sudden deaths" without offering any rational explanation. Generally, they did not. Rather, they made a valiant attempt when possible to determine what actually killed these individuals according to the resources of the time. This is critical because it implies that coroners and their juries were familiar with the leading medical theories of their day. Medieval medicine endorsed miasma and humoral theories as the chief explanations for illness. The coroners' rolls evince a distinct familiarity with both philosophies. Surely, this speaks to a degree of medical aptitude. While the majority of the coroners' records do not construct a confident image of medical expertise, taken as a whole they offer instructive glimpses into the practice of medicine and the English population's knowledge of medicine.

WHAT CAN WE LEARN FROM NAMED SICKNESSES?

An analysis of descriptions of illness in the coroners' reports illustrates best the medical capacity of coroners and jurors. Although the crown did not require jurors to identify the sickness that led to an individual's demise, often coroners' rolls did just that. Enrollments furnish a pool of 370 named sicknesses (see Table 5.2).

Table 5.2 Breakdown of Named Sicknesses (Excluding Mental Sicknesses) in the Coroners' Rolls

Named Sickness	As Written in Coroners' Rolls	Nature of Sickness[i]	Number of Cases
ague	*ague*	acute fever (perhaps malaria)	6
aposteme	*apostume, postume, apostema, apostemato, postumo,*[ii] *postym, impostuma, posteme, postamac*	an abscess; swelling or inflammation	43
blood sickness	*morbo sanguine*	unknown	1
cachexia	*morbus cacus*	general decline in health	1
cardiac	*cardiac, kardiake*	chest pain or heart palpitations	2
cramp	*crampe*	a cramp (perhaps tetanus)	2
debility of the brain	*debilitate cerebris, ex debilitate cerebrum*	unknown	2

(Continued)

Table 5.2 (Continued)

Named Sickness	As Written in Coroners' Rolls	Nature of Sickness[i]	Number of Cases
dropsy	*droppsey, dropeseye*	over-accumulation of fluid or air in the body tissues	2
epilepsy	*morbum caducum, caduco morbo, morbum habens caducum, infirmitationem caducam, falanyvell (falling evil)*	epilepsy	162
fatal spots	*macula mortal*	buboes?	2
felon	*felone*	a suppurative sore or boil	3
fester	*festre*	fistulation, ulceration	1
fever	*febre acute, phrebra*	fever	19
flumens		perhaps a variety of flux?	1
flux (of various kinds)	*flux, flux ventris, flux sang per nasum, flux sanguinis, flix*	excessive flow of blood from the bowels or a from a wound	30
gout	*gutta*	a) gout (or something that presents similarly) b) toothache c) disorder in head and stomach d) painful urination	1
hasty spots	*propuereo maculo*	buboes?	1
hot sickness	*calidus morbus*	a) fever b) skin inflammation c) burning feeling in stomach	1
jaundice	*jauny*	jaundice	1
Le Spreng	*Le Spreng*	unknown	1
lentfever	*lentefever*	slow or prolonged fever (perhaps malaria)	2
maudeflank	*maudeflank*	pain in the groin or abdomen	2
menison	*blodymeneson, meneylun*	dysentery	2
mortality	*mortalite*	unknown	1
narrowness	*Le Narth*	a) labored breathing and feeling of constriction in the chest b) constriction in region of the heart	1

(Continued)

Table 5.2 (Continued)

Named Sickness	As Written in Coroners' Rolls	Nature of Sickness[i]	Number of Cases
palsy	*palsy, palsey, palasye, peralisis, morbum peraliticus*	paralysis	11
pestilence (general)	*pestilencia*	any fatal sickness	40
pestilence (true)	*ex vera pestilencia, bocche*	bubonic plague	9
postpartum illness	*post partum suum . . . infirmitate*	uncertain	1
pox	*pokkes*	sickness characterized by pustules	1
pregnancy	*pregnante*	pregnancy-related	4
quinsy	*squimancia, squinacie, quynesie*	inflammation or swelling of the throat	7
secret infirmity	*infirmitatis secret*	uncertain	1
sickness in the arm	*morbum in brachio dextra*	uncertain	1
sickness in the head	*infirmitatis existentis in capite suo, quedam infirmitatus cepit eum in capite*	uncertain	2
sickness in the tibia	*infirmitatis existentis in tibia*	uncertain	1
tisik	*tysik*	probably pulmonary tuberculosis	2

[i]Definitions in the column "Nature of Sickness" are based on Juhani Norri, *Names of Sicknesses in English, 1400–1550: An Exploration of the Lexical Field* (Helsinki: Suomalainen Tiedeakatemia, 1992).

[ii]Many of the variations of this term omit the initial "a." Norri explains that this is because many clerks believed that it was an indefinite article and omitted it as a result. Norri, *Names of Sicknesses*, p. 120.

This sampling of named illnesses has much to offer in terms of gaining clearer insight into the effectiveness of the inquest at diagnosing death. First, we need to acknowledge that determining cause of death in disease fatalities is not an easy task, and the English crown provided no guidance. William Farr, who developed England's first system of nomenclature for death, lamented in 1839 the poor quality of death certification historically: "Each disease has in many instances been denoted by three or four terms, and each term has been applied to as many different diseases; vague, inconvenient names have been employed, or complications have been registered instead of primary diseases."[79] Farr, who was the compiler of Statistical Abstracts for England's General Register Office, fashioned the system of nomenclature that acted as the foundation for the various incarnations leading up to the current International Classification of Diseases. Even today, with such extensive written instruction on the process, researchers claim that "[s]tatistics from death certificates are so inaccurate that they are unsuitable for use in research or planning."[80] The process of death certification today is fraught with inaccuracies. Because medical education teaches practitioners to address the health concerns of the living and not the dead, physicians are ill equipped to determine cause and manner of death. Consequently, it is often difficult for them to distinguish "immediate cause of death" (the final disease or injury that actually caused the death) from "intermediate cause of death" (the disease or condition preceding death and causing the immediate cause of death) from "underlying cause of death" (the disease or condition present before and resulting in the intermediate or immediate cause of death).[81] Add to this diagnostic differences in opinion, respect for the family of the dead, and a perennial lack of time for paperwork. The point here is to stress that our expectations of medieval death certification need to be realistic. If the process is this poorly executed today with the ready availability of a detailed handbook and a standard nosology, a higher bar must not be set for the medieval coroners and their juries.

As the above table reveals, Farr's concerns were well founded. Coroners and their juries used a wide range of terms to reference the same illness and they often described merely the symptoms of a disease (fever, constriction, rash, abscesses, paralysis) rather than naming the disease itself. Regional variation might explain some of the diversity in recording practices. Yet, what is striking is that most of the terminology was not "vague." Coroners and jurors confidently proceeded with the accepted medical terminology of their day. At times, the presence of a medical practitioner on the jury must account for the precision in terminology. As Chapter Four of this book argues, variations in the terminology for "plague" indicate the contribution of an educated medical professional. It is also plausible that the dead (obviously, before s/he died) supplied the expert vocabulary sometimes found in the coroners' rolls: as Michael McVaugh observes, "attentive patients got the jargon right."[82] In other instances, it is not always clear why coroners and their jurors chose one term over another. For example, the Oxford borough roll of William of Wheatley and Richard of Eynsham reported two fatalities in November 1342 from the same illness, recorded on the same membrane, and yet employing different terminology. While they characterized Stephen Felaw's death as a result of *squimancia in guttur* (quinsy), they stated that Agnes, daughter of John atte Wichege, of Clare died instead from an *aposteme in guttur* (an abscess in the throat).[83] Similarly, a single membrane from the York county roll of John Mapples includes reports of two deaths roughly a week and a half apart in February 1365/66, both resulting from accidents produced by epileptic seizures. Alice of Newbiggin of Godmanham (*Yorks.*) suffered from *morbo caduco* (epilepsy), while Walter Shepherd of Newbald's death was caused by the *falanyvell* ("falling evil," that is, epilepsy).[84] Why the difference in terminology? With so many constants in each of these situations, the one differential is the jury: these discrepancies point to the dominant role played by the jury, rather than the coroner, in assessing the nature of the illness leading to the death. It is not hard to imagine that Alice's jury drafted their enrollment on the advice of a medical practitioner; the inclusion of such a popular term like the "falling evil" in Walter's enrollment, on the other hand, points to a jury working in the absence of technical expertise.

The sheer diversity of medical vocabulary employed in the coroners' rolls is impressive. Medieval jurors demonstrate an awareness of thirty-four different categories of illness, however crudely described. When compared with the findings of other historical studies, this figure indicates a reasonable familiarity with medical vocabulary: that is, medieval coroners and their juries were not resorting repeatedly to the same diagnosis out of convenience. For example, an investigation into causes of death as recorded in Quebec parish registers by priests during the period 1681–1706, revealed a "meager vocabulary" of only twenty terms to identify illnesses.[85] A study of death registration from the city of Sheffield (*Yorks.*) in 1870, where legal officials were working from Farr's recommended nomenclature, produced instead roughly eighty different terms for illness.[86]

Farr would have disparaged the medieval coroners for their preference of symptoms over disease names, even though medicine in the medieval era made no distinction between the two. Yet, what is useful about this approach is the tendency of enrollments to describe the progress of illness. Many historians have lamented the impossibility of tracking the evolution of disease throughout history because of the difficulty of determining whether, for example, the medieval descriptor "leprosy" identifies the same disease that it indicates today (Hanson's Disease).[87] The years of heated debate over the nature of the "Black Death," whether it was bubonic plague, ebola, or some other disease altogether, nicely illustrates this quandary.[88] The resolution to the Black Death dispute came only in October of 2011 after geneticists were able to reproduce the plague genome from DNA found in skeletons uncovered in a mass grave of plague victims at East Smithfield in London.[89] For most other medieval diseases, however, there are no mass graves labeled *aposteme* or *tisik* waiting to be found. The solution to retrospective disease analysis appears instead in the descriptions of symptoms and disease progress in medical treatises and documents such as the coroners' rolls.

On occasion, coroners and their juries furnished precise details about the duration of an illness and the manner of death, even if described in a rudimentary manner. For example, an enrollment from July 1396 remarks that John Roolf of Clawson (*Leics.*) had suffered with an aposteme of an internal variety for many years, reducing him to a weakened condition. The abscess burst while he was roughhousing in a field. Recognizing that death was nigh, he immediately journeyed to a nearby hospital where the vicar administered last rites before he passed away.[90] When John Mortimer died in Staffordshire in 1393, he was riding by carriage through the abbot's forest when an aposteme ruptured in his body. He fell from the carriage, but jurors report that he was dead before he hit the ground.[91] Unfortunately, in these instances, the multiple meanings of the term *aposteme* obstruct an accurate retrospective diagnosis. An internal abscess of this nature might be a cancerous tumor, an ulcer, a hernia, perhaps even a blood clot. Nonetheless, some descriptions do lend themselves to an identification of the disease or underlying condition, or at the very least, offer enough detail about the symptoms to narrow down the pool of possibilities. Consider the following three case studies:

1. When twenty-four-year-old John Clemer of Groton was found dead at Edwardstone (*Suffolk*) in 1363, the enrollment comments that he had been ill for four years before his death suffering from le Palsye (paralysis). He was on his way to church alone when he was seized by the disease, causing him to collapse into a ditch filled with thorns where he died.[92] If the enrollment had told us only that John died from palsy, we would have little to go on in order to identify the nature of his condition. However, the details provided by the enrollment are a virtual goldmine. The pertinent elements include: a) John's youth at the onset of disease, and b) its episodic nature. Conditions that cause intermittent episodes of paralysis are extremely rare. In all likelihood, John was suffering from hypokalemic periodic paralysis, a congenital disorder that typically manifests in adolescence. While John would have been on the late end of that spectrum, his age was probably an estimate anyway. Those who experience hypokalemic periodic paralysis suffer occasional episodes of muscle weakness that would explain his fateful plunge into the thorn-filled ditch.[93]
2. Alice, wife of Richard Dany, of Kessingland (*Suffolk*) died in May 1356. Jurors remarked that she had suffered from an illness called "fever" for half a year and more continuously before she suddenly came down with the flux and died.[94] The relevant details here are: a) fever, b) flux, and c) her place of residence. The fens in southeast England, including parts of Lincolnshire, Cambridgeshire, Norfolk, and Suffolk, were a hotbed of malaria, encouraged by infestations of mosquitoes in naturally marshy areas. John Theilmann contends that recurring fevers resulting from malarial infections were so common it had become a "way of life for people living in the fens almost so much so that a person not suffering from the disease would have stood out."[95] Alice's long-standing fevers, followed by nausea and diarrhea, strongly suggest that the more typical malarial infection evolved into a severe case of malaria, leading to her death.
3. Alice, wife of Bartholomew Sley, was forty years old when her last child was born in June 1378. She underwent the process of purification soon after the birth of her child;[96] however, on the tenth day after delivery, she was gripped by an infirmity and suddenly died.[97]

> In Alice's case, narrowing down the nature of her illness is not as straightforward as the other two examples, only because there are numerous possible explanations. Alice's death might have resulted from something as simple as an infection caused by unsanitary childbirth: however, the absence of any mention of fever argues against this possibility. In developing countries today, the two leading causes of maternal death are a) obstetrical hemorrhaging and b) deep vein thrombosis leading to pulmonary embolism (a blood clot that detaches and travels to the lungs). The length of time after delivery rules out obstetrical hemorrhaging. Deep vein thrombosis leading to pulmonary embolism is a strong possibility: this condition afflicts one in a thousand women, but its incidence increases dramatically in women over the age of thirty-five. Of course, there are other logical explanations: Alice might have suffered from an obstetric fistula (a hole developed between either the rectum and vagina, or the vagina and the bladder), what is today considered a common "disease of poverty." She might also have contracted something else wholly unrelated to pregnancy, but in her weakened condition, her body was unable to fight the accompanying infection.

The goal of these three case studies is to point to the value of coroner's enrollments for historians of disease. The crown may not have obliged coroners and their juries to identify the nature of the illness in natural deaths, yet many chose to do so anyway. The number and variety of disease labels utilized in the coroners' rolls make it clear that they were not constantly resorting to the same cause of death as an easy way out. Moreover, while the coroners' rolls are far from clinical in nature, they contain descriptions of disease progress that help us to better comprehend the kinds of health concerns experienced by medieval English men and women.

ELITE VERSUS NON-ELITE PRACTICES

The vast majority of our knowledge of late medieval English medical practices is drawn from medical treatises, penned by physicians or surgeons—men whose backgrounds, learning, and social rank consigned them to an elite caste of medical practitioners with a fundamentally philosophical outlook on medicine. English physicians were university trained, and more often than not, boasted a European education. England's universities incorporated medicine in only a "limited fashion": it was one component among many in a Bachelor of Arts degree. Consequently, most aspiring physicians preferred instead to pursue their studies on the Continent where they could attend a medical university.[98] English surgeons, unlike their Continental equivalents, were not university trained. Nonetheless, surgeons in late medieval England consciously aligned themselves with physicians precisely in the hopes of elevating their professional status. In forging links with the upper stratum of the medical hierarchy, surgeons as a whole had to refashion their identities, transforming themselves from craftsmen into intellectuals. Disassociating themselves from those they regarded as "little more than rude mechanicals" (that is, the barbers) was the first step in the process. In London, where tensions ran highest, barbers and surgeons developed "separate, mutually hostile mysteries," in constant competition in the marketplace.[99] Surgeons also worked to enter more fully into the literate environment of elite medicine through book ownership, reading, and even writing themselves. This was not an easy endeavor. Despite the vernacularization of late medieval medical treatises, which some have argued opened medicine up to a wider audience,[100] there were numerous obstacles to reading those works. Medical treatises, even in English, inherited a multilingual tradition, and integrated many terms from Greek, Latin, and sometimes Arabic.[101] The willingness of surgeons to embrace the intellectualism of elite medicine is a measure of their ambition.[102]

The aspirations of surgeons and physicians had a profound impact on the practice of late medieval medicine, constructing an unbridgeable chasm between elite and non-elite medical practitioners. The professionalization of English medicine is grounded in this hostility. In order to assert their superiority over London's growing corpus of unlearned medical practitioners and monopolize the late medieval medical marketplace, surgeons and physicians allied themselves with the crown to implement a licensing process that would make them the ultimate medical authorities.[103] This coalition climaxed in the 1423 creation of a joint College of Physicians and Surgeons. All of these enterprises ended in failure: even the College lasted only eighteen months before collapsing under pressure from the significantly more numerous London barbers. England's physicians and surgeons were vastly outnumbered and their services too expensive for the average Englishman. Nonetheless, the ideals of this elite group dominate historians' reconstruction of medieval medical practice because they were literate and sometimes wrote treatises or pharmacological recipes that have survived the rigors of time.

This context makes the coroners' rolls an important window into non-elite medical practices in late medieval England. As Chapter Two argues, even when medical practitioners served on inquest juries, they were usually barbers, not physicians or surgeons, and when physicians and surgeons did participate, they had to communicate with a lay audience, not other elite practitioners. The legal documentation thus supplies an opportunity to view medicine from a populist perspective. This is especially significant in light of the character of late medieval medical treatises. As Julie Ormanski argues, the professionalization of medicine in later medieval England led to an increasing "textual incomprehension," an "obscurity of medical discourse," that was deliberately intended to exclude those outside medicine's elite circles.[104] Accordingly, they offer little insight into how the average medical practitioner, or medieval individual, understood and explained diseases and conditions. Viewing health and healthcare through the lens of the coroners' rolls thus affords a sense of everyday language, attitudes toward the diseased and the disabled, and common medical practices. A discussion of four specific conditions (epilepsy, plague, abscesses, and senescence) will serve to illustrate this point.

A) Epilepsy

Deaths resulting from epilepsy dominate the sampling of named sicknesses at roughly 44%. Epilepsy was such a common vehicle for death that it had its own marginal notation (that is, shorthand) in the coroners' rolls: *caducus*. Much like the highly functional category of "visitation by God," historians have generally assumed that the medieval world had an insufficient understanding of epilepsy and used the term as a grab bag of sorts, comprising any sudden natural death.[105] This argument derives principally from the scores of epileptics reported in chronicles, miracle stories, and legal records. Nonetheless, the popularity of the diagnosis should not lead us to assume that the medieval world regularly mistook other diseases for epilepsy. First, keep in mind the prevalence of epilepsy today and the circumstances that influence it. Epilepsy affects roughly 4 to 10 per 1,000 people.[106] The risk of contracting epilepsy in a developing country, however, is twice as high as it is for those living in a developed nation because of the greater risk of "experiencing conditions that can lead to permanent brain damage." The World Health Organization estimates that close to 80% of the world's 50 million epileptics live in developing countries. The risk of dying prematurely is two to three times higher for an epileptic than for the average person.[107] Medieval England's living conditions, in many respects, resembled today's developing countries in terms of the presence of open wells and fires, and ditches filled with water. Thus, the incidence of epilepsy in the records, as well as the multitude of deaths by misadventure resulting from seizures at inopportune moments, would seem to fall in line with these figures.

Second, medical writers identified epilepsy as a sickness as early as the ancient Greeks, and Gilbertus Anglicus's *Compendium* (*c.* 1180–1220) confirms that medieval medicine had a solid understanding of the illness. They differentiated variants of epilepsy by cause. Epilepsy is caused by moist humors in the brain; analempsy springs from vapors that rise to the head from a sick and feeble stomach; in cathalempsy corrupt vapors ascend from the extremities. They also distinguished epilepsy by behavior. In "more epilepsy" (think of this as a *grand mal* seizure), the patient is rendered unconscious, he foams at the mouth, his body quakes, and he is hard to hold on to. In "less epilepsy" (a *petit mal* seizure), the attack is much less severe. The epileptic is partly conscious ("he feels somewhat"), and the quaking is restricted mostly to the hind part of the head.[108] Gilbertus elaborates on these descriptions by warning that the following indicators are tokens (symptoms) of epilepsy: heaviness of the head, confusion of wits, sloth, dimness of eyes, biting of tongue, involuntary urination, and falling to the ground.[109] With the almost complete emphasis on seizures—it was not called the "falling evil" for nothing—medical practitioners may well have misdiagnosed other seizure-inducing illnesses (diabetes, meningitis, viral encephalitis, hydrocephalus, celiac's disease, among others) as epilepsy. They might also have misunderstood the cause of a seizure—high fevers or head injuries are seizure inducing.

However, there is good reason to believe that coroners' juries were not so easily misled. Coroners' jurors demonstrated a conviction that epilepsy presents as a pattern: they often noted a history of seizures. Jurors remarked that Ralph Stacy was "frequently vexed by epilepsy": a seizure took him by surprise while standing near a river, causing him to fall and drown in the spring of 1394.[110] Robert Sludon often had seizures, in fact, the day he was found dead in the highway leading from Catherington to Cosham (*Southants.*) in August 1390, he had experienced three before dawn.[111] John Osebarn, who drowned in a well in 1415 as a decrepit, old man, had been afflicted with epilepsy since he was a baby (*ab infancia*).[112] Jurors appreciated epilepsy as a condition, apart from the experience of a seizure. Hence, myriad enrollments describe an individual as "having" (*habens*) epilepsy or "suffering" (*vexatur*) from it, but discriminate the disease from the seizure. The seizure is denoted as the moment he was "overcome" (*veniet super eum*) by the disease. The inquest jurors in the death of Roisa, wife of William, son of Henry, note matter-of-factly that she had a sickness called epilepsy: while she was collecting herbs one day in the spring of 1273, "a seizure overcame her," causing her to fall into a well where she drowned.[113] Given the widespread recognition that epilepsy is a life-long condition, rather than a one-time only seizure, jurors were plainly evaluating a sickness that either was epilepsy, or looked a great deal like it. This finding is important also because Mervyn Eadie and Peter Bladin assert that before 1850, medical descriptions of epilepsy were confusing, largely because "the word 'epilepsy' was applied either to the individual epileptic seizure or to the disorder that caused recurrent epileptic seizures."[114] The coroners' rolls, however, discern between the two perfectly well in their context.

Further, as these examples hint, epilepsy was not typically the direct cause of these deaths. Epileptics died by falling into wells and water-filled ditches, falling into fires, falling from ladders and trees, falling under moving carts, and so forth, when a seizure struck unexpectedly. The nature of medieval living conditions heightened opportunities for death by misadventure. Medieval men and women were also aware of the dangers posed to an epileptic by their living conditions. In the 1395 trial of Marguerite de Portu for the death of her husband, Jean Damponcii of the Provencal town of Manosque, the defendant made this point overtly. Marguerite announced that she could not have poisoned her husband as accused because she had deserted him a long time before his death. She abandoned him to return to her "brothers' protection" at home in nearby Beaumont because she suffered from epilepsy and feared she might fall into a fire while having a seizure. Her husband showed little concern for her condition: but her brothers had always been protective of her.[115] Many English men and women realized Marguerite's fear. One of the most horrific tales from the coroners' rolls is that of the death of Amice Gyddan. Her mother, Agnes, was holding the six-month-old child in her lap while warming up by the fire in February 1377/78 at Horsham (*Norfolk*), when Agnes was gripped by a seizure, causing her to drop the baby into the fire. Amice died soon after from the burns extending across the majority of her body.[116]

Gilbertus's explanation for the causes of epilepsy coexisted with a more popular, religiously inspired understanding that a seizure represents the physical expression of a spiritual attack by demons. This conception of epilepsy dates at least to the time of the ancient Greeks, earning epilepsy the moniker of the "sacred disease." The populist explanation of epilepsy so disturbed Hippocrates that he dedicated an entire treatise to the subject, rejecting the association with demons and endorsing only the humoral account. Nonetheless, support for the demonic origins of epilepsy persisted, encouraged in the Christian era by a Biblical adoption of the Greek inheritance connecting epilepsy with lunacy and demon possession. Indeed, the Biblical Jesus regularly exorcised demons from the epileptic.[117] The sporadic nature of seizures cemented the ideological relationship between epilepsy and lunacy, a form of mental incapacity thought to be triggered by lunar cycles, so much so that medieval medicine often defined the epileptic as "one seized by 'the disease of the moon.'"[118] Medieval medical treatises frequently reflect both humoral and demonic origins, or even an amalgam of the two. For example, Hildegard of Bingen writes:

> The first [kind of epilepsy] is associated with wrath, which sets the blood in motion, thus causing an ascent of smoke and humors which touch the brain and cause madness. When individuals of such a disposition are induced to anger aggravated by some worldly troubles, the devil will notice it and frighten them by his suggestions, when their soul becomes tired, succumbs, and withdraws itself. As a result the body falls down and remains thus till the soul has regained its strength.[119]

While one might expect the religiously motivated explanation for epilepsy to prevail in a legal source like the coroners' rolls, only three enrollments forge a link between mental incapacity and epilepsy, and none of them implicates the devil.[120] In the spring of 1367, John, son of Randalph Rykkes, was "out of his mind" and afflicted with epilepsy when he drowned himself in a well.[121] The 1401/02 inquest into the death of John Norfolk described him as both lunatic and epileptic when he broke open the shutters to his apartment, jumped out of the window, and ran to Stokewell for some water. While drinking, a seizure overcame him and he drowned.[122] The third enrollment is much less reliable, primarily because the way it describes disease is highly unsophisticated. The inquest reports that John de Mosbrok "was languishing in an epilepsy called flux" for six weeks. Gravely vexed by the disease, he became "demented, *non compos mentis.*" He grabbed a pair of scissors and stabbed himself in two different places on his body, dying confessed several days later.[123]

What is perhaps more surprising is that the coroners' rolls make an explicit connection between epilepsy and drunkenness, a correlation that is frequently noted today in instructive materials distributed by the Epilepsy Foundation to caution police officers, school officials, and others from rashly diagnosing epileptics as drunks. To the undiscriminating eye, seizures (especially of the *petit mal* variety) may appear drug or alcohol induced, manifesting in bizarre behavior such as speaking in gibberish, shouting, or disrobing. This misdiagnosis may have occurred regularly in the medieval period: however, unless the coroner commented on a history of epilepsy, a death through drunken misadventure would fail to emphasize the connection. Yet, it is striking that a few enrollments distinctly tie the two together. When Roger Canny froze to death in the street after leaving the local tavern late one night in December of 1276, jurors reported that it was because of an epileptic seizure and "his own drunkenness."[124] Jurors attributed also the death of Robert Hore in July 1389 to a combination of epilepsy and alcohol. Drunk while driving his cart, he had a seizure, fell from the cart, and died.[125]

These descriptions of epilepsy imply that medieval coroners and their juries had a more developed understanding of epilepsy than has previously been imagined. As a category of disease, epilepsy was not a "grab bag" of sudden deaths. Rather, the coroners' rolls substantiate a firm awareness of the disease grounded in the medical knowledge of the era. Certainly, they may also have confused other seizure-centered diseases for epilepsy; but at the very least, jurors understood that epilepsy was a life-long affliction, resulting in sporadic seizures. Even when jurors' evaluations of cause of death seem to wander somewhat farther afield—such as in allegations of lunacy or drunkenness—their assessments are explicable in light of the heritage of ideas surrounding epilepsy, or common misconceptions that continue to plague the diseased.

B) *Pestilencia*

When medieval writers employ the term *pestilencia*, historians have been reluctant to translate it as plague (that is, bubonic, septicemic, or pneumonic plague), insisting instead that it was understood more generally to refer to any fatal sickness. As John Theilmann and Frances Cate explain, "[m]edieval authors used the word plague to signify a disease of great proportions with a high mortality rate, not in a clinical sense."[126] One of the few scholars to deviate from this stance was Charles Creighton, the nineteenth-century historian of disease who claimed emphatically that when the English used the term "pestilence," they were referring specifically to "bubo-plague."[127]

More recently, historians have dismissed Creighton's work as being full of errors, claiming that it must be approached with caution. Nonetheless, the coroners' rolls themselves lend credence to Creighton's viewpoint. They imply that there was a distinct correlation between the term and the epidemic. Of the forty deaths ascribed to pestilence in the coroners' rolls (see Table 5.3 below), thirty-one (or 78%) correspond to documented plague outbreaks of a national or regional character. Many of the nine that do not fit neatly into this paradigm correlate with outbreaks nearby—if the victim traveled for work or religious reasons, he may well have come into contact with the virus outside of his immediate locale. Most plague deaths were also of an urban character, again a prominent feature of late medieval bubonic plague.[128]

What is significant about this finding is that it elucidates the popular usage of the term. While "pestilence" originated as a general term for fatal disease, among the English populace it came to mean bubonic plague. Again, it is not

Table 5.3 Documenting the Plague in the Coroners' Rolls

Year	Date	Location	Known Outbreak
1348	Feb. 28	York (*Yorks.*)	Black Death
1357[i]	June 11	Lincoln (*Lincs.*)	
1361	Nov. 14	York (*Yorks.*)	*Pestis Secunda*
1361	Dec. 7	York (*Yorks.*)[ii]	*Pestis Secunda*
1367	June 12	Upthorneton (Thornton, *Yorks.*?)	
1369	June 9	Lincoln (*Lincs.*)	*Pestis Tertia*
1369	July 20	York prison (*Yorks.*)	*Pestis Tertia*
1378	Sept. 14	Carnaby (*Yorks.*)	*Pestis Quarta*[iii]
1379	May 27	Buckingham (*Bucks.*)	*Pestis Quinta*
1380	Oct. 25	Donington (*Lincs.*)	*Pestis Quinta*
1381	Aug. 30	Mansbridge (*Southants.*)	*Pestis Quinta*
1382	June 23	York (*Yorks.*)	*Pestis Quinta*
1384	Oct. 7	Oxford prison (*Oxon.*)	
1384	Nov. 9	Honeybourne (*Worcs.*)[iv]	
1387	Jan. 23	Coventry	
1387	Mar. 16	Oxford prison (*Oxon.*)	
1388	June 1	Coventry	
1389	Jan. 21	Sutton (*Derbys.*)	1389–1393
1389	Jan. 31	Stoke (Stoke End?, *Warks.*)	1389–1393
1389	Feb. 5	Aubourn (*Lincs.*)	1389–1393
1389	July 18	Leicester prison (*Leics.*)	1389–1393
1391	Mar. 30	Derby (*Derbys.*)	1389–1393

(Continued)

Table 5.3 (Continued)

Year	Date	Location	Known Outbreak
1391	*Illegible*	York prison (*Yorks.*)[v]	1389–1393
1391	Oct. 3	Wetherby (*Yorks.*)	1389–1393
1392	Jan. 4	Chaddesden (*Derbys.*)	1389–1393
1392	Mar. 16	Tydd (*Lincs.*)	1389–1393
1392	Dec. 11	Osney (*Oxon.*)	1389–1393
1394	Apr. 4	Gosberkirk (*Lincs.*) (maybe Gosberton?)	1389–1393
1395	July 26	Oxford (*Oxon.*)	1395
1395	Oct. 21	Leicester (*Leics.*)	1395
1395	Nov. 14	Pinchbeck (*Lincs.*)	1395
1395	Dec. 20	Gosberkirk (*Lincs.*) (maybe Gosberton?)	1395
1397	Dec. 13	Saxelbye (*Leics.*)	
1399	Feb. 12	Leicester prison (*Leics.*)	1399–1400
1408[vi]	Aug. 8	Leicester prison (*Leics.*)	
1412	June 15	Leicester prison (*Leics.*)	1411–1412
1451	Mar. 4	The Marshalsea (London)	1447–1451
1451	Apr. 27	The Marshalsea (London)	1447–1451
1451	May 6	The Marshalsea (London)	1447–1451
1451	May 21	The Marshalsea (London)	1447–1451

[i] This particular case was probably not bubonic plague. According to Creighton, there was no record of pestilence in England between 1349 and 1361. See Creighton, *History of Epidemics*, v. 1, p. 202.y

[ii] This outbreak was particularly bad in the north, so much so that it is thought to have developed into a pneumonic outbreak. See Bean, "Plague, Population and Economic Decline," 429.

[iii] According to *The Anonimalle Chronicle*, this is the year the plague reached Yorkshire and lasted roughly a year. See V.H. Gailbraith, ed., *The Anonimalle Chronicle* (Manchester: Manchester UP, 1927), p. 124.

[iv] 1384 was the year of a great epidemic in Ireland and the Low Countries; thus, for Englishmen who traveled regularly, it is certainly not inconceivable for them to have died from plague in this year. See J.F.D. Shrewsbury, *A History of Bubonic Plague in the British Isles* (Cambridge: Cambridge UP, 1970; repr. 2005), p. 137; and W.P. Blockmans, "The Social and Economic Effects of Plague in the Low Countries: 1349–1500," *Revue Belge de Philogie et d'Histoire* 58.4 (1980): 844.

[v] The 1391 outbreak was worst in the north of England. Creighton, *History of Epidemics*, v. 1, p. 207.

[vi] There was a national epidemic in 1407—this case may represent the tail end of that outbreak. See Bean, "Plague, Population and Economic Decline," 428.

surprising that the medical treatises written by medical professionals were more cautious in their use of terminology, but when the average Englishman referred to *pestilencia*, he was talking about the plague. Once again, this conclusion underscores the value of using legal records as a means to unravel medieval medical perceptions: medical treatises tell us little about how the average person described disease.

C) *Apostema*

Deaths relating to abscesses, both internal and external, were so common that they also had their own marginal notation. Unfortunately, because of the symptom's rate of incidence, it is impossible to assess with hindsight precisely what caused these growths. As suggested above, the options are numerous: they could be anything from an allergic reaction, to a staph infection, to a cancerous tumor. The coroners' rolls afford few clues to pinpoint the nature of the illnesses that produced these abscesses. Some enrollments describe a growth as a long-term affliction: Adam of Bridlington was detained "for a long time" with an illness called *apostume* before he was found dead at the vill of Chesterton (*Oxon.*) in March 1344/45 after "the sickness existing inside his body broke" (*morbus infra corpus suum existens fregit*).[129]Adam of Garforth of Ellerton (*Yorks.*) had been suffering from an illness called *apostuma* for six weeks prior to his death in September 1347: he was so debilitated by the illness for the seven days before he died that he fell from a cart, causing the aposteme to burst, instantly killing him.[130] On its own, the prolonged existence of the abscess is not sufficient to narrow down the possibilities effectively. At best, it helps us to rule out bubonic plague.[131] Bubonic plague killed swiftly—purportedly within three days. Thus, when described as long-term, these *apostema* could not have been buboes. Other rapidly developing diseases can also be eliminated. The list of alternative possibilities is so lengthy, however, that this does little to help in the process of retrospective disease diagnosis.

As the two cases above imply, one element that is common to almost all enrollments of deaths relating to *apostema* is the fatal consequences of rupturing one. To offer additional examples: when Warren Dene passed away in Cambridgeshire in the summer of 1377, he did so after an aposteme growing in his ear burst open; without assistance, he died almost immediately.[132] John Weylond of Stondon died in 1337/38. The abscess (*felon*) on his left arm had been there for some time when he accidently ran into the wall of a neighbor's house; the collision caused him to fall on his arm, ripping open the abscess. He died soon after.[133] In the case of Richard Adyngton of Oxfordshire in April 1382, an internal aposteme located in his stomach burst while he was guiding his cart into a field; he died instantly.[134] These enrollments substantiate a strong conviction that rupturing a growth had a deadly cost. What is interesting about this finding is the disjuncture between this conclusion and humoral theory. Medieval medicine contended that an aposteme was the result of the body's attempt to rid itself of poison. Humoral theory viewed illness as a putrefactive process in which the humors slowly corrupted, eventually killing the body. An aposteme, then, was the body's means of expelling unsuccessfully the "poisonous putrefactive by-products from the body."[135] Accordingly, it was standard practice for medical practitioners to treat an abscess through curettage: by lancing it and draining it of pus in the hopes of rebalancing the humors by evacuating corrupt fluids. While the drainage of abscesses probably saved many lives, medieval medicine has been on the receiving end of a great deal of criticism for this practice. In the unsanitary conditions of the medieval world, lancing a bubo, for example, essentially liberated the organisms from the human body, increasing the opportunity for contagion, or mutation into a septicemic form, and transforming the medical practitioner, who had not yet discovered the importance of compulsive hand washing, into the ultimate agent of transmission for epidemic disease.[136] Without proper anesthesia, it was also an exceptionally painful process that may well have resulted in the death of the patient through severe shock.[137] Nonetheless, the evidence of the coroners' rolls offers good reason to question the accepted nature of this practice in the English setting. Medieval England's jurors clearly believed that cutting open an abscess would lead to instant death.

Granted, the English did view the abscess as a pocket of poisonous fluid. This is confirmed by the 1406/07 inquest into the death of William Aldeman. The jury, upon which two of his family members served, reported that William was traveling toward London from Kentish Town carrying a wooden butt full of beer with two gallons of half-beer on his back in order to set up a stand to sell beer on Figs Lane near the church of St Pancreas. In walking he somehow became unbalanced and the butt fell to the ground while it was still attached to his back. In falling, William's body shook so violently that the aposteme around his genitals burst open. The "corruption and poison" oozing forth from the aposteme killed him immediately.[138] This example confirms the English acceptance of humoral theory—the abscess clearly was the body's means of rejecting corrupt blood. However, as William's immediate death confirms, at least some of the English saw releasing the poison to be a life-threatening act.

What can we learn from this observation? Here, the coroners' rolls act as a gentle corrective to the medical treatises. Medical theory recommended curettage and drainage, and under the right conditions, that was indeed the wisest approach for the patient's health and welfare. Yet, the findings of the coroners' rolls suggest that popularly the English may have shied away from such invasive procedures, believing that only the worst could come of it. Admittedly, there is a great distinction between a sudden rupture and the procedure of curettage; yet, the rolls imply immediate death upon bursting, as opposed to death resulting from complications arising from the rupture itself. While this may seem like an inconsequential finding, it may point to a safer approach to addressing bubonic plague. Blame has been heaped upon the medieval medical practitioner for disseminating the epidemic by releasing the disease bacteria to infect the practitioner and his future patients. The English anxiety about curettage suggests that historians may be leaping too quickly to the conclusion that the English followed the advice in medical treatises.

D) Senescence

Coroners' rolls open a window onto the experience and perception of the elderly in later medieval England. Old age is a subject upon which little has been written, primarily because the source material is at best "scarce,"[139] and narrowly focused, concentrating principally on the aged from among the elite, whose diet, access to medical care, and exposure to dangerous living conditions is such that they are demographically atypical. With a focus on the more ordinary English man and woman, the coroners' rolls thus offer a unique perspective of the place of the elderly in the medieval village setting.

In medieval parlance, exactly how old was old? Demographic evidence has often led historians to assume that the medieval world had a much younger vision of the elderly than we do today. Consequently, it is not unusual to find textbooks on medieval life proclaiming communities considered a person to be "very old at forty."[140] Indeed, the life expectancy for those in later medieval England was quite modest. For men who survived the perils of infancy and childhood, one might reasonably hope to reach what the modern world refers to as middle age, that is, around forty years of age.[141] Because of the dangers of childbirth, women's life expectancy was even shorter. Archaeological data proposes an average date of death for adult women of around thirty-three.[142] Of course, those who contend that medieval men and women saw forty years of age as old are assuming a direct correlation between the average life span and social perceptions of senescence. This correspondence makes about as much sense as now-discredited notions that high infant mortality rates persuaded parents to withhold affection from their children until they were certain they were here to stay. Unfortunately, literary sources offer little assistance in discerning the medieval definition of senescence. Medieval authorities from Saint Augustine of Hippo to Isidore of Seville, obsessed with categorizing the ages of man, varied widely in their estimations. While some cynics placed the beginnings of senescence at the age of thirty-five, others more optimistically argued in favor of age seventy.[143] Looking specifically to the English context, surviving legislation relating to retirement from public service supports a more advanced age for the onset of senescence. In the manorial and village setting, by-laws regularly excused men over the age of sixty from participating in the physically demanding labor of bringing in the harvest.[144] Royal law originally aimed even higher showed much less compassion for the elderly. The 1285 Statute of Westminster declared that men over the age of seventy, providing they were "continually sick" or "diseased at the Time of the Summons," might petition for exemption from jury service.[145] The Statute of Labourers (1351) seems to have been more in line with municipal expectations: it also deemed sixty years of age a marker of distinction: those over the age of "threescore" were exempt from compulsory service.[146]

A number of other factors complicate our understanding of medieval perceptions of old age and the place of the elderly in medieval society. The legacy of medieval literature furnishes a conflicting sense of attitudes toward old age. Sermon literature reminds us that ageing itself is a divine punishment. Humankind surrendered its immortality and entered the ageing process upon the fall from Paradise. Had Adam and Eve obediently followed God's directive, refusing to be led into sin by the temptations of the devil, humankind would never have been exposed to such a horrific experience.

The punitive nature of senescence is pronounced by contemporary representations of Hell. Medieval Christianity perpetuated an ideal of Hell as a state of continuous bodily torment. Woodcuts depicting infernal punishment associated with the seven deadly sins remind us that bodies in Hell are grotesque: they are old, haggard, sickly, malformed, and undernourished.[147] Youth and beauty is reserved for those who enter Paradise: freed from the ugliness of sin, the human body once again regains its youthful appearance.[148] This deeply entrenched ideology springs from both theological and medical views of the individual as a unity of body and soul: pure souls reside in beautiful bodies, and beauty (then, as now) is articulated as youth. In line with this mode of thinking, medieval clergymen preaching from the pulpit often included old age "among the great evils to which mankind is subject in this life, such as pestilence, earthquakes, nightmares, depression and human viciousness."[149] And yet, many of the same sources also extolled the benefits of old age, claiming the "old body is a means of drawing close to God because of its suffering and because it no longer has passions."[150]

The historiography of old age is no more consolidated in its conception of the place of the elderly in medieval society. Indeed, historians' positions on the issue represent both ends of the spectrum. Gillian Overing describes the field as laboring in the shadow of the "natural Rosy Family myth," that is, the perception that in the past, the elderly "ha[d] roles to play, [were] granted respect, and [were] sustained by caring intergenerational families."[151] On the contrary, research into the medieval period has emphasized instead the marginal nature of the aged, especially old women, twice marginalized for their age and their gender.[152] More often than not, the historical tradition associates old age with "want and deprivation"[153] and with poverty,[154] rather than the security and comfort propagated by this mythical vision. Julia Baldó also offers a grim assessment, declaring that "those who failed to obtain guarantees of protection from their families or a monastery ended up forming part of the marginal mass forced into mendicity."[155] Gaining support from one's family was not necessarily an easy task. As Barbara Hanawalt writes, "a considerable tension [existed] between the young and the old. The young were desirous of gaining control of the family resources while the old wishes to secure care and comfort."[156] Joel Rosenthal puts forth the most positive appraisal. While he observes that the aged were "never really singled out for special treatment,"[157] at the same time he found no "social currents that worked to sweep the aged aside, to marginalize them because of their exceptional survival."[158] Drawing on Rosenthal, S.H. Rigby writes: "far from being excluded, many of the aged were in positions of power, wealth and culturally endorsed authority."[159] Granted, much of the work in this field is speculative because of the nature of the sources, Rosenthal's meticulous work being the exception here: founded on literary materials, it is difficult to parse out reality from prescription.

The coroners' rolls set us on a firmer footing with respect to the elderly and their place in later medieval England. Admittedly, the data has its limits as a statistical resource. Fatalities among the elderly in the coroners' rolls fall into the category of accidental or sudden deaths. While many of those sudden deaths were, in fact, natural, they represent only a small proportion of natural deaths among the larger population, and thus cannot provide meaningful statistical data for a demographic analysis. Moreover, as records of death investigation, the coroners' rolls are inherently weighted toward a gloomy reality. Nonetheless, as Joel Rosenthal asserts, the elderly were common in medieval England. Indeed, those who made it beyond the average life span sometimes lived to be very old.[160] The coroners' rolls record the deaths of a good number of individuals aged seventy and eighty years.[161] There are even examples of men and women ninety or one hundred years of age. None of this should come as a surprise. Any individual capable of surviving episodic disease, hazardous living conditions compounded by an absence of antibiotics and pain relievers, hardships occasioned by the erratic weather conditions of the Little Ice Age,[162] multiple childbirths (if female), and endemic warfare should indeed be made of sturdy stuff.

The overall impression afforded by death investigations is not wholly positive or negative. When coroners wrote about old age, they typically resorted to terms evoking images of decay, debility, impotence, and ill health. For example, Gloucestershire coroner G. Rowland remarked that when a certain woman identified only as Joanna drowned accidently by falling from a boat into the River Colne, she did so because she was of "decrepit" age.[163] In recounting the death of Isabella Swon in October 1378, who tripped on a plank lying near the water's edge and drowned, Berkshire coroner William Barton reported that she did so "because of old age and debility."[164] The enrollment of the death of Elena Anne of Sutterton (*Lincs.*), aged seventy, described her as "debilitated and sick." Elena fell dead from a fatal infirmity after returning from church in January 1377/78.[165] When Robert Flaxman of Corpusty, aged eighty, expired at Great Yarmouth (*Norfolk*) a few days after Palm Sunday in 1360, again, the record attributes his accidental death to "debility" and "old age" (here described as *antique etat*). Around the ninth hour, Flaxman rose from bed, and walked to the city wall in order to relieve himself; in doing so, he fell into a gravel pit and died.[166] There exists also an impressive corpus of deaths stressing the link between old age and poverty. Seventy-year-old William Gadhill died a beggar when he fell into a well at Whaplode (*Lincs.*) in the spring of 1378.[167] So, too, did Thomas Taskar of Thimbleby (*Yorks.*), who drowned at the age of eighty.[168] Alice Berdholf of Donington (*Lincs.*) was labeled both a pauper and a beggar (*paupercula et mendicans*) when she drunkenly fell into a well and died at the age of seventy in the summer of 1377.[169] The only element seemingly missing from the story of destitution and decrepitude is an emphasis on senility: there are few examples of the mentally unstable among the aged. Agnes de Goyton presents the extreme example. She committed suicide at age eighty years and more, reportedly under the influence of the devil.[170]

Yet, some positive insights into the state of the aged and their living conditions surface in the records. Old age did not necessarily entail poverty. Some elders continued to eke out an independent existence by living in their own houses. Alice Huddoghter, an old, blind woman living at Southburn (*Yorks.*) in 1382/83 was living in her own home when she passed away. The record mentions specifically that she exited her home (*de domo sua*) and went into the street where unwittingly she fell into a well and drowned.[171] Mariota, widow of Richard Pepper, described as infirm, debilitated, and of decrepit age, clearly also lived in her own home. Around the hour of bedtime, she rose from her bed, lantern in her hand, and went to the well in her own courtyard in order to get a drink. Unfortunately, she tripped and plunged into the well. Matilda Mody, John Spayne, and his son, Henry, all witnessed the incident and made diligent efforts to rescue her from the well, but their labors were futile.[172] Others presumably lived on charity. In August 1385, eighty-year-old Sara Andrew failed to fasten the candle near her bed securely. As a result, the candle fell from its holder and set fire to her bed, eventually consuming her in flames. The record identified Sara as a beggar, living in the home of Thomas Banbury at Stratford-at-Bow. Coroners tended to be quite fastidious about remarking on familial relationships, and yet this record mentions no relationship between the two, leaving us with the distinct impression that Sara was living on Thomas's charity at the time of her demise.[173] When Margaret Giler, aged one hundred years, drowned by mistake in the parish of St Botolph's outside Bishopsgate in the spring of 1407, she died near the gates of St Mary Bethlehem's hospital. In all likelihood, much like many other elders, she was receiving assistance from the hospital prior to her death.[174] Still others were involved in fairly normal activities up until the moment of their deaths. Even though she was eighty years and more, Alice, wife of John Robyn, of Finchley was traveling by horse on the highway from London to Finchley near Islington in July of 1410 when she happened upon a cart led by six horses traveling in the opposite direction. Spooked by the pack animals, Alice's horse suddenly reversed, and in doing so threw Alice to the ground and trampled over her body. She died soon after, with at least two broken ribs.[175] For Alice to have been riding by horse on her own at the age of eighty suggests that she must have been in good health. For those who were not in such good shape, there is evidence to argue that medieval family and friends helped to make the elderly as comfortable as possible. When Robert Wylewes, the canon of Missenden Abbey, passed away at the age of one hundred years, he did so in a wheelchair (*cathedra sua rotata*). Parked by the fire to keep him warm on a cold October day in 1378, the aged canon fell asleep in his wheelchair while his servant was fetching his meal, and accidentally slid into the fire. The burns to his face eventually took his life. The coroner's report assessed his wheelchair at a value of 4*d*. as deodand, hinting that comfort for the elderly came at a relatively modest price.[176]

Perhaps most important, the coroners' rolls reveals that elderly women filled an important niche in childcare. Numerous aged women passed away while caring for a small child. Agnes, wife of Richard Couper, who stumbled into the river and drowned in April of 1393, did so through debility and old age: it is significant that she had a child in her arms at the time.[177] Hundred-year-old Meliora atte Persones, who was both blind and deaf, was caring for John, son of Richard "That Was Jonesman" of Fenton, a six-month-old child, when the house went up in flames at Goadby (*Leics.*) in December of 1405. Sensing the danger, Meliora managed to escape the burning home with the infant in her arms: she survived, but the infant John perished from smoke inhalation.[178] Joanna Clount, aged seventy years and more, was presumably caring for one of her grandchildren when she passed away in a house fire at Carlford Hundred (*Suffolk*) in December 1358: five-year-old Margery Clount died with her.[179]

The coroners' rolls thus furnish a body of evidence to solidify scholarly perceptions of the elderly in medieval England, a necessary endeavor given the broad range of scholarly conclusions inspired by literary works. The legal records provide plentiful examples to substantiate that some individuals lived to a ripe old age, despite the many and varied obstacles working against them. The documentation stresses also the variety of experiences awaiting the senescent. For many, old age brought poverty, suffering, and physical impotence; but this was not, by far, a universal experience. The coroners' rolls boast examples of elderly men and women who continued an independent lifestyle, living in their own homes and participating in very ordinary activities. Still others survived on the love and charity of family and friends. More important still, the elderly played an important role in childcare, corroborating in part Overing's "natural Rosy Family myth" by discovering that the medieval world did, at least occasionally, see the elderly as useful and productive members of society.

MEDICINE IN ACTION

Historians of medicine depict medieval medicine as being chiefly domestic in nature, practiced by family members "whose lives and methods remain hidden."[180] In this respect, the narrative style of coroners' enrollments is a boon for historians. Because the more inclusive enrollments incorporate a chronology of the victim's health and welfare leading up to the moment of death, they furnish a view of medieval medicine in action. Admittedly, it must be reiterated that the nature of the records shapes our perceptions. Death investigation inevitably proffers a negative view of healthcare; after all, there were no inquests into deaths narrowly averted by the heroics of medical practitioners. In no way should the coroners' rolls be employed to construct an overall assessment of the effectiveness of medieval medical practice. Nonetheless, they have much to offer in terms of understanding the regular process of healthcare and contemporary expectations.

The domestic nature of medieval medicine is addressed primarily in the significance of the family in monitoring those whose conditions present a danger to themselves. Jurors were quick to emphasize the role of family and friends as the first line of defense against sudden death. Enrollments of natural deaths regularly contain brief turns of phrase to explain how the presence of the dead's family and friends might have prevented his death. Once again, the fatalities of epileptics provide some of the clearest evidence. In 1370, when William Skirk Bercard collapsed in the fields of Blyborough (*Lincs.*) during an epileptic seizure that resulted in his death, jurors commented not only that he was alone, but also that he died through "defect of help" (*defectum auxilii*).[181] Robert Clerk of Garthorpe (*Lincs.*) purportedly stumbled into the River Don and drowned while overcome by a seizure: his death also occurred because there was no one around to help him.[182] Thomas the Pinder was en route from Grassthorpe to Manton (*Notts.*) in 1341 when his body was gripped with a seizure: he, too, was alone, and without help when he died.[183] Jurors deliberately called attention to the solitary state of these individuals as an aspersion on their negligent family and friends. Medieval English men and women "universally dreaded" sudden death.[184] Indeed, the death-obsessed culture of the late Middle Ages led many among the English to attend mass daily, believing wholly that anyone who witnessed the elevation of the host was protected from sudden death that day. The moment of death had huge implications for a Christian's soul and legacy, and thus the deathbed was an occasion with multiple functions. For the family, it was both a moment of farewell and an opportunity to hearten the dying in preparation for his final struggle with Satan. Because the English suspected that writing a will prematurely might usher in death unnecessarily, the deathbed was also the occasion for will making, and thus it was typically a communal event, replete with plenty of family squabbles over the future ownership of goods and properties. For the Christian, the hour of death marked a rite of passage in the penitential process expressed in final confession and absolution, without which one's fate in the afterworld was in jeopardy. In this respect, will making was also an essential part of a Christian death because it provided the dying an opportunity to arrange a funeral and set aside money to pay for prayers to be said for one's soul in purgatory. Accordingly, death and preparation for it was so central to the late medieval English that Eamon Duffy contends it "manifested itself in every aspect of late medieval piety."[185]

In this context, the taunts inserted into the coroners' enrollments were public acknowledgements of the family's failure to care for the diseased, thus depriving the dead of a worry-free journey into the afterworld, as well as increasing the burden for the living in terms of prayers for the dead. Given the magnitude of the implications, it is not surprising that jurors sometimes articulated their blame quite pointedly. At the 1393 inquest of Thomas

Chippinghurst in Oxford, jurors noted that leading up to his death, Thomas was languishing from fever and *flux sanguinis* (dysentery) for some time. He was in such poor health that a priest had already administered last rites. When Thomas awoke thirsty, he was surprised to discover himself alone. In "the absence of his wife and family," he rose from his deathbed and went to the river for a drink. Because of the debility of his body and brain, he fell into the river and drowned.[186] The coroners affirm also that for those without family, the results were bleak. The investigation into the death of William Denelot at Frisby (*Leics.*) in 1372/73 recounts how William, clearly a loner who was hostile to unwelcome intrusions into his home, had been dead for some time before anyone found him. Jurors concluded that he must have experienced a fatal seizure while he was home alone in bed. His body lay there for three days and three nights after the fact, until his neighbors, curious to learn why he had not left his home in days finally decided to check on him. His shutters were closed tight, and when they hollered into his home to ask how he was doing, they received no response. Hesitant to enter without permission, some brave soul finally took the initiative to open the door, finding William lying dead in his bed, his body slowly decomposing.[187]

While medieval medicine was principally domestic, the English were prepared to call on the services of a medical practitioner chiefly in two scenarios: 1) to perform surgical procedures, and 2) when a victim's condition was life threatening. The most popular surgical procedure was preventative: bloodletting to release corrupt blood and/or an excess of blood and thus rebalance the body's fluids was fundamental to medieval Europe's medical practice. Galenic theory privileged bloodletting as a cure-all to restore internal harmony. Medieval medicine inherited this infatuation with phlebotomy from the Greeks. As Shigehisa Kuriyama remarks, "[p]lethora gripped the Greek imagination with an intensity that the bare logic of intake and consumption cannot adequately explain. Physicians sometimes exsanguinated their patients until they fainted and passed feces, so terrible was the perceived danger."[188] Thankfully, their medieval heirs proceeded in a somewhat more restrained fashion, although bloodletting continued to assume a place of privilege. A medieval leechbook expounds the benefits of bloodletting and its inherent versatility:

> Blood letting in measure it clears your thought, it closes your bladder, it tempers your brain, it amends your hearing, it strengthens tears, it closes your "maw", it digests your meat, it clears your voice, it sharpens the wit, it eases your womb, it gathers your sleep, it draws away anguish, it nourishes good blood; wicked blood [it] destroys, and lengthens your life.[189]

The Greeks endorsed topological bleeding: that is, much like the approach adopted by acupuncturists, they mapped the body to discern how letting blood from one vein would treat an illness associated with the corresponding/opposing part of the body. Medieval medicine exercised this ideal much less vigorously than did the Greeks: although "vein man" diagrams marking prospective bloodletting sites on the body existed and circulated, medical practitioners typically let blood from the basilic vein near the elbow. The basilic vein was thought to be tied to the venomous humors emanating from the liver and spleen, thus letting blood from this particular vein was most effectual at cleansing the blood. Despite the seeming crudity of the practice, medieval phlebotomy was, indeed, a science.[190] Surgeons advocated bloodletting only at the appropriate stage of treatment, when the weather was conducive to healing, and at astrologically auspicious times of the year. Bloodletting was also a valuable tool of diagnosis. Physicians not only analyzed the color, heat, texture, and smell of the blood they extracted, they also tasted it. The blood of a healthy individual is sweet; bitter or sour blood is a sure sign of bodily imbalance.[191] Effective bloodletting called for a professional, and the coroners' rolls provide cautionary tales to explain why hiring an experienced phlebotomist was imperative. The sad death of Alice Mason in 1384 is instructive in this respect. In the hope of saving her life, Alice extracted blood from an abscess on her tibia using a pair of scissors; but once the blood began to surge forth, she was incapable of staunching the bleeding. She died later that same day in the home of a relative.[192] While Alice was probably not a medical practitioner, her plan adhered to the medical advice of her era. Galenic theory advised rebalancing the humors by letting blood at the source of illness, in this case, by lancing the abscess itself.[193] Admittedly, as the discussion on *apostema* above proposes, many Englishmen feared that curettage might cause more harm than good. Alice's death clarifies one of the dangers. If the medical practitioner carrying out the procedure was inexpert, bleeding to death was a distinct possibility.

While Alice's death, presumably, resulted from inexperience, engaging the services of a professional might still end tragically. In 1407/08, Thomas, son of John Primus, of Ludlow (*Salop.*) hired Thomas Leche of Staffordshire to "heal him of all the infirmities in his body." With a razor worth 6*d*., the leech sliced him across the abdomen. Given the propensity of stomach injuries to bleed profusely, it is no wonder that he could not halt the flow of blood. Thomas, son of John, died soon after, and the panicked leech fled.[194] The demise of Richard of Stramshall in 1384/85 shares many similarities. Afflicted with an unnamed illness from which he had suffered for two years, Richard took advantage of an unknown physician's visit to Burton (*Staffs.*) by hiring the man to bleed him. Regrettably, due to what the jurors described as the physician's "negligence and lack of good governance," Richard died soon after and the physician disappeared.[195] The record of the 1277 death of William the Palmer is even more succinct, although his death presumably sprang from a similar experience. The coroner's enrollment notes that "having been let blood" the day before, the London skinner died from loss of blood. The record makes no mention whatsoever of whom he hired to perform the service.[196]

Were these medical practitioners quacks? This is entirely possible. Because of the popularity of phlebotomy as a universal remedy, unskilled individuals often practiced it "freelance," or as a "profitable sideline."[197] Carole

Rawcliffe illustrates this point with the unexpected example of Robert Reynes, a parish constable at Acle in fifteenth-century Norfolk, whose commonplace book reveals that he practiced bloodletting alongside his duties as an officer.[198] In the case of Thomas Leche, mentioned above in connection with Thomas, son of John Primus, it is hard to imagine that he had any training in the field. While medical theory recommended at least thirty different veins for topological phlebotomy, none of them is located in the stomach.[199] Yet, it is critical to accept that even genuine medical practitioners sometimes had the unfortunate experience of watching their patients slowly bleed to death before their eyes. For this reason, phlebotomy texts are full of monitions of who not to bleed (children, the elderly, menstruating women, those with cold temperaments), when to avoid bloodletting (according to stage of treatment, the weather, the positions of the stars), and what to do if the bleeding becomes excessive (usually cautery performed in a wide variety of formats).[200] What is perhaps more remarkable is that given the prevalence of the practice, one would expect the coroners' rolls to contain a surfeit of deaths by ill-fated phlebotomy. That these are the only ones is a testament to the general competency of medical practitioners.

When a victim's condition was critical, English men and women with the available means hired the services of a medical practitioner. While a couple of the above examples suggest that medical practitioners sometimes trekked the countryside in search of business, more often than not, professional healthcare in later medieval England meant traveling to an urban center.[201] Physicians (even if educated abroad) ran in university circles, thus Oxford and Cambridge; surgeons, barbers, and other craftsmen worked out of guilds, also tied to urban environments. The coroners' rolls confirm the highly urban nature of medieval medicine. When a 1373 altercation in Worthington (*Leics.*) led to John the Thresher being stabbed with a knife, without delay he left his village to seek the services of a medical practitioner in the borough of Leicester; regrettably, he passed away soon after his arrival.[202] Similarly, after an attack that left him wounded in the arm in 1300, William Wattepas of Essex journeyed to London in the hopes of obtaining a cure: he, too, did not survive long after his arrival in the kingdom's capital.[203] Other victims of assault turned to the medieval hospital. The inquest of Thomas Bateman of Oxton held at Tadcaster (*Yorks.*) reported that John Cooper stabbed him in the left arm with a dagger. Because of the severity of the injury, friends transported Thomas to the city of York to be cured. He languished there for a week, and then died as a result of the wound.[204] In the death of Richard Hunt of Skipwith, jurors commented that a fight between Richard and three of his friends precipitated his death: the altercation produced wounds on Richard's head and right arm inflicted by a staff. The three friends conveyed Richard to the city of York where they hoped he might be cured: he, too, languished for a week before his wounds got the better of him. John Barbour, who served on Richard's inquest, may well have been the medical practitioner engaged by his friends to treat the injuries.[205] In the fatality of John Hendement in 1392/93, jurors did not know where the victim had come from: they explained that he had traveled to the borough of Gloucester to receive medical care. He was staying at the home of William Barbour, recovering from a lesion in his head made with an arrow, when he suddenly contracted *le blodeymeneson* (dysentery) and died.[206]

In all of the above instances, patients journeyed to some of medieval England's major urban centers for medical care. The 1249 inquest into the death of Ughtred Smith illustrates that the services of a medical professional might also be available in smaller urban centers. Ughtred was injured in a hunting accident. He and his companion, Peter Grapere, were in the woods of Dotland, a small rural community in Northumberland. Reportedly, Ughtred went ahead to scout out their hunting prospects while Peter accustomed himself to a new bow. Experimenting with the bow's elasticity, Peter shot a test arrow, but it traveled much further than he expected. He called ahead to Ughtred to ask if he spied where it went: Ughtred responded that it was "stuck in [his] head." Peter's innocence is signaled by his reaction: he immediately fell to the ground "groaning and crying." Seeing this, Ughtred "bade him not grieve since he felt no hurt," but fearing his wife's reaction, he begged Peter to pull the arrow out of his head, which he did. Able to move faster on his own, Peter left Ughtred in the woods and journeyed to the nearby village of Horsley to fetch William the Leech. After inspecting the wound, William announced that Ughtred would recover in a day or two, but his prognosis was wide of the mark. Ughtred died, and the inquest jurors believed the wound was responsible. Nonetheless, because Peter plainly had not intended to shoot Ughtred (and Ughtred himself did not hold Peter responsible), they declared it a death by misadventure.[207]

Many of these instances involve accounts of medicine gone wrong, for one reason or another. Nonetheless, except for the occasional fleeing medical man, who clearly interpreted his own actions as blameworthy, the enrollments do not hold medical practitioners accountable. Certainly, common law recognized the possibility of medical negligence leading to homicide. *Bracton* acknowledged that homicide might result from the "inadequacy" of the victim's physician, "who gave him the wrong medicine."[208] *Britton* warns of the dangers of those who seek medical advice from "false physicians and bad surgeons"; when their counsel ended in death, *Britton* categorized their actions as felony.[209] Nonetheless, both *Bracton* and *Britton* fail to recognize the magnitude of the dilemma. Rather, the *Mirror of Justices* addresses the importance of assessing a medical practitioner's experience and reputation, but also the options set before him. Indeed, the *Mirror* reminds us that sometimes death is unavoidable.

> Physicians and surgeons being learned in their faculties and provably making lawful cures, and having clear consciences, so that in nothing have they failed their patients that to their art belongs, if their patients die, are not homicides or mayhemers; but if they undertake to make a cure which they do not know how to bring to a successful end, or,

> although they have such knowledge, they behave stupidly or negligently, as by applying heat instead of cold, or the reverse, or too little of the cure, or if they do not apply a due diligence, more especially in their cauterisings and amputations, which are things that cannot lawfully be done save at the peril of the practitioners, then, if their patients die or lose a limb, they are homicides or mayhemers.[210]

The *Mirror*, thus, shines a spotlight on one instance in which the law needed to function at the behest of a group of England's elite. Admittedly, this approach served everyone's best interests. If medical practitioners had fears of homicide indictments looming over their heads, they would refuse to take on patients whose health might take a turn for the worse. This legal stance effectively exempted a medical practitioner from homicide allegations, providing he was a legitimate practitioner and the allegations were medically relevant. Instead, disgruntled patients or their families opted to plead trespass suits against negligent medical practitioners: indeed the court of King's Bench provides myriad examples.[211]

As this alliance between medical practitioners and the law implies, coroners and their jurors were more inclined to lay blame at the feet of the patient than the practitioner. The 1371 inquest into the death of Alice, daughter of John, of Spalding epitomizes this tendency. Alice had been suffering from an illness (almost certainly gout) afflicting one of her feet for six years and more. On the advice of a physician and her neighbors, who concluded that there was no likelihood of a cure, she hired a physician to amputate the putrefied foot. She paid him twenty pennies to carry out the operation, not realizing that she was, in fact, financing her death: she passed away a week after the operation. What is striking is that the record offers no hint that her death resulted from medical malpractice. Rather, it goes to great lengths to exonerate Alice and the dispensing apothecary from any implication in her death. The enrollment establishes that she followed the physician's advice: she took her medicine as prescribed and there was no defect in the medicine. Thus, the jury announced that her death was natural.[212] Jurors did not let all individuals off this easily. The 1254 inquest into the death of John Craghe at Bramham (*Yorks.*) denounced the victim for bringing about his own death by disregarding his health needs. The enrollment begins with a quarrel between John and Bartholomew of Bramham. John stalked away angry and went drinking at a local tavern for several hours. Upon his departure from the tavern, he returned to Bartholomew's home and lay in wait for him. Bartholomew must have suspected John's plans, however, because he materialized armed with a hatchet. John struck the first blow, but his pole was no match for a hatchet. When John fled from the quarrel, he did so sporting a great wound on his head. Afterward, while he did receive care for his injury, John "went all about the country to markets and taverns"—in the minds of the jurors, definitive proof that he cared little for his health. When he passed away three weeks later, jurors resolved it happened "because he had neglected the wound."[213] In this enrollment, John is depicted as impulsive, devious, and homicidal: it is no wonder they preferred to hold him accountable rather than the man who actually cast the blow.

Because humoral theory focused so heavily on the ingestion and expulsion of fluids and foods of the appropriate qualities for an individual's temperament, it is not surprising that jurors' expectations in following a medical practitioner's advice extended also to an analysis of a victim's last meals. Jurors in the inquest into the death of Leonard de Casalt Motant, the king's moneyer, did just that. Leonard was sharing an evening meal at the home of Richard le Messager in Reading when the conversation took a turn for the worse. "Like a madman," Leonard shot up from the table, brandished his knife, and stabbed his three dinner companions. "Seeing no way of escape in the narrow house," one of his fellow diners, Albert Guy, drew his knife and thrust it into Leonard's stomach. Leonard survived the attack. He lived for six days after the incident: but because he "would neither eat nor drink anything but cold water, which his surgeon forbade him," he died.[214] Jurors at the inquest into the death of Robert the Provost drew a similar conclusion. When an attack by Richard of Barnby (*Yorks.*) left Robert with a defensive wound, jurors remarked that the wound itself was not mortal, but it became lethal "because of his immoderate eating and drinking."[215]

Inquests supply a view of medicine from a more normative perspective than one might encounter in the medical treatises of the era. While medicine was primarily domestic and family played a critical role in caring for the diseased, English men and women knew when to call in a professional. Surgical procedures, such as bloodletting and amputation, were dangerous enough to necessitate the skill of a medical professional: families and friends also recognized the need for an expert when a victim's condition appeared to be life threatening. Physicians and surgeons sometimes traveled the countryside to sell their services as phlebotomists; however, more often than not when a patient required the advice of a medical practitioner, he needed to travel to an urban center. Granted, the coroners' rolls expand the options available: the documentation suggests that even smaller urban centers boasted the services of medical professionals. What is most striking about the coroners' rolls is the reluctance to hold medical practitioners accountable for their actions and wrong-headed prognoses. In general, coroners and their jurors were much more likely to blame the dead than a medical practitioner.

More generally, the coroners' rolls are a goldmine of insight into popular medical ideas and usage of terminology. Medieval men and women did not view health primarily in religious terms: death was not routinely explained by God's visitation, nor were they likely to blame the devil. For the most part, the coroners' rolls reveal a surprising aptitude for medicine: coroners and jurors grasped the major theories of disease transmission current at that time, and the scope of disease names implies a respectable attempt to identify the illness that resulted in a death, even though the crown did not technically require an inquest to do so. An examination of the documentation's treatment of common conditions highlights popular usage and clears up common misconceptions about medieval medicine. For example: the term "epilepsy" was not a catch-all phrase for all sudden deaths—medical histories supplied by jurors reveal that when jurors employed the term, they were describing epilepsy, or a disease that looked a lot like it. Similarly, despite the reluctance of historians to translate *pestilencia* as bubonic plague, when jurors used the term, that is exactly what they meant. Moreover, contemporary medical practices may not have caused as much harm as some historians have suggested: curettage (and all the dangers that might accompany it in a time prior to the recognition of germ theory) was not a universal practice, despite the inherent logic of humoral theory. Perhaps, most important of all, the medieval English did not alienate the elderly because their deteriorated health made them less productive members of society. While some became beggars in their old age, others lived independently in their own homes. Older women, in particular, filled an important role in childcare. Overall, the coroners' rolls remind us that we have much to learn about healthcare in medieval England, and they offer a new source for historians of medicine to examine in this endeavor.

NOTES

1. Francis B. Brévart, "Between Medicine, Magic, and Religion: Wonder Drugs in German Medico-Pharmaceutical Treatises of the Thirteenth to the Sixteenth Centuries," *Speculum* 83 (2008): 1–57. Walton Schalick addresses this debate in his "To Market, to Market: The Theory and Practice of Opiates in the Middle Ages," *Opiods and Pain Relief: A Historical Perspective* 25 (2003): 5.
2. John M. Riddle, "Contraception and Early Abortion in the Middle Ages," in *Handbook of Medieval Sexuality*, ed. Vern L. Bullough and James A. Brundage (New York: Garland, 1996), p. 261.
3. Nicholas Everett explores the continuity between medieval and modern pharmaceutical practices. See his *The Alphabet of Galen: Pharmacy from Antiquity to the Middle Ages* (Toronto: University of Toronto Press, 2012), pp. 28–31.
4. Marianne Elsakkers, "'In Pain You Shall Bear Children' (Gen. 3:16): Medieval Prayers for a Safe Delivery," in *Women and Miracle Stories: A Multidisciplinary Exploration*, ed. Anne-Marie Korte (Leiden: Brill, 2001), pp. 179–209; see also Lea T. Olson, "Charms and Prayers in Medieval Medical Theory and Practice," *SHoM* 16.3 (2003): 343–66.
5. Carole Rawcliffe, *Medicine and Society in Later Medieval England* (London: Sandpiper Books, 1999), p. 72.
6. Nutton's account does not consider the variety of pain relievers that existed in later medieval culture. See Linda E. Voigts and Robert P. Hudson, "A drynke þat men callen dwale to make a man to slepe whyle men kerven him: A Surgical Anesthetic from Late Medieval England," in *Health, Disease, and Healing in Medieval Culture*, ed. Sheila Diana Campbell, Bert S. Hall, and David N. Klausner (New York: St Martin's Press, 1992), pp. 34–52; Shalick, "To Market, to Market," 5–20; and Esther Cohen, *The Modulated Scream: Pain in Late Medieval Culture* (Chicago: University of Chicago Press, 2010), pp. 87–92.

7. Vivian Nutton, "Medicine in Medieval Western Europe, 1000–1500," in *The Western Medical Tradition 800 BC to AD 1800*, ed. Lawrence I. Conrad, *et al.* (Cambridge: Cambridge UP, 1995), p. 161.
8. As Chaucer puts it in the General Prologue: "And yet he was but easy of dispense; / He kept what he won in pestilence. / For gold in physic is a cordial, / Therefore he loved gold in special" (lines 441–44).
9. Rosanne Gasse, "The Practice of Medicine in *Piers Plowman*," *The Chaucer Review* 39.2 (2004): 188.
10. Pasquale Accardo, "Dante and Medicine: The Circle of Malpractice," *Southern Medical Journal* 82.5 (1989): 625.
11. Lisi Oliver, *The Body Legal in Barbarian Law* (Toronto and Buffalo: University of Toronto Press, 2011), p. 4.
12. Oliver, *Body Legal*, p. 132.
13. Oliver, *Body Legal*, p. 5.
14. Thomas Fayreford is certainly less well known than John Arderne. See Peter Murray Jones, "Thomas Fayreford: An English Fifteenth-Century Medical Practitioner," in *Medicine from the Black Death to the French Disease*, ed. Roger French (Aldershot: Ashgate, 1998), pp. 156–83.
15. This discussion applies exclusively to English medicine. Because the records for Continental legal medicine are more meticulous and prolific, there has been more overlap in the disciplines. Continental historians of medicine received Guido Ruggiero's 1978 landmark study ["The Cooperation of Physicians and the State in the Control of Violence in Renaissance Venice," *JHMAS* 33 (1978): 156–66] as a call to arms for historians to begin looking to legal sources for a greater understanding of medical history. Since that time, much has been published on the subject, although the histories for some regions (such as the Italian city-states, Christian Spain, and France) are better researched than others (the Holy Roman Empire, for example).
16. Madeleine P. Cosman has written a number of articles on this subject drawn from the same grouping of cases. See her "Medieval Medical Malpractice and Chaucer's Physician," *New York State Journal of Medicine* 72.19 (1972): 2439–44; "Medieval Medical Malpractice: The Dicta and The Dockets," *Bulletin of New York Academy of Medicine* 49.1 (1973): 1–47; "Medical Practice and Peer Review in Medieval England," *Trans Sect Otolaryngol American Academy of Ophthalmol Otolaryngol* 80.3 (1975), pt. 1: 293–37; "Surgical Malpractice in the Renaissance and Today," *Plastic and Reconstructive Surgery* 86.5 (1990): 1017–29; "The Medieval Medical Third Party: Compulsory Consultation and Malpractice Insurance: Risk Management," *Clinical Orthopaedics and Related Research* 407 (2003): 3–10. See also: C.B. Chapman, "Stratton vs. Swanlond: The Fourteenth-Century Ancestor of the Law of Malpractice," *The Pharos of Alpha Omega Alpha-Honor Medical Society* 45.4 (1982): 20–24; M.T. Walton, "The Advisory Jury and Malpractice in 15th century London," *JHMAS* 40.4 (1985): 478–82; C.L. Wood, "Historical Perspectives on Law, Medical Malpractice, and the Concept of Negligence," *Medical-Legal Issues* 11.4 (1993): 819–32; J.B. Post, "Doctor versus Patient: Two Fourteenth-Century Lawsuits," *MH* 16.3 (1972): 296–300; and finally, Thomas R. Forbes, *Surgeons at the Bailey: English Forensic Medicine to 1878* (New Haven: Yale UP, 1985), Chapter One.
17. An exception to the rule: Sara M. Butler, "Medicine on Trial: Regulating the Health Professions in Later Medieval England." *Florilegium* 28 (2011): 71–94.
18. Elizabeth and John Towner similarly argue in favor of the use of coroners' rolls for medical purposes. See their "Developing the History of Unintentional Injury: The Use of Coroners' Records in Early Modern England," *Injury Prevention* 6 (2000): 102–05. Inspired by the Towners' article, Steven Gunn wrote

a fascinating study of safety relating to archery practice. See Steven Gunn, "Archery Practice in Early Tudor England," *P&P* 209 (2010): 53–81.

19. Thomas R. Forbes, "A Mortality Record for Colbath Fields Prison, London, in 1795–1829," *Bulletin of the New York Academy of Medicine* 53.7 (1977): 668.
20. James Sharpe and J.R. Dickinson, "Coroners' Inquests in an English County, 1600–1800: A Preliminary Survey," *Northern History* 48.2 (2011): 260.
21. P. Fisher, "Getting Away with Murder? The Suppression of Coroners' Inquests in Early Victorian England and Wales," *Local Population Studies* 78 (2007): 50.
22. Thomas R. Forbes, "Coroners' Inquisitions on the Deaths of Prisoners in the Hulks at Portsmouth, England in 1817–27," *JHMAS* 33.3 (1978): 364. This viewpoint derives from the modern legal treatises. Writing in 1761, coroner for the county of Middlesex, Edward Umfreville, explained: "What is said of a dying by the Visitation of God in a natural way, is to be understood of Persons *at large*, and not under any Restraint or Confinement at the Timc, as in the Case of a *Prisoner's* dying in Gaol, as is the Office or Duty of the Gaoler to send for the Coroner, to inquire how the Deceased came by his Death, the better to remove a possible Presumption, that the Prisoner died "*per dure Gard*," the ill Usage or Severity of his Gaoler." See Edward Umfreville, *Lex Coronatoria* (London: R. Griffiths, 1761), v. 1, fos. 209–10, ch. 148.
23. A. Dally, "*Status Lymphaticus*: Sudden Death in Children from 'Visitation of God' to Cot Death," *MH* 41.1 (1997): 70; Sharpe and Dickinson, "Coroners' Inquests," 265; Cathy Smith, "'Visitation by God': Rationalizing Death in the Victorian Asylum," *History of Psychiatry* 23.104 (2012): 104.
24. As cited in Mary Beth Emmerichs, "Getting Away with Murder? Homicide and the Coroners in Nineteenth-Century London," *Social Science History* 25.1 (2001): 95.
25. Lindsay Prior, "The Good, the Bad and the Unnatural: A Study of Coroners' Decisions in Northern Ireland," *Sociological Review* 33.1 (1985): 83.
26. Matthew Hale, *History of the Pleas of the Crown: Concerning the Coroner and His Court, and His Authority in the Pleas of the Crown* (London: T. Payne, 1800), p. 61. Sharpe and Dickinson's study of the palatinate of Chester persists in this categorization. See Sharpe and Dickinson, "Coroners' Inquests," 260.
27. F.W. Maitland and W.J. Whittaker, eds., *The Mirror of Justices* (*SS*, v. 7, 1895), p. 31.
28. TNA PRO JUST 1/690, m. 5d, death of John, son of Hugh Harding, of Rampton (*Notts.*), a four-year-old boy; TNA PRO JUST 1/690, m. 6, death of Thomas Robert le Cartere; TNA PRO JUST 1/690, m. 1d, death of John Belle of Shireoaks (*Notts.*).
29. TNA PRO JUST 1/690, m. 6d, death of John Dirland, a mendicant pauper; TNA PRO JUST 1/690, m. 8d, death of Richard Burbage of Granby (*Notts.*); TNA PRO JUST 1/690, m. 5, death of Hugh Ryling of Normanton (*Notts.*).
30. TNA PRO JUST 1/692, m. 3, death of Agnes, wife of William of Leicester.
31. TNA PRO JUST 1/690, m. 3, death of William, son of Richard Gyles, of Cottam (*Notts.*).
32. TNA PRO JUST 2/31, m. 8d, death of Thomas, servant of William, of Riddings (*Derbys.*); TNA PRO JUST 2/189, m. 2, death of Nicholas of Isingdon.
33. "*[P]er dispositionem divina videlicet per pestilencie.*" TNA PRO JUST 2/31, m. 8d.
34. TNA PRO JUST 2/23, m. 2.
35. TNA PRO JUST 2/133, m. 5.
36. K.J. Kesselring has proposed that decreasing literacy in Latin may also account for a more static account of death investigation in the medieval period, as well

as increased concerns about funds disbursed for parchment and scriveners' fees. Many thanks to Dr. Kesselring for this suggestion.

37. Seven prisoners at Southwark alone died from the plague in the years 1450–1451. See TNA PRO KB 9/265, m. 33. See also, TNA PRO JUST 2/135, m. 2, death of John Soly.
38. TNA PRO JUST 2/179A, m. 7, death of Robert Gryffin Walshman at Melton.
39. TNA PRO JUST 2/34, m. 15, death of John Cole.
40. TNA PRO JUST 2/17, m. 27, death of Hugh, son of John Patenmer.
41. TNA PRO JUST 2/17, m. 27d, death of William Knyght.
42. TNA PRO JUST 2/61, m. 2.
43. TNA PRO JUST 2/110, m. 3 includes a list of fourteen prison deaths at Northampton that covers the whole gamut of explanations.
44. TNA PRO JUST 2/9, m. 1.
45. For example, TNA PRO JUST 2/276, m. 1, death of Matilda, daughter of John Clement, of Reading, or Richard, son of Robert, of Boughton.
46. Anthony J. Musson, *Public Order and Law Enforcement: The Local Administration of Criminal Justice, 1294–1350* (Woodbridge: Boydell, 1996), p. 202.
47. A few examples: TNA PRO JUST 2/123, m. 6, death of John Kylnelhirst; TNA PRO JUST 2/195, m. 13d; death of John Flexham; TNA PRO JUST 2/217, m. 6d, death of Peter Syward of Londesborough (*Yorks*.).
48. Y.B., term uncertain, 40 Edw. III, fo. 250a; TNA PRO JUST 2/217, m. 11d (death of William Bateman). For the medieval definition of *penitencia*, see R.E. Latham, *Revised Medieval Latin Word-List from British and Irish Sources: With Supplement* (London: Oxford UP, 1965; repr. 1994), p. 339, headword "*penit/entia*." Earliest usage is 1315.
49. P.E. Hair, "Deaths from Violence in Britain: A Tentative Secular Survey," *Population Studies* 25.1 (1971): 16. Hair's article inspired the research of S.J. Stevenson, whose work centers on the premise that early modern jurors regularly concealed suicides as drownings. See his "The Rise of Suicide Verdicts in South-East England, 1530–1590: The Legal Process," *C&C* 2.1 (1987): 37–75, and "Social and Economic Contributions to the Pattern of 'Suicide' in South-East England, 1530–1590," *C&C* 2.2 (1987): 225–62.
50. Alexander Murray, *Suicide in the Middle Ages* (Oxford: Oxford UP, 1998), v. 1, p. 123.
51. Hildegard of Bingen, *On Natural Philosophy and Medicine: Selections from Cause and Cure* (Cambridge: D.S. Brewer, 1999), pp. 70–71.
52. See Basil Clarke, *Mental Disorder in Earlier Britain: Exploratory Studies* (Cardiff: University of Wales Press, 1975), p. 96.
53. TNA PRO JUST 2/113, m. 16. Agnes, widow of Walter of Ragnall (*Notts*.), went to the tavern around vespers in January 1345/46, where she reportedly died a sudden death after being vexed by an (unnamed) illness. See TNA PRO JUST 1/690, m. 5.
54. TNA PRO JUST 2/113, m. 16.
55. TNA PRO JUST 2/57, m. 8.
56. TNA PRO JUST 2/155, m. 15.
57. TNA PRO JUST 2/242, m. 1d.
58. TNA PRO JUST 2/177, m. 3.
59. TNA PRO JUST 2/133, m. 36. Andrew Cottusworthe's demise sprang from a "certain infirmity" from which he had suffered for two weeks prior to his death. See TNA PRO JUST 2/133, m. 5.
60. TNA PRO JUST 2/129, m. 1.
61. TNA PRO JUST 2/116, m. 3.
62. Naomi Williams has made a similar point about mid-nineteenth-century coroners. She writes, "Coroners' returns were notorious for their vagueness

and were a source of continual frustration for those attempting to classify and interpret these data. The ambiguity reflected the fact that most coroners generally regarded their principal role to be that of establishing whether the deaths referred to them had been caused by either natural or unnatural (i.e. violent) causes, and as such they tended to avoid any attempt to identify the actual disease responsible for death." See her, "The Reporting and Classification of Causes of Death in Mid-Nineteenth-Century England," *Historical Methods* 29.2 (1996): 58–72. For another interesting discussion of this problem, see Rebecca Kippen, "'Incorrect, loose and coarse terms': Classifying Nineteenth-Century English Language Causes of Death for Modern Use: An Example Using Tasmanian Data," *Journal of Population Research* 28 (2011): 267–91.

63. Charles-Edward A. Winslow, *The Conquest of Epidemic Disease: A Chapter in the History of Ideas* (Princeton: Princeton UP, 1943; repr. 1971), p. 88.
64. John Henderson, "The Black Death in Florence: Medical and Communal Response." This article appeared originally in Steven Bassett, *Deaths and Towns: Urban Responses to the Dying and the Dead 100–1600* (Leicester: Leicester UP, 1992), pp. 136–47; repr. in Elizabeth A. Lehfeldt, ed., *Problems in European Civilization: The Black Death* (New York: Houghton Mifflin, 2005), p. 49.
65. Winslow, *Conquest of Epidemic Disease*, p. 267.
66. TNA PRO JUST 2/61, m. 2.
67. "*[A]d capiendum aerem.*" TNA PRO JUST 2/61, m. 17/3.
68. This absence is probably best explained by the scrivener's training: medieval scriveners were far more comfortable with legal than medical terms. The simple fact that the scriveners resorted to a Latinization of an English term tells us that they were not familiar with the term *halit*.
69. Reginald R. Sharpe, ed., *Calendar of Coroners' Rolls of the City of London, A.D. 1300–1378* (London: R. Clay & Sons, Limited, 1913), pp. 198–99. In January 1279 a well maker arranged for Thomas Dust to be let down in a well when he accidently tumbled out of the bucket, falling to the bottom. Jurors blamed the corrupt air at the bottom of the well for his immediate death. The phrase used was "*per corrupcionem aeris.*" See William Hudson and John C. Tingey, eds., *The Records of the City of Norwich* (Norwich: Jarrold & Sons, 1906), v. 1, p. 219.
70. Personal communication with William Walkenhorst, Department of Chemistry, Loyola University New Orleans, November 2, 2012.
71. TNA PRO JUST 2/194, m. 1. Although the jurors do not blame miasma-bearing air in the death of John de Hynkele in 1297, he seems to have died in a similar fashion. The inquest determined that he was hired to dig in Henry of Thornton's croft at the borough of Leicester. While digging he suddenly died, and jurors had no idea what caused his death. See Mary Bateson, ed., *Records of the Borough of Leicester*, v. 1 (London: Clay & Sons, 1899), p. 359.
72. "*[P]er defectum aeris totaliter suffocatus.*" TNA PRO JUST 2/137, m. 1.
73. TNA PRO JUST 2/124, m. 4. In August 1383, Nicholas Fouler also descended into the operational well of John Glede (although the record does not explain why). He died abruptly upon contact with a certain air (*quendam ayerem*) called "Dampe." See TNA PRO JUST 2/123, m. 3.
74. TNA PRO JUST 2/164, m. 5. The record for the death of John of Hull in August 1390 is almost identical. See TNA PRO JUST 2/164, m. 8.
75. Bryon Grigsby, *Pestilence in Medieval and Early Modern English Literature* (New York: Routledge, 2004), p. 132.
76. TNA PRO JUST 2/3, m. 16. A 1288 inquisition also refers to a man suffering from the "hot sickness." See *CIM*, v. 1, pp. 410–11, no. 1445.

77. TNA PRO JUST 2/92, m. 4.
78. *CIM*, v. 1, p. 397.
79. William Farr, *Vital Statistics: A Memorial Volume from the Reports and Writings of William Farr* (New York: New York Academy of Medicine, 1885; repr. 1975), p. 234.
80. Michael Bloor, "A Minor Office: The Variable and Socially Constructed Character of Death Certification in a Scottish City," *Journal of Health and Social Behavior* 32 (1991): 273–74.
81. Doug Campos-Outcalt, "Cause-of-Death Certification: Not as Easy as It Seems," *The Journal of Family Practice* 54.2 (2005): 135.
82. Michael R. McVaugh, *Medicine before the Plague: Practitioners and Their Patients in the Crown of Aragon 1285–1345* (Cambridge: Cambridge UP, 1993), p. 142.
83. TNA PRO JUST 2/129, m. 2.
84. TNA PRO JUST 2/220, m. 9.
85. Yves Landry and Renald Lessard, "Causes of Death in Seventeenth- and Eighteenth-Century Quebec as recorded in the Parish Registers," *Historical Methods* 29.2 (1996): 49–57.
86. Williams, "Reporting and Classification," Appendix B.
87. For more on this subject, see Andrew Cunningham, "Identifying Disease in the Past: Cutting the Gordian Knot," *Asclepio* 54.1 (2002): 13–34; Jon Arrizabalaga, "Problematizing Retrospective Diagnosis in the History of Disease," *Asclepio* 54.1 (2002): 51–70.
88. Highlights of this debate include Graham Twigg, *The Black Death: A Biological Reappraisal* (Batsford: Schocken Books, 1985); Samuel K. Cohn, *The Black Death Transformed: Disease and Culture in Early Renaissance Europe* (London: Hodder Arnold, 2003); Susan Scott and Christopher Duncan, *The Biology of Plagues: Evidence from Historical Populations* (Cambridge: Cambridge UP, 2005); Vivian Nutton, ed., *Pestilential Complexities: Understanding Medieval Plague* (London: Wellcome Trust for the History of Medicine, 2008); and Ole J. Benedictow, *What Disease Was Plague? On the Controversy over the Microbiological Identity of Plague Epidemics of the Past* (Leiden: Brill, 2010).
89. "Researchers Reconstruct Genome of the Black Death," Press Release (Hamilton, McMaster University, October 12, 2011), http://fhs.mcmaster.ca/mcmastermedia/documents/black_death_mcmaster_press_release.pdf. Accessed Apr. 3, 2013.
90. TNA PRO JUST 2/61, m. 16.
91. TNA PRO JUST 2/164, m. 4.
92. TNA PRO JUST 2/178, m. 3d.
93. For more information on this subject, see P.F. Chinnery, "Muscle Diseases," in *Cecil Medicine*, ed. L. Goldman and A.L. Shafer, 24th ed. (Philadelphia: Saunders Elsevier, 2011), ch. 429.
94. TNA PRO JUST 2/177, m. 2.
95. John Theilmann, "Disease or Disability? The Conceptual Relationship in Medieval and Early Modern England," in *The Treatment of Disabled Persons in Medieval Europe: Examining Disability in the Historical, Legal, Literary, Medical, and Religious Discourses of the Middle Ages*, ed. Wendy J. Turner and Tory Vanderventer Pearman (Lewiston: Edwin Mellon Press, 2010), p. 222.
96. Alice's purification occurred much earlier that I would have imagined possible after her child's birth. Churching—a Catholic ceremony in which a blessing is granted to mothers after recovery from childbirth—usually took place roughly thirty days after birth, at a point when post-partum bleeding should have ceased. Unfortunately, the record offers no sense as to why she was purified so soon after the birth of her child.

97. TNA PRO JUST 2/105, m. 7d.
98. Bryon Grigsby, "The Social Position of the Surgeon in London, 1350–1450," *Essays in Medieval Studies* 13 (1996): 75.
99. Rawcliffe, *Medicine and Society*, p. 133.
100. Luke Demaitre, "Medical Writing in Transition: Between *Ars* and *Vulgus*," *Early Science and Medicine* 3.2 (1998): 88–102; Louise Bishop, *Words, Stones, and Herbs: The Healing Word in Medieval and Early Modern England* (Syracuse: Syracuse UP, 2007), pp. xi, 2.
101. Julie Ormanski, "Jargon and the Matter of Medicine in Middle English," *JMEMS* 42.2 (2012): 398.
102. In an interesting spin on this ideology, late medieval surgeon John of Arderne consciously associated surgery with a knightly ethos. See Jeremy J. Citrome, *The Surgeon in Medieval English Literature* (New York: Palgrave Macmillan, 2006), p. 113.
103. In 1421, Thomas Morstede petitioned on behalf of surgeons and physicians for a licensing process; this was approved and entered into law by Henry V. Grigsby, "Social Position of the Surgeon," 77.
104. Ormanski, "Jargon and the Matter of Medicine," 398, 396.
105. For example, see Faye Getz, *Medicine in the English Middle Ages* (Princeton: Princeton UP, 1998), p. 76; and Oswei Temkin, *The Falling Sickness: A History of Epilepsy from the Greeks to the Beginnings of Modern Neurology* (Baltimore: Johns Hopkins, 1945; repr. 1994), p. 86.
106. World Health Organization, www.who.int/mediacentre/factsheets/fs999/en/index.html. Accessed November 27, 2012.
107. World Health Organization.
108. Faye Getz, ed., *Healing and Society in Medieval England: A Middle English Translation of the Pharmaceutical Writings of Gilbertus Anglicus* (Madison: University of Wisconsin Press, 1991), pp. 20–21.
109. Getz, *Gilbertus Anglicus*, p. 21.
110. TNA PRO JUST 2/127, m. 1.
111. TNA PRO JUST 2/155, m. 18. John Porter had been afflicted with the "falling evil" for many years before he suffered the fatal seizure that caused him to fall into a pit and drown in 1395/96. See TNA PRO JUST 2/61, m. 14/1.
112. TNA PRO JUST 2/101, m. 1.
113. TNA PRO JUST 2/106, m. 4. The jury described eleven-year-old Thomas le Personesman also as having epilepsy: the disease "overcame him" when he was standing near a well in Holme Hale (*Norfolk*) in 1367, prompting him to fall into the well and drown. See TNA PRO JUST 2/104, m. 47d.
114. Mervyn Eadie and Peter Bladin, "The Idea of Epilepsy as a Disease *Per Se*," *Journal of the History of the Neurosciences* 19 (2010): 209.
115. See Andrée Courtemanche, "The Judge, the Doctor and the Poisoner: Medical Expertise in Manosquin Judicial Rituals at the End of the Fourteenth Century," in *Medieval and Early Modern Ritual: Formalized Behavior in Europe, China, and Japan*, ed. Joëlle Rollo-Koster (Leiden: Brill, 2002), p. 112.
116. TNA PRO JUST 2/105, m. 1d.
117. Matthew 17: 15–17.
118. Temkin, *Falling Sickness*, p. 92.
119. As cited in Temkin, *Falling Sickness*, p. 97. See also Donald F. Scott, *The History of Epileptic Therapy: An Account of How Medication was Developed* (Carnforth, UK: CRC Press, 1993), p. 30; See also J. Lascaratus and P.V. Zis, "The Epilepsy of Emperor Michael IV, Paplagon (1034–1041 A.D.): Accounts of Byzantine Historians and Physicians," *Epilepsia* 41.7 (2000): 915; and Anna Vanzan Paladin, "Epilepsy According to the Christian, Jewish, and Islamic Religions: An Overview," *Epilepsia* 1 (1995): 39.

120. Chapter Four also discusses the link between insanity and epilepsy.
121. TNA PRO JUST 2/104, m. 47.
122. TNA PRO JUST 2/61, m. 7.
123. TNA PRO JUST 2/217, m. 16d.
124. H.T. Riley, ed., *Memorials of London and London Life in the 13th, 14th, and 15th Centuries* (London: Longmans, Green, and Co., 1868), p. 9. In November 1288, an epileptic, William Pechus of Oxendon (*Northants.*), went into the forest of Benefield while inebriated. Jurors were not entirely sure how he died, but they argued that his death resulted from the disease and the alcohol. See TNA PRO JUST 2/106, m. 10. The inquest into the death of Peter of Hatton (*Northants.*) in June 1342 drew much the same conclusion. They noted only that he was an epileptic who died suddenly while drunk; unfortunately, no one discovered his body until a week after his demise, undoubtedly part of the reason why jurors had difficulty identifying cause of death. See. TNA PRO JUST 1/690, m. 8d.
125. TNA PRO JUST 2/155, m. 17.
126. John Theilmann and Frances Cate, "A Plague of Plagues: The Problem of Plague Diagnosis in Medieval England," *Journal of Interdisciplinary History* 37.3 (2007): 390. See also, Benedictow, *What Disease was Plague?*, p. 326; and Rosemary Horrox, ed., *The Black Death* (Manchester: Manchester UP, 1994), p. 4.
127. Charles Creighton, *A History of Epidemics in Britain: From A.D. 664 to the Extinction of Plague*, 2 vols. (Cambridge: Cambridge UP, 1891), v.1, p. 226.
128. J.M.W. Bean, "Plague, Population and Economic Decline in England in the Later Middle Ages," *EHR*, n.s., 15.3 (1963): 432.
129. TNA PRO JUST 2/18, m. 5.
130. TNA PRO JUST 2/214, m. 15.
131. Continental writers of plague tracts frequently employed the term *aposteme* for a bubo. Cohn, *Black Death Transformed*, Chapter Four, *passim*.
132. TNA PRO JUST 2/24, m. 16d.
133. TNA PRO JUST 2/17, m. 8d.
134. TNA PRO JUST 2/133, m. 3.
135. Ann Carmichael, "Contagion Theory and Contagion Practice in Fifteenth-Century Milan," *Renaissance Quarterly* 44.2 (1991): 223.
136. Carmichael, "Contagion Theory," 252.
137. William Naphy and Andrew Spicer, *The Black Death: A History of Plagues, 1345–1730* (Stroud: Tempus, 2000), p. 146; Andrew Wear, *Knowledge and Practice in English Medicine, 1550–1680* (Cambridge: Cambridge UP, 2000), p. 346.
138. TNA PRO KB 9/195/1, m. 12. Roger Aldenam and Hugh Aldenam junior both served as jurors on this inquest. In this situation, because the abscess was located in the genital region, William Aldeman may have been suffering from bubonic plague.
139. Erik D. Spindler, "Youth and Old Age in Late Medieval London," *The London Journal* 36.1 (2011): 10.
140. Nigel Kelly, Rosemary Rees, and Jane Shuter, *Medieval Realms* (Portsmouth, NH: Heinemann, 1997), p. 18.
141. Estimates with respect to life expectancy vary more than one would expect. The earlier sources offer a more positive assessment. Josiah Cox Russell estimates a life expectancy between forty-five and fifty-three. See Russell, *British Medieval Population* (Albuquerque: University of New Mexico Press, 1948), pp. 182–86. More cautiously, Erik Spindler proposes a lower estimation of forty years of age (Spindler, "Youth and Old Age," 13). Gillian Overing notes that life expectancy in a developed nation only reached forty-five years of age

in the nineteenth-century. See her "A Body in Question: Aging, Community, and Gender in Medieval Iceland," *JMEMS* 29.2 (1999): 213.

142. Carole Rawcliffe, "Women, Childbirth, and Religion in Later Medieval England," in *Women and Religion in Medieval England*, ed. Diana Wood (Oxford: Oxbow Books, 2003), p. 94.
143. Luke Demaitre, "The Care and Extension of Old Age in Medieval Medicine," in *Aging and the Aged in Medieval Europe*, ed. Michael M. Sheehan (Toronto: PIMS, 1983), p. 8.
144. Richard M. Smith, "The Manorial Court and the Elderly Tenant in Late Medieval England," in *Life, Death, and the Elderly: Historical Perspectives*, ed. Smith and Margaret Pelling (London: Routledge, 1991), pp. 33–51.
145. "Statute of Westminster, I" 13 Edw. I, c. 38 (1275); *SR*, v. 1, p. 89.
146. "Statute of Labourers," 23 Edw. III, c. 1 (1349); *SR*, v. 1, p. 307.
147. For example, see Anon., *Le grant kalendrier des Bergiers* (Troyes: Nicolas le Rouge, 1496).
148. Shulamith Shahar, "The Old Body in Medieval Culture," in *Framing Medieval Bodies*, ed. Sarah Kay and Miri Rubin (Manchester: Manchester UP, 1994), p. 171.
149. Shulamith Shahar, *Growing Old in the Middle Ages: Winter Clothes Us in Shadow and Pain* (London: Routledge, 1997), p. 8.
150. Shahar, "Old Body in Medieval Culture," p. 175.
151. Overing, "Body in Question," 216.
152. Overing concludes: "The stigma attached to old women is profound and profoundly negative overall" (Overing, "Body in Question," 221). The subject of women and old age has been one of the most productive within the discipline. See Gretchen Mieszkowski, "Old Age and Medieval Misogyny: The Old Woman," in *Old Age in the Middle Ages and the Renaissance: Interdisciplinary Approaches to a Neglected Topic*, ed. Albrecht Classen (Berlin: de Gruyter, 2007), pp. 299–319; and Michael Solomon, "Women Healers and the Power to Disease in Late Medieval Spain," in *Women Healers & Physicians: Climbing a Long Hill*, ed. Lillian R. Furst (Lexington: UP of Kentucky, 1997), pp. 79–92.
153. David Herlihy, "Age, Property, and Career in Medieval Society," in Sheehan, *Aging and the Aged*, p. 143.
154. Shahar, *Growing Old*, p. 9.
155. Julia Baldó, "Quonstituido en Estrema Vejez: Old Age and Life Expectancy in Late Medieval Navarre," *Imago Temporis: Medium Aevum* 2 (2008): 198. Elaine Clark makes the same argument. See Clark, "The Quest for Security in Medieval England," in Sheehan, *Aging and the Aged*, p. 189.
156. Barbara A. Hanawalt, *The Ties That Bound: Peasant Families in Medieval England* (New York: Oxford UP, 1986), p. 242.
157. Joel T. Rosenthal, *Old Age in Late Medieval England* (Philadelphia: University of Pennsylvania Press, 1996), p. 185.
158. Rosenthal, *Old Age in Late Medieval England*, p. 190.
159. S.H. Rigby, "Death and Old Age in the Middle Ages," *Journal of Early Modern History* 3.1 (1999): 81.
160. Rosenthal, *Old Age in Late Medieval England*, p. 171.
161. As I suggested in Chapter Three, the medieval English were not terribly precise about age. Thus, it seems likely that the ages listed in the coroners' rolls were rounded up or down to the nearest decade.
162. The Little Ice Age was a period of cooling temperatures lasting from roughly 1350 to 1850.
163. TNA PRO JUST 2/46, m. 1.
164. TNA PRO JUST 2/14, m. 3.

165. TNA PRO JUST 2/83, m. 4.
166. TNA PRO JUST 2/102, m. 1.
167. TNA PRO JUST 2/82, m. 4.
168. TNA PRO JUST 2/221, m. 1.
169. TNA PRO JUST 2/82, m. 3. Stephen Gagnebald, aged ninety, was thought to have died precisely because of his circumstances: his Norfolkshire jurors characterized him as poor, debilitated, and old. See TNA PRO JUST 2/102, m. 1.
170. TNA PRO JUST 2/67, m. 23.
171. TNA PRO JUST 2/236, m 5.
172. TNA PRO JUST 2/1/, m. 3.
173. TNA PRO JUST 2/96, m. 6d. Julia Baldó argues that sometimes individuals took in elderly neighbors who were down on their luck. See Baldó, "Quonstituido en Estrema Vejez," 210. The 1339/40 inquest into the death of David ap Madoc bolsters this impression. David was a blind beggar who died in the home of Tuder ap Ad ap Ririd. Tuder claimed that David had come for lunch, but was feeling poorly. Out of his love for God, Tuder put David in his bed, where he passed away. See CHES 18/1, m. 2.
174. TNA PRO KB 9/195/1, m. 12.
175. TNA PRO KB 9/197, m. 21.
176. TNA PRO JUST 2/14, m. 16.
177. TNA PRO JUST 2/32, m. 3d.
178. TNA PRO JUST 2/61, m. 9/2.
179. TNA PRO JUST 2/179A, m. 7.
180. Faye Getz, *Medicine in the English Middle Ages* (Princeton: Princeton UP, 1998), p. 6.
181. TNA PRO JUST 2/73, m. 2d.
182. TNA PRO JUST 2/73, m. 3.
183. TNA PRO JUST 1/690, m. 12.
184. Eamon Duffy, *The Stripping of the Altars: Traditional Religion in England 1400–1580* (New Haven: Yale UP, 1992; repr. 2005), p. 310.
185. Duffy, *Stripping of the Altars*, p. 318.
186. TNA PRO JUST 2/138, m. 3.
187. TNA PRO JUST 2/55, m. 9.
188. Shigehisa Kuriyama, "Interpreting the History of Bloodletting," *JHMAS* 50.1 (1995): 31.
189. *A Leechbook or Collection of Medicinal Recipes*, pp. 62–63, English modernized. As cited in Rawcliffe, *Medicine and Society*, p. 64.
190. Modern medicine is beginning to recognize once again the benefits of bloodletting. Bloodletting is the most uncomplicated method of lowering levels of stored iron in the body. An excess of iron can produce dangerous molecules, referred to as free radicals, which damage the cells. This is a common health concern in a society that overindulges in red meat. As a result, physicians advocate its use in the treatment of cardiovascular health, liver disease, genetic hemochromatosis, even staph infections. For a useful general summary, see Jeffrey S. Jhang and Joseph Schwartz, "Phlebotomy or Bloodletting: From Tradition to Evidence-Based Medicine," *Transfusion* 52 (March 2012): 460–62. Somewhat more experimentally, physicians also employ phlebotomy as preventative medicine to reduce cholesterol levels and prevent cancer. See Andreas Michaelsen, *et al.*, "Effects of Phlebotomy-Induced Reduction of Body Iron Stores on Metabolic Syndrome: Results from a Randomized Clinical Trial," *BMC Medicine* 10:54 (2012): 1–8; and L.R. Zacharski, *et al.*, "Decreased Cancer Risk after Iron Reduction in Patients with Peripheral Arterial Disease: Results from a Randomized Trial," *Journal of National Cancer Institute* 100.14 (2008): 996–1002.

191. Rawcliffe, *Medicine and Society*, p. 51. "Grease" in the blood was thought to be a telltale sign of leprosy.
192. TNA PRO JUST 2/14, m. 9d.
193. Leif Søndergaard, "Imagining Plague: The Black Death in Medieval Mentalities," in *Living with the Black Death*, ed. Søndergaard and Lars Bisgaard (Odense: UP of Southern Denmark, 2009), p. 223.
194. TNA PRO JUST 2/150, m. 1.
195. TNA PRO JUST 2/162, m. 8.
196. Reginald R. Sharpe, ed., *Calendar of Letter-Books of the City of London, A-L (1275–1497)* (London: John Edward Francis, 1899–1912), v. B, p. 272. The same death is recorded in Riley, *Memorials of London*, p. 14; however, Riley transcribes his name as "William le Pannere."
197. Rawcliffe, *Medicine and Society*, p. 64.
198. Rawcliffe, *Medicine and Society*, p. 64.
199. See "Drawing of Vein Man. In the Guildbook of the Barber Surgeons of York," "Online Gallery," British Library. www.bl.uk/onlinegallery/onlineex/illmanus/egermanucoll/d/011ege000002572u00050000.html. Accessed March 27, 2013.
200. Rawcliffe, *Medicine and Society*, pp. 63–68.
201. Vern L. Bullough, "Medical Practice in the Middle Ages, or Who Treated Whom," in his *Universities, Medicine, and Science in the Medieval West* (Aldershot: Ashgate, 2004), pp. 277–88.
202. TNA PRO JUST 2/53, m. 4.
203. Sharpe, *Calendar of Coroners' Rolls*, p. 1.
204. TNA PRO JUST 2/242, m. 2.
205. TNA PRO JUST 2/242, m. 2.
206. TNA PRO JUST 2/40, m. 4.
207. *CIM*, v. 1, pp. 553–54.
208. Henri de Bracton, *De Legibus et Consuetudinibus Angliae*, ed. George Woodbine, ed. and trans. Samuel E. Thorne, 4 vols. (*SS*, 1968–1976), v. 2, p. 356.
209. F.M. Nichols, ed., *Britton: The French Text Revised with an English Translation* (Oxford: Clarendon Press, 1865), v. 1, p. 34.
210. F.W. Maitland and W.J. Whittaker, eds., *Mirror of Justices* (*SS*, v. 7, 1895), p. 137.
211. Butler, "Medicine on Trial," 71–94.
212. TNA PRO JUST 2/67, m. 30.
213. *CIM*, v. 1, p. 563.
214. *CIM*, v. 1, p. 597.
215. *CIM*, v. 1, p. 643.

Conclusion

Simon of Watford, the perpetual vicar for the church of Conway (in northern Wales, under English administration), offered an instructive story of death investigation from the later Middle Ages when testifying before an ecclesiastical commission in the canonization trial of Saint Thomas de Cantilupe, once the Bishop of Hereford. A young boy named Roger, aged two years and three months, son of Gervase the cook and Dionisia de Paytefin, wandered out of his parents' house during the night of September 6, 1303. His parents were merely a "stone's throw away" (*ad jactum unius lapidis*) at the local parish church for an all-night vigil after the recent deaths of two fellow villagers. According to his mother, Roger and his sisters were sleeping soundly when she left for the night, closing the door (but not locking it) securely behind her. Because he was still an infant, she and her female servant had taken the usual precaution of swaddling Roger and tying him to his cradle for safety. Waking during the night, he somehow escaped his cloth bonds and exited the house undressed, setting himself on the path to the castle where his father worked as a cook for the constable, William de Cycons. His vision obscured by the dark of night, he stumbled on the bridge joining the vill to the castle, falling twenty-eight feet to the bottom of the moat. His small, naked body was dashed against the icy rocks below.

William de Cycons and his men discovered the nude, frost-encrusted boy the following morning. On the constable's order, the first finder, John de Gistyn, climbed down into the barren moat to inspect the boy. After feeling Roger's body and seeing the expression on his face, John believed the boy was dead: Roger was not crying, he emitted no sound, and he appeared rigid, holding one shin out erect and in an unnatural position. The man's instinctive reaction was to bring the boy back to his parents, but the seneschal called out to him to stop what he was doing, reminding him that the body needed to remain in place while they waited for the arrival of the coroners. It was the coroners' job to determine whether he had died through accident or homicide; therefore, the boy's body could not be removed from its resting place—and so John returned the boy to the rocks. The constable sent for the coroners, and not long after, Stephen de Ganvy and William of Nottingham, the king's county coroners, arrived accompanied by William, a cleric who worked as their scribe (*clericus & scriptor dictorum coronatorum*). Without delay, they climbed down into the moat and "touched and felt" (*tetigerunt et palpaverunt*) the boy's body, inspecting diligently (*perquinentes*) into the needs of their office, trying to determine the number of his wounds, as well as their length, width, and depth, their clerk busily recording all the evidence as they worked. Miraculously, the boy's body was physically intact. They were unable to find any wounds; nor did they discover any broken limbs, broken bones, effusion or emission of blood, or broken skin. He did, however, sport a great bruise on his left jaw in the place where it was lying on the rocks, but in no other part of his body did there appear any sign of violence. After the physical inspection, the coroners and their scribe moved away from Roger's body to confer over their notes. Another deponent at the canonization trial reveals that all of this was done in the presence of the coroners' jury; one of those jurors, Simon of Flint—who claimed to "have been drafted for jury duty at the clamor of Roger's mother"—was later brought to testify as a witness before the canonization trial.[1]

While the coroners and jurors were otherwise occupied, John Seward, another burgher of the vill, defied the coroners' prohibition from entering the ditch, descended into it, and approached Roger's body. He, too, felt the body and found Roger to be dead. With a penny he drew from his purse, he made the sign of the cross on Roger's forehead; he then bent the penny (a distinctly British votive ritual) and prayed to Saint Thomas to perform a miracle and resuscitate this boy. In return, he promised that the boy would visit the saint at his tomb. After the sign of the cross and his prayer, he opened Roger's mouth to feel his tongue, and spoke to the coroners and others standing around the moat, telling them to give thanks to God and Saint Thomas. After a little while, Roger began to move his right arm ever so slightly, causing the coroners to halt their investigation. They returned the boy to his mother, who was nearly out of her mind with worry—until that time she had had to be physically restrained by her neighbors from throwing herself into the ditch alongside her beloved son. The tearful mother held his naked body to her warm flesh and huddled next to the fire, and eventually more signs of life began to return to the boy's body. Around the hour of prime, they brought two-year-old Roger to the church to celebrate the miracle of his return to the living. As one witness tells it, it was a joyous occasion: at least two hundred villagers, as well as the coroners, the inquest jury, the constable, and the local clergy joined the procession to the church, all gratefully singing *Te Deum Laudamus*.[2]

Because of its successful conclusion, record of this inquest never made it into the coroners' rolls. Nonetheless, this miracle story clarifies just how human was the process of death investigation. Coroners were not universally corrupt, money-grubbing crown officials intent only on exploiting the local population. These coroners were diligent and hard working. They arrived at once after the discovery of the body, duly accompanied by a clerk to record their findings, and multiple witnesses testified that they followed proper procedure. The physical examination adhered to the requirements articulated in the statutes. The decision-making process was highly democratic: coroners and jurors removed from the scene of death together to deliberate on the nature of their findings from the post-mortem examination. Presumably, they were discussing the next step in the investigative process—who best to interview in order to discover exactly how the toddler found himself alone on a dark bridge, naked, late at night. This was also a communal event. Neighbors comforted the distraught mother; one of the jurors agreed to serve only because the boy's mother asked him to; another neighbor prayed for intercession to Saint Thomas on the boy's behalf; up to two hundred villagers participated in the final procession of celebration; and many of those same villagers were also present as spectators at the moat during the inquest. The miracle story discloses also that the villagers were aware of the rules of death investigation, and (with one, well-intentioned exception) they consciously kept back so that the coroners and their jury might perform their work uninterrupted. The humanity of the coroners is revealed particularly in the conclusion: upon discovering that the boy was, in fact, alive, they did not pack up and go home, grumbling at a lost opportunity to blackmail the parents into paying for a child's burial. Rather, they joined the procession, joyfully singing their thanks to God for the miraculous recovery of one of the village's youngest members.

The resuscitation of two-year-old Roger acts as a useful corrective to scholarly perceptions of medieval death investigation; the miracle story also echoes many of the findings of this study. There are no grounds to believe that corruption ran rampant among the medieval coroners; that they had little incentive to work other than graft; or that without a regular salary (also a disputed point), a rainy day was enough to discourage them from carrying out their jobs. Nor is there any reason to believe that all they cared about was the king's profits: indeed, the statutes and the legal treatises themselves give the opposite impression. The crown focused on the needs of an effective investigation, but certainly not at the expense of profit. Rather, efficient investigation produces sound profits. None of this should come as a surprise. Keeping peace in the kingdom was one of the central duties of the king, and effective law enforcement is an essential facet of that agenda. The seriousness with which the legal tradition approached death investigation is confirmed by the attention to detail in terms of process. Segregating witnesses, examining the body for ligature marks and other signs of attack, tracking the perpetrator's movements leading up to the homicide, questioning family and neighbors about an assault victim's willingness to follow medical advice—all of these directives substantiate an earnest desire to see justice served. The records themselves paint much the same picture. Scene integrity was guaranteed by crown prohibition. The king forbade anyone from touching or moving the body of the dead, and men and women all across England obeyed this ruling, even when it meant tolerating the stench of a decomposing corpse, or returning a body to the scene of the attack when the victim was not yet dead. Coroners headed legitimate investigations into deaths of all forms. Even though the English rejected the European model of post-mortem dissection, crown requirements to measure the width, length, and depth of injuries ensured a thorough and fruitful physical examination. Coroners and their juries spent copious amounts of time interviewing witnesses (even if the records do not always clearly show it), collecting material evidence, and testing that proof against the evidence of the body itself. Coroners and their juries used all the resources available to them: indeed, one ambitious coroner even arranged a medieval version of a police line-up. And when they hit a wall in their investigations, it was not unusual for coroners and/or juries to argue in favor of new investigative strategies, or at the very least, more time to uncover evidence before drawing their conclusions. Coroners may not always have adhered to the democratic ideals of death investigation boldly proclaimed in the surviving London coroner's oath. Certainly, due diligence may sometimes have been lacking when the cause of death seemed obvious. Yet, in general, there is little reason to believe that medieval death investigation was typically anything less than thorough and efficient according to the standards of the day.

Of course, the quality of any investigation relies heavily on the personnel who carry it out. Not only were coroners *not* unanimously corrupt, but more often than not they were qualified (in terms of experience, if not land holdings) and eager to hold office (indeed, to die in office). Coroners regularly hailed from families deeply entrenched in the world of law enforcement. Moreover, the coronership was usually the last in a long string of offices: many coroners were ex-sheriffs or ex-bailiffs (sometimes even ex-mayors). They knew exactly what was expected of them and how to go about fulfilling the needs of the office. Of course, coroners only headed up the investigation; inquest jurors performed most of the heavy lifting. Being an inquest juror was a position of authority in medieval England. Those who served often were drawn from the upper middling ranks, men who hoped to guide the morality of their communities and who saw the office as an opportunity to enhance their social credit by taking charge in a moment of crisis. Nevertheless, coroners did not allow the prestige of jury service to undermine the value of the investigation. Inquest juries also included men who knew best the circumstances surrounding a death: friends, family, co-workers, neighbors, even parish clergy, whose knowledge of the local underworld was unparalleled, and whose background in terms of medicine and literacy were beneficial to the investigation. In the same vein, when a coroner believed medical expertise might shine valuable light on a death, he made certain to enlist the services of a medical practitioner.

The presence of medical practitioners on inquest juries is a vital discovery, but again, it should not come as a surprise. Both before and after the later medieval period, the courts sought the counsel of medical men in cases of assault, mayhem, and homicide. Why should the later medieval period have been an exception to this rule? Moreover, the medieval English were well aware of the role medical practitioners played in legal medicine on the Continent. While they disparaged the Continental approach to paying physicians for their work (seeing that compensation for labor jeopardized their impartiality), they nonetheless must have appreciated the value of their expertise. England's own clerical judges, who often did double-duty as royal justices, were trained in canon law, which advocated summoning medical men as witnesses when the situation necessitated anatomical proficiency. More important still: none of this takes into account the context of an assault. The crown mandated the victim of an assault participate in the view of wounds. The purpose of this procedure was twofold. The view was a useful step to determine compensation in the event of future litigation for wounding or mayhem; it was also a necessary process for the local authorities to determine whether they had an impending homicide investigation on their hands. Because of the need for a prognosis and emergency medical assistance, medical practitioners were often already involved in an investigation long before the coroner even arrived.

If this is the case, why has it taken historians so long to recognize that medical men played a part in medieval death investigation? Foremost, the records typically make no mention of it. The purpose of the records was chiefly financial: to record what was owed to the king, and to clarify that due process was followed. Consequently, there was no need for the coroner to record every step he and his jurors took in the process of investigation. That any coroner bothered to include more than the statutes required him to document must be greeted as a windfall, rather than an opportunity to disparage the medieval coroner. A laissez-faire approach to the jury lists exacerbates this problem: yet, even if bailiffs had meticulously recorded the full names and occupations of each potential juror, we would not necessarily be much further ahead. The ubiquitous plurality of vocations in medieval England prevents us from discovering whether a chandler was also an apothecary, whether a blacksmith was also a surgeon. The London coroners' inquests demonstrate that in an ideal situation, medical professionals (that is, physicians, surgeons, and barbers) served on 38% of inquests. Yet, the uncertainty perpetuated by occupational plurality and the general dissemination of domestic medicine strongly supports the hypothesis that this figure is a vast underestimate of the reality of medical practitioners and their involvement in death investigation.

From a modern perspective, it is hard to shake the deep-rooted belief that a medical practitioner should have been involved in every inquest. In the modern West, we have medicalized death to the point where only a physician is capable of pronouncing death. While certainly physicians were better equipped to do so, in medieval England it was not their responsibility to do so. And, in many instances (some deaths by misadventure, for example), local authorities may have believed the cause of death was so obvious, it did not warrant the time and energies of a medical professional who likely had better things to do. Granted, when coroners did empanel medical men on juries, they typically chose barbers—a group of men who were highly civic minded and by far the most qualified to offer medical expertise because of their hands-on approach to the discipline.

One reason to stack an inquest jury with men of local authority and high social standing was that jury service called for confident men capable of making decisions with weighty implications for their home communities. The crown left communities largely to their own discretion to interpret statute requirements: investigation into unnatural death makes this abundantly clear. While the crown was pleased to collect fines for a failure to report a death, nowhere did it define what it meant by unnatural death, constructing a reactive system of justice that awarded tremendous power to the locality. Yet, even determining when to summon the coroner was a judgment with potentially explosive political ramifications. An inquest transformed death into a spectacle: undoubtedly, the family and friends of the dead (if a suicide, or afflicted with a stigmatized disease) may have advocated in favor of a quiet burial, contrary to crown expectations or communal needs. Far from being mere "judges of fact," inquest jurors had to negotiate the needs of the community alongside those of the law and the crown in order to produce a just judgment. Thus, the nature of the medieval inquest called for jurors to don many hats: figuratively, they were detectives, witnesses, lawyers for the defense and the prosecution, local representatives, neighbors, friends, and doctors all at once.

The complexities of the medical side of the coroner's inquest, especially, produced some of the greatest challenges. Determining cause of death commonly involved assessing the severity of an injury to discern whether it was, indeed, life threatening, and hence a causal connection existed between assault and homicide. This challenge was magnified when the victim of an assault was pregnant. Jurors had to calculate exactly how much force was necessary to produce a miscarriage. Despite the seeming impossibility of drawing such a conclusion in the absence of modern technologies, medieval jurors crafted a useful methodology evident in their enrollments. They looked for specific indicators in order to discern any link between assault and abortion: bodily injuries on the woman and the fetus, the length of time between events, the woman's behavior after the assault. While jurors might have benefitted from regular solicitation of the counsel of midwives, at the very least their approach was systematic and rational. The same can be said for their procedure in addressing the crimes of the mentally ill. The legal tradition categorized the mentally disabled by the onset and duration of the illness: not only were jurors fully aware of the legal classification, but the coroners' rolls took all of it a step further, foreshadowing later developments such as the Trial of Lunatics Act or the Guilty but Mentally Ill verdict by recognizing that only some mentally ill should indeed be excused from their actions.

This study highlights the many similarities between the modern and medieval approaches to death investigation. Yet, it is critical to acknowledge that some elements were distinctly medieval and speak to their understanding of how best to achieve a just verdict. To offer some examples: a) although officially prohibited, in practice the medieval English tolerated overlaps between indicting and trial juries; b) law enforcement officials regularly served on trial juries, even when trying defendants whom they themselves had indicted; c) jurors were sometimes related to the victim or to the accused felon; and d) often jurors were related to each other. While any one of these practices would today lead to a mistrial, for the medieval period it is evidence of a determination to see justice served. Medieval jurors, not paid lawyers or police, bore the weight of the investigative process: if they had shared in the modern valorization of impartiality, there is little hope that any felon would ever have been convicted. In many respects, all of this is a testament to the power of local agency.

Perhaps the greatest distinction between medieval and modern lies in the documentation itself. Today, we compulsively record every aspect of an investigation; the medieval coroners, with fewer resources at their disposal, were far more concerned about completing the investigation than they were about keeping detailed records. Not only were the records primarily financial in nature, but in all likelihood, the coroner viewed the official record as primarily a mnemonic device, to prompt his memory in court. Moreover, the enrollment itself was not a systematic record of the investigation; it was a narrative account of a death or homicide—and the historian needs to look deeply and comparatively to ferret out the investigation behind the narrative.

Death investigation in medieval England required jurors, a minority of whom were also medical practitioners (usually barbers), to journey repeatedly into the world of medicine. Inquest records thus are an ideal source for the study of medicine on the ground, broadening the scope of a discipline that relies principally on the works of elite practitioners, wholly unrepresentative of the larger field, and whose academic works were becoming progressively more obscure and jargon ridden. Coroners and jurors exhibited a solid understanding of contemporary theories of disease transmission, and the range of disease names included in the documentation implies that many jurors endeavored to identify the nature of the disease involved, even if theoretically this task was outside the scope of crown expectations. This populist medical perspective is capable of providing an alternative medical discourse and a fresh understanding of contemporary medical practices. To offer some examples: when medieval men and women employed the term "epilepsy," it was not a catch-all phrase for sudden death; rather they were referring to epilepsy, or at the very least, a disease of a long-standing nature with a history of seizures. Along the same lines, when the average medieval man or woman referred to pestilence, they did indeed mean bubonic plague, and not just any fatal disease. The coroners' rolls are capable also of highlighting distinctions between theory and practice: while humoral theory advocated curettage as a necessary practice to eliminate corrupt humors and restore bodily balance, in practice the English suspected that releasing those humors meant instant death for the patient. Inquest records are particularly illuminating with respect to the elderly. Not only do they remind us that some hardy individuals lived a very long time, but they suggest that senescence did not necessarily usher in destitution and marginalization.

Because of the prohibitive costs of medicine, it has often been assumed that only the upper ranks enlisted the services of a medical professional, while the majority of the English population relied chiefly on the benevolence of local saints, women, priests, and healers. The coroners' rolls substantiate that medicine was primarily domestic in nature, yet, it helps us to understand the circumstances in which professional help was deemed necessary. English men and women called in a professional for preventative medicine (bloodletting) and when a condition or injury was life threatening. While phlebotomists might travel in search of customers, in general, the services of a medical profession were available only in urban environments; however, the distance did not necessarily discourage the ill or injured from making a potentially life-saving journey. Perhaps the most striking observation is that when medical intervention failed to save a patient's life, the law was on the side of the practitioner, not the patient. All of this insight reminds us of the value of legal sources for the history of medicine: although the two disciplines have normally coexisted with little cross-over, the results of this study imply that cooperation between the fields promises to teach us much about medicine in practice.

NOTES

1. See Ronald C. Finucane, "The Toddler in the Ditch: A Case of Parental Neglect?" in *Voices from the Bench: The Narratives of Lesser Folk in Medieval Trials*, ed. Michael Goodich (New York: Palgrave Macmillan, 2006), p. 129. Finucane has looked at the original documents in the Vatican Library, rather than relying on the *Acta Sanctorum*'s transcription. This case is also discussed in Valerie I.J. Flint, "The Saint and the Operation of the Law: Reflections upon the Miracles of St Thomas Cantilupe," in *Belief and Culture in the Middle Ages: Studies Presented to Henry Mayr-Harting*, ed. Richard Gameson and Henrietta Leyser (Oxford: Oxford UP, 2001), pp. 342–57.
2. *AS*, pp. 626–28. The file includes depositions from a number of witnesses, and their stories are not entirely consistent. For the sake of consistency, most of this summary is drawn from the testimony of Simon of Watford.

Glossary

Abjuration of the Realm An oath taken by an accused felon in sanctuary before the coroner, swearing to leave the realm and never return without the king's permission.

Amercement A fine.

Appeal A private accusation.

Approver A confessed felon who "turned king's evidence" and appealed his former criminal accomplices in the hopes of evading his own execution.

Assize Visitation of royal justices of the shires to adjudicate in civil and criminal matters.

Attach To arrest and secure future appearance in court by means of pledges.

Bane A weapon used to commit homicide; forfeit to the king.

Chattels Personal possessions.

Common Bench Also, Court of Common Pleas. Resident at Westminster, this common law court addressed "common pleas," private pleas between two subjects (that is, civil suits).

Coroner's Inquest The proceedings through which the coroner and his jury investigate any sudden or unnatural death.

County Court Also, shire court. Communal court presided by the sheriff, addressing both civil suits and trespasses. Coroners were often chosen at these courts.

Crown Pleas All criminal actions or proceedings.

Deodand An object or animal forfeit to the king because a coroner's inquest jury found it had caused a person's death.

Distraint Seizure of a person's property in order to compel payment of an outstanding debt.

Englishry See *murdrum fine*.

Escheator A crown official responsible for "escheats," that is, lands and goods forfeit to the king.

Eyre An itinerant court presided by a justice in eyre (a judge) who rode in circuit from county to county.

Felo De Se A verdict of "felony of self," that is, suicide.

Felony A serious crime punishable by death. At this time, felony included: homicide, robbery, larceny, rape (at times), arson, and escape from prison.

First Finder The individual who discovered a corpse that later became the subject of an inquest.

Freehold An estate for life or in fee.

Gaol (Jail) Delivery The trial of prisoners held in jail upon felony charges.

General Eyre The periodic visitation of the counties by royal justices empowered to hear all pleas, both civil and criminal.

Grand Jury A jury of presentment.

Halmote A manorial court.

Hue And Cry A loud outcry meant to signal the pursuit of a felon.

Hundred A subdivision of the county, possessing its own court. Formerly, a hundred represented a unit of land large enough to support a hundred peasant families.

Indictment A formal, written accusation of a crime produced by a coroner's inquest, at a sheriff's tourn, or by a jury of presentment at sessions of the peace.

Inquisition Post-Mortem Following the death of a tenant-in-chief, a formal query executed by the escheator to establish the next heir, as well as the extent of the lands held.

Inquisitorial Justice A system of justice in which the court, or representatives of the court, are actively involved in investigating the facts of the case.

Justice Of The Peace Members of the local gentry commissioned by the king to administer justice within their county. Their competency varied with their commission.

King's Bench An itinerant court that followed the king, although most often it sat at Westminster. King's Bench was divided into two parts: the crown side had unlimited criminal jurisdiction. The plea side addressed actions of trespass, appeals of felony, and writs of error. King's Bench acted as England's superior court, capable of addressing cases removed from local inferior courts.

Leet Court A manorial court that exercised view of frankpledge in quasi-criminal matters.

Mainpernor/Mainprise A surety pledged to be responsible for an individual's future appearance in court, or for that individual's future good behavior. Also, manucaption.

Mayhem An injury that permanently incapacitated the victim of an assault from fighting.

Misadventure An accidental death.

Misdemeanor A criminal offense of a lesser nature than felony, usually punishable by fine.

Mortuary Fee The ecclesiastical version of the heriot. A customary gift claimed by and due to the parish priest upon the death of one of his parishioners.

***Murdrum* Fine** A fine paid by the hundred when its representatives were not able to prove that a victim of homicide was of English descent.

Nisi Prius A commission empowering justices to hear civil cases in the locality rather than at Westminster.

Non Compos Mentis Not of sound mind and thus not legally responsible for one's actions.

Ordeal Also, *judicium Dei*. A test to determine one's innocence or guilt by calling for divine judgment.

Outlawry Repeated failure to appear in court to answer a charge of felony led to the accused being ousted from the protections of the law.

Oyer And Terminer A commission empowering justices of assize to "hear and determine" certain cases relating to the requested commission.

Partible Inheritance An inheritance pattern in which all the sons share in the inheritance of their father's estate.

Peine Forte Et Dure Physical duress imposed on an accused felon who refused to submit himself to jury trial.

Petty Jury Trial jury.

Presentment The written record of a presenting jury's formal accusation concerning a crime.

Primogeniture An inheritance pattern in which the eldest son inherits his father's estate.

Recognizance An obligation of record entered before a court containing a promise to perform a particular act, such as the repayment of a debt or reappearance in court.

Sanctuary A church or sacred space with the right to grant immunity from arrest for an accused felon for up to forty days.

Scrivener A scribe with expertise in court hand.

Sheriff's Tourn A court held twice a year at the sheriff's behest within a hundred. The proceedings are called the "view of frankpledge."

Surety A person who undertakes the responsibility of ensuring the performance of another's good behavior or future appearance in court by promising to surrender a payment of debt in the event of a failure to do so.

Tithing A group of ten men bound together by a mutual vow to ensure each others' good behavior, and to present offences at the Sheriff's Tourn.

Tithingman The head of the tithing.

Trailbaston A commission empowering justices of assize to hear and determine cases involving violence, breaches of peace, and/or abuses of legal procedure.

Treasure Trove Any gold, silver, or bullion buried and then rediscovered, which appeared to be without an owner.

Trespass A wrong committed against person or property.

Unfree See *villein*.

Verderer A judicial officer assigned to a royal forest.

View Of Frankpledge The proceedings of the Sheriff's Tourn.

Vill Village or township.

Villein An unfree tenant, "tied to the land." Villeins did not own the land they farmed, but they were allowed to reside there in exchange for labor services and taxes paid to their lords.

Visne Neighborhood or vicinity.

Waivery The female equivalent of outlawry.

Wergeld Body-price in Anglo-Saxon law.

Wreck Of The Sea Goods washed ashore from a shipwreck and not claimed by the owner within a year's time.

Bibliography

MANUSCRIPT SOURCES: THE NATIONAL ARCHIVES, PUBLIC RECORD OFFICE (SURREY, UK)

CHES 18/1: Palatinate of Chester, Coroners' Inquisitions Files (1339–1714)
JUST 1/689 and 692: includes Nottinghamshire Coroners' Rolls (1380–1389; 1347–1349)
JUST 2: Coroners' Rolls and Files, with Cognate Documents (1228–1426)
KB 9: Court of King's Bench, Crown Side (various dates)
SC 8: Ancient Petitions (various dates)

PRINTED PRIMARY SOURCES

Acta Sanctorum, Tomus Octobris I. Antwerp: Petrum Joannem Vander Plassche, 1765.
Anon. *The Boke of Justices of Peas* (1506). London: Professional Books Limited, 1972.
Bateson, Mary, ed. *Records of the Borough of Leicester.* 3 vols. London: Clay & Sons, 1899–1905.
Benedict of Peterborough. *Miracula Sancti Thomae Cantuariensis.* In *Materials for the History of Thomas Becket.* Ed. James Craigie Robertson. Rolls Series, no. 67, v. 2, 1876.
Blancus, Antonius. *Tractatus de Indiciis Homicidii.* Venice: Lugduni Beringi, 1547.
Boatwright, Lesley, ed. *Inquests and Indictments from Late Fourteenth Century Buckinghamshire.* Buckinghamshire Archaeological Society, v. 29, 1994.
Bolland, William Craddock, ed. *Year Books of Edward II*, v. 5. *SS*, v. 24, 1910.
Bowker, M., ed. *An Episcopal Court Book for the Diocese of Lincoln 1514–1520.* Lincoln Record Society, v. 61, 1967.
Bracton, Henri de. *De Legibus et Consuetudinibus Angliae*, ed. George Woodbine, ed. and trans. Samuel E. Thorne, 4 vols. *SS*, 1968–1976.
Brown, William, and A. Hamilton Thompson, eds. *The Register of William Greenfield Lord Archbishop of York 1306–1315*, 4 vols. Surtees Society, 1931–1940.
Calendar of Close Rolls, 1273–1485. 45 vols. London: HMSO, 1911–1963.
Calendar of Inquisitions Miscellaneous, 1216–1422. 7 vols. London: HMSO, 1916–1969.
Calendar of Inquisitions Post Mortem. 26 vols. London: HMSO, 1898–2009.
Calendar of Patent Rolls, 1216–1509. 55 vols. London: HMSO, 1891–1916.
Cam, Helen M., ed. *Year Books of Edward II*, v. 26, pt. 2. *SS*, v. 86, 1969.
Chew, Helena M., and Martin Weinbaum, eds. *The London Eyre of 1244.* London: London Record Society, 1970.

Collins, Francis, ed. *Register of the Freemen of the City of York*, v. 1. Surtees Society, v. 96, 1897.

A Descriptive Catalogue of Ancient Deeds. London: HMSO, 1894.

Drinkwater, Rev. C.H., ed. "Records of Proceedings before the Coroners of Salop (temp. Edward I, 1295 to 1306." *Shropshire Archaeological & Natural History Society*, 3rd ser., 5 (1905): 149–87.

Durandus, Guillelmus. *Speculum iuris*. Venice: 1576.

Everett, Nicholas, ed. *The Alphabet of Galen: Pharmacy from Antiquity to the Middle Ages*. Toronto: University of Toronto Press, 2012.

Farr, William. *Vital Statistics: A Memorial Volume from the Reports and Writings of William Farr.* New York: New York Academy of Medicine, 1975.

Fenwick, Carolyn C., ed. *The Poll Taxes of 1377, 1379, and 1381: Part 3: Wiltshire-Yorkshire*. Oxford: Oxford UP for the British Academy, 2005.

Fitzherbert, Anthony. *La Graunde Abridgement*. London: John Rastell and Wynkyn de Worde, 1516.

Fortescue, John. *De Laudibus Legum Angliae*, ed. S.B. Chrimes. 2nd ed. Cambridge: Cambridge UP, 2011.

Fraser, Russell A., and Norman Rabkin, eds. *Drama of the English Renaissance, I: The Tudor Period*. New York: Macmillan, 1976.

Gailbraith, V.H., ed. *The Anonimalle Chronicle, 1333 to 1381: From a Ms. Written at St Mary's Abbey, York*. Manchester: Manchester UP, 1927.

Getz, Faye, ed. *Healing and Society in Medieval England: A Middle English Translation of the Pharmaceutical Writings of Gilbertus Anglicus*. Madison: University of Wisconsin Press, 1991.

Given-Wilson, C. *et al.*, eds. *Parliament Rolls of Medieval England*. 16 vols. Woodbridge: Boydell Press, 2005.

Gross, Charles, ed. *Select Cases from the Coroners' Rolls 1265–1413, with a Brief Account of the History of the Office of the Coroner. SS*, v. 9, 1896.

Hale, Matthew. *History of the Pleas of the Crown: Concerning the Coroner and His Court, and His Authority in the Pleas of the Crown*. London: T. Payne, 1800.

Hall, G.D.G., ed. *The Treatise on the Laws and Customs of the Realm of England Commonly Called Glanvill*. Oxford: Clarendon Press, 1993.

Halsall, Paul, ed. "Twelfth Ecumenical Council: Lateran IV." *Internet History Sourcebook*. New York: Fordham University, 1996, www.fordham.edu/halsall/basis/lateran4.asp. Accessed Apr. 3, 2013.

Harris, Mary Dormer, ed. *The Coventry Leet Book: Or Mayor's Register: Containing the Records of the City Court Leet or View of Frankpledge, A.D. 1420–1555, with Divers other Matters*. 2 parts. London: Kegan Paul, Trench, Trübner, Co., Ltd., 1908.

Hatto, A.T., trans. *The Nibelungenlied*. London: Penguin, 1965; rev. 1969.

Hershey, Andrew H., ed. *The 1258–9 Special Eyre of Surrey and Kent*. Surrey Record Society, v. 38, 2004.

Hildegard of Bingen. *On Natural Philosophy and Medicine: Selections from Cause and Cure*. Cambridge: D.S. Brewer, 1999.

Hudson, William, and John C. Tingey, eds. *The Records of the City of Norwich*. 2 vols. Norwich: Jarrold & Sons, 1906–1910.

Hunnisett, R.F., ed. *Bedfordshire Coroners' Rolls*. Bedfordshire Historical Record Society, v. 61, 1960.

Jeayes, Isaac Herbert, ed. *Court Rolls of the Borough of Colchester*. 3 vols. Colchester: Town Council of the Borough of Colchester, 1921–1941.

Jennings, Abraham. *Digit Dei, Or an Horrid Murther Strangely Detected*. London, 1664.

Jervis, John. *The Office and Duties of Coroners*. 9th ed. London: Sweet & Maxwell, 1957.

Kaye, J.M., ed. *Placita Corone, or La Corone Pledee Devant Justices. SS*, supplementary series, v. 4, 1966.

Kibler, William W., ed. *Arthurian Romances*. London: Penguin, 1991; rev. 2004.

Libarius, Andreas, of Halle. *De Cruentatione Cadaverum*. Magdeburg: Hendel, 1594.

List of Sheriffs for England and Wales from the Earliest Times to A.D. 1831, Compiled from Documents in the Public Record Office. London: HMSO, 1898; repr. New York: Kraus, 1963.

Lyndwood, William. *Provinciale (seu Constitutiones Angliae)*. Oxford: H. Hall, 1679.

Maitland, F.W., ed. *Pleas of the Crown for the County of Gloucester*. London: Macmillan, 1884.

———, and W.J. Whittaker, eds. *The Mirror of Justices. SS*, v. 7, 1893.

Martin, Charles Trice, ed., *Registrum Epistolarum Fratris Johannis Peckham Archiepiscopi Cantuariensis*. Princeton: Princeton UP, 1885.

Nichols, F.M., ed. *Britton: The French Text Revised with an English Translation*. 2 vols. Oxford: Clarendon Press, 1865.

———, ed. "Original Documents Illustrative of the Administration of Criminal Law at the Time of Edward I." *Archaeologia* 40.1 (1866): 89–105.

Noorthouck, John. *A New History of London: Including Westminster and Southwark*. London: R. Baldwin, 1773.

Oliver, Lisi, ed. *The Beginnings of English Law*. Toronto and Buffalo: University of Toronto Press, 2002.

Owen, D., ed. *The Making of King's Lynn*. Records of Social and Economic History, n.s., v. 9, 1984.

Plucknett, T.F.T., and J.L. Barton, eds. *St. German's Doctor and Student. SS*, v. 91, 1974.

Rastell, John. *An Exposition of Certain Difficult and Obscure Words and Terms of the Laws of this Realm*. London: John Russell, 1579; repr. Clark, NJ: Lawbook Exchange, 2003.

Records of the Borough of Nottingham. 3 vols. London: Quaritch, 1882–1885.

Richardson, H.G., and G.O. Sayles, eds. *Fleta. SS*, vols. 72, 89, 99, 1953–1983.

Riley, H.T., ed. *Liber Albus: The White Book of the City of London*. London: Richard Griffith & Co., 1861.

———, ed. *Chronicles of the Mayors and Sheriffs of London: 1188–1274*. London: Trübner, 1863.

———, ed. *Memorials of London and London Life: In the 13*th, *14th and 15th Centuries*. London: Longmans, 1868.

Rogers, J.E., ed. *Oxford City Documents, 1268–1665*. Oxford Historical Society, v. 18, 1891.

Salter, H.E., ed. *Records of Mediaeval Oxford: Coroners' Inquests, the Walls of Oxford, etc*. Oxford: Oxford Chronicle Co., Ltd., 1912.

———, ed. *Snappe's Formulary and Other Records*. Oxford Historical Society, v. 80, 1924.

Schroeder, H.J., ed. *Disciplinary Decrees of the General Councils: Text, Translation and Commentary*. St. Louis: B. Herder, 1937.

Scott, Walter. *The Fair Maid of Perth*, ed. Andrew Hook and Donald MacKenzie. Edinburgh: Edinburgh UP, 1999.

Shakespeare, William. *Richard III*, ed. David Bevington. New York: Bantam Books, 1951; rev. 1980.

Sharpe, Reginald R., ed. *Calendar of Letter-Books of the City of London, A-L (1275–1497)*. 11 vols. London: John Edward Francis, 1899–1912.

———, ed. *Calendar of Coroners' Rolls of the City of London, A.D. 1300–1378*. London: R. Clay & Sons, Limited, 1913.

Shatzmiller, Joseph, ed. *Médecine et Justice en Provence Médiévale: Documents de Manosque, 1262–1348*. Aix-en-Provence: Publications de l'Université de Provence, 1989.

Statutes of the Realm, ed. A. Luders, *et al*. London: Record Commission, 1810–1827.

Stubbs, William, ed. *Chronicles of the Reigns of Edward I and Edward II: Annales londonienses and Annales paulini edited from mss. in the British Museum and in the Archiepiscopal Library at Lambeth*. London: Longman, 1882.

———, ed. *Select Charters and Other Illustrations of English Constitutional History*. 8th ed. Oxford: Clarendon Press, 1900.

Sutherland, Donald W., ed. *The Eyre of Northamptonshire, 3–4 Edward III (1329–30)*. *SS*, v. 97, 1983.

Thomas, A.H., ed. *Calendar of Early Mayor's Court Rolls of the City of London. A.D. 1298–1307*. Cambridge: Cambridge UP, 1924.

———, ed. *Calendar of Plea and Memoranda Rolls, Preserved among the Archives of the Corporation of the City of London at the Guildhall, Rolls A1a–A9, A.D. 1323–1364*. Cambridge: Cambridge UP, 1926.

———, ed. *Calendar of Plea and Memoranda Rolls of the City of London, 1413–1437*. Cambridge: Cambridge UP, 1943.

Thompson, Edward M., ed. *Chronicon Galfridi le Baker de Swynebroke*. Oxford: Clarendon Press, 1899.

Tobin, Frank, Kim Vivian, and Richard H. Lawson, eds. *Arthurian Romances, Tales and Lyric Poetry: The Complete Works of Hartmann Von Aue*. Philadelphia: Pennsylvania State UP, 2001.

Umfreville, Edward. *Lex Coronatoria*. London: R. Griffiths, 1761.

Vicary, Thomas. *The Anatomie of the Bodie of Man*, pt. 1. London: Early English Texts Society, 1888.

Wallis, Faith, ed. *Medieval Medicine: A Reader*. Toronto: University of Toronto Press, 2010.

Weinbaum, Martin, ed. *The London Eyre of 1276*. London: London Record Society, 1976.

Wenzel, Siegfried, ed. *Fasciculus Morum: A Fourteenth-Century Preacher's Handbook*. University Park: Pennsylvania State UP, 1989.

Wilkins, David, ed. *Concilia Magnae Brittaniae et Hiberniae*, v. 1. London: R. Gosling, 1734.

Woolgar, C.M., ed. "A Lincolnshire Coroner's Roll." *Lincolnshire History and Archaeology* 16 (1981): 13–17.

Year Books. 11 vols. London: George Sawbridge, William Rawlins, Samuel Roycroft, 1679–1680.

SECONDARY SOURCES

Accardo, Pasquale. "Dante and Medicine: The Circle of Malpractice." *Southern Medical Journal* 82.5 (1989): 624–28.

Alter, George C., and Ann G. Carmichael. "Classifying the Dead: Towards a History of the Registration of Causes of Death." *JHMAS* 54 (1999): 114–32.

Arnold, Morris S. "Law and Fact in the Medieval Jury Trial: Out of Sight, Out of Mind." *AJLH* 18.4 (1974): 267–80.

Arrizabalaga, Jon. "Medical Causes of Death in Preindustrial Europe: Some Historiographical Considerations." *JHMAS* 54 (1999): 241–60.

———. "Problematizing Retrospective Diagnosis in the History of Disease." *Asclepio* 54.1 (2002): 51–70.

Baldó, Julia. "Quonstituido en Estrema Vejez: Old Age and Life Expectancy in Late Medieval Navarre." *Imago Temporis: Medium Aevum* 2 (2008): 191–225.

Bandy, Stephen C. "Cain, Grendel, and the Giants of *Beowulf*." *Papers on Language and Literature* 9 (1973): 235–49.

Barber, Eric. "Judicial Discretion, Sentencing Guidelines and Lessons from Medieval England, 1066–1215." *Western New England Law Review* 27.1 (2005): 1–40.

Bardsley, Sandy. "Sin, Speech, and Scolding in Late Medieval England." In *Fama: The Politics of Talk and Reputation in Medieval Europe*, ed. Thelma Fenster and Daniel Lord Smail. Ithaca: Cornell UP, 2003, pp. 145–64.

Bartlett, Robert. *Trial by Fire and Water: The Medieval Judicial Ordeal.* Oxford: Clarendon Press, 1986.

Barton, J.L. *Roman Law in England.* Mediolani: Giuffrè, 1971.

———. "The Authorship of *Bracton*: Again." *JLH* 30.2 (2009): 117–74.

Bassett, William W. "Canon Law and the Common Law." *Hastings Law Journal* 29 (1977–1978): 1383–1420.

Bean, J.M.W. "Plague, Population and Economic Decline in England in the Later Middle Ages." *EHR*, n.s., 15.3 (1963): 423–37.

Beck, R. Theodore. *The Cutting Edge: Early History of the Surgeons of London.* London: Lund Humphries, 1974.

Behlmer, George K. "Grave Doubts: Victorian Medicine, Moral Panic, and the Signs of Death." *JBS* 42.2 (2003): 206–35.

Bellamy, J.G. *Crime and Public Order in England in the Later Middle Ages.* London: Routledge & Kegan Paul, 1972.

———. *The Criminal Trial in Later Medieval England: Felony before the Courts from Edward I to the Sixteenth Century.* Toronto and Buffalo: University of Toronto Press, 1998.

Benedictow, Ole J. *What Disease Was Plague? On the Controversy over the Microbiological Identity of Plague Epidemics of the Past.* Leiden: Brill, 2010.

Bennett, Judith M. "Writing Fornication: Medieval *Leyrwite* and Its Historians." *Transactions of the Royal Historical Society*, 6th ser., 13 (2003): 131–62.

———. "Compulsory Service in Late Medieval England." *P&P* 209.1 (2010): 7–51.

Bildhauer, Bettina. "Blood in Medieval Cultures." *History Compass* 4 (2006): 1–11.

Bishop, Louise. *Words, Stones, and Herbs: The Healing Word in Medieval and Early Modern England.* Syracuse: Syracuse UP, 2007.

Blanshei, Sarah Rubin. "Crime and Law Enforcement in Medieval Bologna." *Journal of Social History* 16.1 (1982): 121–38.

Blockmans, W.P. "The Social and Economic Effects of Plague in the Low Countries: 1349–1500." *Revue Belge de Philogie et d'Histoire* 58.4 (1980): 833–63.

Blomefield, Francis. *An Essay towards a Topographical History of the County of Norfolk.* London: William Miller, 1806.

Bloor, Michael. "A Minor Office: The Variable and Socially Constructed Character of Death Certification in a Scottish City." *Journal of Health and Social Behavior* 32 (1991): 273–87.

Boureau, Alain. "La Preuve par le Cadavre qui Saigne au XIIIe Siècle: Entre Expérience Commune et Savoir Scolastique." *Micrologus* 7 (1999): 24–81.

Brand, Paul. "Courtroom and Schoolroom: The Education of Lawyers in England prior to 1400." *Historical Research* 60.142 (1987): 147–65.

———. "The Date and Authorship of *Bracton*: A Response." *JLH* 31.3 (2010): 217–44.

Brenner, Elma. "Recent Perspectives on Leprosy in Medieval Western Europe." *History Compass* 8.5 (2010): 388–406.

Brévart, Francis B. "Between Medicine, Magic, and Religion: Wonder Drugs in German Medico-Pharmaceutical Treatises of the Thirteenth to the Sixteenth Centuries." *Speculum* 83 (2008): 1–57.

Britnell, Richard. "Town Life." In *A Social History of England 1200–1500*, ed. Rosemary Horrox and W. Mark Ormrod. Cambridge: Cambridge UP, 2006, pp. 134–78.

Brittain, Robert P. "Cruentation in Legal Medicine and in Literature." *MH* 9.1 (1965): 82–88.
Brock, Helen and Catherine Crawford. "Forensic Medicine in Early Colonial Maryland, 1633–83." In *Legal Medicine in History*, ed. Crawford and Michael Clark. Cambridge: Cambridge UP, 1994, pp. 25–44.
Brooke, Rosalind and Christopher. *Popular Religion in the Middle Ages: Western Europe 1000–1300*. London: Thames and Hudson, 1984.
Brundage, James A. "Full and Partial Proofs in Classical Canonical Procedures." *The Jurist* 67 (2007): 58–71.
Bryson, William Hamilton. "Witnesses: A Canonist's View." *AJLH* 13.1 (1969): 57–67.
Bullough, Vern L. *Universities, Medicine, and Science in the Medieval West*. Aldershot: Ashgate, 2004.
Butler, Sara M. "A Case of Indifference? Child Murder in Later Medieval England." *Journal of Women's History* 19.4 (2004): 59–82.
———. "Abortion by Assault: Violence against Pregnant Women in Thirteenth- and Fourteenth-Century England." *Journal of Women's History* 17.4 (2005): 9–31.
———. "Degrees of Culpability: Suicide Verdicts, Mercy, and the Jury in Medieval England." *JMEMS* 36.2 (2006): 263–90.
———. "Local Concerns: Suicide and Jury Behavior in Medieval England." *History Compass* 4.5 (2006): 820–35.
———. "Women, Suicide, and the Jury in Later Medieval England." *Signs: Journal of Women in Culture and Society* 32.1 (2006): 141–66.
———. *The Language of Abuse: Marital Violence in Later Medieval England*. Leiden: Brill, 2007.
———. "Cultures of Suicide? Regionalism and Suicide Verdicts in Medieval England." *The Historian* 69.3 (2007): 427–49.
———. "Medicine on Trial: Regulating the Health Professions in Later Medieval England." *Florilegium* 28 (2011): 71–94.
———. "Discourse on the Nature of Coverture in the Later Medieval Courtroom." In *Married Women and the Law: Coverture in England and the Common Law World*, ed. K.J. Kesselring and Tim Stretton. Montreal: McGill-Queen's UP, 2013, pp. 24–44.
———. *Divorce in Medieval England: From One to Two Persons in Law*. New York: Routledge, 2013.
Bynum, Carolyn Walker. *Wonderful Blood: Theology and Practice in Late Medieval Northern Germany and Beyond*. Philadelphia: University of Pennsylvania Press, 2007.
Cairns, John W. and Grant McLeod, eds. '*The Dearest Birth Right of the People of England': The Jury in the History of the Common Law*. Oxford: Hart Pub., 2002.
Cam, Helen. *Liberties and Communities in Medieval England: Collected Studies in Local Administration and Topography*. Cambridge: Cambridge UP, 1944.
Campos-Outcalt, Doug. "Cause-of-Death Certification: Not as Easy as It Seems." *The Journal of Family Practice* 54.2 (2005): 134–38.
Carmichael, Ann. "Contagion Theory and Contagion Practice in Fifteenth-Century Milan." *Renaissance Quarterly* 44.2 (1991): 213–56.
Carter, John M. *Rape in Medieval England: An Historical and Sociological Study*. Lanham, MD: UP of America, 1985.
Cartilidge, Neil. "Alas, I go with Chylde: Representations of Extra-Marital Pregnancy in the Middle English Lyric." *English Studies* 79.2 (1998): 395–414.
Cawthon, Elisabeth. "New Life for the Deodand: Coroner's Inquests and Occupational Deaths in England, 1830–46."*AJLH* 33.2 (1989): 137–47.
Challis, Keith. "Drowned in 'A Whyrlepytte': The River Trent in the Nottinghamshire Coroners' Inquests of 1485–1558." *Transactions of the Thoroton Society of Nottinghamshire* 108 (2004): 115–23.

Chapman, C.B. "Stratton vs. Swanlond: The Fourteenth-Century Ancestor of the Law of Malpractice." *The Pharos of Alpha Omega Alpha-Honor Medical Society* 45.4 (1982): 20–24.

Chinnery, P.F. "Muscle Diseases." In *Cecil Medicine*. 24th ed., ed. L. Goldman and A.L. Shafer. Philadelphia: Saunders Elsevier, 2011, Chapter 429.

"The Changing Profile of Autopsied Deaths in the United States, 1972–2007." Atlanta, GA: National Center for Health Statistics Data Brief, 2011, www.cdc.gov/nchs/data/databriefs/db67.pdf. Accessed Nov. 27, 2012.

Citrome, Jeremy J. *The Surgeon in Medieval English Literature*. New York: Palgrave Macmillan, 2006.

Clanchy, M.T. *From Memory to Written Record: England 1066–1307*. 3rd ed. Malden, MA: John Wiley & Sons, 2013.

Clark, Elaine. "The Quest for Security in Medieval England." In *Aging and the Aged in Medieval Europe*, ed. Michael M. Sheehan. Toronto: PIMS, 1983, pp. 189–200.

Clarke, Basil F.L. *Mental Disorder in Earlier Britain: Exploratory Studies*. Cardiff: University of Wales' Press, 1975.

Cockburn, J.S. and Thomas A. Green, eds. *Twelve Good Men and True: The Criminal Trial Jury in England, 1200–1800*. Princeton: Princeton UP, 1988.

Cohen, Esther. "Law, Folklore and Animal Lore." *P&P* 110 (1986): 10–37.

———. *The Modulated Scream: Pain in Late Medieval Culture*. Chicago: University of Chicago Press, 2010.

Cohn, Samuel K., Jr. *The Black Death Transformed: Disease and Culture in Early Renaissance Europe*. London: Hodder Arnold, 2003.

Colaizzi, Janet. *Homicidal Insanity, 1800–1985*. Tuscaloosa: University of Alabama Press, 1989.

Collections for a History of Staffordshire, ser. 3. Stafford: Staffordshire History Society, 1917–1918.

Collins, Arthur. *Collins's Peerage of England: Genealogical, Biographical, and Historical*. London: F.C. & J. Rivington, Otridge & Son, 1812.

Cooper, Janet. *A History of the County of Essex: Volume 9: The Borough of Colchester*. Oxford: Institute of Historical Research, 1994.

Cosman, Madeleine P. "Medieval Medical Malpractice and Chaucer's Physician." *New York State Journal of Medicine* 72.19 (1972): 2439–44.

———. "Medieval Medical Malpractice: The Dicta and the Dockets." *Bulletin of New York Academy of Medicine* 49.1 (1973): 1–47.

———. "Medieval Practice and Peer Review in Medieval England." *Trans Sect Otolaryngol American Academy of Ophthalmol Otolaryngol* 80.3 (1975): pt. 1, 293–97.

———. "Surgical Malpractice in the Renaissance and Today." *Plastic and Reconstructive Surgery* 86.6 (1990): 1017–29.

———. "The Medieval Medical Third Party: Compulsory Consultation and Malpractice Insurance: Risk Management." *Clinical Orthopaedics and Related Research* 407 (2003): 3–10.

Courtemanche, Andrée. "The Judge, the Doctor and the Poisoner: Medical Expertise in Manosquin Judicial Rituals at the End of the Fourteenth Century." In *Medieval and Early Modern Ritual: Formalized Behavior in Europe, China, and Japan*, ed. Joëlle Rollo-Koster. Leiden: Brill, 2002, pp. 105–23.

Crawford, Catherine. "Legalizing Medicine: Early Modern Legal Systems and the Growth of Medico-legal Knowledge." In *Legal Medicine in History*, ed. Crawford and Michael Clark. Cambridge: Cambridge UP, 1994, pp. 89–116.

Creighton, Charles. *A History of Epidemics in Britain: From A.D. 664 to the Extinction of Plague*. 2 vols. Cambridge: Cambridge UP, 1891.

Crook, David. *Records of the General Eyre*. Public Record Office Handbooks, no. 20. London: PRO, 1982.

Crossley, Alan, and C.R. Elrington. *A History of the County of Oxford*. London: Oxford UP, 1939.

Cunningham, Andrew. "Identifying Disease in the Past: Cutting the Gordian Knot." *Asclepio* 54.1 (2002): 13–34

Dally, A. "*Status Lymphaticus*: Sudden Death in Children from 'Visitation of God' to Cot Death." *MH* 41.1 (1997): 70–85.

Daniell, Christopher. *Death and Burial in Medieval England 1066–1550*. London and New York: Routledge, 1997.

Dean, Trevor. *Crime in Medieval Europe 1200–1550*. Edinburgh: Longman, 2001.

Demaitre, Luke. "The Care and Extension of Old Age in Medieval Medicine." In *Aging and the Aged in Medieval Europe*, ed. Michael M. Sheehan. Toronto: PIMS, 1983, pp. 3–22.

———. "Medical Writing in Transition: Between *Ars* and *Vulgus*." *Early Science and Medicine* 3.2 (1998): 88–102.

Department for Constitutional Affairs. "Coroners Service Reform Briefing Note." February 2006, webarchive.nationalarchives.gov.uk/+/http://www.dca.gov.uk/corbur/reform_coroner_system.pdf. Accessed December 18, 2013.

De Renzi, Silvia. "Medical Expertise, Bodies, and the Law in Early Modern Courts." *Isis* 98.2 (2007): 315–22.

DeWindt, Anne Reiber. "Local Government in a Small Town: A Medieval Leet Jury and its Constituents." *Albion* 23.4 (1991): 627–54.

———, and Edwin Brezette DeWindt. *Royal Justice and the Medieval English Countryside: The Hungtindonshire Eyre of 1286, the Ramsey Abbey Banlieu Court of 1287, and the Assizes of 1287–88*. 2 parts. Toronto: PIMS, 1981.

Dinzelbacher, Peter. "Animal Trials: A Multidisciplinary Approach." *Journal of Interdisciplinary History* 32.3 (2003): 405–21.

Dobson, R.B. "Admission to the Freedom of the City of York in the Later Middle Ages." *EHR* 26.1 (1973): 1–22.

Donahue, Charles, Jr. "Female Plaintiffs in Marriage Cases in the Court of York in the Later Middle Ages: What Can We Learn from the Numbers?" In *Wife and Widow in Medieval England*, ed. Sue Sheridan Walker. Ann Arbor: University of Michigan Press, 1993, pp. 183–214.

———. "Biology and the Origins of the English Jury." *L&HR* 17 (1999): 591–96.

Duffy, Eamon. *The Stripping of the Altars: Traditional Religion in England 1400–1580*. New Haven: Yale UP, 1992; repr. 2005.

Dwyer, Déirdre M. "Expert Evidence in the English Civil Courts, 1550–1800." *JLH* 28.1 (2007): 93–118.

Eadie, Mervyn, and Peter Bladin. "The Idea of Epilepsy as a Disease *Per Se*." *Journal of the History of the Neurosciences* 19 (2010): 209–20.

Egmond, Florike. "Execution, Dissection, Pain and Infamy—A Morphological Investigation." In *Bodily Extremities: Preoccupation with the Human Body in Early Modern European Culture*, ed. Egmond and Robert Zwignenberg. Aldershot: Ashgate, 2003, pp. 92–128.

Eigen, Joel. "Diagnosing Homicidal Mania: Forensic Psychiatry and the Purposeless Murder." *MH* 54.4 (2010): 433–56.

———. "Lesion of the Will: Medical Resolve and Criminal Responsibility in Victorian Insanity Trials." *Law and Society Review* 33.2 (1999): 425–60.

———. "Sense and Sensibility: Fateful Splitting in the Victorian Insanity Trial." In *Domestic and International Trials. Trials in History, v. 2*, ed. Rose Anne Melikan. Manchester: Manchester UP, 2003, pp. 21–35.

Elsakkers, Marianne. "'In Pain You Shall Bear Children' (Gen. 3:16): Medieval Prayers for a Safe Delivery." In *Women and Miracle Stories: A Multidisciplinary Exploration*, ed. Anne-Marie Korte. Leiden: Brill, 2001, pp. 179–209.

Emmerichs, Mary Beth. "Getting Away with Murder? Homicide and the Coroners in Nineteenth-Century London." *Social Science History* 25.1 (2001): 93–100.

Ernst, Daniel R. "The Moribund Appeal of Death: Compensating Survivors and Controlling Jurors in Early Modern England." *AJLH* 28.2 (1984): 164–88.

Fahmy, Khaled. "The Anatomy of Justice: Forensic Medicine and Criminal Law in Nineteenth-Century Egypt." *Islamic Law and Society* 6.2 (1999): 224–71.

Finch, Andrew. "The Nature of Violence in the Middle Ages: An Alternative Perspective." *Historical Research* 70.173 (1997): 249–68.

Finucane, Ronald C. "The Toddler in the Ditch: A Case of Parental Neglect?" In *Voices from the Bench: The Narratives of Lesser Folk in Medieval Trials*, ed. Michael Goodich. New York: Palgrave Macmillan, 2006, pp. 127–48.

Fisher, P. "Getting Away with Murder? The Suppression of Coroners' Inquests in Early Victorian England and Wales." *Local Population Studies* 78 (2007): 47–62.

Flint, Valerie I.J. "The Saint and the Operation of the Law: Reflections upon the Miracles of St Thomas Cantilupe." In *Belief and Culture in the Middle Ages: Studies Presented to Henry Mayr-Harting*, ed. Richard Gameson and Henrietta Leyser. Oxford: Oxford UP, 2001, pp. 342–57.

Forbes, Thomas R. "By What Disease or Casualty? The Changing Face of Death in London." *JHMAS* 31.4 (1976): 395–420.

———. "A Mortality Record for Colbath Fields Prison, London, in 1795–1829." *Bulletin of the New York Academy of Medicine* 53.7 (1977): 666–70.

———. "Coroners' Inquisitions on the Deaths of Prisoners in the Hulks at Portsmouth, England in 1817–27." *JHMAS* 33.3 (1978): 356–66.

———. "The Crowners Quest," *Transactions of the American Philosophical Society* 68.1 (1978): 1–52.

———. *Surgeons at the Bailey: English Forensic Medicine to 1878*. New Haven: Yale UP, 1985.

———. "A Jury of Matrons." *MH* 32 (1988): 23–33.

Forrest, Ian. "Defamation, Heresy and Late Medieval Social Life." In *Image, Text and Church, 1380–1600: Essays for Margaret Aston*, ed. Linda Clark, Maureen Jurkowski, and Colin Richmond. Toronto: PIMS, 2009, pp. 142–61.

Fraher, Richard M. "Conviction According to Conscience: The Medieval Jurists' Debate Concerning Judicial Discretion and the Law of Proof." *L&HR* 7.1 (1989): 23–88.

Freeman, Jessica. "And He Abjured the Realm of England, Never to Return." In *Freedom of Movement in the Middle Ages: Proceedings of the 2003 Harlaxton Symposium*, ed. Peregrine Horden. Donington: Shaun Tyas, 2007, pp. 287–304.

French, Katherine L. *The Good Women of the Parish: Gender and Religion after the Black Death*. Philadelphia: University of Pennsylvania Press, 2008.

Frisch, Andrea. *The Invention of the Eyewitness: Witnessing and Testimony in Early Modern France*. Chapel Hill: North Carolina Studies in the Romance Languages and Literatures, 2004.

Gaskill, Malcolm. "Reporting Murder: Fiction in the Archives in Early Modern England." *Social History* 23.1 (1998): 1–30.

———. *Crime and Mentalities in Early Modern England*. Cambridge: Cambridge UP, 2000.

Gasse, Rosanne. "The Practice of Medicine in *Piers Plowman*." *The Chaucer Review* 39.2 (2004): 177–97.

Gauvard, Claude. "*De Grace Especial*": *Crime, Etat et Société à la Fin du Moyen Age*. 2 vols. Paris: Publications de la Sorbonne, 1991.

Gerrard, Daniel. "The Military Activities of Bishops, Abbots and Other Clergy in England, c. 900–1200." Ph.D. Diss., University of Glasgow, 2011.

Getz, Faye. *Medicine in the English Middle Ages*. Princeton: Princeton UP, 1998.

Gibson, Gail McMurray. "Scene and Obscene: Seeing and Performing Late Medieval Childbirth." *JMEMS* 29.1 (1999): 7–24.

Gibson, Jeremy, and Colin Rogers. *Coroners' Records in England and Wales*. 3rd ed. Bury, Lancs.: The Family History Partnership, 2000.

Given, J.B. *Society and Homicide in Thirteenth-Century England*. Stanford: Stanford UP, 1977.

Goheen, R.B. "Peasant Politics? Village Community and the Crown in Fifteenth-Century England." *AHR* 96.1 (1991): 42–62.

Goldberg, P.J.P. "'I Know What You Did Last Summer': Knowledge and Power among Parochial Clergy in Later Medieval England." In *Aspects of Power and Authority in the Middle Ages*, ed. Brenda Bolton and Christine E. Meek. Turnhout: Brepols, 2007, pp. 185–96.

Gorski, Richard. *The Fourteenth-Century Sheriff: English Local Administration in the Late Middle Ages*. Woodbridge: Boydell, 2003.

Gottfried, Robert S. *Doctors and Medicine in Medieval England 1340–1530*. Princeton: Princeton UP, 1986.

Green, Monica H. "Women's Medical Practice and Health Care in Medieval Europe." *Signs: Journal of Women in Culture and Society* 14.2 (1988): 434–73.

———. *Making Women's Medicine Masculine: The Rise of Male Authority in Pre-Modern Gynaecology*. Oxford: Oxford UP, 2008.

———. "Integrative Medicine: Incorporating Medicine and Health into the Canon of Medieval European History." *History Compass* 7.4 (2009): 1218–45.

Green, Richard Firth. *A Crisis of Truth: Literature and Law in Ricardian England*. Philadelphia: University of Pennsylvania Press, 1998.

Green, Thomas A. *Verdict According to Conscience: Perspectives on the English Criminal Trial Jury, 1200–1800*. Chicago: University of Chicago Press, 1985.

Grigsby, Bryon. "The Social Position of the Surgeon in London, 1350–1450." *Essays in Medieval Studies* 13 (1996): 71–80.

———. *Pestilence in Medieval and Early Modern English Literature*. New York: Routledge, 2004.

Gunn, Steven. "Archery Practice in Early Tudor England." *P&P* 209 (2010): 53–81.

Hair, P.E. "Deaths from Violence in Britain: A Tentative Secular Survey." *Population Studies* 25.1 (1971): 5–24.

Halliday, Robert. "The Roadside Burial of Suicides: An East Anglian Study." *Folklore* 121 (2010): 81–93.

Hanawalt, Barbara A. "Violent Death in Fourteenth- and Early Fifteenth-Century England." *Comparative Studies in Society and History* 18 (1976): 297–320.

———. *Crime and Conflict in English Communities, 1300–1348*. Cambridge, MA: Harvard UP, 1979.

———. *The Ties That Bound: Peasant Families in Medieval England*. New York: Oxford UP, 1986.

———. "The Voices and Audiences of Social History Records." *Social Science History* 14.2 (1991): 159–75.

———. *Growing up in Medieval London: The Experience of Childhood in History*. New York: Oxford UP, 1993.

———. "Good Governance in the Medieval and Early Modern Context." *JBS* 37 (1998): 246–57.

Haneef, Sayed Sikandar Shah. "Forensic Evidence: A Comparative Analysis of the General Position in Common Law and Sharī'ah." *Islamic Studies* 46.2 (2007): 199–216.

Harding, Alan. *A Social History of English Law*. Gloucester, MA: Peter Smith, 1973.

Harvey, Margaret. "Some Comments on Northern Mortuary Customs in the Later Middle Ages." *Journal of Ecclesiastical History* 59.2 (2008): 272–80.

Hasted, Edward. *The History and Topographical Survey of the County of Kent*. 2 vols. Canterbury: W. Bristow, 1797.

Havard, J.D.J. *The Detection of Secret Homicide: A Study of the Medico-Legal System of Investigation of Sudden and Unexplained Deaths*. London: Macmillan, 1960.

Havens, Jill C. "'As Englishe is comoun langage to oure puple': The Lollards and Their Imagined 'English' Community." In *Imagining a Medieval English Nation*, ed. Kathy Lavezzo. Minneapolis and London: University of Minnesota Press, 2004, pp. 96–131.

Henderson, John. "The Black Death in Florence: Medical and Communal Response." In *Deaths and Towns: Urban Responses to the Dying and the Dead 100–1600*, ed. Steven Bassett. Leicester: Leicester UP, 1992, pp. 136–147.

Herlihy, David. "Age, Property, and Career in Medieval Society." In *Aging and the Aged in Medieval Europe*, ed. Michael M. Sheehan. Toronto: PIMS, 1983, pp. 143–158.

Hill, LaMar. "The Two-witness Rule in English Treason Trials: Some Comments on the Emergence of Procedural Law." *AJLH* 12.2 (1968): 95–111.

Hindle, Steve. "'Bleeding Afreshe'?: The Affray and Murder at Nantwich, 19 December 1572." In *The Extraordinary and the Everyday in Early Modern England: Essays in Celebration of the Work of Bernard Capp*. Houndmills and Basingstoke: Palgrave Macmillan, 2010, pp. 224–45.

Holford, Matthew. "Thrifty Men of the Country? The Jurors and their Role." In *The Fifteenth-Century Inquisitions Post-Mortem: A Companion*, ed. Michael Hicks. Woodbridge: Boydell, 2012, pp. 201–22.

———, and Keith J. Stringer, eds. *Border Liberties and Loyalties: North-East England, c. 1200 to c. 1400*. Edinburgh: Edinburgh UP, 2010.

Horrox, Rosemary, ed. *The Black Death*. Manchester: Manchester UP, 1994.

Houston, Rab. *Punishing the Dead?: Suicide, Lordship, and Community in Britain, 1500–1830*. Oxford: Oxford UP, 2010.

Hunnisett, R.F. "An Early Coroner's Roll." *Bulletin of the Institute of Historical Research* 30 (1957): 225–31.

———. "Sussex Coroners in the Middle Ages. In 3 parts." *Sussex Archaeological Collections* 95 (1957): 42–58, 96; (1958): 17–34; and 98 (1960): 44–70.

———. "The Origin of the Office of the Coroner." *Transactions of the Royal Historical Society* 5th series, v. 8 (1958): 84–104.

———. "The Medieval Coroners' Roll." *AJLH* 3 (1959): 95–124, 205–21, 324–59.

———. "Pleas of the Crown and the Coroner." *Bulletin of the Institute of Historical Research* 32 (1959): 117–37.

———. *The Medieval Coroner*. Cambridge: Cambridge UP, 1961.

———. "The Reliability of Inquisitions as Historical Evidence." In *The Study of Medieval Records: Essays in Honor of Kathleen Major*, ed. D.A. Bullough and R.L. Storey. Oxford: Oxford UP, 1971, pp. 206–35.

Hunting, Penelope. *A History of the Society of Apothecaries*. London: The Society of Apothecaries, 1998.

Huot, Sylvia. *Madness in Medieval French Literature: Identities Found and Lost*. Oxford: Oxford UP, 2003.

Hurnard, Naomi D. *The King's Pardon for Homicide Before AD 1307*. Oxford: Oxford UP, 1969.

Hurren, Elizabeth. "Remaking the Medico-Legal Scene: A Social History of the Late-Victorian Coroner in Oxford." *JHMAS* 65.2 (2010): 207–52.

Ireland, Richard W. "Theory and Practice within the Medieval English Prison." *AJLH* 31.1 (1987): 56–67.

Jenks, Susanne. "*occidit . . . inter brachia sua*: Change in a Woman's Appeal of Murder of her Husband." *Legal History* 21.2 (2000): 119–122.

Jewell, Helen. *English Local Administration in the Middle Ages*. New York: Newton Abbot, David and Charles, 1972.

Jhang, Jeffrey S., and Joseph Schwartz. "Phlebotomy or Bloodletting: From Tradition to Evidence-Based Medicine." *Transfusion* 52 (Mar. 2012): 460–62.

Jillings, Karen. "Plague, Pox, and the Physician in Aberdeen, 1495–1516." *Journal of the Royal College of Physicians in Edinburgh* 40.1 (2010): 70–76.

Jones, Carol A.G. *Expert Witnesses: Science, Medicine, and the Practice of Law*. Oxford: Clarendon Press, 1994.

Jones, Karen. *Gender and Petty Crime in Late Medieval England: The Local Courts in Kent, 1460–1560*. Woodbridge: Boydell, 2006.

Jones, Peter Murray. "Thomas Fayreford: An English Fifteenth-Century Medical Practitioner." In *Medicine from the Black Death to the French Disease*, ed. Roger French. Aldershot: Ashgate, 1998, pp. 156–83.

———. "Witnesses to Medieval Medical Practice in the Harley Collection." *Electronic British Library Journal* (2008): 1–13.

———. "Medical Literacies and Medical Culture in Early Modern England." In *Medical Writing in Early Modern English*, ed. Irma Taavitsainen and Päivi Pahta. Cambridge: Cambridge UP, 2011, pp. 30–43.

Jones, William R. "Sanctuary, Exile, and Law: The Fugitive and Public Authority in Medieval England and Modern America." In *Essays on English Law and the American Experience*, ed. Elisabeth A. Cawthon. College Station: Texas A&M UP, 1994, pp. 19–41.

Jordan, William C. "A Fresh Look at Medieval Sanctuary." In *Law and the Illicit in Medieval Europe*, ed. Ruth Mazo Karras, Joel Kaye, and E. Ann Matter. Philadelphia: University of Pennsylvania Press, 2008, pp. 17–32.

Karras, Ruth Mazo. *Sexuality in Medieval Europe: Doing unto Others*. New York: Routledge, 2005.

Kaye, J.M. "The Early History of Murder and Manslaughter. 2 pts." *Law Quarterly Review* 83.3 (1967): 365–95 and 83.4 (1967): 569–601.

Kellaway, William. "The Coroner in Medieval London." In *Studies in London History Presented to Philip Edmund Jones*, ed. Albert E.J. Hollaender and Kellaway. London: Hodder Stoughton, 1969, pp. 75–95.

Kermode, Jenny. *Medieval Merchants: York, Beverley and Hull in the Later Middle Ages*. Cambridge: Cambridge UP, 1998.

Kerr, Heather. "'Romancing the Handbook': Scenes of Detection in *Arden of Faversham*." In *'This Earthly Stage': World and Stage in Late Medieval and Early Modern England*, ed. Brett Hirsch and Christopher Wortham. Turnhout: Brepols, 2010, pp. 173–92.

Kesselring, K.J. "Abjuration and Its Demise: The Changing Face of Royal Justice in the Tudor Period." *Canadian Journal of History* 34.3 (1999): 345–58.

———. "Detecting 'Death Disguised.'" *History Today* 56.4 (2000): 20–26.

———. "Felony Forfeiture in England, c. 1170–1870." *JLH* 30.3 (2009): 201–26.

Kippen, Rebecca. "'Incorrect, loose and coarse terms': Classifying Nineteenth-Century English-Language Causes of Death for Modern Use: An Example Using Tasmanian Data." *Journal of Population Research* 28 (2011): 267–91.

Klerman, Daniel. "Women Prosecutors in Thirteenth-Century England." *Yale Journal of Law and Humanities* 14.2 (2002): 271–319.

———. "Was the Jury Ever Self-Informing?" *Southern California Law Review* 77:123 (2004): 123–49.

Krummel, Miriamne A. "Getting Even: Social Control and Uneasy Laughter in *The Play of the Sacrament*." In *Medieval English Comedy*, ed. Sandra M. Hordis and Paul Hardwick. Turnhout: Brepols, 2007, pp. 171–94.

Kümper, Hiram. "Learned Men and Skillful Matrons: Medical Expertise and the Forensics of Rape in the Middle Ages." In *Medicine and the Law in the Middle Ages*, ed. Wendy J. Turner and Sara M. Butler. Leiden: Brill, 2014, pp. 88–108.

Kuriyama, Shigehisa. "Interpreting the History of Bloodletting." *JHMAS* 50.1 (1995): 11–46.

Landry, Yves, and Renald Lessard. "Causes of Death in Seventeenth- and Eighteenth-Century Quebec as Recorded in the Parish Registers." *Historical Methods* 29.2 (1996): 49–58.

Langbein, John H. "Historical Foundations of the Law of Evidence: A View from the Ryder Sources." *Columbia Law Review* 96 (1996): 1168–1202.

Larson, Peter L. "Village Voice or Village Oligarchy? The Jurors of the Durham Halmote Court, 1349–1424." *L&HR* 28.3 (2010): 675–709.

Lascaratus, J., and P.V. Zis. "The Epilepsy of Emperor Michael IV, Paphlagon (1034–1041 A.D.): Accounts of Byzantine Historians and Physicians." *Epilepsia* 41.7 (2000): 913–17.

Lloyd, Philip. "The Coroners of Leicestershire in the Early Fourteenth Century." *Transactions of the Leicestershire Archaeological and Historical Society* 56 (1980–1981): 18–32.

Loar, Carol. "Medical Knowledge and the Early Modern English Coroner's Inquest." *SHoM* 23.3 (2010): 475–91.

Lyman, Michael. *Criminal Investigation: The Art and the Science*. 6th ed. Upper Saddle River, NJ: Pearson, 2011.

Maeder, Thomas. *Crime and Insanity: The Origins and Evolution of the Insanity Defense*. New York: Harper & Row, 1985.

Magherini, Graziella, and Vittorio Biotti. "Madness in Florence in the 14th–18th Centuries: Judicial Inquiry and Medical Diagnosis, Care, and Custody." *International Journal of Law and Psychiatry* 21.4 (1998): 355–68.

Marrone, Steven P. "Magic and the Physical World in Thirteenth-Century Scholasticism." *Early Science and Medicine* 14 (2009): 158–85.

Masschaele, James. "Space of the Marketplace in Medieval England." *Speculum* 77.2 (2002): 383–421.

———. *Jury, State, and Society in Medieval England*. New York: Palgrave Macmillan, 2008.

Matthews, Paul. "Involuntary Manslaughter: A View from the Coroners' Court." *Journal of Criminal Law* 60 (1996): 189–200.

McDonough, Susan Alice. *Witnesses, Neighbors, and Community in Late Medieval Marseille*. New York: Palgrave Macmillan, 2013.

McGlynn, Margaret. "Idiots, Lunatics and the Royal Prerogative in Early Tudor England." *JLH* 26. 1 (2005): 1–20.

———. "Memory, Orality and Life Records: Proofs of Age in Tudor England." *Sixteenth Century Journal* 40 (2009): 679–97.

McIntosh, Marjorie K. *Controlling Misbehavior in England, 1370–1600*. Cambridge: Cambridge UP, 2002.

McKinley, R.A. *A History of British Surnames*. New York: Longman, 1990.

McLane, Bernard W. "Juror Attitudes toward Local Disorder: The Evidence of the 1328 Trailbaston Proceedings." In *Twelve Good Men and True: The Criminal Trial Jury in England, 1200–1800*, ed. J.S. Cockburn and Thomas A. Green. Princeton: Princeton UP, 1988, pp. 36–64.

McNab, B. "Obligations of the Church in English Society: Military Arrays of the Clergy 1369–1418." In *Order and Innovation in the Middle Ages: Essays in Honor of Joseph R. Strayer*, ed. W.C. Jordan, *et al*. Princeton: Princeton UP, 1976, pp. 293–314.

McNair, Mike. "Law, Politics and the Jury." *L&HR* 17 (1999): 603–07.

———. "Vicinage and the Antecedents of the Jury." *L&HR* 17 (1999): 537–90

McSheffrey, Shannon. "Jurors, Respectable Masculinity, and Christian Morality: A Comment on Marjorie McIntosh's *Controlling Misbehavior*." *JBS* 37 (1998): 269–78.

———. "Men and Masculinity in Late Medieval London Civic Culture: Governance, Patriarchy, and Reputation." In *Conflicted Identities and Multiple Masculinities: Men in the Medieval West*, ed. Jacqueline Murray. New York: Taylor & Francis, 1999, pp. 243–78.

———. "Sanctuary and the Legal Topography of Pre-Reformation London." *L&HR* 27.3 (2009): 483–514.

McVaugh, Michael R. *Medicine before the Plague: Practitioners and Their Patients in the Crown of Aragon 1285–1345*. Cambridge: Cambridge UP, 1993.

———. "Cataracts and Hernias: Aspects of Surgical Practice in the Fourteenth Century." *MH* 45.3 (2001): 319–40.

Mellen, P.F. "Coroners' Inquests in Colonial Massachusetts." *JHMAS* 40.4 (1985): 462–72.

Michaelsen, Andreas, *et al*. "Effects of Phlebotomy-Induced Reduction of Body Iron Stores on Metabolic Syndrome: Results from a Randomized Clinical Trial." *BMC Medicine* 10.54 (2012): 1–8.

Midelfort, H.C. Erik. *A History of Madness in Sixteenth-Century Germany*. Stanford: Stanford UP, 1999.

Mieszkowski, Gretchen. "Old Age and Medieval Misogyny: The Old Woman." In *Old Age in the Middle Ages and the Renaissance: Interdisciplinary Approaches to a Neglected Topic*, ed. Albrecht Classen. Berlin: de Gruyter, 2007, pp. 299–319.

Milsom, S.F.C. *Historical Foundations of the Common Law*. 2nd ed. London: Butterworths, 1981.

Mitchell, Piers D. *Medicine in the Crusades: Warfare, Wounds and the Medieval Surgeon*. Cambridge: Cambridge UP, 2004.

Mitnik, John Marshall. "Neighbor-Witness to Judge of Proofs: The Transformation of the English Civil Juror," *AJLH* 32.3 (1988): 201–35.

Moran, Jenny. "By the Instigation of the Devil: The Doncaster Borough Coroner's Records." In *Aspects of Doncaster: Discovering Local History*, ed. Brian Elliott. 2 vols. Barnsley: Wharncliffe, 1997, v. 1, pp. 209–28.

Mulholland, Maureen. "The Jury in English Manorial Courts." In *'The Dearest Birth Right of the People of England': The Jury in the History of the Common Law*, ed. John W. Cairns and Grant McLeod. Oxford: Hart Pub., 2002, pp. 63–74.

———. "Trials in Manorial Courts in Late Medieval England." In *Judicial Tribunals in England and Europe, 1200–1700: Vol. 1*, ed. Mulholland and Brian Pullan. Manchester: Manchester UP, 2003, pp. 81–101.

Müller, Miriam. "Social Control and the Hue and Cry in Two Fourteenth-Century Villages." *Journal of Medieval History* 31 (2005): 29–53.

Munkhoff, Richelle. "Searchers of the Dead: Authority, Marginality, and the Interpretation of Plague in England, 1574–1665." *Gender & History* 11.1 (1999): 1–29.

Murray, Alexander. *Suicide in the Middle Ages*. v. 1. Oxford: Oxford UP, 1998.

Murray, Jacqueline. "On the Origins and Role of 'Wise Women' in Causes of Annulment on the Grounds of Male Impotence." *Journal of Medieval History* 16.3 (1990): 235–49.

Musson, Anthony J. *Public Order and Law Enforcement: The Local Administration of Criminal Justice, 1294–1350*. Woodbridge: Boydell, 1996.

———. "Twelve Good Men and True? The Character of Early Fourteenth-Century Juries." *L&HR* 15.1 (1997): 115–44.

———. "Turning King's Evidence: The Prosecution of Crime in Late Medieval England." *Oxford Journal of Legal Studies* 19.3 (1999): 467–79.

Muzzarelli, Maria G. "Reconciling the Privilege of a Few with the Common Good: Sumptuary Laws in Medieval and Early Modern Europe." *JMEMS* 39.3 (2009): 597–617.

Naphy, William, and Andrew Spicer. *The Black Death: A History of Plagues, 1345–1730*. Stroud: Tempus, 2000.

Neal, Derek G. *The Masculine Self in Late Medieval England*. Chicago and London: University of Chicago Press, 2008.

Neville, C.J. "Common Knowledge of the Common Law in Later Medieval England." *Canadian Journal of History* 29.3 (1994): 461–78.

———. *Violence, Custom and Law: The Anglo-Scottish Border Lands in the Later Middle Ages*. Edinburgh: Edinburgh UP, 1998.

———. "'The Bishop's Ministers': The Office of Coroner in Late Medieval Durham." *Florilegium* 18.2 (2001): 47–60.

Norri, Juhani. *Names of Sicknesses in English, 1400–1550: An Exploration of the Lexical Field*. Helsinki: Suomalainen Tiedeakatemia, 1992.

Nutton, Vivian, ed. "Medicine in Medieval Western Europe, 1000–1500." In *The Western Medical Tradition 800 BC to AD 1800*, ed. Lawrence I. Conrad, *et al.* Cambridge: Cambridge UP, 1995, pp. 139–214.

———. *Pestilential Complexities: Understanding Medieval Plague*. London: Wellcome Trust for the History of Medicine, 2008.

Oldham, James C. "On Pleading the Belly: A History of the Jury of Matrons." *Criminal Justice History* 6 (1985): 1–64.

Oliver, Lisi. "Sick-Maintenance in Anglo-Saxon Law." *The Journal of English and Germanic Philology* 107.3 (2008): 303–26.

———. *The Body Legal in Barbarian Law*. Toronto and Buffalo: University of Toronto Press, 2011.

Olson, Lea T. "Charms and Prayers in Medieval Medical Theory and Practice." *SHoM* 16.3 (2003): 343–66.

Olson, Sherri. *A Chronicle of All That Happens: Voices from the Village Court in Medieval England*. Toronto: PIMS, 1996.

Ormanski, Julie. "Jargon and the Matter of Medicine in Middle English." *JMEMS* 42.2 (2012): 395–420.

Ormrod, W. Mark. "The English Government and the Black Death of 1348–49." In *England in the Fourteenth Century: Proceedings of the 1985 Harlaxton Symposium*, ed. Ormrod. Woodbridge: Boydell, 1986, pp. 175–88.

———. "The Politics of Pestilence: Government in England after the Black Death." In *The Black Death in England*, ed. Ormrod and Phillip Lindley. Stamford: Watkins, 1996, pp. 147–77.

Orr, Patricia R. "*Non Potest Appellum Facere*. Criminal Charges Women Could Not—but Did—Bring in Thirteenth-Century English Royal Courts of Justice." In *The Final Argument: The Imprint of Violence on Society in Medieval and Early Modern Europe*, ed. Donald J. Kagay and L.J. Andrew Villalon. Woodbridge: Boydell, 1998, pp. 141–60.

Overing, Gillian R. "A Body in Question: Aging, Community, and Gender in Medieval Iceland." *JMEMS* 29.2 (1999): 211–26.

Paladin, Anna Vanzan. "Epilepsy According to the Christian, Jewish, and Islamic Religions: An Overview." *Epilepsia* 1 (1995): 38–41.

Palliser, D.M. *Tudor York*. Oxford: Oxford UP, 1979.

Palmer, C.A., and M. Hazelrigg. "The Guilty but Mentally Ill Verdict: A Review and Conceptual Analysis of Intent and Impact." *Journal of the American Academy of Psychiatry and the Law* 28.1 (2000): 47–54.

Palmer, Robert C. *English Law in the Age of the Black Death, 1348–1381: A Transformation of Governance and Law*. Chapel Hill, NC: University of North Carolina Press, 2001.

Park, Katharine. "Medicine and Society in Medieval Europe, 500–1500." In *Medicine in Society: Historical Essays*, ed. Andrew Wear. Cambridge: Cambridge UP, 1992, pp. 59–90.

———. "The Life of the Corpse: Division and Dissection in Late Medieval Europe." *JHMAS* 50.1 (1995): 111–32.

———. "Holy Autopsies: Saintly Bodies and Medical Expertise, 1300–1600." In *The Body in Early Modern Italy*, ed. Julia L. Hairston and Walter Stephens. Baltimore: Johns Hopkins, 2010, pp. 61–73.

Pattenden, Rosemary. "The Exclusion of the Clergy from Criminal Trial Juries: An Historical Perspective." *Ecclesiastical Law Journal* 5.24 (1999): 151–63.

Payling, Simon. *Political Society in Lancastrian England: The Greater Gentry of Nottinghamshire*. Oxford: Clarendon Press, 1991.

Pedersen, Frederik. "Demography in the Archives: Social and Geographical Factors in Fourteenth-Century York Cause Paper Marriage Litigation." *C&C* 10.3 (1995): 405–36.

Pelling, Margaret. "Knowledge Common and Acquired: The Education of Unlicensed Medical Practitioners in Early Modern London." In *The History of Medical Education in Britain*, ed. Vivian Nutton and Roy Porter. Amsterdam: Rodopi, 1995, pp. 250–79.

———. *Medical Conflicts in Early Modern London: Patronage, Physicians and Irregular Practitioners 1550–1640*. Oxford: Clarendon Press, 2003.

———. "Politics, Medicine and Masculinity: Physicians and Office-Bearing in Early Modern England." In *The Practice of Reform in Health, Medicine, and Science, 1500–2000: Essays for Charles Webster*, ed. Pelling and Scott Mandelbrote. Aldershot: Ashgate, 2005, pp. 81–106.

Pennington, Kenneth. "Innocent until Proven Guilty: The Origins of a Legal Maxim." *The Jurist* 63 (2003): 106–24.

Pervukhin, Anna. "Deodands: A Study in the Creation of Common Law Rules." *AJLH* 47.3 (2005): 237–56.

Peters, Edward. *Torture*. New York: Basil Blackwell, 1996.

Plucknett, Theodore. *A Concise History of the Common Law*. 5th ed. London: Butterworths, 1956.

Pollock, F. "Anglo-Saxon Law." *The English Historical Review* 8.30 (1893): 239–71.

———, and F.W. Maitland. *A History of English Law before the Time of Edward I*. 2 vols. 2nd ed. Cambridge: Cambridge UP, 1898.

Post, J.B. "Doctor versus Patient: Two Fourteenth-Century Lawsuits." *MH* 16.3 (1972): 296–300.

———. "Crime in Later Medieval England: Some Historiographical Limitations." *C&C* 2.2 (1987): 211–24.

———. "Jury Lists and Juries in the Late Fourteenth Century." In *Twelve Good Men and True: The Criminal Trial Jury in England, 1200–1800*, ed. J.S. Cockburn and Thomas A. Green. Princeton: Princeton UP, 1988, pp. 65–77.

Powell, Edward. "Jury Trial at Gaol Delivery in the Late Middle Ages: The Midland Circuit, 1400–1429." In *Twelve Good Men and True: The Criminal Trial Jury in England, 1200–1800*, ed. J.S. Cockburn and Thomas A. Green. Princeton: Princeton UP, 1988, pp. 78–116.

Prestwich, Michael, ed. *Liberties and Identities in the Medieval British Isles*. Woodbridge: Boydell, 2008.

Prior, Lindsay. "The Good, the Bad and the Unnatural: A Study of Coroners' Decisions in Northern Ireland." *Sociological Review* 33.1 (1985): 64–90.

———. *The Social Organization of Death: Medical Discourse and Social Practices in Belfast*. New York: St Martin's, 1989.

———, and Mick Bloor. "Why People Die: Social Representations of Death and Its Causes." *Science as Culture* 3.3 (1993): 346–75.

Pugh, R.B. "The Duration of Criminal Trials in Medieval England." In *Law, Litigants and the Legal Profession*, ed. E.W. Ives and A.H. Manchester. London: Royal Historical Society, 1983, pp. 104–15.

Pugliese, Joseph. "*Super visum corporis*: Visuality, Race, Narrativity and the Body of Forensic Pathology." *Law and Literature* 14.2 (2002): 367–96.

Ramsey, Nigel. "Scriveners and Notaries as Legal Intermediaries in Later Medieval England." In *Enterprise and Individuals in Fifteenth-Century England*, ed. Jenny Kermode. Gloucester: Sutton, 1991, pp. 118–31.

Rawcliffe, Carole. "The Profits of Practice: The Wealth and Status of Medical Men in Later Medieval England." *SHoM* 1.1 (1988): 61–78.

———. *Medicine and Society in Later Medieval England.* London: Sandpiper Books, 1995.

———. "Women, Childbirth, and Religion in Later Medieval England." In *Women and Religion in Medieval England,* ed. Diana Wood. Oxford: Oxbow Books, 2003, pp. 91–117.

———. "Sickness and Health." In *Medieval Norwich,* ed. Rawcliffe and Richard Wilson. London and New York: Hambledon, 2004, pp. 301–26.

———. *Leprosy in Medieval England.* Woodbridge: Boydell, 2006.

"Researchers Reconstruct Genome of the Black Death." Press Release. Hamilton, ON: McMaster University, October 12, 2011, http://fhs.mcmaster.ca/mcmaster media/documents/black_death_mcmaster_press_release_pdf. Accessed April 3, 2013.

Richards, Jeffrey. *Sex, Dissidence and Damnation: Minority Groups in the Middle Ages.* London and New York: Routledge, 1991.

Richards, Mary. "The Body as Text in Early Anglo-Saxon Law." In *Naked Before God: Uncovering the Body in Anglo-Saxon England*, ed. Benjamin C. Withers and Jonathan Wilcox. Morgantown: West Virginia UP, 2003, pp. 97–115.

Riddle, John M. "Contraception and Early Abortion in the Middle Ages." In *Handbook of Medieval Sexuality*, ed. Vern L. Bullough and James A. Brundage. New York: Garland, 1996, pp. 261–78.

Rigby, S.H. "Death and Old Age in the Middle Ages." *Journal of Early Modern History* 3.1 (1999): 80–83.

———. "Introduction: Social Structure and Economic Change in Late Medieval England." In *A Social History of England 1200–1500*, ed. Rosemary Horrox and W. Mark Ormrod. Cambridge: Cambridge UP, 2006, pp. 1–30.

Rose, Jonathan. "Feodo de Compedibus Vocato le Sewet: The Medieval Prison 'Oeconomy.'" In *Law in the City: Proceedings of the Seventeenth British Legal History Conference*, ed. Paul Brand, Andrew Lewis and Paul Mitchell. London: Four Courts Press, 2005, pp. 72–94.

Rosenmerkel, Sean, Matthew Durose, and Donald Farole. "Felony Sentences in State Courts, 2006—Statistical Tables." *Bureau of Justice Statistics* (December 2009), http://bjs.gov/index.cfm?ty=pbdetail&iid=2152. Accessed April 3, 2013.

Rosenthal, Joel T. "Retirement and the Life Cycle in Fifteenth-Century England." In *Aging and the Aged in Medieval Europe*, ed. Michael M. Sheehan. Toronto: PIMS, 1983, pp. 173–88.

———. *Old Age in Late Medieval England.* Philadelphia: University of Pennsylvania State Press, 1996.

Roskell, J.S., L. Clark, and C. Rawcliffe, eds. *The History of Parliament: the House of Commons 1386–1421.* Woodbridge: Boydell, 1993, www.historyofparliamen tonline.org/volume/1386-1421/constituencies/gloucester. Accessed March 12, 2013.

Rosser, Gervase. "Sanctuary and Social Negotiation in Medieval England." In *The Cloister and the World: Essays in Medieval History in Honour of Barbara Harvey*, ed. J. Blair and B. Golding. Oxford: Clarendon Press, 1996, pp. 57–79.

Ruggiero, Guido. "The Cooperation of Physicians and the State in the Control of Violence in Renaissance Venice." *JHMAS* 33 (1978): 156–66.

Russell, Josiah Cox. *British Medieval Population.* Albuquerque: University of New Mexico Press, 1948.

Schalick, Walton. "To Market, to Market: The Theory and Practice of Opiates in the Middle Ages." *Opiods and Pain Relief: A Historical Perspective* 25 (2003): 5–20.

Scott, Donald F. *The History of Epileptic Therapy: An Account of How Medication Was Developed.* Carnforth, Lancs.: CRC Press, 1993.

Scott, Susan, and Christopher Duncan. *The Biology of Plagues: Evidence from Historical Populations*. Cambridge: Cambridge UP, 2005.

Scull, Andrew. "The Domestication of Madness." *MH* 27.3 (1983): 233–48.

Seabourne, Gwen, and Alice Seabourne. "The Law on Suicide in Medieval England." *JLH* 21.1 (2000): 21–48.

Seipp, David J. "The Reception of Canon Law and Civil Law in the Common Law Courts before 1600." *Oxford Journal of Legal Studies* 13.1 (1993): 388–420.

———. "Crime in the Year Books." In *Law Reporting in Britain*, ed. Chantal Stebbings. London and Rio Grande, OH: Hambledon, 1995, pp. 15–34.

———. "The Mirror of Justices." In *Learning the Law: Teaching and the Transmission of the Law in England, 1150–1900*, ed. Jonathan A. Bush and Alain A. Wijffels. London and Rio Grande, OH: Hambledon, 1999, pp. 85–112.

———. "Jurors, Evidence and the Tempest of 1499." In *'The Dearest Birth Right of the People of England': The Jury in the History of the Common Law*, ed. John W. Cairns and Grant McLeod. Oxford: Hart Pub., 2002, pp. 75–92.

Shahar, Shulamith. "The Old Body in Medieval Culture." In *Framing Medieval Bodies*, ed. Sarah Kay and Miri Rubin. Manchester: Manchester UP, 1994, pp. 160–86.

———. *Growing Old in the Middle Ages: Winter Clothes Us in Shadow and Pain*. London: Routledge, 1997.

Shapiro, Barbara J. *A Culture of Fact: England, 1550–1720*. Ithaca: Cornell UP, 2000.

Sharpe, James, and J.R. Dickinson. "Coroners' Inquests in an English County, 1600–1800: A Preliminary Survey." *Northern History* 48.2 (2011): 253–69.

Sharpe, R.R. *London and the Kingdom: A History Derived Mainly from the Archives at Guildhall in the Custody of the Corporation of the City of London*. London: Longmans, Green, & Co., 1895.

Shatzmiller, Joseph. "The Jurisprudence of the Dead Body: Medical Practition at the Service of Civic and Legal Authorities." *Micrologus* 7 (1999): 223–30.

Shojania, K.G., and E.C. Burton. "The Vanishing Nonforensic Autopsy." *New England Journal of Medicine* 358.9 (2008): 873–75.

Shrewsbury, J.F.D. *A History of Bubonic Plague in the British Isles*. Cambridge: Cambridge UP, 1970; repr. 2005.

Siraisi, Nancy G. "Girolamo Cardano and the Art of Medical Narrative." *Journal of the History of Ideas* 52.4 (1991): 581–602.

Slack, Paul. *Plague: A Very Short Introduction*. Oxford: Oxford UP, 2012.

Smith, Carrie. "Medieval Coroners' Rolls: Legal Fiction or Historical Fact?" In *Courts, Counties and the Capital in the Later Middle Ages*, ed. Diana E.S. Dunn. New York: St Martin's Press, 1996, pp. 93–115.

———, and Brian Barraclough. "Suicide in Hampshire and Wiltshire 1327–1399." *History of Psychiatry* 6.1 (1995): 105–17.

Smith, Cathy. "'Visitation by God': Rationalizing Death in the Victorian Asylum." *History of Psychiatry* 23.104 (2012): 104–16.

Smith, Richard M. "The Manorial Court and the Elderly Tenant in Late Medieval England." In *Life, Death, and the Elderly: Historical Perspectives*, ed. Smith and Margaret Pelling. London: Routledge, 1991, pp. 33–51.

Smith, Steven M., Veronica Stinson, and Marc W. Patry. "Fact or Fiction? The Myth and Reality of the *CSI* Effect." *Court Review* 47.1 (2011): 4–7.

Solomon, Michael. "Women Healers and the Power to Disease in Late Medieval Spain." In *Women Healers & Physicians: Climbing a Long Hill*, ed. Lillian R. Furst. Lexington: UP of Kentucky, 1997, pp. 79–92.

Søndergaard, Leif. "Imaging Plague: The Black Death in Medieval Mentalities." In *Living with the Black Death*, ed. Søndergaard and Lars Bisgaard. Odense: UP of Southern Denmark, 2009, pp. 207–33.

Spindler, Erik D. "Youth and Old Age in Late Medieval London." *The London Journal* 36.1 (2011): 1–22.

Steadman, Henry J., *et al. Before and after Hinckley: Evaluating Insanity Defense Reform*. New York: Guildford Press, 1993.

Stell, Philip. "Medical Practice in Medieval York." *BIHR* no. 90 (1996): 1–29.

Stevenson, S.J. "The Rise of Suicide Verdicts in South-East England, 1530–1590: The Legal Process." *C&C* 2.1 (1987): 37–75.

———. "Social and Economic Contributions to the Pattern of 'Suicide' in South-East England, 1530–1590." *C&C* 2.2 (1987): 225–262.

Summerson, H.T. "The Structure of Law Enforcement in Thirteenth Century England." *AJLH* 23.313 (1979): 313–28.

Sutton, Teresa. "Nature of the Early Law of Deodand." *Cambrian Law Review* 30 (1999): 9–20.

Swanson, Heather. "Craftsmen and Industry in Late Medieval York." Ph.D. diss., York University, 1980.

———. "Building Craftsmen in Late Medieval York." *BIHR* no. 63 (1983): 1–45.

———. "The Illusion of Economic Structure: Craft Guilds in Late Medieval English Towns." *P&P* 121 (1988): 29–48.

Talbot, C.H., and E.A. Hammond. *The Medical Practitioners in Medieval England*. London: Wellcome Historical Medical Library, 1965.

Tankard, Danae. "Defining Death in Early Tudor England." *Cultural and Social History* 3 (2006): 1–20.

Temkin, Oswei. *The Falling Sickness: A History of Epilepsy from the Greeks to the Beginnings of Modern Neurology*. Baltimore: Johns Hopkins, 1945; repr. 1994.

Theilmann, John. "Disease or Disability? The Conceptual Relationship in Medieval and Early Modern England." In *The Treatment of Disabled Persons in Medieval Europe: Examining Disability in the Historical, Legal, Literary, Medical, and Religious Discourses of the Middle Ages*, ed. Wendy J. Turner and Tory Vandeventer Pearman. Ceredigion: Edwin Mellen, 2010, pp. 197–230.

———, and Frances Cate. "A Plague of Plagues: The Problem of Plague Diagnosis in Medieval England." *Journal of Interdisciplinary History* 37.3 (2007): 371–93.

Thiery, Daniel. "Welcome to the Parish. Remove Your Cap and Stop Assaulting Your Neighbor." In *Reputation and Representation in Fifteenth-Century Europe*, ed. Douglas Biggs, Sharon D. Michalove, and Compton Reeves. Leiden: Brill, 2004, pp. 235–65.

Thrupp, Sylvia. *The Merchant Class of Medieval London*. Chicago: University of Chicago Press, 1948.

Towner, Elizabeth, and John Towner. "Developing the History of Unintentional Injury and the Use of Coroners' Records in Early Modern England." *Injury Prevention* 6 (2000): 102–105.

Turner, Ralph V. "Clerical Judges in English Secular Courts: The Ideal versus the Reality." *Medievalia et Humanistica*, n.s. 3 (1972): 75–98.

Turner, Wendy J. "'Afflicted with Insanity': The Care and Custody of the Feeble Minded in Late Medieval England." Ph.D. Diss., University of California, Los Angeles, 2000.

Twigg, Graham. *The Black Death: A Biological Reappraisal*. Batsford: Schocken Books, 1985.

Uszkalo, Kirsten C. "Rage Possession: A Cognitive Science Approach to Early English Demon Possession." In *Bodies of Knowledge: Cultural Interpretations of Illness and Medicine in Medieval Europe*, ed. Sally Crawford and Christina Lee. Oxford: Archaeopress, 2010, pp. 5–17.

Vekerdy, Lilla. "Paracelsus's *Great Wound Surgery*." In *Textual Healing: Essays on Medieval and Early Modern Medicine*, ed. Elizabeth Lane Furdell. Leiden: Brill, 2005, pp. 77–100.

Vitiello, Joanna Carraway. "Forensic Evidence, Lay Witnesses and Medical Expertise in the Criminal Courts of Late Medieval Italy." In *Medicine and the Law in the Middle Ages*, ed. Wendy J. Turner and Sara M. Butler. Leiden: Brill, 2014, pp. 133–156.

Voigts, Linda E., and Robert P. Hudson. "A drynke þat men callen dwale to make a man to slepe whyle men kerven him: A Surgical Anesthetic from Late Medieval England." In *Health, Disease, and Healing in Medieval Culture*. ed. Sheila Diana Campbell, Bert S. Hall, and David N. Klausner. New York: St Martin's Press, 1992, pp. 34–52.

Walker, Nigel. *Crime and Insanity in England: Volume One: The Historical Perspective*. Edinburgh: Edinburgh UP, 1968.

Walker, Simon. "Order and Law." In *A Social History of England 1200–1500*, ed. Rosemary Horrox and W. Mark Ormrod. Cambridge: Cambridge UP, 2006, pp. 91–113.

Wallis, Faith. "Signs and Senses: Diagnosis and Prognosis in Medieval Pulse and Urine Texts." *SHoM* 13.2 (2000): 265–78.

Walton, M.T. "The Advisory Jury and Malpractice in 15th Century London." *JHMAS* 40.4 (1985): 478–82.

Watson, Katherine D. *Forensic Medicine in Western Society*. London and New York: Routledge, 2011.

Waugh, Scott. "Reluctant Knights and Jurors: Respites, Exemptions, and Public Obligations in the Reign of Henry III." *Speculum* 58.4 (1983): 937–86.

Wear, Andrew. *Knowledge and Practice in English Medicine, 1550–1680*. Cambridge: Cambridge UP, 2000.

White, Stephen. "The Insanity Defense in England and Wales since 1843." *Annals of the American Academy of Political and Social Science* 477 (1985): 43–57.

Wilkinson, Louise. "Women as Sheriffs in Early Thirteenth Century England." In *English Government in the Thirteenth Century*, ed. A. Jobson. Woodbridge: Boydell, 2004, pp. 111–24.

Williams, Naomi. "The Reporting and Classification of Causes of Death in Mid-Nineteenth-Century England." *Historical Methods* 29.2 (1996): 58–72.

Williams, William Retlaw. *The Parliamentary History of the County of Oxford*. Brecknock, Priv. Print. for the author by E. Davies, 1899.

Wilson, Dudley. *Signs and Portents: Monstrous Births from the Middle Ages to the Enlightenment*. London and New York: Routledge, 1993.

Winslow, Charles-Edward A. *The Conquest of Epidemic Disease: A Chapter in the History of Ideas*. Princeton: Princeton UP, 1943; repr. 1971.

Wodderspoon, John. *Memorials of the Ancient Town of Ipswich*. London: Pawsey, 1850.

Wood, C.L. "Historical Perspectives on Law, Medical Malpractice, and the Concept of Negligence." *Medical-Legal Issues* 11.4 (1993): 819–32.

Woolgar, C.M. *The Senses in Late Medieval England*. New Haven: Yale UP, 2006.

Wormald, Patrick. "Neighbors, Courts and Kings: Reflections on Michael McNair's *Vicini*." *L&HR* 17 (1999): 597–601.

Wray, Shona Kelly. "Boccaccio and the Doctors: Medicine and Compassion in the Face of the Plague." *Journal of Medieval History* 30.3 (2004): 301–22.

———. "Tracking Families and Flight in Bologna during the Black Death." *Medieval Prosopography* 25 (2004): 145–60.

Wright, Thomas. *The History and Topography of the County of Essex*. London: George Virtue, 1836.

Wrottsely, G. *Staffordshire Historical Collections*. London: Harrison and Sons, 1889.

Yoshikawa, Naoë. "Holy Medicine and Diseases of the Soul: Henry of Lancaster and *Le Livre de Seyntz Medicines*." *MH* 53 (2009): 397–414.

Zacharski, L.R., *et al.* "Decreased Cancer Risk after Iron Reduction in Patients with Peripheral Arterial Disease: Results from a Randomized Trial." *Journal of National Cancer Institute* 100.14 (2008): 996–1002.

Ziegler, J. "Practitioners and Saints: Medical Men in Canonization Processes in the Thirteenth to Fifteenth Centuries." *SoHM* 12.2 (1999): 191–225.

REFERENCE TEXTS

Black's Law Dictionary. 6th ed. St. Paul, MN: West Publishing, 1990.
Latham, R.E., ed. *Revised Medieval Latin Word-List from British and Irish Sources with Supplement*. London: The British Academy, 1965; rev. 1995.
Martin, Charles Trice. *The Record Interpreter*. Chichester, Sussex: Phillimore & Co. Ltd, 1892; repr. 1999.
Oxford English Dictionary. Oxford: Oxford UP, 2013, www.oed.com/.

Index

Note: 'f' after a page number indicates a figure; 't' indicates a table.